The
International
Law of
Pollution

The INTERNATIONAL LAW of POLLUTION

 James Barros

A N D

Douglas M. Johnston

THE FREE PRESS
A Division of Macmillan Publishing Co., Inc.
NEW YORK

Collier Macmillan Publishers
LONDON

241182

The Free Press
A Division of Macmillan Publishing Co., Inc.
866 Third Avenue, New York, New York 10022

Collier–Macmillan Canada Ltd.

Library of Congress Catalog Card Number: 73-6491

Printed in the United States of America

printing number
1 2 3 4 5 6 7 8 9 10

Library of Congress Cataloging in Publication Data

Barros, James, comp.
   The international law of pollution.

  Includes bibliographies.
   1. Environmental law. 2. Marine pollution--Law
and legislation. I. Johnston, Douglas M., joint
comp. II. Title.
Law   341.7'62   73-6491
ISBN 0-02-901910-9

Contents

PART II

The Emerging International Law of Pollution

PART III
SELECTED ISSUES IN INTERNATIONAL
ENVIRONMENTAL LAW

Prohibition of Ecocidal Weapons and Weapons of Mass Destruction (with suggested reading list)

Preface

Few libraries in the world are arranged so as to be of maximum convenience to students of pollution control policy. Policy problems of this kind cut across familiar disciplinary lines, and the relevant materials usually have to be flushed out with the greatest difficulty from different sections of the library system. In part, therefore, this collection is designed as a practical research tool for students of international pollution control problems. We hope it will be equally useful to undergraduates, graduate students, and professional researchers, whether they are located in law schools, political science departments, research institutes, government departments, international agencies, or multinational corporations involved in pollution problems.

Because the international law of pollution has only recently been conceived as a legitimate new-comer to the teaching curriculum, we have tried to avoid the mistake of over-organization of these materials within a tightly constructed framework. We believe the book will be more widely useful during the next few years in this relatively loose form, especially to teachers who will want to add supplementary materials as new developments in the international law of pollution unfold.

We have, however, attempted to impose some degree of logical sequence by providing introductory comments and materials in Part I as a background to the central concern with the international problems of pollution control policy. We have also provided brief explanatory introductions to Parts II and III and short reading lists at the beginning of each section of materials.

We are grateful to Professor Walter Berns of the Department of

Political Economy, University of Toronto, and to Professor George Alexandrowicz of the Faculty of Law, Queen's University, for their advice on the choice of materials. The collecting of materials was much easier than it might have been because of the helpfulness of many Canadian government officials in Ottawa. Last, but certainly not least, we wish to thank the secretarial staffs of the University of Toronto Department of Political Economy and of Dalhousie University Faculty of Law for their yeoperson services in helping to compile and reproduce the contents of this collection.

James Barros
Douglas M. Johnston

Introduction

Pollution is not a modern phenomenon. It is not peculiar to man and may indeed have preceded him. Pollution by man in the twentieth century is a reflection of population growth, development of technology and the resulting increase in living standards, and consumption habits associated with economic growth. The most serious effects of these trends include the increasing spread of waste and the destruction of nature. Since pollution can be traced to many causes, some of which are political and highly emotional, its solution will not come easily. Most pollution problems are further complicated by the fact that merely national approaches, though important, are too limited to provide lasting assurance of prevention and control. Most forms of pollution are transnational in scope and must be treated within a modern system of international law suitable to the needs of the interdependent world community in the late twentieth century.

The critical reader of this collection will have no difficulty in pointing out serious omissions in this volume. In addition to yielding to the usual constraints of space and printing costs, we have undoubtedly made his task easier by opting for a broad definition of pollution and by including materials on environmental issues that might be regarded by some as tangential, rather than central, to the problems of pollution. But at this stage in the development of the law of nations, it is unnecessarily arbitrary to adopt restrictive definitions: there is often disagreement as to what constitutes "waste" and scientists themselves have difficulty in determining what constitutes "pollution." Indeed, this factor of scientific uncertainty has already played a judicially negative role, as shown in some of the decisions of the United States Supreme Court and in the *Trail Smelter* Arbitration reproduced in this volume. Because of the importance of scientific uncertainty we have included in Part I of this volume not only recent examples of legal definitions, such as that of marine pollution provided by the Joint Group of Experts on the Scientific Aspects of Marine Pollution (GESAMP), but also specific examples of precise scientific criteria and quality standards, such as those annexed to the 1972 Agreement between Canada and the United States on Great Lakes Water Quality. Our own approach to the concept of pollution is sufficiently inclusive to embrace the impairment of scenic beauty which was, for example, the joint concern that led to the signing of the 1950 Treaty between the United States and Canada Relating to the Uses of the Waters of the Niagara River.

Just as science and law are bound together in the international treatment of pollution problems, so too are the contributions of international law meshed with the heritage of national legal systems. The collective experience of municipal law may be relevant through analogical reasoning or as the fund from which "general principles of law recognized by civilized nations" may be derived. In Part I of this volume we have, therefore, included a note on pollution-related doctrines of public and private law and referred to other works where analysis of these legal concepts can be found. In no sense are these concepts held out as representative of all legal systems in the world. Other national materials included in Part I, chosen from United States Supreme Court decisions, mirror judicial attempts in this century to resolve pollution issues that involved quasi-sovereign entities. These attempts have attracted the attention of international tribunals and, as shown in this volume, the famous *Trail Smelter* Arbitration between the United States and Canada accepted them as relevant to the settlement of a pollution dispute between sovereign entities.

It is, of course, one of the features of contemporary international law that its treatment of environmental issues has been extremely uneven. It is noticeable, for example, that very little has so far been accomplished among states in the treatment of air pollution, whereas there has been a considerable concern, especially in recent years, with legal development to preserve water quality. Why has this been so? Apparent reasons include the subjacent state's fear of further restrictions on its sovereignty over its airspace and the late recognition by states that airspace constitutes an internationally shared resource in the same sense as water. The materials collected in Part II show that there already exists a considerable body of established international law pertaining to the protection of the environment but also that there exists a variety of international approaches in the treatment of pollution problems. The collection runs the gamut from bilateral arrangements to regional and global agreements, and it also includes references to relevant principles of customary international law. It is only in the last few years, however, that the organized world community has placed world pollution problems in the context of the human environment and adopted a holistic approach to these problems, as described in the materials on the United Nations Conference on the Human Environment held in Stockholm in July 1972. It should also be noted that Part II contains materials which show recent national initiatives that reflect or anticipate trends in international law, or which represent intranational arrangements within a federal state for the implementation of national and international environment policy.

Lastly, we have felt it necessary to include materials that go beyond the scope of pollution, strictly defined, but might be regarded as belonging to the field of international environmental law. First, we recognize that it is unrealistic to divorce pollution issues from the larger issues of international resource use and development. Perhaps the most relevant area, in this sense, is that of the law of the sea, viewed as the juridical context in which marine pollution has to be treated. Obviously, we have had to limit ourselves in extracting from that body of law, not only because of the mass of material involved but also because of the transformation now being proposed for the law of the sea in the name of modernization. By contrast, the evolving regime of outer space is entirely modern and should not have to be altered fundamentally in order to become conducive to the legal treatment of pollution problems. Antarctica is something of a special case as the only substantial body of land not subject to national sovereignty and, therefore, open to a higher degree of international cooperation in environmental protection. Moreover, we believe that it may be useful to view the prospective development of international pollution law in juxtaposition with recent developments in the prohibition of environmentally dangerous ("ecocidal") weapons or weapons of mass destruction: that is, nuclear and thermonuclear, bacteriological (biological), and chemical weapons. To those who argue that the prohibition of nuclear weapons belongs to the international law and politics of disarmament and not to that of pollution control, we would point out that since the signing of the 1968 Treaty on the Non-Proliferation of Nuclear Weapons these two areas have in effect been conjoined by specific treaty references to the need for regulating the use of atomic energy for peaceful purposes. Accordingly, we conclude with a section consisting of documents that trace the development of safety precautions in this field.

PART I

The Pollution Problem in Science, Law, and Policy

Problems of Definition

It is possible to define "pollution" so widely as to make the term practically unmanageable: for example, by including in it the overuse and misuse of resources. The current preference is to focus on "environment" rather than "resources." Pollution might then be defined as any kind of environmental impairment. But this definition simply replaces the problem of defining "pollution" with the more difficult problems of defining "environment" and "impairment." One for the price of two is a bad bargain.

A better approach to defining a general term is to translate it into a combination of more precise terms. As the identification of pollution often depends upon the presentation of credible, scientifically testable evidence, the ideal scientific definition would be a lengthy list of scientific standards and criteria by which it could be precisely determined in what sense a specific environment can be regarded as impaired and at what point the impairment should be regarded as intolerable. Obviously, it will be a long time before an ideal scientific definition of pollution in general can be expected along these lines.

For the foreseeable future, however, short-form definitions of pollution and related concepts will continue to be proposed for the usual purposes of legal reference. In specific contexts, such as that of marine pollution, short-form definitions already coexist with lists of scientific standards and criteria. In recent treaties dealing with the prevention and control of marine pollution, to be referred to later, it has become customary to attach Annexes that specify the standards and criteria applicable under the treaty. In accordance with this practice, we have included in Part I of this volume both examples of relevant short-form definitions and references to detailed scientific standards and criteria.

Although a comprehensive definition of pollution is impossible, it is possible to find a general consensus on the different kinds of pollution and on the different ways in which pollution can be viewed. The present scientific consensus is probably reflected in the following extract from a document prepared for the United Nations Conference on the Human Environment ("Identification and Control of Pollutants of International Significance," Doc. A/CONF. 48/8).

Human activities inevitably and increasingly introduce material and energy into the environment; *when that material or energy endangers or is liable to endanger man's health, his well-being or his resources, directly or indirectly, it is called a pollutant.* This definition suggests that desirable activities can produce undesirable side effects, and indeed that is true even of great achievements in preventive medicine, in agriculture and in industrial development that have benefited mankind. To look at it in another way, a *substance may be considered a pollutant simply because it is in the wrong place, at the wrong time, and in the wrong quantity.*

It must also be appreciated that air, water and food always contain varying amounts of "foreign" matter, and in this sense, the potential for pollution has always been present. *When we say that something is polluted, we are in fact making a value judgement about the quality or quantity of foreign matter present. This judgement may be based on objective facts, but it also depends on other value judgements that vary with social and economic circumstances.* [Emphasis added.] Similarly, the subsequent decisions as to what to do about any given pollution situation also depend on local value judgements.

Finally, it must be emphasized that one of the most widespread, and the oldest, forms of pollution is that arising from contamination of the environment, and especially of food and water supplies, by pathogenic organisms. Despite the advances that have made it possible to control many of the diseases that afflicted mankind in the past, the problem of "biological" pollution has been amplified, particularly in developing countries, by increasing population and urbanization, with the attendant need for large-scale disposal of human waste, and by changes in land use and irrigation practices.

* * *

There are many ways of thinking about pollution hazards, but probably the first requirement is to recognize the different ways in which pollutants can affect man, directly or indirectly.

Among the *direct* effects are the following:

—acute effects from exposure to a toxic pollutant reaching man through air, water or food;

—long-term effects due to prolonged exposure to a pollutant at levels lower than those giving rise to overt toxic effects;

—acute or long-term effects due to synergistic interaction between pollutants or between a pollutant and such factors as malnutrition and disease;

—genetic effects that a pollutant may induce in the germ cells of an exposed individual but that manifest themselves in his descendants, sometimes several generations removed.

Indirect effects on man may result from reduction of the food supply, deterioration of the habitat, or alteration of the climate. Such effects include:

—actual reduction of the food supply when a pollutant kills food plants or animals, renders them liable to disease, or makes the product unfit for consumption;

—elimination by a pesticide or herbicide of the natural enemies of a hitherto harmless species, allowing it to proliferate and become a pest;

—damage to the human habitat resulting from air pollution that destroys forests or corrodes buildings; from oil that fouls beaches or industrial wastes that make inland waters unusable for recreation; etc.

—alteration of the global climate from a number of causes. This however is generally considered as a threat for the future rather than an actual effect of present pollution.

* * *

Pollution can be viewed in a number of ways, each of which may be useful at one time or another. One may start by considering the the polluting agents—biological agents, chemical pesticides, excess heat, noise—and group them accordingly. The polluting activity may be examined on a geographical basis . . . is it local, regional, global? Pollutants may be considered with regard to a specific part of the biosphere . . . the air, the land, or the oceans. They may be classified by their direct or indirect effects, perhaps through a whole biological cycle or food chain, or on individual elements such as a local human population. Moreover, while the ultimate effect on man is usually the paramount point of interest, the nature of the biosphere is such that the effect on some other organism or natural resource may be of immediate concern.

Given these general considerations, there are two different approaches to the identification of individual pollutants. One is to assume that the substance under examination is not harmful, until the evidence indicates otherwise. The other method is to consider any such substance, or at least any new chemical substance, as potentially harmful, and to treat it as such until found otherwise. The debate as to which approach should be followed is a fruitful and essential part of the whole decision-making process and involves economic and political considerations as much as scientific knowledge.

Finally, in attempting to foresee future pollution problems one should consider the particular properties of substances that are likely to make them significant pollutants. In the case of chemical substances, particularly new ones, widespread or large-scale input into the biosphere is at once suggestive of hazard when associated with toxicity to plants or animals, including man, persistence in the environment or in tissues, and mobility (through atmospheric or oceanic transport, weathering or leaching from soils, or transmission through food chains).

Selected Definitions

Marine Pollution

The most widely invoked definition of marine pollution is that agreed upon in 1970 by the United Nations Group of Experts on the Scientific Aspects of Marine Pollution (GESAMP), a body of experts drawn from a number of UN agencies. It became the generally accepted working definition of marine pollution during the preparations for the 1972 UN Conference on the Human Environment held at Stockholm.

The introduction by man, directly or indirectly, of substances or energy into the marine environment (including estuaries) resulting in such deleterious effects as harm to living resources, hazards to human health, hindrance to marine activities including fishing, impairment of quality or use of sea water, and reduction of amenities.

It will be noted that this definition is limited to pollution by man, but it is sufficiently inclusive, in its reference to causes, to embrace thermal pollution arising from the increase in temperature caused by hydroelectric works. It is also sufficiently inclusive, in its reference to effects, to embrace pollution resulting in the "reduction of amenities," which would certainly include deterioration of the sea for recreational purposes and might be construed to include the additional rise in the cost of desalinization of seawater for irrigation that can be attributed to pollution.

From a scientific, as distinguished from a legal, viewpoint, it may be questioned whether it is worth while to labor over definitions of marine pollution, for it is almost impossible to separate marine pollution from pollution of the biosphere as a whole. For one thing, pollutants are transferred continuously among the atmosphere, the water, and the soil; the ocean plays the major role in this transfer mechanism through its influence on world weather patterns. Here again we are confronted with man's imperfect knowledge of the planet he inhabits and should remember that it may be dangerous to treat marine pollution separately simply because it is politically convenient and legally feasible to do so.

Waste

An alternative to defining marine pollution as such was provided in Canada's *Arctic Waters Pollution Prevention Act* of 1970. This statute defines "waste," the discharge of which in designated areas is expressly prohibited under the Act. Section 2(h) provides that waste is:

  (i) any substance that, if added to any waters, would degrade or alter or form part of a process of degradation or alteration of the quality of those waters to an extent that is detrimental to their use by man or by any animal, fish or plant that is useful to man, and
 (ii) any water that contains a substance in such a quantity or concentration, or that has been so treated, processed or changed, by heat or other means, from a natural state that it would, if added to any waters, degrade or alter or form part of a process of degradation or alteration of the quality of those waters to an extent that is detrimental to their use by man or by any animal, fish or plant that is useful to man,

and without limiting the generality of the foregoing, includes anything that, for the purposes of the *Canada Water Act,* is deemed to be waste.

The definition of waste in section 2(k) of the Canada Water Act is, it should be noted, similar to that in the Arctic Waters Pollution Prevention Act.

Hazardous Polluting Substance

Applicable to boundary waters of the Great Lakes system—all fresh water areas—the 1972 U.S.–Canadian Agreement on Great Lakes Water Quality in Article 1 defines "hazardous polluting substance" as any element or compound identified by the Parties which, when discharged in any quantity into or upon receiving waters or adjoining shorelines, present an imminent and substantial danger to public health or welfare; for this purpose, "public health or welfare" encompasses all factors affecting the health and welfare of man including but not limited to human health and the conservation and protection of fish, shellfish, wildlife, public and private property, shorelines and beaches.

This definition differs from the two preceding it in two important respects. First, it implies that there may also be "non-hazardous polluting substances," whereas marine pollution and waste are defined, by GESAMP and the Canadian government respectively, as harmful by nature. Second, the U.S.-Canadian definition of a hazardous polluting substance, focusing on the need to prove "an imminent and substantial danger to public health or welfare," is rather more prospective in its terms, allowing an earlier critical date for determining on scientific evidence whether there is pollution or whether it has reached an intolerable level.

Identification of Pollutants

As noted in the extract from the United Nations document previously cited, virtually any natural substance may be considered a pollutant if introduced into the wrong place, at the wrong time, and in the wrong quantity. Similarly, almost any human activity could result in pollution as a function of error. The growth of technology has greatly increased pollution by man, especially during the last century through the development and manufacture of synthetic materials, such as plastics, detergents and solvents, food additives, and pesticides. It is obvious, however, that many of the most serious pollution problems can be attributed directly to the introduction of specific substances. A list of the most familiar substances contributing to pollution has been compiled recently by the Secretariat of the UN Conference on the Human Environment. This list, partly reproduced below from Document A/CONF. 48/8, contains twenty-eight categories of pollutants, but this list is neither exhaustive nor arranged in order of relative importance.

Pollutant	Principal Man-Made Sources	Distribution in the Environment
Carbon dioxide (CO_2)	Carbonaceous fuel combustion for energy production, heating and transport.	Air and water (global)
Carbon monoxide (CO)	Incomplete combustion of carbonaceous matter (motor vehicles, industrial processes, solid waste disposal, forest fires).	Air (local and regional)
Sulphur dioxide (SO_2)	Energy and heat production from sulphur containing fuel. Industrial processes.	Air (water) (local and regional)
Airborne particles	Fuel combustion for heating and energy production, industrial processes, solid waste incineration, motor vehicles and other transport. Agriculture and forestry burning.	Air (local, regional and global)
Oxides of nitrogen (NO_2)	Oxidation of atmospheric nitrogen at high temperature (internal combustion engines, furnaces, incinerators), industrial processes; forest fires.	Air (local and regional)
Volatile hydrocarbons and their products	Partial combustion of carbonaceous fuels (motor vehicles, stationary fuel combustion); industrial processes; solid waste disposal; solvents; forest fires.	Air (local and regional)
Oxidants including ozone	Emissions from motor vehicles. Photochemical reactions of oxides of nitrogen and reactive hydrocarbons.	Air (local)
Fluorides	Industrial processes (production of aluminum, steel, phosphate fertilizers, fluorinated hydrocarbons, brickmaking). Combustion of coal. Industrial liquid wastes and agricultural run-off.	Air (local) water, soil, food
Odourous air pollutants	Industrial processes. Fuel combustion. Processing of animal products. Improper disposal of liquid and solid wastes.	Air (local)

Mercury (Eg)	Chlor-alkali plants. Mercurial catalysts. Pulp and paper industry (slimicides). Seed treatment. Burning of fossil fuels. Mining and refining processes. Medical and research laboratories.	Food, fresh water and marine environment, soil, air (local, regional and global)
Lead (Pb)	Anti-knock ingredients of motor fuels. Lead smelting. Chemical industry. Pesticides. Burning of fossil fuels. Lead paints, glazes, and enamels.	Air, water and food (local, regional and global)
Cadmium (Cd)	Mining and metallurgy (lead, copper, and zinc smelters). Chemical industry (alkaline accumulators, alloys, paints, and plastics).	Air, soil, water (local), food
Phosphates	Sewage. Agricultural run-off. Detergent "builders."	Fresh water and marine environment (local, regional)
Nitrates and nitrites	Sewage. Fossil fuel burning. Nitrate fertilizers. Industry.	Fresh water and marine environment, food (local and regional)
Alkyl sulfonates (AS)	Detergents in sewage and industrial wastes.	Fresh water and marine environment (local)
Chlorinated hydrocarbon (organo-chlorine) pesticides	Application in agriculture and public health. Industrial wastes (e.g. pesticide manufacture, wool and carpet manufacture).	Soil, food, water, including marine environment, air (local, regional, global)
Polychlorinated biphenyls (POB)	Electrical industry; plastics industry, lubricants, industrial effluents and sewage, uncontrolled disposal (including incineration) of POB-containing products.	Water, including marine environment (local, regional and global)
Asbestos	Mining operations, fibre production from the ore. Manufac-	Air and water (local, but

	ture of brake linings and insulated pipes (asbestos-cement industry). Abrasion of brake linings in motor vehicles. Asbestos-lined water pipes, asbestos filters.	widespread)
Mycotoxins	Prepared food for man and feed for animals.	Peanuts, beans, and corn are principal food products contaminated with aflatoxins.
Polycyclic aromatic hydrocarbons (PAH)	Combustion of organic materials. Exhausts from gasoline and diesel engines. Atmospheric soot, cigarette smoke. Wastes from gasworks, refineries, chemical industry.	Air, water, food (local and regional)
Oil	Shipping accidents. Run-off from transport wastes. Polluted land drainage. Refineries. Offshore oil production.	Fresh water, sea, and land (local and regional)
Degradable organic matter	Sewage. Garbage. Industrial wastes. Agricultural wastes.	Fresh water and marine environment, land, and soil (local)
Solid wastes	Domestic, municipal, commercial, industrial, and agricultural activities.	Land, fresh water, and marine environment (local)
Pathogenic organisms	Human and animal excreta (sewage, agricultural run-off, etc.). Contaminated food and water.	Fresh water and marine environment, soil (air)
Ionizing radiation (including radionuclides)	Medical uses. Weapon production and testing. Nuclear power production. Uses of radio-isotopes and radiation sources in industry and research.	Air, fresh water and marrine environment, land, and soil (local, regional and global)

Non-ionizing radiation	A variety of electronic devices such as microwave ovens, lasers, medical diathermy equipment, high-power radio and radar transmitters.	Not applicable
Heat	Fossil-fuel and nuclear power stations. Large urban areas.	Water, air (local)
Noise	Transportation—especially aircraft and motor vehicles. Industry. Building construction. Occupational and domestic sources.	Air (local)

The reader will note that one of these substances, namely oil, has been dealt with extensively in the context of marine pollution and has been the subject of several agreements. Other agreements not limited to one specific substance have, however, given rise to scientific studies that focus on substances that are regarded as primarily responsible for the pollution problem in question, for example, studies of the problems of pollution by mercury and phosphates arising out of the general treaty responsibilities of the International Joint Commission between Canada and the U.S.

Scientists will continue to differ among themselves on how to rank pollutants by virtue of their dangerous and toxic properties. There is still a wide disparity of scientific views, for example, on the toxic effect of oil on marine organisms. There seems to be general agreement, however, that problems of marine pollution need to be approached by reference to the following classification of dangerous and toxic pollutants:

1. Halogenated hydrocarbons and polychlorinated biphenyls (DDT, dieldrin, etc.).
2. Urban sewage containing pathogens, biological oxygen-demanding substances, absorbed metals such as zinc and lead.
3. Heavy metals—mercury, cadmium, copper, chromium, zinc, arsenic, and selenium.
4. Solid and bulky wastes.

A picture of growing scientific agreement on the identification of pollutants is presented in the Annexes to the U.S.–Canadian Agreement on Great Lakes Water Quality, to the Oslo Convention on the Control of Marine Pollution by Dumping from Ships and Aircraft, and to the London Convention on the Prevention of Marine Pollution by Dumping of Wastes and Other Matter.

Criteria of Pollution Assessment and Control

More difficult than the identification of the major pollutants is the question of how to decide that pollution has occurred, that it is getting worse, or that it has reached a degree unacceptable to society. It is interesting, and amusing, to note the condescension which Mr. Justice Holmes dispensed in *Missouri* v. *Illinois* (1906) in suggesting that the courts fifty years earlier would have been limited to the tests of the "unassisted senses." Today we are apt to look back with equal condescension, though the scientific experts today, as in that case, are still often unable to agree on the elementary scientific facts. In scientific matters our own sophistication is destined to be considered primitive by our children—at least, the scientific criteria they apply are likely to be more complicated. In the case of *New York* v. *New Jersey* (1921) Mr. Justice Clarke stated that there was

> only one point upon which all the experts called for the opposing parties agree, viz.: that in the present state of learning upon the subject the amount of dissolved oxygen [DO] in water is the best index or measure of the degree to which it is polluted by organic substances, it seemingly being accepted by them all that upon the oxygen content of water depends its capacity for digesting sewage— that is, for converting organic matters into inorganic and harmless substances by direct oxidation and by sustaining bacteria which assist in such conversion.

This should be contrasted with the more sophisticated approach to the question of water quality reflected in the Annexes to the 1972 U.S.-Canadian Agreement on Great Lakes Water Quality and the related 1971 Memorandum of Agreement between Canada and the Province of Ontario, both influenced by the 1950, 1960, and 1970 Reports of the International Joint Commission of Canada and the United States.[1]

---

[1] On the traditional dissolved-oxygen (DO) test of water quality, see Ackerman, B., and Sawyer, J., "The Uncertain Search for Environmental Policy: Scientific Fact-finding and Rational Decision-making along the Delaware River," 120 *U. Penn. L. Rev.* 419 (1972).

In the past it was common to approach the question of pollution through the legal concept of nuisance, which was often determined by reference to the value criteria of human health and welfare, property rights, and commercial interests. In *New York* v. *New Jersey* (1921) the court was asked to go further and consider the *right* of the United States to protect public property and the welfare of its employees. Following current trends in political philosophy, we are more likely today to consider these criteria as obligatory, falling within the powers of governments and public agencies as a matter of social responsibility.

This question of government prerogative and responsibility for environmental control has arisen first not in international law but in constitutional law, with which this volume is only tangentially concerned. But it is interesting to note that in *Georgia* v. *Tennessee Copper* (1906), the State of Georgia was awarded an injunction to prevent the defendant from polluting Georgian territory from the State of Tennessee. In writing the Supreme Court's opinion, Mr. Justice Holmes declared: "It is a fair and reasonable demand on the part of a sovereign that the air over its territory should not be polluted on a great scale by sulphurous acid gas, that the forests on its mountains, be they better or worse, and whatever domestic destruction they have suffered, should not be further destroyed or threatened by the act of persons beyond its control . . . ." Holmes appears to have been a consistent environmentalist: for example, in the second *Missouri* v. *Illinois* case (1906) he pungently observed that it is a "question of the first magnitude whether the destiny of the great rivers is to be the sewers of the cities along their banks or to be protected against everything that threatens their purity." However, Mr. Justice Harlan, in a separate concurring judgment in the Georgia case, disagreed with Holmes' contention that the court was authorized to treat Georgia differently by virtue of its powers of sovereignty and grant it an injunction even if this would not have been possible on the same facts if Georgia had been a private party. "Georgia," Harlan asserted, "is entitled to the relief sought not because it is a State, but because it is a *party* which has established its right to such relief by proof."

The question of the extent of a sovereign entity's special responsibility for environmental protection is, of course, of great significance in international law. Moreover, delay in the exercise of government responsibility gives rise to moral issues that transcend questions of jurisdiction and procedure. For example, given the lack of an appropriate government initiative, should a private party be allowed to initiate a suit in the public interest in order to protect the environment, even though he cannot show that he has suffered direct personal economic loss? The most recent answer of the United States Supreme Court, in *Sierra Club* v. *Morton* (1972), is in the negative, despite three vigorous dissents. It should be observed that in this particular case the alleged threat of pollution was to the scenic beauty of the Sierra Nevada Mountains in California. Though the negative decision of the majority was on procedural grounds, on the issue of standing, the court did not reject the notion that this alleged threat would constitute a kind of pollution. This at least is a contribution to environmental law, which may be compared with the decision of the governments of the United States and Canada to act together to combat scenic pollution under the 1950 Treaty Relating to the Uses of the Waters of the Niagara River, in which the parties acknowledged "their primary obligation to preserve and enhance the scenic beauty of the Niagara Falls and River."

Today, of course, it is obvious that lawyers on their own cannot be expected to provide the criteria of pollution assessment and control. This is primarily a scientific question that can be approached only on an interdisciplinary basis. Normally, lawyers, economists, and other kinds of specialists have to be added to the mix of disciplines in order to achieve a well-rounded view of what is essentially a matter of social policy. Considerable experience in this kind of collaboration is now being consolidated to provide criteria for the prevention and control of marine pollution. For example, in determining how industrial and other wastes are to be disposed of, dumped, or discharged into the ocean, there appears to be a growing consensus among scientists, lawyers, and administrators that the following criteria should be considered:

1. The area in which waste materials are to be disposed of.
2. The total amount of waste materials to be disposed of.
3. The amount of material to be deposited in a given period of time.
4. The concentration of the substances.
5. The method of disposal.
6. The physical, chemical, and biochemical properties of the substances.
7. The bacteriological properties of the substances.
8. The solubility of the substances in sea water.
9. The density of the substances.
10. The toxicity and the potential danger of the substances for the fauna and flora of the sea and for man, including accumulation in the food chain.
11. The chemical reactions of substances with sea water.
12. The speed of chemical or biological reactions during the process or the formation of new compounds, including their breakdown.

13. The potential dangers of the substances to shipping and other marine activities.

In establishing criteria of pollution assessment, as distinguished from criteria of pollution control, it may be sufficient to adopt a simple test that will enable the potential polluter to determine at the critical point, with his "unassisted senses," whether his activity involves pollution. Pollution-control treaties that can be enforced only through national penal legislation can sometimes be strengthened by the inclusion of definitions containing criteria that consist of simple empirical tests. In the 1972 United States–Canadian Agreement on Great Lakes Water Quality, for example, a "harmful quantity of oil" is defined in Annex 7 to mean

> any quantity of oil that, if discharged into receiving waters, would produce a film or sheen upon, or discoloration of, the surface of the water or adjoining shoreline, or that would cause a sludge or emulsion to be deposited beneath the surface of the water or upon adjoining shoreline.

Obviously, however, where the treaty deals with forms of pollution caused only by large-scale organizations (e.g., factory emissions), there is less reason for avoiding the use of more sophisticated scientific criteria of pollution assessment.

Priority of Uses

The difficulty of determining socially acceptable criteria in pollution prevention and control is magnified when the threatened resource has multiple uses. Most of the early river-basin agreements, especially in Europe, gave precedence to the interests of navigation. In these early agreements there was no explicit acceptance of the need to prevent these great rivers from becoming the "sewers of the cities along their banks," though many of them contained provisions to safeguard other uses of the waters.[2] In North America, however, the

---

[2] The preference for navigation over other uses was evident also in general conventions governing the use of international rivers, such as the 1921 Barcelona Convention and Statute on the Regime of Navigable Waterways of International Concern. But in the absence of an international commission for any such waterway, it was provided that one of the riparian states might close the waters to navigation, if the navigation on them was of very small importance and if the state in question could show an economic interest clearly greater than that of navigation.

United States and Canada, under the 1909 Boundary Waters Treaty, gave highest preference to the "domestic and sanitary" uses of the boundary waters of the two countries. The parties agreed in Article 4 that boundary waters "shall not be polluted on either side to the injury of health or property on the other," and the International Joint Commission established by the parties was instructed under Article 8 to give lesser priority to navigation, power, and irrigation. This order of priorities was ostensibly followed in the 1925 Agreement and Protocol to Regulate the Level of Lake of the Woods and in the 1944 Exchange of Notes with respect to the I.J.C.'s study of the Upper Columbia River Basin, but it is only in recent years that the Commission has become chiefly preoccupied with pollution, as noted in our Introduction to Part Two.

Even earlier, in 1889, the United States and Mexico established an International Boundary Commission (later called the International Boundary and Water Commission) to discharge responsibilities with respect to utilization of the waters of the Colorado and Tijuana Rivers and the Rio Grande. In the treaty of 1944 between the same parties this Commission was required to follow an order of preference that gave highest priority to "domestic and municipal uses" and to "agriculture and stock-raising." There followed electric power, other industrial uses, navigation, fishing and hunting, and "any other beneficial uses which may be determined by the Commission."

A similar order of precedence, favorable to the interests of environmental protection, is becoming more generally accepted in other parts of the world. This can be seen, for instance, in the 1960 Indus Waters Treaty between India and Pakistan which is especially protective of agricultural and domestic uses.

Quality Standards

Perhaps the most challenging problem in the international law of pollution is that of securing widespread agreement among nations on the establishment of environmental quality standards. It is unlikely that this can be done on a universal basis in the near future. There are, however, some important developments on a regional and common user basis. The 1972 United States–Canadian Agreement on Great Lakes Water Quality contains articles on general and specific water quality objectives and Annexes that translate these objectives into scientific terms. On the Canadian side, this international accord was preceded by the 1971 Memorandum of Agreement between Canada and the Province of Ontario, with similar water quality objectives also translated into scientific terms. These objectives are largely based on, though not identical to, the objectives proposed by the I.J.C. in its 1970 Report, and they represent a much tougher approach to pollution of the Great Lakes than previously taken. This new policy should be contrasted with the "reasonable use" approach adopted by the Commission as recently as 1965 in its Report on the Pollution of Rainy River and Lake of the Woods. Extensive portions of the 1965 and 1970 Reports are reproduced to show the recent tightening of standards by an international agency that has been closely studied and accepted as a model in many parts of the world.

It is also interesting to compare these developments in water-quality standards with earlier approaches to the establishment of health and safety standards in the handling of radioactive materials by international agencies such as the International Atomic Energy Agency, Euratom, and the International Labour Organization. It is, however, beyond the scope of this collection to illustrate the full range of international experience in the establishment of technical standards with which most countries, rich and poor, have been able to comply.

The Doctrine of Municipal Law

The emerging international law of pollution owes something, at least indirectly, to the existing doctrine of national (municipal) law. Even though most international measures in pollution prevention and control represent fresh efforts in treaty-making, those engaged in these lawmaking exercises have been furnished by training with relevant, cognate, or analogous concepts that have evolved within national legal systems. At least in this sense, the international law of pollution has a municipal law heritage. Moreover, in certain aspects of the international law of pollution, such as the control of pollution in international rivers and lakes and the liability of shipowners for marine pollution by oil, the public and private principles of municipal law are directly applicable, providing the primary concepts for the treatment of these problems on the international level.

It is not our intention to trace these principles in detail, nor can we provide an overview of municipal law heritage that would be representative of all major legal systems. Instead we have limited ourselves to two objectives that are much more modest. For readers interested in the Anglo-American common law system, we have attached a brief list of readings, which provide at most a suggested point of departure. For readers unlikely even to sample the literature of common law doctrine, we have drawn from the suggested readings some of the more familiar legal concepts, which provide as it were some of the furnishings of the legal mind trained in the Anglo-American system.

Much of the pollution litigation today in the common law world is affected, if not controlled, by the existence of statutes; but in most cases the plaintiff's chance of a remedy, such as damages, depends upon the court's interpretation of (unlegislated) common law doctrine that has evolved over decades, even centuries, of legal development. The relevant doctrine is likely to fall within the area of tortious liability or property rights or both. The four main heads of pollution-related doctrine in the common law are negligence, strict (or absolute) liability, nuisance, and riparian rights.

Negligence (or fault) is the usual basis of liability for tortious conduct under the common law, that is, for wrongful conduct that causes an injury and gives rise to a claim for damages. The plaintiff suing for pollution damage on the basis of negligence would have to show that the defendant, the alleged polluter, had fallen short of the standard of conduct imputed (by the court) to a hypothetical "reasonable man" and could have foreseen that his conduct might result in damage like that which has occurred. In pollution cases based on negligence it is often difficult for the plaintiff to show what standard should be expected of a prudent operator, and he will have to contend with the usual difficulties of proving negligence, such as establishing cause and effect and applying the test of foreseeability. In some pollution cases, however, the court has lightened the plaintiff's burden of proof by applying the doctrine of *res ipsa loquitur,* which permits an inference of negligence upon a showing that the action, activity, or omission causing injury is of a kind that ordinarily does not occur in the absence of negligence, that the injury was caused by an instrumentality within the defendant's exclusive control, and that the injury was not due to the voluntary action of the plaintiff.

The doctrine of *strict (or absolute) liability* has evolved in modern times in certain kinds of situations where injury has been caused by an activity that is not wrongful but gives rise to liability even in the absence of an allegation of negligence or fault. A familiar example is the situation where the defendant has created a peril on his own property or has engaged in a lawful but ultrahazardous activity that results in an injury to the plaintiff. In these circumstances, under the doctrine of strict liability, the defendant is obligated to compensate the plaintiff for all damage that is the natural result of the peril or activity, regardless of a finding that the defendant exercised due care. A good example, of special importance in international law, is the application of the doctrine of strict or absolute liability to operators or agencies responsible for the manufacture, transportation, or use of radioactive materials, activities that may result in injuries in the form of pollution by radiation.

Nuisance may be defined as substantial and unreasonable interference with the use and enjoyment of another's property. To be a nuisance, the pollution complained of would have to be regarded as offensive to a reasonable person of ordinary sensibilities. A nuisance action can be based upon a negligent, intentional, or ultrahazardous act. Though negligence can be the basis of a nuisance action, it is not a requirement for assigning liability; and negligence and nuisance are generally treated as separate fields of tortious liability. On the question of proof, the court looks primarily to the *effect*, rather than the nature, of the act complained of, in determining whether a nuisance exists.

The concept of nuisance is sometimes divided into three categories: private nuisance, public nuisance, and statutory nuisance (or nuisance *per se*).

Private nuisance involves the defendant's unreasonable use of his property in such a way as to cause substantial interference with the use and enjoyment of the plaintiff's property. The plaintiff must show not only that the defendant's conduct was the proximate cause of the interference but also that the defendant's conduct was either intentional and unreasonable or unintentional and actionable under the rules governing liability for negligent, reckless, or ultrahazardous conduct.

Public nuisance, on the other hand, is an interference with the right of the public at large. Logically, this concept seems more relevant to the social problem of environmental damage, but it is less developed doctrinally than the concept of private nuisance. Historically, there is no connection between the two, but the two classes are frequently treated as if they were generically linked. It is often said that public nuisance actions must proceed, *mutatis mutandis,* subject to the same doctrinal requirements as private nuisance suits. As public nuisances affect private individuals, often in the same way as private nuisances, they may give rise to procedural issues such as the basic question of the private right to represent the public interest, a highly pertinent and controversial question in the context of environmental damage as long as statutory law in this field is underdeveloped.

The third category, *statutory nuisance,* is of course a kind of nuisance created by legislation. In this case the plaintiff need only show that the statute has been violated in order to recover on the basis of nuisance. Most statutory nuisances are minor criminal offences. For example, in industrial societies where factory smoke constitutes a serious pollution problem there are statutes declaring such emissions to be a public nuisance and punishable as such. In the absence of an express provision in the statute, statutory intention to create the type of nuisance complained of might be inferred by the court from the express prohibition of the kind of activity that has caused pollution, if it seems to satisfy the normal common law criteria of nuisance.

In the past most water pollution nuisance cases have followed the doctrine of private rather than public nuisance. It is quite possible that this trend will be reversed under pressure from environmental groups and agencies, allowing the courts to develop the doctrine of public nuisance that recognizes rights in the public to be free from certain forms of interference with the public safety, health, comfort, and convenience. Actions to abate a public nuisance can be brought by public agencies and, in certain common law jurisdictions, also by private individuals. For a private plaintiff (or complainant) to bring an action to abate a public nuisance he will normally have to show that he has suffered an injury different in kind and degree from that suffered by the public at large.

The doctrine of *riparian rights* is applicable to questions concerning the reasonable quantity and quality of water. Essentially, it limits the right to use running water to those who have access to it by virtue of their ownership of land. Roman in origin, the doctrine evolved in different versions in both civil law and common law countries. By the time of the Code Napoleon, in early 19th-century France, the doctrine was highly developed; and since then it has spread to most countries in Western Europe, many countries in Asia, and all countries in Latin America, though in many different versions. Riparianism was also inherent in medieval English common law and seems to have come to the British American colonies as part of that heritage. As the English version of riparian rights spread also to other parts of the British Empire, in one form or another the doctrine has become an important feature of property law in most areas of the world.

In most countries, therefore, it is often possible for a private land-owner to sue for water pollution damage on the ground that the defendant has infringed the plaintiff's riparian rights. In most common law countries, however, confusion has arisen out of the evolution of two distinct branches of riparian doctrine. On the one hand, it has been recognized since the 19th century, when the Industrial Revolution made its impact on land law, that riparian owners had a right to the *reasonable use* of water flowing past their land. To facilitate testing the reasonableness of water use there was a trend toward categorical distinctions and *a priori* criteria. For example, a distinction was made between domestic and nondomestic uses. Domestic uses included drinking, washing, cleaning, and the watering of livestock belonging to the riparian owner and family. Domestic uses were declared in advance to be reasonable, and riparians in supplying the needs of the family dwelling were permitted to consume as much water as was necessary for those purposes without regard for the needs of the downstream neighbor. Other uses, such as for industry and irrigation, were unreasonable if they interfered with the existing domestic uses of other riparians.

These and related developments led to what is called the *natural flow* version of riparian rights doctrine. There is a great deal of variation and confusion in the common law countries with respect to the relationship between *reasonable use* and *natural flow* versions of riparianism. It is enough here to observe that they are, strictly interpreted, incompatible with each other. *Natural flow* logic begins with the policy that there should be no adulteration of water quality and that absolute natural purity should be maintained. *Reasonable use* represents a flexible, relativist, broadbased policy approach to the problem of multiple use, which tolerates solutions that might involve the acceptance of some lessening of water quality. Under the pressure of environmental dangers and fears, the natural flow version of riparian rights doctrine has been revised, but in view of the growing urgency for tighter social control of water management it seems that riparian doctrine as a whole will continue to decline as a legal approach to problems of water pollution. For one reason, natural flow doctrine is often used by common law courts as a means of confining permissible uses to those that are "natural in character," that is, to those traditionally associated with the land, which is quite a different focus from that on "pure" water quality. Similarly, the concept of reasonable use is employed in diverse ways, sometimes, for example, to uphold the prevailing usage custom, sometimes to refer to the degree of traditional domestic usage. In short, the riparian doctrine seems to have run out of control.

A fifth remedial approach to pollution problems in common law jurisdictions, by actions in trespass, raises technical considerations that need not be explained in this summary intended for lay readers.

Suggested Reading List

General: Legal Aspects of Environmental Protection Policy

Mayda, Jaro, *Environment and Resources: From Conservation to Eco-management* (1968).

Baldwin, Malcolm F., and Page, James K., Jr., *Law and the Environment* (1970).

Gray, Oscar S., *Cases and Materials of Environmental Law* (1970).

Grad, F. P., *Environmental Control: Priorities, Policies and the Law* (1971).

Jaffe, Louis L., and Tribe, Lawrence H., *Environmental Protection* (1971).

Sloan, Irving J., *Environment and the Law* (1971).

Landau, Norman J., and Rheingold, Paul D., *The Environmental Law Handbook* (1971).

Lohrman, Robert R., "The Environmental Lawsuit: Traditional Doctrines and Evolving Theories to Control Pollution," 16 *Wayne L. Rev.* 1085 (1970).

McLaughlin, J., *The Law Relating to Pollution: An Introduction* (1972).

Lucas, A. R., "Legal Control of Pollution in Canada," 8 *Col. int. de droit compare* (Centre Can. Droit compare) 11 (1970).

Juergensmeyer, J. C., "American Legal System and Environmental Pollution," 23 *U. Fla. L. Rev.* 439 (1971).

Krier, James E., "The Pollution Problem and Legal Institutions: A Conceptual Overview," 18 *UCLA L. Rev.* 429 (1971).

Caponera, Dante A., "Towards a New Methodological Approach in Environmental Law," 12 *Nat. Resources Journal* 133 (1972).

Thompson Andrew R., "Legal Responses to Pollution Problems: Their Strengths and Weaknesses," *ibid.* 227.

Calabresi, Guido, and Melamed, A. Douglas, "Property Rules, Liability Rules, and Inalienability: One View of the Cathedral," 85 *Harv. L. Rev.* 1089 (1972).

Bryson, J. E., and Macbeth, A., "Public Nuisance, the Restatement (Second) of Torts, and Environmental Law," 2 *Ecol. L. Q.* 241 (1972).

Garton, W. A., "The State versus Extraterritorial Pollution-States' Environmental Rights Under Federal Common Law," *ibid.* 313.

General: Non-Legal Aspects of Environmental Protection Policy

Dales, John, *Pollution, Property and Prices: An Essay in Policy-making and Economics* (1968).

Stepp, J. M., and Macauley, H. H., *The Pollution Problem* (1968).

Davies, J. Clarence, III, *The Politics of Pollution* (1970).

Ehrlich, Paul R., *Population Resources, Environment: Issues in Human Ecology* (1970).

Bohm, Peter, and Kneese, Allen V., eds., *The Economics of Environment* (1971).

Marx, Wesley, *Man and His Environment: Waste* (1971).

Boulding, Kenneth E., and others, *Economics of Pollution* (1971).

Murdoch, William W., ed., *Environment: Resources, Pollution and Society* (1971).

Kneese, A. V., and Bower, Blair T., *Environmental Quality Analysis* (1972).

Meyers, Charles J., and Tarlock, A. Dan, *Selected Legal and Economic Aspects of Environmental Protection* (1971).

Kneese, A. V., "*Environmental Pollution: Economics and Policy*," *Amer. Econ. Rev. and Procs. (83rd Annual Mtg. Amer. Econ. Assoc.,* May, 1971), pp. 153–66.

Solow, R. M., "The Economist's Approach to Pollution and its Control," *Science,* Aug. 6, 1971.

Chase, R. X., "Economic Analysis and Environmental Quality," 31 *Amer. J. Econ.* 271 (1972).

Lowenthal, John, "Research in Environmental Perception and Behavior: Perspectives on Current Problems," 4 *Environ. and Behav.* 333 (1972).

Water Pollution: Legal Aspects

Davis, Peter N., "Theories of Water Pollution Litigation," 1971 *Wisc. L. Rev.* 738 (1971).

Ackerman, Bruce and Sawyer, James, "The Uncertain Search for Environmental Policy: Scientific Fact-finding and Rational Decision-making along the Delaware River," 120 *U. Penn. L. Rev.* 419 (1972).

Teclaff, Ludwik A., "What You Have Always Wanted to Know about Riparian Rights but Were Afraid to Ask," 12 *Nat. Resources J.* 30 (1972).

Meyers, C. J., and Tarlock, A. D., *Water Resources Management: A Coursebook in Law and Public Policy* (1971).

Curlin, J. W., "The Interstate Water Pollution Compact—Paper Tiger or Effective Regulatory Device?" 2 *Ecol. L. Q.* 333 (1972).

Air Pollution: Legal Aspects

Edelman, Sidney, *The Law of Air Pollution Control* (1970).

Krier, James E., *Environmental Law and Policy: Readings, Materials and Notes on Air Pollution and Related Problems* (1971).

Schuck, Benedict A., III, "Air Pollution as a Private Nuisance," 3 *Nat. Resources Lawyer* 475 (1970).

Koen, Robert G., and Ain, Sanford K., "The Availability of Individual or Class Actions for Damages as a Deterrent to Air Pollution," 16 *N.Y. Law Forum* 751 (1970).

Trumbull, T. A., "Federal Control of Statutory Source Air Pollution," 2 *Ecol. L. Q.* 283 (1972).

Aircraft Noise and Sonic Boom: Legal Aspects

Logan, George B., "The Recent Trend of Aeronautical Litigation," 4 *J. Air Law* 462 (1933).

(Case Note), 18 *J. Air Law* 486 (1951).

Roth, Allen J., "Sonic Boom: A Definition and Some Legal Implications," 25 *J. Air Law and Commerce* 68 (1958).

Calkins, G. Nathan, "The Landowner and the Aircraft—1958," *ibid.* 373.

Tondel, Lyman M., Jr., "Noise Litigation at Public Airports," 32 *J. Air Law and Commerce* 378 (1966).

Munro, James, "Aircraft Noise as a Taking of Property," 13 *N.Y. Law Forum* 476 (1967).

McNairn, C. H., "Airport Noise Pollution: The Problem and the Regulatory Response," 50 *Can. Bar Rev.* 248 (1972).

Offshore Oil Spills: Legal Aspects

Krueger, Robert B., "International and National Regulation of Pollution from Offshore Oil Production," 7 *San Diego L. Rev.* 541 (1970).

Nanda, Ved P., and Stiles, Kenneth R., "Offshore Oil Spills: An Evaluation of Recent United States Responses," *ibid.* 519.

Walmesley, David J., "Oil Pollution Problems Arising out of the Exploitation of the Continental Shelf: the Santa Barbara Disaster," 9 *San Diego L. Rev.* 514 (1972).

Decisions of the United States Supreme Court

◢ MISSOURI V. ILLINOIS AND THE SANITARY DISTRICT OF CHICAGO (1900)

This suit was brought by the State of Missouri against the State of Illinois and the Sanitary District of Chicago. The latter is alleged to be "a public corporation, organized under the laws of the State of Illinois and located in part in the city of Chicago, and in the county of Cook, in the State of Illinois, and a citizen of the State of Illinois." The remedy sought for is an injunction restraining the defendants from receiving or permitting any sewage to be received or discharged into the artificial channel or drain constructed by the Sanitary District, under authority derived from the State of Illinois, in order to carry off and eventually discharge into the Mississippi the sewage of Chicago, which had been previously discharged into Lake Michigan, and from permitting the same to flow through said channel or drain into the Des Plaines River, and thence by the river Illinois into the Mississippi. The bill alleged that the nature of the injury complained of was such that an adequate remedy could only be found in this court, at the suit of the State of Missouri. The object of the bill was to subject this public work to judicial supervision, upon the allegation that the method of its construction and maintenance will create a continuing nuisance, dangerous to the health of a neighboring State and its inhabitants, and the bill charged that the acts of the defendants, if not restrained, would result in the transportation, by artificial means, and through an unnatural channel, of large quantities of undefecated sewage daily, and of accumulated deposits in the harbor of Chicago, and in the bed of the Illinois River, which will poison the water supply of the inhabitants of Missouri, and injuriously affect that portion of the bed or soil of the Mississippi River which lies within its territory. The bill did not assail the drainage canal as an unlawful structure, nor aim to prevent its use as a waterway, but it sought relief against the pouring of sewage and filth through it by artificial arrangements into the Mississippi River, to the detriment of the State of Missouri and its inhabitants. The defendants demurred to the bill for want of jurisdiction and for reasons set forth in the demurrer. This court *held* that the demurrer could not be sustained, and required the defendants to appear and answer.

Mr. Justice Shiras delivered the opinion of the court.

In January, 1900, the State of Missouri filed in this court a bill of complaint against the State of Illinois and the Sanitary District of Chicago, a corporation of the latter State. . . .

An inspection of the bill discloses that the nature of the injury complained of is such that an adequate remedy can only be found in this court at the suit of the State of Missouri. It is true that no question of boundary is involved, nor of direct property rights belonging to the complainant State. But it must surely be conceded that, if the health and comfort of the inhabitants of a State are threatened, the State is the proper party to represent and defend them. If Missouri were an independent and sovereign State all must admit that she could seek a remedy by negotiation, and, that failing, by force. Diplomatic powers and the right to make war having been surrendered to the general government, it was to be expected that upon the latter would be devolved the duty of providing a remedy and that remedy, we think, is found in the constitutional provisions we are considering.

The allegations of the bill plainly present such a case. The health and comfort of the large communities inhabiting those parts of the State situated on the Mississippi River are not alone concerned, but contagious and typhoidal diseases introduced in the river communities may spread themselves throughout the territory of the State. Moreover substantial impairment of the health and prosperity of the towns and cities of the State situated on the Mississippi River, including its commercial metropolis, would injuriously affect the entire State.

That suits brought by individuals, each for personal injuries, threatened or received, would be wholly inadequate and disproportionate remedies, requires no argument.

It is further contended, in support of the demurrer, that even if the State of Missouri be the proper party to file such a bill, yet that the proper defendant is the Sanitary District of Chicago solely, and that the State of Illinois should not have been made a party, and that, as to her, the demurrer ought to be sustained.

It can scarcely be supposed, in view of the express provisions of the Constitution and of the cited cases, that it is claimed that the State of Illinois is exempt from suit because she is a sovereign State which has not consented to be sued. The contention rather seems to be that, because the matters complained of in the bill proceed and will continue to proceed from the acts of the Sanitary District of Chicago, a corporation of the State of Illinois, it therefore follows that the State, as such, is not interested in the question, and is improperly made a party.

We are unable to see the force of this suggestion. The bill does not allege that the Sanitary District is acting without or in excess of lawful authority. The averment and the conceded facts are that the corporation is an agency of the State to do the very things which, according to the theory of the complainant's case, will result in the mischief to be apprehended. It is state action and its results that are complained of—thus distinguishing this case from that of *Louisiana* v. *Texas*, where the acts sought to be restrained were alleged to be those of officers or functionaries proceeding in a wrongful and malevolent misapplication of the quarantine laws of Texas. The Sanitary District of Chicago is not a private corporation, formed for purposes of private gain, but a public corporation, whose existence and operations are wholly within the control of the State.

The object of the bill is to subject this public work to judicial supervision, upon the allegation that the method of its construction and maintenance will create a continuing nuisance, dangerous to the health of a neighboring State and its inhabitants. Surely, in such a case, the State of Illinois would have a right to appear and traverse the allegations of the bill, and, having such a right, might properly be made a party defendant.

It is further contended that, even if this court has original jurisdiction of the subject-matter, and even if the respective States have been properly made parties, yet the case made out by the bill does not entitle the State of Missouri to the equitable relief prayed for.

This proposition is sought to be maintained by several considerations. In the first place, it is urged that the drawing, by artificial means, of the sewage of the city of Chicago into the Mississippi River may or may not become a nuisance to the inhabitants, cities and towns of Missouri; that the injuries apprehended are merely eventual or contingent, and may, in fact, never be inflicted. Can it be gravely contended that there are no preventive remedies, by way of injunction or otherwise, against injuries not inflicted or experienced, but which would appear to be the natural result of acts of the defendant, which he admits or avows it to be his intention to commit?

The bill charges that the acts of the defendants, if not restrained, will result in the transportation, by artificial means and through an unnatural channel, of large quantities of undefecated sewage daily, and of accumulated deposits in the harbor of Chicago and in the bed of the Illinois River, which will poison the water supply of the inhabitants of Missouri and injuriously affect that portion of the bed or soil of the Mississippi River which lies within its territory.

In such a state of facts, admitted by the demurrer to be true, we do not feel it necessary to enter at large into a discussion of this part of the defendants' contention. . . .

It is finally contended [by counsel] that, if the bill was not prematurely filed, then it was filed too late; that, by standing by for so long a period, the complainant was guilty of such laches that a court of equity will not grant relief.

The inconsistency between these contentions is manifest, and on consideration, we are of opinion that the suggestion that the complainant's remedy has been lost by delay, is not founded in fact or reason.

In *Goldsmid* v. *Tunbridge Wells Commissioners,* L. R. 1 Eq. 161 answering a similar contention, it was said by Romilly, M. R.:

If the plaintiff comes to the court and complains very early, then the evidence is that the pollution is not preceptible, it is wholly inappreciable, and you get evidence after evidence for the defendants, (the pollution being slight and perhaps only observable at some times and on some occasions,) saying you have no proof at all that there is any appreciable pollution, and you must wait until it becomes a nuisance. Then he waits for five or six years, until it is obvious to everybody's sense that the pollution is considerable, and then they say "you have come too late, you have allowed this to continue on for twenty years, and we have acquired an easement over your property, and the right of pouring the sewage into it." My opinion is that any person who has a water course flowing through his land, and sewage which is preceptible is brought into that water course, has a right to come here to stop it; and that when the pollution is increasing, and gradually increasing from time to time, by the additional quantity of sewage poured into it, the persons who allow the polluted matter to flow into the stream are not at liberty to claim any right or prescription against him. . . .

This is a matter of very great importance, and it has been suggested to me in argument as a matter that ought to be regarded that private interests must give way to public interests; that the court ought to regard what the advantage to the public is, and that some little sacrifice ought to be made by private individuals. I do not assent to that view of the law on the subject, and I apprehend that the observations which were quoted to me of Vice Chancellor Sir William Page Wood, in the *Attorney General* v. *The Mayor of Kingston,* 13 W. R. 888, are perfectly accurate, and that private rights are not to be interfered with. But my firm conviction is that in this, as in all the great dispensations and operations of nature, the interests of the individuals are not only compatible with but identical with the interests of the public; and although in this case I have only to consider an injury to the private individual, the plaintiff in the present action, yet I believe that the injury to the public may be extremely great by polluting a stream which flows for a considerable distance, the water of which cattle are in the habit of drinking, the exhalations from which persons who reside on the banks must necessarily inhale, and this at a time when the attention of the people and the court is necessarily called to the fact that the most scientific men who have examined the subject are unable to say whether great diseases among cattle and contagious diseases affecting human beings, such as cholera or typhus, and the like, may not in a great measure be communicated or aggravated by the absorption of particles of feculent matter into the system, which are either inappreciable or scarcely appreciable by the most minute chemical analysis. It is impossible in that state of things to say what amount of injury may be done by polluting even partially a stream which flows a considerable distance. I am of opinion that Mr. Goldsmid was not bound to remain quiet until this stream had become such a nuisance that it was obvious to everybody near its banks; and the result is that in my opinion he is entitled to a decree for an injunction to restrain the defendants from causing or permitting the sewage and other offensive matters from the town of Tunbridge Wells to be discharged into the Calverly Brook, or stream, in such a manner as to affect the waters of the brook as it flows through the plaintiff's land.

This decree of the Master of the Rolls was subsequently affirmed on appeal. L. R. 1 Ch. App. 349. . . .

Cases cited by defendants' counsel, where injunctions were refused to aid in the suppression of public nuisances, were cases where the act complained of was fully completed, and where the nuisance was not one resulting from conduct repeated from day to day. Most of them were cases of purpresture, and concerned permanent structures already existing when courts in equity were appealed to.

The bill in this case does not assail the drainage canal as an unlawful structure, nor aim to prevent its use as a waterway. What is sought is relief against the pouring of sewage and filth through it, by artificial arrangements, into the Mississippi River, to the detriment of the State of Missouri and her inhabitants, and the acts are not merely those that have been done, or which when done cease to operate, but acts contemplated as continually repeated from day to day. The relief prayed for is against not merely the creation of a nuisance but against its maintenance.

Our conclusion, therefore, is that the demurrers filed by the respective defendants cannot be sustained. We do not wish to be understood as holding that, in a case like the present one, where the injuries complained of grow out of the prosecution of a public work, authorized by law, a court of equity ought to interpose by way of preliminary or interlocutory injunction, when it is denied by answer that there is any reasonable foundation for the charges contained in the bill. We are dealing with the case of a bill alleging, in explicit terms, that damage and irreparable injury will naturally and necessarily be occasioned by acts of the defendants, and where the defendants have chosen to have their rights disposed of, so far as the present hearing is concerned, upon the assertions of this bill.

We fully agree with the contention of defendants' counsel that it is settled that an injunction to restrain a nuisance will issue only in cases where the fact of nuisance is made out upon determinate and satisfactory evidence; that if the evidence be conflicting and the injury be doubtful, that conflict and doubt will be a ground for withholding an injunction; and that, where interposition by injunction is sought, to restrain that which is apprehended will create a nuisance of which its complainant may complain, the proofs must show such a state of facts as will manifest the danger to be real and immediate. But such observations are not relevant to the case as it is now before us.

The demurrers are overruled, and leave is given to the defendants to file answers to the bill.

Mr. Chief Justice Fuller, with whom concurred Mr. Justice Harlan and Mr. Justice White, dissenting:

Controversies between the States of this Union are made justiciable by the Constitution because other modes of determining them were surrendered; and before that jurisdiction, which is intended to supply the place of the means usually resorted to by independent sovereignties to terminate their differences, can be invoked, it must appear that the States are in direct antagonism as States. Clearly this bill makes out no such state of case.

If, however, on the case presented, it was competent for Missouri to implead the State of Illinois, the only ground on which it can be rested is to be found in the allegation that its Governor was about to authorize the water to be turned into the drainage channel.

The Sanitary District was created by an act of the General Assembly of Illinois, and the only authority of the State having any control and supervision over the channel is that corporation. Any other control or supervision lies with the law-making power of the State of Illinois, and I cannot suppose that complainant seeks to coerce that. It is difficult to conceive what decree could be entered in this case which would bind the State of Illinois or control its action.

The Governor, it is true, was empowered by the act to authorize the water to be let into the channel on the receipt of a certificate, by commissioners appointed by him to inspect the work, that the channel was of the capacity and character required. This was done, and the water was let in on the day when the application was made to this court for leave to file the bill. The Governor had discharged his duty, and no official act of Illinois, as such, remained to be performed.

Assuming that a bill could be maintained against the Sanitary District in a proper case, I cannot agree that the State of Illinois would be a necessary or proper party, or that this bill can be maintained against the corporation as the case stands.

The act complained of is not a nuisance, *per se,* and the injury alleged to be threatened is contingent. As the channel has been in operation for a year, it is probable that the supposed basis of complaint can now be tested. But it does not follow that the bill in its present shape should be retained.

In my opinion both the demurrers should be sustained, and the bill dismissed, without prejudice to a further application, as against the Sanitary District, if authorized by the State of Missouri.

My brothers Harlan and White concur with me in this dissent.

📧 MISSOURI v. ILLINOIS AND THE SANITARY DISTRICT OF CHICAGO (1906)

Mr. Justice Holmes delivered the opinion of the court.

. . . A supplemental bill alleges that since the filing of the original bill the drainage canal has been opened and put into operation and has produced and is producing all the evils which were apprehended when the injunction first was asked. The answers deny the plaintiff's case, allege that the new plan sends the water of the Illinois River into the Mississippi much purer than it was before, that many towns and cities of the plaintiff along the Missouri and Mississippi discharge their sewage into those rivers, and that if there is any trouble the plaintiff must look nearer home for the cause.

The decision upon the demurrer discussed mainly the jurisdiction of the court, and, as leave to answer was given when the demurrer was overruled, naturally there was no very precise consideration of the principles of law to be applied if the plaintiff should prove its case. That was left to the future with the general intimation that the nuisance must be made out upon determinate and satisfactory evidence, that it must not be doubtful and that the danger must be shown to be real and immediate. The nuisance set forth in the bill was one which would be of international importance—a visible change of a great river from a pure stream into a polluted and poisoned ditch. The only question presented was whether as between the States of the Union this court was competent to deal with a situation which, if it arose between independent sovereignties, might lead to war. Whatever differences of opinion there might be upon matters of detail, the jurisdiction and authority of this court to deal with such a case as that is not open to doubt. But the evidence now is in, the actual facts have required for their establishment the most ingenious experiments, and for their interpretation the most subtle speculations, of modern science, and therefore it becomes necessary at the present stage to consider somewhat more nicely than heretofore how the evidence is to be approached.

The first question to be answered was put in the well known case of the Wheeling bridge. *Pennsylvania* v. *Wheeling & Belmont Bridge Co.*, 13 How. 518. In that case, also, there was a bill brought by a State to restrain a public nuisance, the erection of a bridge alleged to obstruct navigation, and a supplemental bill to abate it after it was erected. The question was put most explicitly by the dissenting judges but it was accepted by all as fundamental. The Chief Justice observed that if the bridge was a nuisance it was an offence against the sovereignty whose laws had been violated, and he asked what sovereignty that was. 13 How. 581; Daniel, J., 13 How. 599. See also *Kansas* v. *Colorado*, 185 U. S. 125. It could not be Virginia, because that State had purported to authorize it by statute. The Chief Justice found no prohibition by the United States. 13 How. 580. No third source of law was suggested by any one. The majority accepted the Chief Justice's postulate, and found an answer in what Congress had done.

It hardly was disputed that Congress could deal with the matter under its power to regulate commerce. The majority observed that although Congress had not declared in terms that a State should not obstruct the navigation of the Ohio, by bridges, yet it had regulated navigation upon that river in various ways and had sanctioned the compact between Virginia and Kentucky when Kentucky was let into the Union. By that compact the use and navigation of the Ohio, so far as the territory of either State lay thereon, was to be free and common to the citizens of the United States. The compact, by the sanction of Congress, had become a law of the Union. A state law which violated it was unconstitutional. Obstructing the navigation of the river was said to violate it, and it was added that more was not necessary to give a civil remedy for an injury done by the obstruction. 13 How. 565, 566. At a later stage of the case, after Congress had authorized the bridge, it was stated again in so many words that the ground of the former decision was that "the act of the Legislature of Virginia afforded no authority or justification. It was in conflict with the acts of Congress, which were the paramount law." 18 How. 421, 430.

In the case at bar, whether Congress could act or not, there is no suggestion that it has forbidden the action of Illinois. The only ground on which that State's conduct can be called in question is one which must be implied from the words of the Constitution. The Constitution extends the judicial power of the United States to controversies between two or more States and between a State and citizens of another State, and gives this court original jurisdiction in cases in which a State shall be a party. Therefore, if one State raises a controversy with another, this court must determine whether there is any principle of law and, if any, what, on which the plaintiff can recover. But the fact that this court must decide does not mean, of course, that it takes the place of a legislature. Some principles it must have power to declare. For instance, when a dispute arises about boundaries, this court must determine the line, and in doing so must be governed by rules explicitly or implicitly recognized. *Rhode Island* v. *Massachusetts,* 12 Pet. 657, 737. It must follow and apply those rules, even if legislation of one or both of the States seems to stand in the way. But the words of the Constitution would be a narrow ground upon which to construct and apply to the relations between States the same system of municipal law in all its details which would be applied between individuals. If we suppose a case which did not fall within the power of Congress to regulate, the result of a declaration of rights by this court would be the establishment of a rule which would be irrevocable by any power except that of this court to reverse its own decision, an amendment of the Constitution, or possibly an agreement between the States sanctioned by the legislature of the United States.

The difficulties in the way of establishing such a system of law might not be insuperable, but they would be great and new. Take the question of prescription in a case like the present. The reasons on which prescription for a public nuisance is denied or may be granted to an individual as against the sovereign power to which he is subject have no application to an independent state. See 1 Oppenheim, International Law, 293, §§ 242, 243. It would be contradicting a fundamental principle of human nature to allow no effect to the lapse of time, however long, *Davis* v. *Mills,* 194 U. S. 451, 457, yet the fixing of a definite time usually belongs to the legislature rather than the courts. The courts did fix a time in the rule against perpetuities, but the usual course, as in the instances of statutes of limitation, the duration of patents, the age of majority, etc., is to depend upon the lawmaking power.

It is decided that a case such as is made by the bill may be a ground for relief. The purpose of the foregoing observations is not to lay a foundation for departing from that decision, but simply to illustrate the great and serious caution with which it is necessary to approach the question whether a case is proved. It may be imagined that a nuisance might be created by a State upon a navigable river like the Danube, which would amount to a *casus belli* for a State lower down, unless removed. If such a nuisance were created by a State upon the Mississippi the controversy would be resolved by the more peaceful means of a suit in this court. But it does not follow that every matter which would warrant a resort to equity by one citizen against another in the same jurisdiction equally would warrant an interference by this court with the action of a State. It hardly can be that we should be justified in declaring statutes ordaining such action void in every instance where the Circuit Court might intervene in a private suit, upon no other ground than analogy to some selected system of municipal law, and the fact that we have jurisdiction over controversies between States.

The nearest analogy would be found in those cases in which an easement has been declared in favor of land in one State over land in another. But there the right is recognized on the assumption of a concurrence between the two States, the one, so to speak, offering the right, the other permitting it to be accepted. *Manville Co.* v. *Worcester,* 138 Massachusetts, 89. But when the State itself is concerned and by its legislation expressly repudiates the right set up, an entirely different question is presented.

Before this court ought to intervene the case should be of serious magnitude, clearly and fully proved, and the principle to be applied should be one which the court is prepared deliberately to maintain against all considerations on the other side. See *Kansas* v. *Colorado,* 185 U. S. 125.

As to the principle to be laid down the caution necessary is manifest. It is a question of the first magnitude whether the destiny of the great rivers is to be the sewers of the cities along their banks or to be protected against everything which threatens their purity. To decide the whole matter at one blow by an irrevocable fiat would be at least premature. If we are to judge by what the plaintiff itself permits, the discharge of sewage into the Mississippi by cities and towns is to be expected. We believe that the practice of discharging into the river is general along its banks, except where the levees of Louisiana have led to a different course. The argument for the plaintiff asserts it to be proper within certain limits. These are facts to be considered. Even in cases between individuals some consideration is given to the practical course of events. In the black country of England parties would not be expected to stand upon extreme rights. *St. Helen's Smelting Co.* v. *Tipping,* 11 H. L. C. 642. See *Boston Ferrule Co.* v. *Hills,* 159 Massachusetts, 147, 150. Where, as here, the plaintiff has sovereign powers and deliberately permits discharges similar to those of which it complains, it not only offers a standard to which the defendant has the right to appeal, but, as some of those discharges are above the intake of St. Louis, it warrants the defendant in demanding the strictest proof that the plaintiff's own conduct does not produce the result, or at least so conduce to it that courts should not be curious to apportion the blame.

We have studied the plaintiff's statement of the facts in detail and have perused the evidence, but it is unnecessary for the purposes of decision to do more than give the general result in a very simple way. At the outset we cannot but be struck by the consideration that if this suit had been brought fifty years ago it almost necessarily would have failed. There is no pretence that there is a nuisance of the simple kind that was known to the older common law. There is nothing which can be detected by the unassisted senses—no visible increase of filth, no new smell. On the contrary, it is proved that the great volume of pure water from Lake Michigan which is mixed with the sewage at the start has improved the Illinois River in these respects to a noticeable extent. Formerly it was sluggish and ill smelling. Now it is a comparatively clear stream to which edible fish have returned. Its water is drunk by the fishermen, it is said, without evil results. The plaintiff's case depends upon an inference of the unseen. It draws the inference from two propositions. First, that typhoid fever has increased considerably since the change and that other explanations have been disproved, and second, that the bacillus of typhoid can and does survive the journey and reach the intake of St. Louis in the Mississippi.

We assume the now prevailing scientific explanation of typhoid fever to be correct. But when we go beyond that assumption everything is involved in doubt. The data upon which an increase in the deaths from typhoid fever in St. Louis is alleged are disputed. The elimination of other causes is denied. The experts differ as to the time and distance within which a stream would purify itself. No case of an epidemic caused by infection at so remote a source is brought forward, and the cases which are produced are controverted. The plaintiff obviously must be cautious upon this point, for if this suit should succeed many others would follow, and it not improbably would find itself a defendant to a bill by one or more of the States lower down upon the Mississippi. The distance which the sewage has to travel (357 miles) is not open to debate, but the time of transit to be inferred from experiments with floats is estimated at varying from eight to eighteen and a half days, with forty-eight hours more from intake to distribution, and when corrected by observations of bacteria is greatly prolonged by the defendants. The experiments of the defendants' experts lead them to the opinion that a typhoid bacillus could not survive the journey, while those on the other side maintain that it might live and keep its power for twenty-five days or more, and arrive at St. Louis. Upon the question at issue, whether the new discharge from Chicago hurts St. Louis, there is a categorical contradiction between the experts on the two sides.

The Chicago drainage canal was opened on January 17, 1900. The deaths from typhoid fever in St. Louis, before and after that date, are stated somewhat differently in different places. We give them mainly from the plaintiff's brief: 1890, 140; 1891, 165; 1892, 441; 1893, 215; 1894, 171; 1895, 106; 1896, 106; 1897, 125; 1898, 95; 1899, 131; 1900, 154; 1901, 181; 1902, 216; 1903, 281. It is argued for the defendant that the numbers for the later years have been enlarged by carrying over cases which in earlier years would have been put into a miscellaneous column (intermittent, remittent, typho-malaria, etc., etc.), but we assume that the increase is real. Nevertheless, comparing the last four years with the earlier ones, it is obvious that the ground for a specific inference is very narrow, if we stopped at this point. The plaintiff argues that the increase must be due to Chicago, since there is nothing corresponding to it in the watersheds of the Missouri or Mississippi. On the other hand, the defendant points out that there has been no such enhanced rate of typhoid on the banks of the Illinois as would have been found if the opening of the drainage canal were the true cause.

Both sides agree that the detection of the typhoid bacillus in the water is not to be expected. But the plaintiff relies upon proof that such bacilli are discharged into the Chicago sewage in considerable quantities; that the number of bacilli in the water of the Illinois is much increased, including the *bacillus coli communis*, which is admitted to be an index of contamination, and that the chemical analyses lead to the same inference. To prove that the typhoid bacillus could make the journey an experiment was tried with the *bacillus prodigiosus*, which seems to have been unknown, or nearly unknown, in these waters. After preliminary trials, in which these bacilli emptied into the Mississippi near the mouth of the Illinois were found near the St. Louis intake and in St. Louis in times varying from three days to a month, one hundred and seven barrels of the same, said to contain one thousand million bacilli to the cubic centimeter, were put into the drainage canal near the starting point on November 6, and on December 4 an example was found at the St. Louis intake tower. Four others were found on the three following days, two at the tower and two at the mouth of the Illinois. As this bacillus is asserted to have about the same length of life in sunlight in living waters as the *bacillus typhosus*, although it is a little more hardy, the experiment is thought to prove one element of the plaintiff's case, although the very small number found in many samples of water is thought by the other side to indicate that practically no typhoid germs would get through. It seems to be conceded that the purification of the Illinois by the large dilution from Lake Michigan (nine parts or more in ten) would increase the danger, as it now generally is believed that the bacteria of decay, the saprophytes, which flourish in stagnant pools, destroy the pathogenic germs. Of course the addition of so much water to the Illinois also increases its speed.

On the other hand, the defendant's evidence shows a reduction in the chemical and bacterial accompaniments of pollution in a given quantity of water, which would be natural in view of the mixture of nine parts to one from Lake Michigan. It affirms that the Illinois is better or no worse at its mouth than it was before, and makes it at least uncertain how much of the present pollution is due to Chicago and how much to sources further down, not complained of in the bill. It contends that if any bacilli should get through they would be scattered and enfeebled and would do no harm. The defendant also sets against the experiment with the *bacillus prodigiosus* a no less striking experiment with typhoid germs suspended in the Illinois River in permeable sacs. According to this the duration of the life of these germs has been much exaggerated, and in that water would not be more than three or four days. It is suggested, by way of criticism, that the germs may not have been of normal strength, that the conditions were less favorable than if they had floated down in a comparatively unchanging body of water, and that the germs may have escaped, but the experiment raises at least a serious doubt. Further, it hardly is denied that there is no parallelism in detail between the increase and decrease of typhoid fever in Chicago and St. Louis. The defendants' experts maintain that the water of the Missouri is worse than that of the Illinois, while it contributes a much larger proportion to the intake. The evidence is very strong that it is necessary for St. Louis to take preventive measures, by filtration or otherwise, against the dangers of the plaintiff's own creation or from other sources than Illinois. What will protect against one will protect against another. The presence of causes of infection from the plaintiff's action makes the case weaker in principle as well as harder to prove than one in which all came from a single source.

Some stress was laid on the proposition that Chicago is not on the natural watershed of the Mississippi, because of a rise of a few feet between the Desplaines and the Chicago Rivers. We perceive no reason for a distinction on this ground. The natural features relied upon are of the smallest. And if under any circumstances they could affect the case, it is enough to say that Illinois brought Chicago into the Mississippi watershed in pursuance not only of its own statutes, but also of the acts of Congress of March 30, 1822, c. 14, 3 Stat. 659, and March 2, 1827, c. 51, 4 Stat. 234, the validity of which is not disputed. *Wisconsin v. Duluth*, 96 U. S. 379. Of course these acts do not grant the right to discharge sewage, but the case stands no differently in point of law from a suit because of the discharge from Peoria into the Illinois, or from any other or all the other cities on the banks of that stream.

We might go more into detail, but we believe that we have said enough to explain our point of view and our opinion of the evidence as it stands. What the future may develop of course we cannot tell. But our conclusion upon the present evidence is that the case proved falls so far below the allegations of the bill that it is not brought within the principles heretofore established in the cause.

Bill dismissed without prejudice.

⚄ GEORGIA v. TENNESSEE COPPER CO. AND DUCKTOWN SULPHUR, COPPER & IRON CO. (1906)

Mr. Justice Holmes delivered the opinion of the court.

This is a bill in equity filed in this court by the State of Georgia, in pursuance of a resolution of the legislature and by direction of the Governor of the State, to enjoin the defendant Copper Companies from discharging noxious gas from their works in Tennessee over the plaintiff's territory. It alleges that in consequence of such a discharge a wholesale destruction of forests, orchards and crops is going on, and other injuries are done and threatened in five counties of the State. It alleges also a vain application to the State of Tennessee for relief. A preliminary injunction was denied, but, as there was ground to fear that great and irreparable damage might be done, an early day was fixed for the final hearing and the parties were given leave, if so minded, to try the case on affidávits. This has been done without objection, and, although the method would be unsatisfactory if our decision turned on any nice question of fact, in the view that we take we think it unlikely that either party has suffered harm.

The case has been argued largely as if it were one between two private parties; but it is not. The very elements that would be relied upon in a suit between fellow-citizens as a ground for equitable relief are wanting here. The State owns very little of the territory alleged to be affected, and the damage to it capable of estimate in money, possibly, at least, is small. This is a suit by a State for an injury to it in its capacity of *quasi*-sovereign. In that capacity the State has an interest independent of and behind the titles of its citizens, in all the earth and air within its domain. It has the last word as to whether its mountains shall be stripped of their forests and its inhabitants shall breathe pure air. It might have to pay individuals before it could utter that word, but with it remains the final power. The alleged damage to the State as a private owner is merely a makeweight, and we may lay on one side the dispute as to whether the destruction of forests has led to the gullying of its roads.

The caution with which demands of this sort, on the part of a State, for relief from injuries analogous to torts, must be examined, is dwelt upon in *Missouri v. Illinois,* 200 U. S. 496, 520, 521. But it is plain that some such demands must be recognized, if the grounds alleged are proved. When the States by their union made the forcible abatement of outside nuisances impossible to each, they did not thereby agree to submit to whatever might be done. They did not renounce the possibility of making reasonable demands on the ground of their still remaining *quasi*-sovereign interests; and the alternative to force is a suit in this court. *Missouri* v. *Illinois*, 180 U.S. 208, 241.

Some peculiarities necessarily mark a suit of this kind. If the State has a case at all, it is somewhat more certainly entitled to specific relief than a private party might be. It is not lightly to be required to give up *quasi*-sovereign rights for pay; and, apart from the difficulty of valuing such rights in money, if that be its choice it may insist that an infraction of them shall be stopped. The States by entering the Union did not sink to the position of private owners subject to one system of private law. This court has not quite the same freedom to balance the harm that will be done by an injunction against that of which the plaintiff complains, that it would have in deciding between two subjects of a single political power. Without excluding the considerations that equity always takes into account, we cannot give the weight that was given them in argument to a comparison between the damage threatened to the plaintiff and the calamity of a possible stop to the defendants' business, the question of health, the character of the forests as a first or second growth, the commercial possibility or impossibility of reducing the fumes to sulphuric acid, the special adaptation of the business to the place.

It is a fair and reasonable demand on the part of a sovereign that the air over its territory should not be polluted on a great scale by sulphurous acid gas, that the forests on its mountains, be they better or worse, and whatever domestic destruction they have suffered, should not be further destroyed or threatened by the act of persons beyond its control, that the crops and orchards on its hills should not be endangered from the same source. If any such demand is to be enforced this must be, notwithstanding the hesitation that we might feel if the suit were between private parties, and the doubt whether for the injuries which they might be suffering to their property they should not be left to an action at law.

The proof requires but a few words. It is not denied that the defendants generate in their works near the Georgia line large quantities of sulphur dioxide which becomes sulphurous acid by its mixture with the air. It hardly is denied and cannot be denied with success that this gas often is carried by the wind great distances and over great tracts of Georgia land. On the evidence the pollution of the air and the magnitude of that pollution are not open to dispute. Without any attempt to go into details immaterial to the suit, it is proper to add that we are satisfied by a preponderance of evidence that the sulphurous fumes cause and threaten damage on so considerable a scale to the forests and vegetable life, if not to health, within the plaintiff State as to make out a case within the requirements of *Missouri* v. *Illinois*, 200 U. S. 496. Whether Georgia by insisting upon this claim is doing more harm than good to her own citizens is for her to determine. The possible disaster to those outside the State must be accepted as a consequence of her standing upon her extreme rights.

It is argued that the State has been guilty of laches. We deem it unnecessary to consider how far such a defense would be available in a suit of this sort, since, in our opinion, due diligence has been shown. The conditions have been different until recent years. After the evil had grown greater in 1904 the State brought a bill in this court. The defendants, however, already were abandoning the old method of roasting ore in open heaps and it was hoped that the change would stop the trouble. They were ready to agree not to return to that method, and upon such an agreement being made the bill was dismissed without prejudice. But the plaintiff now finds, or thinks that it finds, that the tall chimneys in present use cause the poisonous gases to be carried to greater distances than ever before and that the evil has not been helped.

If the State of Georgia adheres to its determination, there is no alternative to issuing an injunction, after allowing a reasonable time to the defendants to complete the structures that they now are building, and the efforts that they are making, to stop the fumes. The plaintiff may submit a form of decree on the coming in of this court in October next.

Injunction to issue.

Mr. Justice Harlan, concurring.

The State of Georgia is, in my opinion, entitled to the general relief sought by its bill, and, therefore, I concur in the result. With some things, however, contained in the opinion, or to be implied from its language, I do not concur. When the Constitution gave this court original jurisdiction in cases "in which a State shall be a party," it was not intended, I think, to authorize the court to apply in its behalf, any principle or rule of equity that would not be applied, under the same facts, in suits wholly between private parties. If this was a suit between private parties, and if under the evidence, a court of equity would not give the plaintiff an injunction, then it ought not to grant relief, under like circumstances, to the plaintiff, because it happens to be a State possessing some powers of sovereignty. Georgia is entitled to the relief sought, not because it is a State, but because it is a *party* which has established its right to such relief by proof. The opinion, if I do not mistake its scope, proceeds largely upon the ground that this court, sitting in this case as a court of equity, owes some special duty to Georgia as a State, although it is a party, while under the same facts, it would not owe any such duty to the plaintiff, if an individual.

⌘ GEORGIA v. TENNESSEE COPPER COMPANY AND DUCKTOWN SULPHUR, COPPER & IRON COMPANY, LIMITED (1915)

Mr. Justice McReynolds delivered the opinion of the court.

Both defendants are smelting copper ores in Polk County, East Tennessee, near the Georgia line. The works of the Tennessee Company, much the larger of the two, are situated within half a mile of the line; those of the Ducktown Company are some two and one-half miles away. The ores contain a very large amount of sulphur—around 20%—and in the process of smelting great quantities of sulphur dioxide are formed; if allowed to escape into the air this becomes sulphurous acid, a poisonous gas destructive of plant life.

In October, 1905, the State of Georgia began this original proceeding alleging that defendants permitted discharge from their works of noxious gases which being carried by air currents ultimately settled upon its territory and destroyed the vegetation, and asking for appropriate relief. The case was heard on the merits and the issues determined in complainant's favor, May, 1907. We then said: "If the State of Georgia adheres to its determination, there is no alternative to issuing an injunction, after allowing a reasonable time to the defendants to complete the structures that they now are building, and the efforts that they are making, to stop the fumes. The plaintiff may submit a form of decree on the coming in of this court in October next." 206 U. S. 230, 239.

Hope was entertained that some practical method of subduing the noxious fumes could be devised and by consent the time for entering a final decree was enlarged. Both companies installed purifying devices. The Tennessee Company and the State finally entered into a stipulation whereby the former undertook annually to supply a fund to compensate those injured by fumes from its works, to conduct its plant subject to inspection in specified ways, and between April 10th and October 1st not to "operate more green ore furnaces than it finds necessary to permit of operating its sulphuric acid plant at its normal full capacity." The State agreed to refrain from asking an injunction prior to October, 1916, if the stipulation was fully observed. The Ducktown Company and the State were unable to agree, and in February, 1914, the latter moved for a decree according a perpetual injunction. Consideration of the matter was postponed upon representation that conditions had materially changed since 1907, and leave was granted to present additional testimony "to relate solely to the changed conditions, if any, which may have arisen since the case was here decided." A mass of conflicting evidence has been submitted for our consideration.

The Ducktown Company has spent large sums—$600,000 and more—since the former opinion in constructing purifying works (acid plant); and a much smaller proportion of the sulphur contained in the ores now escapes into the air as sulphur dioxide—possibly only 41½% as against 85½% under former conditions. Similar improvements have been installed by the Tennessee Company at great expense, but we are without adequate information concerning the effect produced by them. As it asked and was granted opportunity to show material changes the burden is upon the Ducktown Company. A full and complete disclosure of the improvements installed by it and the results continuously obtained has not been presented.

Counsel maintain that escaping sulphur fumes now produce no substantial damage in Georgia, and further that if any such damage is being done the Tennessee Company alone is responsible therefor. We think the proof fails to support either branch of the defense, and the State should have a decree adequate to diminish materially the present probability of damage to its citizens.

The evidence does not disclose with accuracy the volume or true character of the fumes which are being given off daily from the works of either company. Averages may not be relied on with confidence since improper operations for a single week or day might destroy vegetation over a large area, while the emission of great quantities of fumes during a short period would affect but slightly the average for a month or year.

It appears that in 1913 the total ores smelted by the Ducktown Company amounted to 152,249 tons, or 304,498,000 pounds—20% sulphur; total matte shipped was 12,537,000 pounds—about 4% of the ore; the total sulphur in the smelted ores not accounted for and which escaped into the air in the form of sulphur dioxide was 13,102 tons, or 26,204,000 pounds—over two pounds of sulphur for each pound of matte and an average of more than 35 tons per day.

During July, 1913, the total matte shipped (approximately the production) was 846,000 pounds—more was shipped in June and less in August. The July production was thus approximately 7% of the year's total. The sulphur in the fumes generated in connection with the production for this month, not redeemed by the acid plant and emitted into the air, may be fairly estimated as not less than 7% of 13,102 or 917 tons—substantially 30 tons per day. This amount produced harmful results and must be diminished.

It is impossible from the record to ascertain with certainty the reduction in the sulphur content of emitted gases necessary to render the territory of Georgia immune from injury therefrom; but adequate relief, we are disposed to think, will follow a decree restraining the Ducktown Company from continuing to operate its plant otherwise than upon the terms and conditions following: (1) It shall keep daily records showing fully and in detail the course and result of the operations. (2) A competent inspector to be appointed by this court shall have access to all the books and records of the Company, shall make frequent careful observations of the conditions—at least once each fortnight—during the next six months, and at the end of that time shall make full report with appropriate recommendations. An adequate sum to cover the necessary costs and expenses must be deposited with the Clerk by the Company. (3) It shall not permit the escape into the air of fumes carrying more than 45% of the sulphur contained in the green ore subjected to smelting. (4) It shall not permit escape into the air of gases the total sulphur content of which shall exceed 20 tons during one day from April 10th to October 1st of each year or exceed 40 tons in one day during any other season.

The cause will be retained for further action and either party may apply hereafter for appropriate relief.

Within ten days either side may present a decree in conformity herewith, together with such suggestions as seem desirable.

Mr. Justice Hughes, dissenting: I do not think that the evidence justifies the decree limiting production as stated.

The Chief Justice and Mr. Justice Holmes join in this dissent.

DECREE

On consideration of the motion of complainant for final injunction, the application of defendant Ducktown Sulphur, Copper & Iron Company, Limited, to show changed conditions, the proof submitted thereon, and of the argument of counsel thereupon had, and the Court being of opinion that by reducing the amount of sulphur discharged into the air said defendant probably can operate its plant without subjecting the territory of Georgia to serious danger of immediate injury, and deeming it desirable to be more fully informed concerning the true conditions and results which may be obtained by subduing the noxious gases discharged,

IT IS ACCORDINGLY ordered, adjudged and decreed:

(1) That the defendant Ducktown Sulphur, Copper & Iron Company, Limited, shall hereafter keep daily records showing fully and in detail the course and result of its operations.

(2) That Dr. John T. McGill, of Vanderbilt University, Nashville, Tennessee, is hereby appointed Inspector to observe the operations of said defendant's plant and works. He shall be given by it at all times free and full access to its books, records and premises, and during the next six months he shall make frequent and careful observations—at least one each fortnight—of the conditions of the plant and works, the manner of

their operation, the quantity and character of smoke emitted therefrom, and the resulting effect upon vegetation within the vicinity and in the State of Georgia. At the end of that time he shall make a full report of his observations accompanied by recommendations as to appropriate future action. To cover necessary costs and expenses incident to these services and the reasonable compensation of the Inspector, the defendant Ducktown Sulphur, Copper & Iron Company, Limited, is hereby directed to deposit with the Clerk of this Court, within ten days, the sum of five thousand dollars. Of this sum not exceeding two thousand dollars shall be paid from time to time, prior to October 12th next, by the Clerk to the Inspector, upon his written application, to cover costs, expenses, and on account of his services, etc.

(3) That said defendant hereafter shall not permit the escape into the air from its works of fumes carrying more than 45% of the sulphur contained in the green ore subjected to smelting.

(4) That it shall not hereafter permit the escape into the air of gases the total sulphur content of which shall exceed twenty tons during one day from April 10th to October 1st of each year or exceed forty tons in one day during any other season.

(5) That the cause will be retained upon the docket for such further action as may be proper and either party may at any time hereafter apply for relief as it may be advised.

▶ NEW YORK v. NEW JERSEY AND PASSAIC VALLEY SEWERAGE COMMISSIONERS (1921)

Mr. Justice Clarke delivered the opinion of the court.

The People of the State of New York, in their bill filed in this suit, pray that the defendants, the State of New Jersey and the Passaic Valley Sewerage Commissioners, be permanently enjoined from discharging, as it is averred they intend to discharge, a large volume of sewage into that part of New York Harbor known as the Upper Bay, for the reason, as it is alleged, that such pollution of the waters of the harbor will be caused thereby as to amount to a public nuisance, which will result in grave injury to the health, to the property, and to the commercial welfare, of the people of the State and City of New York. . . .

For the purpose of showing its right to maintain the suit, the bill thus filed sets out, with much detail, an agreement between the States of New York and New Jersey, approved by Congress in 1834, establishing the boundary line between the two States and giving to New York, to the extent therein written, exclusive jurisdiction over the waters of the Bay of New York.

But we need not inquire curiously as to the rights of the State of New York derived from this compact, for, wholly aside from it, and regardless of the precise location of the boundary line, the right of the State to maintain such a suit as is stated in the bill is very clear. The health, comfort and prosperity of the people of the State and the value of their property being gravely menaced, as it is averred that they are by the proposed action of the defendants, the State is the proper party to represent and defend such rights by resort to the remedy of an original suit in this court under the provisions of the Constitution of the United States. *Missouri* v. *Illinois*, 180 U. S. 208, 241, 243; *Georgia* v. *Tennessee Copper Co.*, 206 U. S. 230.

Also, for the purpose of showing the responsibility of the State of New Jersey for the proposed action of the defendant, the Passaic Valley Sewerage Commissioners, the bill sets out, with much detail, the acts of the legislature of that State authorizing and directing such action on their part.

Of this it is sufficient to say that the averments of the bill, quite undenied, show that the defendant sewerage commissioners constitute such a statutory, corporate agency of the State that their action, actual or intended, must be treated as that of the State itself, and we shall so regard it. 180 U. S. 208, *supra*.

The remaining essential allegations of the bill are that the defendants are about to construct the sewer we have described and to discharge the sewage thereby collected into the Upper New York Bay, . . . that such sewage would be carried by the currents and tides into the Hudson and East Rivers and would be deposited on the bottom and shores of the Bay and upon and adjacent to the wharves and docks of New York City, thereby so polluting the water as to render it: a public nuisance offensive and injurious to persons living near it or using it for bathing or for purposes of commerce, damaging to vessels using the waters, and so poisonous to the fish and oysters subsisting within it as to render them unfit for food. To prevent the public nuisance, which it is averred would thus be created, a permanent injunction was prayed for. . . .

After the defendants had answered, the Government of the United States, by leave of court, filed a Petition of Intervention. The warrant assigned for this intervention was, the power and duty of the Government with respect to navigation and interstate commerce, and the inherent power which it has to act for the protection of the health of government officials and employees at the Brooklyn navy yard, and its duty to protect from damage the Government property bordering upon New York Bay. . . .

The coming of the Government into the case was followed by conferences between its officials and the Sewerage Commissioners, with the result that a method of treatment of the sewage was decided upon much more thorough, comprehensive and definite in character than had been adopted before and the manner of dispersion of it at the outlet was so changed as to secure a much greater diffusion, at a great depth, in the adjacent waters.

These changes were ultimately embodied in a stipulation between the United States, acting through its Attorney General, and the Passaic Valley Sewerage Commissioners, acting under authority of a special act of the New Jersey legislature. It was agreed that upon the filing of this stipulation, properly executed, with the Clerk of this Court, the Petition of Intervention of the Government should be dismissed, without prejudice —which was done on May 16, 1910. . . .

Having regard to the large powers of the Government over navigation and commerce, its right to protect adjacent public property and its officers and employees from damage and disease, and to the duty and authority of the Attorney General to control and conduct litigation to which the Government may be a party (Rev. Stats., §§ 359, 367), we cannot doubt that the intervention of the Government was proper in this case and that it was within the authority of the Attorney General to agree that the United States should retire from the case upon the terms stated in the stipulation, which were plainly approved by the Secretary of War, who afterwards embodied them in the construction permit issued to the Sewerage Commissioners. . . .

It is much to be regretted that any forecast as to what the effect would be of the treatment and deeply submerged discharge through multiple outlets proposed for this large volume of sewage must depend almost entirely upon the conflicting opinions of expert witnesses, for experience with such treatment and dispersion under even approximately like conditions seems entirely wanting. It is, however, of much significance that the authorities of the City of New York, after many years of investigation of the subject of sewage disposal, in their latest plans propose to adopt a treatment of screening and sedimentation and dispersal in deep water very similar to, but not so extensive and thorough as, that provided for in the stipulation between the defendants and the United States.

There is only one point upon which all the experts called for the opposing parties agree, viz.: that in the present state of learning upon the subject the amount of dissolved oxygen in water is the best index or measure of the degree to which it is polluted by organic substances, it seemingly being accepted by them all that upon the oxygen content in water depends its capacity for digesting sewage—that is for converting organic matter into inorganic and harmless substances by direct oxidation and by sustaining bacteria which assist in such conversion. . . .

Considering all of this evidence, and much more which we cannot detail, we must conclude that the complainants have failed to show by the convincing evidence which the law requires that the sewage which the defendants intend to discharge into Upper New York Bay, even if treated only in the manner specifically described in the stipulation with the United States Government, would so corrupt the water of the Bay as to create a public nuisance by causing offensive odors or unsightly deposits on the surface or that it would seriously add to the pollution of it.

We cannot withhold the suggestion, inspired by the consideration of this case, that the grave problem of sewage disposal presented by the large and growing populations living on the shores of New York Bay is one more likely to be wisely solved by coöperative study and by conference and mutual concession on the part of representatives of the States so vitally interested in it than by proceedings in any court however constituted.

The court, recognizing the importance of the ruling which it is making to the great populations interested, as well in the State of New Jersey as in the State of New York, will direct that the decree denying the relief prayed for shall be without prejudice to the instituting of another suit for injunction if the proposed sewer in operation shall prove sufficiently injurious to the waters of the Bay to lead the State of New York to conclude that the protection of the health, welfare or commerce of its people requires another application to this court.

It results that the bill of complainant will be dismissed but without prejudice to a renewal of the application for injunction if the operation of the sewer of defendants shall result in conditions which the State of New York may be advised requires the interposition of this court.

Bill dismissed without prejudice.

⚓ NEW YORK v. NEW JERSEY AND PASSAIC VALLEY SEWERAGE COMMISSIONERS (1931)

Mr. Justice Holmes delivered the opinion of the court.

❋ ❋ ❋

New York proposes to divert a large amount of water from the above-named tributaries of the Delaware and from the watershed of that river to the watershed of the Hudson River in order to increase the water supply of the City of New York. *New Jersey insists on a strict application of the rules of the common law governing private riparian proprietors subject to the same sovereign power.* Pennsylvania intervenes to protect its interests as against anything that might be done to prejudice its future needs.

We are met at the outset by the question what rule is to be applied. It is established that a more liberal answer may be given than in a controversy between neighbors members of a single State. Connecticut v. Massachusetts, 282 U. S. 660. Different considerations come in when we are dealing with independent sovereigns having to regard the welfare of the whole population and when the alternative to settlement is war. In a less degree, perhaps, the same is true of the quasi-sovereignties bound together in the Union. [Emphasis supplied by the editors.] A river is more than an amenity, it is a treasure. It offers a necessity of life that must be rationed among those who have power over it. New York has the physical power to cut off all the water within its jurisdiction. But clearly the exercise of such a power to the destruction of the interest of lower States could not be tolerated. And on the other hand equally little could New Jersey be permitted to require New York to give up its power altogether in order that the River might come down to it undiminished. Both States have real and substantial interests in the River that must be reconciled as best they may be. The different traditions and practices in different parts of the country may lead to varying results, but the effort always is to secure an equitable apportionment without quibbling over formulas. See *Missouri* v. *Illinois,* 200 U. S. 496, 520. *Kansas* v. *Colorado,* 206 U. S. 46, 98, 117. *Georgia* v. *Tennessee Copper Co.,* 206 U. S. 230, 237. *Wyoming* v. *Colorado,* 259 U. S. 419, 465, 470. *Connecticut* v. *Massachusetts,* 282 U. S. 660, 670.

This case was referred to a Master and a great mass of evidence was taken. In a most competent and excellent report the Master adopted the principle of equitable division which clearly results from the decisions of the last quarter of a century. Where that principle is established there is not much left to discuss. The removal of water to a different watershed obviously must be allowed at times unless States are to be deprived of the most beneficial use on formal grounds. In fact it has been allowed repeatedly and has been practiced by the States concerned. *Missouri* v. *Illinois,* 200 U. S. 496, 526. *Wyoming* v. *Colorado,* 259 U. S. 419, 466. *Connecticut* v. *Massachusetts,* 282 U. S. 660, 671.

New Jersey alleges that the proposed diversion will transgress its rights in many respects. That it will interfere with the navigability of the Delaware without the authority of Congress or the Secretary of War. That it will deprive the State and its citizens who are riparian owners of the undiminished flow of the stream to which they are entitled by the common law as adopted by both States. *That it will injuriously affect water power and the ability to develop it. That it will injuriously affect the sanitary conditions of the River. That it will do the same to the industrial use of it. That it will increase the salinity of the lower part of the River and of Delaware Bay to the injury of the oyster industry there.*

That it will injure the shad fisheries. That it will do the same to the municipal water supply of the New Jersey towns and cities on the River. That by lowering the level of the water it will injure the cultivation of adjoining lands; and finally, that it will injuriously affect the River for recreational purposes. [Emphasis added.] The bill also complains of the change of watershed, already disposed of; denies the necessity of the diversion; charges extravagant use of present supplies, and alleges that the plan will violate the Federal Water Power Act, 16 USCA §§ 791–823 (but see U. S. Code, tit. 16, § 821 [16 USCA § 821]), interfere with interstate commerce, prefer the ports of New York to those of New Jersey and will take the property of New Jersey and its citizens without due process of law. . . .

The Master finds that the taking of 600 millions of gallons daily from the tributaries will not materially affect the River or its sanitary condition, or as a source of municipal water supply, or for industrial uses, or for agriculture, or for the fisheries for shad. The effect or the use for recreation and upon its reputation in that regard will be somewhat more serious as will be the effect of increased salinity of the River upon the oyster fisheries. [Emphasis added.] The total is found to be greater than New Jersey ought to bear, but the damage can be removed by reducing the draft of New York to 440 million gallons daily; . . .

1. The injunction prayed for by New Jersey so far as it would restrain the State of New York or City of New York from diverting from the Delaware River or its tributaries to the New York City water supply the equivalent of 440 million gallons of water daily is denied, but is granted to restrain the said State and City from diverting water in excess of that amount.

*   *   *

2. The diversion herein allowed shall not constitute a prior appropriation and shall not give the State of New York and City of New York any superiority of right over the State of New Jersey and Commonwealth of Pennsylvania in the enjoyment and use of the Delaware River and its tributaries.

3. The prayer of the intervenor, Commonwealth of Pennsylvania, for the present allocation to it of the equivalent of 750 million gallons of water daily from the Delaware River or its Pennsylvania tributaries is denied without prejudice.

4. The prayer of the Commonwealth of Pennsylvania for the appointment of a river master is denied without prejudice.

5. This decree is without prejudice to the United States and particularly is subject to the paramount authority of Congress in respect to navigation and navigable waters of the United States and subject to the

powers of the Secretary of War and Chief of Engineers of the United States Army in respect to navigation and navigable waters of the United States.

6. Any of the parties hereto, complainant, defendants or intervenor, may apply at the foot of this decree for other or further action or relief and this Court retains jurisdiction of the suit for the purpose of any order or direction or modification of this decree, or any supplemental decree that it may deem at any time to be proper in relation to the subject matter in controversy.

7. The costs of the cause shall be divided and shall be paid by the parties in the following proportions: State of New Jersey 35 per cent, City of New York 35 percent, State of New York 15 per cent, Commonwealth of Pennsylvania 15 per cent.

The Chief Justice and Mr. Justice Roberts took no part in the consideration or decision of this case.

✔ SIERRA CLUB v. MORTON (1972)

Mr. Justice Stewart delivered the opinion of the Court.

I

The Mineral King Valley is an area of great natural beauty nestled in the Sierra Nevada Mountains in Tulare County, California, adjacent to Sequoia National Park. It has been part of the Sequoia National Forest since 1926, and is designated as a National Game Refuge by special Act of Congress. Though once the site of extensive mining activity, Mineral King is now used almost exclusively for recreational purposes. Its relative inaccessibility and lack of development have limited the number of visitors each year, and at the same time have preserved the valley's quality as a quasi-wilderness area largely uncluttered by the products of civilization.

The United States Forest Service, which is entrusted with the maintenance and administration of national forests, began in the late 1940's to give consideration to Mineral King as a potential site for recreational development. Prodded by a rapidly increasing demand for skiing facilities, the Forest Service published a prospectus in 1965, inviting bids from private developers for the construction and operation of a ski resort that would also serve as a summer recreation area. The proposal of Walt Disney Enterprises, Inc., was chosen from those of six bidders, and Disney received a three-year permit to conduct surveys and explorations in the valley in connection with its preparation of a complete master plan for the resort.

The final Disney plan, approved by the Forest Service in January, 1969, outlines a $35 million complex of motels, restaurants, swimming pools, parking lots, and other structures designed to accommodate 14,000 visitors daily. This complex is to be constructed on 80 acres of the valley floor under a 30-year use permit from the Forest Service. Other facilities, including ski lifts, ski trails, a cog-assisted railway, and utility installations, are to be constructed on the mountain slopes and in other parts of the valley under a revocable special use permit. To provide access to the resort, the State of California proposes to construct a highway 20 miles in length. A section of this road would traverse Sequoia National Park, as would a proposed high-voltage power line needed to provide electricity for the resort. Both the highway and the power line require the approval of the Department of the Interior, which is entrusted with the preservation and maintenance of the national parks.

Representatives of the Sierra Club, who favor maintaining Mineral King largely in its present state, followed the progress of recreational planning for the valley with close attention and increasing dismay. They unsuccessfully sought a public hearing on the proposed development in 1965, and in subsequent correspondence with officials of the Forest Service and the Department of the Interior, they expressed the Club's objections to Disney's plan as a whole and to particular features included in it. In June of 1969 the Club filed the present suit in the United States District Court for the Northern District of California, seeking a declaratory judgment that various aspects of the proposed development contravene federal laws and regulations governing the preservation of national parks, forests, and game refuges, and also seeking preliminary and permanent injunctions restraining the federal officials involved from granting their approval or issuing permits in connection with the Mineral King project. The petitioner Sierra Club sued as a membership corporation with "a special interest in the conservation and sound maintenance of the national parks, game refuges, and forests of the country," and invoked the judicial review provisions of the Administrative Procedure Act, 5 U.S.C. § 701 et seq.

After two days of hearings, the District Court granted the requested preliminary injunction. It rejected the respondents' challenge to the Sierra Club's standing to sue, and determined that the hearing had raised questions "concerning possible excess of statutory authority, sufficiently substantial and serious to justify a preliminary injunction. . . ." The respondents appealed, and the Court of Appeals for the Ninth Circuit reversed. 433 F.2d 24. With respect to the petitioner's standing, the court noted that there was "no allegation in the complaint that members of the Sierra Club would be affected by the actions of [the respondents] other than the fact that the actions are personally displeasing or distasteful to them," id., at 33, and concluded:

We do not believe such club concern without a showing of more direct interest can constitute standing in the legal sense sufficient to challenge the exercise of responsibilities on behalf of all the citizens by two cabinet level officials of the government acting under Congressional and Constitutional authority. *Id.*, at 30.

Alternatively, the Court of Appeals held that the Sierra Club had not made an adequate showing of irreparable injury and likelihood of success on the merits to justify issuance of a preliminary injunction. The court thus vacated the injunction. The Sierra Club filed a petition for a writ of certiorari which we granted, 401 U.S. 907, 91 S.Ct. 870, 27 L.Ed.2d 805, to review the questions of federal law presented.

II

[1–4] The first question presented is whether the Sierra Club has alleged facts that entitle it to obtain judicial review of the challenged action. Whether a party has a sufficient stake in an otherwise justiciable controversy to obtain judicial resolution of that controversy is what has traditionally been referred to as the question of standing to sue. Where the party does not rely on any specific statute authorizing invocation of the judicial process, the question of standing depends upon whether the party has alleged such a "personal stake in the outcome of the controversy," Baker v. Carr, 369 U.S. 186, 204, 82 S.Ct. 691, 703, 7 L.Ed.2d 663, as to ensure that "the dispute sought to be adjudicated will be presented in an adversary context and in a form historically viewed as capable of judicial resolution." Flast v. Cohen, 392 U.S. 83, 101, 88 S.Ct. 1942, 1953, 20 L.Ed.2d 947. Where, however, Congress has authorized public officials to perform certain functions according to law, and has provided by statute for judicial review of those actions under certain circumstances, the inquiry as to standing must begin with a determination of whether the statute in question authorizes review at the behest of the plaintiff.

The Sierra Club relies upon § 10 of the Administrative Procedure Act (APA), 80 Stat. 392, 5 U.S.C. § 702, which provides:

A person suffering legal wrong because of agency action, or adversely affected or aggrieved by agency action within the meaning of a relevant statute, is entitled to judicial review thereof.

Early decisions under this statute interpreted the language as adopting the various formulations of "legal interest" and "legal wrong" then prevailing as constitutional requirements of standing. But, in Association of Data Processing Service Organizations, Inc. v. Camp, 397 U.S. 150, 90 S.Ct. 827, 25 L.Ed.2d 184, and Barlow v. Collins, 397 U.S. 159, 90 S.Ct. 832, 25 L.Ed.2d 192, decided the same day, we held more broadly that persons had standing to obtain judicial review of federal agency action under § 10 of the APA where they had alleged that the challenged action had caused them "injury in fact," and where the alleged injury was to an interest "arguably within the zone of interests to be protected or regulated" by the statutes that the agencies were claimed to have violated.

In *Data Processing*, the injury claimed by the petitioners consisted of harm to their competitive position in the computer servicing market through a ruling by the Comptroller of the Currency that national banks might perform data processing services for their customers. In *Barlow*, the petitioners were tenant farmers who claimed that certain regulations of the Secretary of Agriculture adversely affected their economic position vis-à-vis their landlords. These palpable economic injuries have long been recognized as sufficient to lay the basis for standing, with or without a specific statutory provision for judicial review. Thus, neither *Data Processing* nor *Barlow* addressed itself to the question, which has arisen with increasing frequency in federal courts in recent years, as to what must be alleged by persons who claim injury of a noneconomic nature to interests that are widely shared. That question is presented in this case.

III

[5] The injury alleged by the Sierra Club will be incurred entirely by reason of the change in the uses to which Mineral King will be put, and the attendant change in the aesthetics and ecology of the area. Thus, in referring to the road to be built through Sequoia National Park, the complaint alleged that the development "would destroy or otherwise affect the scenery, natural and historic objects and wildlife of the park and would impair the enjoyment of the park for future generations." We do not question that this type of harm may amount to an "injury in fact" sufficient to lay the basis for standing under § 10 of the APA. Aesthetic and environmental well-being, like economic well-being, are important ingredients of the quality of life in our society, and the fact that particular environmental interests are shared by the many rather than the few does not make them less deserving of legal protection through the judicial process. But the "injury in fact" test requires more than an injury to a cognizable interest. It requires that the party seeking review be himself among the injured.

The impact of the proposed changes in the environment of Mineral King will not fall indiscriminately upon every citizen. The alleged injury will be felt directly only by those who use Mineral King and Sequoia National Park, and for whom the aesthetic and recreational values of the area will be lessened by the highway and ski resort. The Sierra Club failed to allege that it or its members would be affected in any of their

activities or pastimes by the Disney development. Nowhere in the pleadings or affidavits did the Club state that its members use Mineral King
for any purpose, much less that they use it in any that would be significantly affected by the proposed actions of the respondents.[1]

The Club apparently regarded any allegations of individualized injury
as superfluous, on the theory that this was a "public" action involving
questions as to the use of natural resources, and that the Club's long-
standing concern with and expertise in such matters were sufficient to
give it standing as a "representative of the public."[2] This theory reflects
a misunderstanding of our cases involving so-called "public actions" in
the area of administrative law.

The origin of the theory advanced by the Sierra Club may be traced
to a dictum in Scripps-Howard Radio, Inc. v. FCC, 316 U.S. 4, 62 S.Ct.
875, 86 L.Ed. 1229, in which the licensee of a radio station in Cincinnati,
Ohio, sought a stay of an order of the FCC allowing another radio station
in a nearby city to change its frequency and increase its range. In discuss-
ing its power to grant a stay, the Court noted that "these private litigants
have standing only as representatives of the public interest." Id., at 14,
62 S.Ct. at 882. But that observation did not describe the basis upon

---

[1] The only reference in the pleadings to the Sierra Club's interest in the dispute is
contained in paragraph 3 of the complaint, which reads in its entirety as follows:
"Plaintiff Sierra Club is a non-profit corporation organized and operating under the
laws of the State of California, with its principal place of business in San Francisco,
California since 1892. Membership of the Club is approximately 78,000 nationally,
with approximately 27,000 members residing in the San Francisco Bay area. For many
years the Sierra Club by its activities and conduct has exhibited a special interest in
the conservation and sound maintenance of the national parks, game refuges and
forests of the country, regularly serving as a responsible representative of persons
similar interested. One of the principal purposes of the Sierra Club is to protect and
conserve the national resources of the Sierra Nevada Mountains. Its interests would
be vitally affected by the acts hereinafter described and would be aggrieved by those
acts of the defendants as hereinafter more fully appears."
In an *amici curiae* brief filed in this Court by the Wilderness Society and others,
it is asserted that the Sierra Club has conducted regular camping trips into the
Mineral King area, and that various members of the Club have used and continue to
use the area for recreational purposes. These allegations were not contained in the
pleadings, nor were they brought to the attention of the Court of Appeals. Moreover,
the Sierra Club in its reply brief specifically declines to rely on its individualized
interest, as a basis for standing. . . . Our decision does not, of course, bar the Sierra
Club from seeking in the District Court to amend its complaint by a motion under
Rule 15, Federal Rules of Civil Procedure.

[2] This approach to the question of standing was adopted by the Court of Appeals
for the Second Circuit in Citizens Committee for Hudson Valley v. Volpe, 425 F.2d
97, 105:
"We hold, therefore, that the public interest in environmental resources—an interest
created by statutes affecting the issuance of this permit—is a legally protected interest
affording these plaintiffs, as responsible representatives of the public, standing to
obtain judicial review of agency action alleged to be in contravention of that public
interest."

which the appellant was allowed to obtain judicial review as a "person aggrieved" within the meaning of the statue involved in that case, since Scripps-Howard was clearly "aggrieved" by reason of the economic injury that it would suffer as a result of the Commission's action. The Court's statement was rather directed to the theory upon which Congress had authorized judicial review of the Commission's action. That theory had been described earlier in FCC v. Sanders Bros. Radio Station, 309 U.S. 470, 477, 60 S.Ct. 693, 698, 84 L.Ed. 869, as follows:

> Congress had some purpose in enacting section 402(b) (2). It may have been of opinion that one likely to be financially injured by the issue of a license would be the only person having a sufficient interest to bring to the attention of the appellate court errors of law in the action of the Commission in granting the license. It is within the power of Congress to confer such standing to prosecute an appeal.

[6] Taken together, *Sanders* and *Scripps-Howard* thus established a dual proposition: the fact of economic injury is what gives a person standing to seek judicial review under the statute, but once review is properly invoked, that person may argue the public interest in support of his claim that the agency has failed to comply with its statutory mandate. It was in the latter sense that the "standing" of the appellant in *Scripps-Howard* existed only as a "representative of the public interest." It is in a similar sense that we have used the phrase "private attorney general" to describe the function performed by persons upon whom Congress has conferred the right to seek judicial review of agency action. See *Data Processing, supra,* 397 U.S., at 154, 90 S.Ct., at 830.

The trend of cases arising under the APA and other statutes authorizing judicial review of federal agency action has been towards recognizing that injuries other than economic harm are sufficient to bring a person within the meaning of the statutory language, and towards discarding the notion that an injury that is widely shared is *ipso facto* not an injury sufficient to provide the basis for judicial review.[3] We noted this develop-

---

[3] See, e. g., Environmental Defense Fund, Inc. v. Hardin, 138 U.S.App.D.C. 391, 428 F.2d 1093, 1097, (interest in health affected by decision of Secretary of Agriculture refusing to suspend registration of certain pesticides containing DDT); Office of Communication of United Church of Christ v. FCC, 123 U.S.App.D.C. 328, 359 F.2d 994, 1005 (interest of television viewers in the programming of a local station licensed by the FCC); Scenic Hudson Preservation Conf. v. FPC, 2 Cir., 354 F.2d 608, 615–616 (interests in aesthetics, recreation, and orderly community planning affected by FPC licensing of a hydroelectric project); Reade v. Ewing, 2 Cir., 205 F.2d 630, 631–632 (interest of consumers of oleomargarine in fair labeling of product regulated by Federal Security Administration); Crowther v. Seaborg, D.C., 312 F.Supp. 1205, 1212 (interest in health and safety of persons residing near the site of a proposed atomic blast).

ment with approval in *Data Processing, supra*, at 154, 90 S.Ct., at 830, in saying that the interest alleged to have been injured "may reflect 'aesthetic, conservational, and recreational' as well as economic values." But broadening the categories of injury that may be alleged in support of standing is a different matter from abandoning the requirement that the party seeking review must have himself suffered an injury.

[7, 8] Some courts have indicated a willingness to take this latter step by conferring standing upon organizations that have demonstrated "an organizational interest in the problem" of environmental or consumer protection. Environmental Defense Fund, Inc. v. Hardin, 138 U.S.App.D.C. 391, 428 F.2d 1093, 1097.[4] It is clear that an organization whose members are injured may represent those members in a proceeding for judicial review. See, *e. g.*, NAACP v. Button, 371 U.S. 415, 428, 83 S.Ct. 328, 335, 9 L.Ed.2d 405. But a mere "interest in a problem," no matter how long-standing the interest and no matter how qualified the organization is in evaluating the problem, is not sufficient by itself to render the organization "adversely affected" or "aggrieved" within the meaning of the APA. The Sierra Club is a large and long-established organization, with an historic commitment to the cause of protecting our Nation's natural heritage from man's depredations. But if a "special interest" in this subject were enough to entitle the Sierra Club to commence this litigation, there would appear to be no objective basis upon which to disallow a suit by any other bona fide "special interest" organization however small or short-lived. And if any group with a bona fide "special interest" could initiate such litigation, it is difficult to perceive why any individual citizen with the same bona fide special interest would not also be entitled to do so.

[9, 10] The requirement that a party seeking review must allege facts showing that he is himself adversely affected does not insulate executive action from judicial review, nor does it prevent any public interests from being protected through the judicial process. It does serve as at least a rough attempt to put the decision as to whether review will be sought in the hands of those who have a direct stake in the outcome. That goal

---

[4] See Citizens Committee for Hudson Valley v. Volpe, n. 8, *supra*; Environmental Defense Fund, Inc. v. Corps of Engineers, D.C., 325 F.Supp. 728, 734–736; Izaak Walton League of America v. St. Clair, D.C., 313 F.Supp. 1312, 1317. See also Scenic Hudson Preservation Conf. v. FPC, *supra*, 354 F.2d at 616:

"In order to ensure that the Federal Power Commission will adequately protect the public interest in the aesthetic, conservational, and recreational aspects of power development, those who by their activities and conduct have exhibited a special interest in such areas, must be held to be included in the class of 'aggrieved' parties under § 313(b) [of the Federal Power Act]."

In most, if not all of these cases, at least one party to the proceeding did assert an individualized injury either to himself or, in the case of an organization, to its members.

would be undermined were we to construe the APA to authorize judicial review at the behest of organizations or individuals who seek to do no more than vindicate their own value preferences through the judicial process.[5] The principle that the Sierra Club would have us establish in this case would do just that.

[11] As we conclude that the Court of Appeals was correct in its holding that the Sierra Club lacked standing to maintain this action, we do not reach any other questions presented in the petition, and we intimate no view on the merits of the complaint. The judgment is

Affirmed.

Mr. Justice Powell and Mr. Justice Rehnquist took no part in the consideration or decision of this case.

Mr. Justice Douglas, dissenting.

I share the views of my Brother Blackmun and would reverse the judgment below.

The critical question of "standing" would be simplified and also put neatly in focus if we fashioned a federal rule that allowed environmental issues to be litigated before federal agencies or federal courts in the name of the inanimate object about to be dispoiled, defaced, or invaded by roads and bulldozers and where injury is the subject of public outrage. Contemporary public concern for protecting nature's ecological equilibrium should lead to the conferral of standing upon environmental objects to sue for their own preservation. See Stone, Should Trees Have Standing? Toward Legal Rights for Natural Objects, 45 S.Cal.L.Rev. 450 (1972). This suit would therefore be more properly labeled as Mineral King v. Morton.

Inanimate objects are sometimes parties in litigation. A ship has a legal personality, a fiction found useful for maritime purposes. The corporation sole—a creature of ecclesiastical law—is an acceptable adversary and

---

[5] Every school boy may be familiar with de Tocqueville's famous observation, written in the 1830's, that "Scarcely any political question arises in the United States that is not resolved, sooner or later, into a judicial question." 1 Democracy in America 280 (Alfred A. Knopf, 1945). Less familiar, however, is de Tocqueville's further observation that judicial review is effective largely because it is not available simply at the behest of a partisan faction, but is exercised only to remedy a particular, concrete injury.

"It will be seen, also, that by leaving it to private interest to censure the law, and by intimately uniting the trial of the law with the trial of an individual, legislation is protected from wanton assaults and from the daily aggressions of party spirit. The errors of the legislator are exposed only to meet a real want; and it is always a positive and appreciable fact that must serve as the basis for a prosecution." *Id.*, at 102.

large fortunes ride on its cases. The ordinary corporation is a "person" for purposes of the adjudicatory processes, whether it represents proprietary, spiritual, aesthetic, or charitable causes.

So it should be as respects valleys, alpine meadows, rivers, lakes, estuaries, beaches, ridges, groves of trees, swampland, or even air that feels the destructive pressures of modern technology and modern life. The river, for example, is the living symbol of all the life it sustains or nourishes—fish, aquatic insects, water ouzels, otter, fisher, deer, elk, bear, and all other animals, including man, who are dependent on it or who enjoy it for its sight, its sound, or its life. The river as plaintiff speaks for the ecological unit of life that is part of it. Those people who have a meaningful relation to that body of water—whether it be a fisherman, a canoeist, a zoologist, or a logger—must be able to speak for the values which the river represents and which are threatened with destruction.

I do not know Mineral King. I have never seen it nor travelled it, though I have seen articles describing its proposed "development," notably Hano, Protectionists v. Recreationists—the Battle of Mineral King, N.Y. Times Mag., Aug. 17, 1969; and Browning, Mickey Mouse in the Mountains, Harper's, March 1972, p. 65. The Sierra Club in its complaint alleges that "One of the principal purposes of the Sierra Club is to protect and conserve the national resources of the Sierra Nevada Mountains." The District Court held that this uncontested allegation made the Sierra Club "sufficiently aggrieved" to have "standing" to sue on behalf of Mineral King.

Mineral King is doubtless like other wonders of the Sierra Nevada such as Tuolumne Meadows and the John Muir Trail. Those who hike it, fish it, hunt it, camp in it, or frequent it, or visit it merely to sit in solitude and wonderment are legitimate spokesmen for it, whether they may be a few or many. Those who have that intimate relation with the inanimate object about to be injured, polluted, or otherwise despoiled are its legitimate spokesmen.

The Solicitor General, whose views on this subject are in the Appendix to this opinion, takes a wholly different approach. He considers the problem in terms of "government by the Judiciary." With all respect, the problem is to make certain that the inanimate objects, which are the very core of America's beauty, have spokesmen before they are destroyed. It is, of course, true that most of them are under the control of a federal or state agency. The standards given those agencies are usually expressed in terms of the "public interest." Yet "public interest" has so many differing shades of meaning as to be quite meaningless on the environmental front. Congress accordingly has adopted ecological standards in the National Environmental Policy Act of 1969, Pub.L. 91–90, 83 Stat. 852, 42 U.S.C. § 4321, et seq., and guidelines for agency action have been provided by the Council on Environmental Quality of which Russell E. Train is Chairman. See 36 Fed.Reg. 7724.

Yet the pressures on agencies for favorable action one way or the other are enormous. The suggestion that Congress can stop action which is undesirable is true in theory; yet even Congress is too remote to give meaningful direction and its machinery is too ponderous to use very often. The federal agencies of which I speak are not venal or corrupt. But they are notoriously under the control of powerful interests who manipulate them through advisory committees, or friendly working relations, or who have that natural affinity with the agency which in time develops between the regulator and the regulated. As early as 1894, Attorney General Olney predicted that regulatory agencies might become "industry-minded," as illustrated by his forecast concerning the Interstate Commerce Commission:

> The Commission is or can be made of great use to the railroads. It satisfies the public clamor for supervision of the railroads, at the same time that supervision is almost entirely nominal. Moreover, the older the Commission gets to be, the more likely it is to take a business and railroad view of things. M. Josephson, The Politicos 526 (1938).
>
> Years later a court of appeals observed, the recurring question which has plagued public regulation of industry [is] whether the regulatory agency is unduly oriented toward the interests of the industry it is designed to regulate, rather than the public interest it is supposed to protect. Moss v. CAB, 139 U.S.A.App.D.C. 150, 430 F.2d 891, 893 (1970).

See also Office of Communication of United Church of Christ v. FCC, 123 U.S.App.D.C. 328, 359 F.2d 994, 1003–1004; Udall v. FPC, 387 U.S. 428, 87 S.Ct. 1712, 18 L.Ed.2d 869; Calvert Cliffs' Coordinating Committee, Inc. v. AEC, D.C.Cir., 449 F.2d 1109; Environmental Defense Fund, Inc. v. Ruckelshaus, 142 U.S.App.D.C. 74, 439 F.2d 584; Environmental Defense Fund, Inc. v. United States Dept. of HEW, 138 U.S.App.D.C. 381, 428 F.2d 1083; Scenic Hudson Preservation Conf. v. FPC, 354 F.2d 608, 620. But see Jaffe, The Federal Regulatory Agencies In a Perspective: Administrative Limitation In A Political Setting, 11 Bos. C. I. & C. Rev. 565 (1970) (labels "industry-mindedness" as "devil" theory).

The Forest Service—one of the federal agencies behind the scheme to despoil Mineral King—has been notorious for its alignment with lumber companies, although its mandate from Congress directs it to consider the various aspects of multiple use in its supervision of the national forests.

The voice of the inanimate object, therefore, should not be stilled. That does not mean that the judiciary takes over the managerial functions from the federal agency. It merely means that before these priceless bits of

Americana (such as a valley, an alpine meadow, a river, or a lake) are forever lost or are so transformed as to be reduced to the eventual rubble of our urban environment, the voice of the existing beneficiaries of these environmental wonders should be heard.

Perhaps they will not win. Perhaps the bulldozers of "progress" will plow under all the aesthetic wonders of this beautiful land. That is not the present question. The sole question is, who has standing to be heard?

Those who hike the Appalachian Trail into Sunfish Pond, New Jersey, and camp or sleep there, or run the Allagash in Maine, or climb the Guadalupes in West Texas, or who canoe and portage the Quetico Superior in Minnesota, certainly should have standing to defend those natural wonders before courts or agencies, though they live 3,000 miles away. Those who merely are caught up in environmental news or propaganda and flock to defend these water or areas may be treated differently. That is why these environmental issues should be tendered by the inanimate object itself. Then there will be assurances that all of the forms of life which it represents will stand before the court—the pileated woodpecker as well as the coyote and bear, the lemmings as well as the trout in the streams. Those inarticulate members of the ecological group cannot speak. But those people who have so frequented the place as to know its values and wonders will be able to speak for the entire ecological community.

Ecology reflects the land ethic; and Aldo Leopold wrote in A Sand County Almanac 204 (1949), "The land ethic simply enlarges the boundaries of the community to include soils, waters, plants, and animals, or collectively, the land."

That, as I see it, is the issue of "standing" in the present case and controversy.

APPENDIX TO
OPINION OF DOUGLAS, J.

Statement of the Solicitor-General:

*   *   *

As far as I know, no case has yet been decided which holds that a plaintiff which merely asserts that, to quote from the complaint here, its interest would be widely affected, and that 'it would be aggrieved,' by the acts of the defendant, has standing to raise legal questions in court.

But why not? Do not the courts exist to decide legal questions? And are they not the most impartial and learned agencies we have in our governmental system? Are there not many questions which must be decided by courts? Why should not the courts decide any question which any citizen wants to raise? As the tenor of my argument indicates, this raises, I think, a true question, perhaps a somewhat novel question, in the separation of powers. . . .

Ours is not a government by the Judiciary. It is a government of three branches, each of which was intended to have broad and effective powers subject to checks and balances. In litigable cases, the courts have great authority. But the Founders also intended that the Congress should have wide powers, and that the executive branch should have wide powers. All these officers have great responsibilities. They are no less sworn than are the members of this Court to uphold the Constitution of the United States.

This, I submit, is what really lies behind the standing doctrine, embodied in those cryptic words 'case' and 'controversy' in Article III of the Constitution. Analytically, one could have a system of government in which every legal question arising in the course of government would be decided by the courts. It would not be, I submit, a good system. More important, it is not the system which was ordained and established in our Constitution, as it has been understood for nearly 200 years.

Over the past 20 or 25 years there has been a great shift in the decision of legal questions in our governmental operations into the courts. This has been the result of continuous whittling away of the numerous doctrines which have been established over the years, designed to minimize the number of governmental questions which it was the responsibility of the courts to consider.

I have already mentioned the most ancient of all, case or controversy, which was early relied on to prevent the presentation of feigned issues to the court. But there are many other doctrines, which I cannot go into in detail: reviewability, justiciability, sovereign immunity, mootness in various aspects, statutes of limitations and laches, jurisdictional amount, real party in interest and various questions in relation to joinder. Under all of these headings, limitations which previously existed to minimize the number of questions decided in courts have broken down in varying degrees. I might also mention the explosive development of class actions which has thrown more and more issues into the courts. . . .

If there is standing in this case, I find it very difficult to think of any legal issue arising in government which will not have to await one or more decisions of the court before the administrator sworn to uphold the law, can take any action. I'm not sure that this is good for the government. I'm not sure that it is good for the courts. I do find myself more and more sure that it is not the kind of allocation of governmental power in our tripartite constitutional system that was contemplated by the Founders. . . .

I do not suggest that administrators can act at their whim and without any check at all. On the contrary, in this area they are subject to continuous check by the Congress. Congress can stop this development any time it wants to.

Mr. Justice Brennan, dissenting.

I agree that the Sierra Club has standing for the reasons stated by my Brother Blackmun in Alternative No. 2 of his dissent. I therefore would reach the merits. Since the Court does not do so, however, I simply note agreement with my Brother Blackmun that the merits are substantial.

Mr. Justice Blackmun, dissenting.

The Court's opinion is a practical one espousing and adhering to traditional notions of standing as somewhat modernized by Association of Data Processing Service Organizations, Inc. v. Camp, 397 U.S. 150, 90 S.Ct. 827, 25 L.Ed.2d 184 (1970); Barlow v. Collins, 397 U.S. 159, 90 S.Ct. 832, 25 L.Ed.2d 192 (1970); and Flast v. Cohen, 392 U.S. 83, 88 S.Ct. 1942, 20 L.Ed.2d 947 (1968). If this were an ordinary case, I would join the opinion and the Court's judgment and be quite content.

But this is not ordinary, run-of-the-mill litigation. The case poses—if only we choose to acknowledge and reach them—significant aspects of a wide, growing and disturbing problem, that is, the Nation's and the world's deteriorating environment with its resulting ecological disturbances. Must our law be so rigid and our procedural concepts so inflexible that we render ourselves helpless when the existing methods and the traditional concepts do not quite fit and do not prove to be entirely adequate for new issues?

The ultimate result of the Court's decision today, I fear, and sadly so, is that the 35.3-million-dollar complex, over 10 times greater than the Forest Service's suggested minimum, will now hastily proceed to comple-tion; that serious opposition to it will recede in discouragement; and that Mineral King, the "area of great natural beauty nestled in the Sierra Nevada Mountains," to use the Court's words, will become defaced, at least in part, and, like so many other areas, will cease to be "uncluttered by the products of civilization."

I believe this will come about because: (1) The District Court, although it accepted standing for the Sierra Club and granted preliminary injunctive relief, was reversed by the Court of Appeals, and this Court now upholds that reversal. (2) With the reversal, interim relief by the District Court is now out of the question and a permanent injunction becomes most unlikely. (3) The Sierra Club may not choose to amend its complaint or, if it does desire to do so, may not, at this late date, be granted permission. (4) The ever-present pressure to get the project underway will mount. (5) Once underway, any prospect of bringing it to a halt will grow dim. Reasons, most of them economic, for not stopping the project will have a tendency to multiply. And the irreparable harm will be largely inflicted in the earlier stages of construction and development.

Rather than pursue the course the Court has chosen to take by its affirmance of the judgment of the Court of Appeals, I would adopt one of two alternatives:

1. I would reverse that judgment and, instead, approve the judgment·of the District Court which recognized standing in the Sierra Club and granted preliminary relief. I would be willing to do this on condition that the Sierra Club forthwith amend its complaint to meet the specifications the Court prescribes for standing. If Sierra Club fails or refuses to take that step, so be it; the case will then collapse. But if it does amend, the merits will be before the trial court once again. As the Court's footnote 2, p. 1364, so clearly reveals, the issues on the merits are substantial and deserve resolution. They assay new ground. They are crucial to the future of Mineral King. They raise important ramifications for the quality of the country's public land management. They pose the propriety of the "dual permit" device as a means of avoiding the 80-acre "recreation and resort" limitation imposed by Congress in 16 U.S.C. § 497, an issue that apparently has never been litigated, and is clearly substantial in light of the congressional expansion of the limitation in 1956 arguably to put teeth into the old, unrealistic five-acre limitation. In fact, they concern the propriety of the 80-acre permit itself and the consistency of the entire, enormous development with the statutory purposes of the Sequoia Game Refuge, of which the Valley is a part. In the context of this particular development, substantial questions are raised about the use of National Park area for Disney purposes for a new high speed road and a 66,000-volt power line to serve the complex. Lack of compliance with existing administrative regulations is also charged. These issues are not shallow or perfunctory.

2. Alternatively, I would permit an imaginative expansion of our traditional concepts of standing in order to enable an organization such as the Sierra Club, possessed, as it is, of pertinent, bona fide and well-recognized attributes and purposes in the area of environment, to litigate environmental issues. This incursion upon tradition need not be very extensive. Certainly, it should be no cause for alarm. It is no more progressive than was the decision in *Data Processing* itself. It need only recognize the interest of one who has a provable, sincere, dedicated, and established status. We need not fear that Pandora's box will be opened or that there will be no limit to the number of those who desire to participate in environmental litigation. The courts will exercise appropriate restraints just as they have exercised them in the past. Who would have suspected 20 years ago that the concepts of standing enunciated in *Data Processing* and *Barlow* would be the measure for today? And Mr. Justice Douglas, in his eloquent opinion, has imaginatively suggested another means and one, in its own way, with obvious, appropriate and self-imposed limitations as

to standing. As I read what he has written, he makes only one addition to the customary criteria (the existence of a genuine dispute; the assurance of adversariness; and a conviction that the party whose standing is challenged will adequately represent the interests he asserts), that is, that the litigant be one who speaks knowingly for the environmental values he asserts.

I make two passing references:

1. The first relates to the Disney figures presented to us. The complex, the Court notes, will accommodate 14,000 visitors *a day* (3,100 overnight; some 800 employees; 10 restaurants; 20 ski lifts). The State of California has proposed to build a new road from Hammond to Mineral King. That road, to the extent of 9.2 miles, is to traverse Sierra National Park. It will have only two lanes, with occasional passing areas, but it will be capable, it is said, of accommodating 700–800 vehicles per hour and a peak of 1,200 per hour. We are told that the State has agreed not to seek any further improvement in road access through the park.

If we assume that the 14,000 daily visitors come by automobile (rather than by helicopter or bus or other known or unknown means) and that each visiting automobile carries four passengers (an assumption, I am sure, that is far too optimistic), those 14,000 visitors will move in 3,500 vehicles. If we confine their movement (as I think we properly may for this mountain area) to 12 hours out of the daily 24, the 3,500 automobiles will pass any given point on the two-lane road at the rate of about 300 per hour. This amounts to five vehicles per minute, or an average of one every 12 seconds. This frequency is further increased to one every six seconds when the necessary return traffic along that same two-lane road is considered. And this does not include service vehicles and employees' cars. Is this the way we perpetuate the wilderness and its beauty, solitude and quiet?

2. The second relates to the fairly obvious fact that any resident of the Mineral King area—the real "user"—is an unlikely adversary for this Disney-governmental project. He naturally will be inclined to regard the situation as one that should benefit him economically. His fishing or camping or guiding or handyman or general outdoor prowess perhaps will find an early and ready market among the visitors. But that glow of anticipation will be short-lived at best. If he is a true lover of the wilderness—as is likely, or he would not be near Mineral King in the first place —it will not be long before he yearns for the good old days when masses of people—that 14,000 influx per day—and their thus far uncontrollable waste were unknown to Mineral King.

Do we need any further indication and proof that all this means that the area will no longer be one "of great natural beauty" and one "uncluttered by the products of civilization?" Are we to be rendered helpless to consider and evaluate allegations and challenges of this kind because of procedural limitations rooted in traditional concepts of standing? I suspect that this may be the result of today's holding. As the Court points out, p. 1367, other federal tribunals have not felt themselves so confined. I would join those progressive holdings.

The Court chooses to conclude its opinion with a footnote reference to de Tocqueville. In this environmental context I personally prefer the older and particularly pertinent observation and warning of John Donne.[6]

---

[6] "No man is an Iland, intire of itselfe; every man is a peece of the Continent, a part of the maine; if a Clod bee washed away by the Sea, Europe is the lesse, as well as if a Promontorie were, as well as if a Mannor of thy friends or of thine owne were; any man's death diminishes me, because I am involved in Mankinde; And therefore never send to know for whom the bell tolls; it tolls for thee." Devotions XVII.

PART II

The Emerging International Law of Pollution

Introduction

It is generally agreed that the existing principles of international law, as described by the leading jurists, provide an inadequate legal basis for the effective treatment of international pollution problems. Until very recently there has been little, if any, agreement, for example, on what principles of customary international law are directly applicable to the question of a state's liability for pollution damage, despite frequent references to the *Trail Smelter* arbitration between the United States and Canada, which proceeded from the assumption of liability by Canada for its discharge of noxious gases over American territory. In a sense, the paucity of legal principles in the field might be considered a blessing in that a clean slate should allow states to negotiate an appropriate matrix of environmental rights and responsibilities. Yet it would be naïve to suggest that there is a complete juridical vacuum. In addition to the heritage of municipal law outlined in Part I and the long line of relevant interstate arrangements documented in Part II, there exists international legal doctrine supporting the notion that one state may be required to compensate another for injury. Although they occurred in a case far removed from the problem of environmental damage, some of the comments of the International Court of Justice in the *Corfu Channel* case (1949) can be interpreted as an important judicial affirmation of state responsibility from which one today can infer the obligation of each state not to allow the nationals of other states to suffer pollution damage that might reasonably be prevented and the liability of providing appropriate compensation to the injured party when that obligation is violated.

69

In the case of international rivers and lakes there is growing support in state practice for the doctrine of *equitable utilization* along the lines proposed in the unofficial Helsinki Rules. But the problems of pollution control in internationally shared waters are essentially regional and subject to different treaty arrangements. It is perhaps unlikely that the doctrine of equitable utilization, whose chief virtue resides in its flexibility, will be applied with the degree of uniformity that would permit the evolution of more specific principles of environmental responsibility in the use of such waters. It should be noted, however, that at the 1972 Stockholm Conference on the Human Environment the participating governments endorsed the idea that it is incumbent upon all coadjacent states in international river basins to develop appropriate regimes for the prevention and control of pollution.

Particularly interesting regional experiments in pollution control have been attempted in North America, where the United States shares a number of international rivers and lakes with Canada and Mexico. Of special relevance is the history of the International Joint Commission established under the 1909 Boundary Waters Treaty between Canada and the United States. The Commission is limited to investigative and recommendatory roles in relation to specific questions referred to it by the two governments, and even under the 1972 Agreement the Commission has only the sanction of publicity to spur the governments to implement its recommendations. Yet in its 60 years the I.J.C. has accumulated expertise in pollution problems unequalled by any other international body. As early as 1912 the two federal governments, alarmed by the prevalence of typhoid fever, sent the Commission a wide-ranging reference to examine and report "to what extent and by what causes and in what localities have the boundary waters . . . been polluted. . . ." In 1918 the Commission reported its findings of a "situation along the frontier which is generally chaotic, everywhere perilous, and in some cases disgraceful." Yet no action upon the I.J.C.'s recommendations was taken by either government, mainly because of the advent of chlorination of municipal water supplies, which eliminated typhoid, and because of the continuing general belief that there was an inexhaustible supply of clean, fresh water. Thereafter, except for its involvement in air pollution studies, which culminated in the famous *Trail Smelter* Arbitration, the Commission turned away from pollution problems until 1946, when it was asked to investigate the St. Clair River, Lake St. Clair, and the Detroit River, and later the Niagara River. In response to this reference the Commission recommended "objectives" for maintaining the quality of the boundary waters in question, which were approved by the two governments. Since then the I.J.C. has been chiefly pre-occupied with pollution problems along the United States–Canadian boundary. Most important of all was its study, conducted between 1964 and 1970, of the state of pollution in Lake Erie, Lake Ontario, and the international section of the St. Lawrence River. Reputedly the most extensive international pollution study undertaken to date anywhere in the world, it provided the basis for the 1972 Agreement on Great Lakes Water Quality.

Although the International Joint Commission of North America is held out as a model for the future, it may be questioned how many neighboring countries in other parts of the world have a comparable degree of technical and financial capability for effective joint treatment of shared environmental problems. Even in Europe it will be more difficult to get intergovernmental participation in costly pollution control programs entrusted, say, to the International Commission for the Protection of the Rhine against Pollution. In this example, of course, several states are involved that lack the advantage of cultural similarity, which has contributed to successful cooperation between the federal governments of Canada and the United States. The North American experiments are, however, of additional interest for comparison with experiments elsewhere that are also complicated by the involvement of subfederal governments and agencies, but no effort has been made in this book to provide materials that focus specifically on the political and legal problems of cooperation between federal states.

The *Trail Smelter* Arbitration occupies a special niche in the emerging international law of pollution, not only because it provides a quasi-judicial comment on the environment responsibility of one state toward another, but also because it apparently represents the only international adjudication of a pollution dispute. Yet this famous case has not yet been accepted as a precedent for the establishment of similar arbitral tribunals. Indeed, it is scarcely an exaggeration to say that until very recently it was regarded as something of a juridical oddity, even though the tribunal did not purport to establish the principle of Canada's liability. Liability was already accepted by Canada with respect to the period up to January 1, 1932, in Article I of the convention signed by the parties in April 1935 for establishing the arbitration tribunal. In fact, under Article I Canada undertook to pay the United States $350,000 for the damage caused prior to January 1, 1932. One of the most important results of the 1972 Stockholm Conference on the Human Environment is the general acceptance, in Principle 21 of the Stockholm Declaration, of the principle of state responsibility for environmental damage beyond territorial limits, similar to that acknowledged by Canada prior to the *Trail Smelter* Arbitration.

Quite clearly, the most active area of environmental treaty-making is that of marine pollution. Its development can be divided into three categories: agreements dealing solely with the problem of marine pollution by oil; agreements on the prohibition and regulation of dumping practices of ships at sea; and lastly, the elaboration of general principles and guidelines for the preservation of the marine environment. The first-named category was the earliest to develop, beginning with the 1954 Convention for the Prevention of Pollution of the Sea by Oil. Most of the agreements in this category concluded since then have been negotiated under the auspices of the Intergovernmental Maritime Consultative Organization (IMCO), a specialized agency of the United Nations in London. Since then IMCO has become the leading international agency on the technical aspects of shipping and marine pollution by oil.[1] The second category, that of dumping agreements, is of very recent date, beginning with a regional rather than a user approach such as taken under IMCO in the first category. More recently, however, dumping arrangements have been developed further along more universal lines under the impetus of the Stockholm Conference. Even more ambitious are those developments which belong to the third category, where a more comprehensive approach is taken to the problem of pollution of the marine environment. These efforts represent an attempt to define new or emerging principles of state responsibility and rights for the prevention and control of marine pollution in general. The Ottawa guidelines and principles have not yet acquired the force of established international law, but their endorsement at the Stockholm Conference on the Human Environment suggests that there is sufficient international consensus to enable the members of the United Nations to incorporate most of these principles in the form of an international convention, perhaps as part of the difficult lawmaking exercises beginning in 1974 at the Third Law of the Sea Conference. Because of the Stockholm endorsement of the Ottawa principles, it

---

[1] Also belonging to this category but omitted from this volume are arrangements by the oil companies themselves, such as the 1969 Tanker Owners Voluntary Agreement concerning Liability for Oil Pollution (TOVALOP) and the 1971 Contract regarding an interim supplement ("Cristal"). These texts are reproduced in International Legal Materials in vol. 7, p. 497, and vol. 10, p. 137, respectively.

seems appropriate to include them in the section devoted to global approaches to international environmental cooperation.

From their beginning most of the U.N. specialized agencies have been involved in environmental studies and projects: UNESCO (with its sponsored groups, like the International Union for the Conservation of Nature and the International Oceanographic Commission), WHO, WMO, FAO, IAEA, ILO, ICAO, and IMCO are conspicuous examples. Various United Nations conferences have also been held to discuss certain aspects of global environment problems, such as the 1966 U.N. Conference on New Sources of Energy, and a number of committees have met, such as the U.N. Scientific Committee on the Effects of Atomic Radiation set up in 1955.

However it was not until 1966 that the concept of the "problems of the human environment" emerged in debate in the General Assembly, promoting the view that a bold response from the organized world community was needed to stave off ecocatastrophe. Finally, in December 1968, the 23rd session of the General Assembly approved a Swedish proposal, endorsed by the Economic and Social Council, to convene a worldwide conference on the problems of the human environment at Stockholm in 1972. It soon became evident that the preparations for this conference would be on an unprecedented scale and that particular pollution issues, however serious, could only be treated within a much larger context.

In advance of the Stockholm Conference the Preparatory Committee established five intergovernmental working groups: on the Declaration on the Human Environment, on marine pollution, on monitoring and surveillance, on soil reclamation and preservation, and on conservation. It was in the Intergovernmental Working Group on Marine Pollution that the Ottawa Guidelines and Principles for the Preservation of the Marine Environment (see readings from Conference) were drawn up, based on a Canadian working paper, and submitted for approval at Stockholm. We have also included an excerpt from the Stockholm Declaration that upholds the *Trail Smelter* principle of state responsibility for environmental damage extending beyond territorial limits and selected recommendations directly relevant to the emerging international law of pollution. It might be ventured that the most important result of Stockholm will be a much more general acceptance of the need to adopt a global environmental approach to many forms of international pollution and to develop appropriate principles, institutions, and procedures in international law.

Principles of Responsibility for Environmental Damage Beyond Territorial Limits

It is commonly asserted that the international law of pollution is still at the embryonic stage of development. What is normally meant by this statement is that legal development in this area has not yet been evidenced by any growing acceptance of general principles of state responsibility for environmental injury beyond territorial limits. One may quarrel with this emphasis on general principles on the ground that it represents an unduly narrow view of how international law evolves, especially in an area that is likely to be characterized by a growing proliferation of environmental agreements. On the other hand, it is unlikely that an international law of pollution will emerge holistically from universal lawmaking conventions in the near future. International legal principles of environmental responsibility are likely to emerge chiefly from two sources: from international declarations and resolutions that lack the form and, arguably, the effect of lawmaking treaties and from the express commitments and implied assumptions common to a growing variety of international environmental agreements of limited scope. But it will be easier to derive generally binding principles from either of these sources if they can be shown to be a development or modification of existing principles of international responsibility.

The textbooks show that the doctrine of international responsibility is not highly developed. Primarily it deals with the responsibility of a state for injuries to aliens in its territory and only marginally with state responsibility for direct injury to the rights of other states. Even in the latter category, there are few references to general principles that pertain specifically to situations of environmental injury. It is generally assumed that liability for such an injury would arise upon proof of an "international delinquency," an unlawful act or omission by one state resulting in loss or damage to another. But the injury need not be accompanied by fault or negligence on the part of the individual or agency whose delinquent conduct is ascribed to the state. The doctrine of strict or absolute liability in international law is, however, limited to a few areas designated by treaty under arrangements for the allocation of risks associated with extremely dangerous activities.

Recent examples are found in the 1960 and 1963 treaties on third-party liability for nuclear damage and the 1962 Brussels Convention on the Liability of Operators of Nuclear Ships. In these instances the provisions deal with civil liability under the applicable domestic law, and state responsibility under international law is not a primary concern. The activities themselves are dangerous but not unlawful. Although those agreements on risk distribution are certainly part of the evolving international law of pollution, they are marginal to the basic question of state responsibility for environmental damage extending beyond territorial limits.

Earlier approaches to that basic question are found rather in applications of the principle of noninterference established by customary international law and described in the vague maxim *sic utere tuo ut alienum non laedas* (use your property in such a manner as not to injure that of another). Obviously this maxim is of minimal utility in the assessment of international environmental responsibility without the provision of specific criteria. It belongs to an even more nebulous order of vagueness than the civil law doctrine of abuse of rights (*abus de droit*). The observations in the *Trail Smelter* Arbitration and the *Corfu Channel* case, reproduced below, belong essentially to this category. In the latter case, although the "environmental" danger lay hidden *within* territorial limits, the state's responsibility would have been recognized if the danger had "escaped" beyond these limits.

Another source of general principles of state responsibility for extraterritorial injury might be traced by analogy with the doctrine of equitable utilization applied to international rivers and lakes. This doctrine, enunciated in the unofficial Helsinki Rules adopted by the nongovernmental International Law Association in 1966, has evolved in state practice in most areas of the world, but it really does little more than introduce the "reasonable man" test for determining what is a lawful share in the beneficial uses of the waters of an international drainage basin. Thus, according to the Helsinki Rules, a state causing pollution of such waters is not under a duty to take prevention or control measures that would deprive it of equitable utilization; and liability arises only where the water use is inconsistent with that principle and causes substantial injury in the territory of another state.

The famous *Trail Smelter* decision has been interpreted in many ways. Some, for example, have argued that it introduced the concept of strict (or absolute) liability into international law. Some maintain that it merely invokes the rudimentary principle of *sic utere tuo*. Others have suggested that it hints at an acceptance of the doctrine of equitable utilization. As this decision was an arbitral award and not a judicial decision, the controversy will never be authoritatively resolved. More important, the *Trail Smelter* heritage has now been appropriated by the international community in the Stockholm Declaration on the Human Environment. Whether the language of the Declaration is wholly faithful to the *Trail Smelter* doctrine is now academic: it has transcended it.

◤ THE TRAIL SMELTER ARBITRATION: UNITED STATES AND CANADA *

The Tribunal, therefore, finds . . . under the principles of international law, as well as of the law of the United States, no State has the right to use or permit the use of its territory in such a manner as to cause injury by fumes in or to the territory of another or the properties or persons therein, when the case is of serious consequence and the injury is established by clear and convincing evidence.

◤ THE CORFU CHANNEL CASE: UNITED KINGDOM AND ALBANIA †

From all the facts and observations mentioned above, the Court draws the conclusion that the laying of the minefield which caused the explosions on October 22nd, 1946, could not have been accomplished without the knowledge of the Albanian Government.

The obligations resulting for Albania from this knowledge are not disputed between the Parties. Counsel for the Albanian Government expressly recognized that [*translation*] "if Albania had been informed of the operation before the incidents of October 22nd, and in time to warn the British vessels and shipping in general of the existence of mines in the Corfu Channel, her responsibility would be involved. . . ."

The obligations incumbent upon the Albanian authorities consisted in notifying, for the benefit of shipping in general, the existence of a minefield in Albanian territorial waters and in warning the approaching British warships of the imminent danger to which the minefield exposed them. Such obligations are based, not on the Hague Convention of 1907, No. VIII, which is applicable in time of war, but on certain general and well-recognized principles, namely: elementary considerations of humanity, even more exacting in peace than in war; the principle of the freedom of maritime communication; *and every State's obligation not to allow knowingly its territory to be used for acts contrary to the rights of other States.* [Emphasis added.]

* Final decision, March 11, 1941.
† Extract from the International Court of Justice Decision, April 9, 1949.

In fact, Albania neither notified the existence of the minefield, nor warned the British warships of the danger they were approaching.

But Albania's obligation to notify shipping of the existence of mines in her waters depends on her having obtained knowledge of that fact in sufficient time before October 22nd; and the duty of the Albanian coastal authorities to warn the British ships depends on the time that elapsed between the moment that these ships were reported and the moment of the first explosion.

⚑ HELSINKI RULES ON THE USES OF THE WATERS OF INTERNATIONAL RIVERS

Chapter 2

EQUITABLE UTILIZATION OF THE WATERS OF AN INTERNATIONAL DRAINAGE BASIN

ARTICLE IV

Each basin State is entitled, within its territory, to a reasonable and equitable share in the beneficial use of the water of an international drainage basin.

Comment:

(a) GENERAL

This Article reflects the key principle of international law in this area that every basin State in an international drainage basin has the right to the reasonable use of the waters of the drainage basin. It rejects the unlimited sovereignty position, exemplified by the "Harmon Doctrine," which has been cited as supporting the proposition that a State has the unqualified right to utilize and dispose of the waters of an international river flowing through its territory; such a position imports its logical corollary, that a State has no right to demand continued flow from co-basin States.

The Harmon Doctrine has never had a wide following among States and has been rejected by virtually all States which have had occasion to speak out on the point. . . .

This Article recognizes that each basin State has rights equal in kind and correlative with those of each co-basin State. Of course, equal and

Adopted by the non-governmental International Law Association (ILA) on Aug. 20, 1966, in Helsinki at its 52nd Conference.

correlative rights of use among the co-basin States does not mean that each such State will receive an identical share in the uses of the waters. Those will depend upon the weighing of factors considered in Article V of this Chapter.

A use of a basin State must take into consideration the economic and social needs of its co-basin States for use of the waters, and *vice-versa*. This consideration may result in one co-basin State receiving the right to use water in quantitatively greater amounts than its neighbors in the basin. The idea of equitable sharing is to provide the maximum benefit to each basin State from the uses of the waters with the minimum detriment to each.

(b) BENEFICIAL USE

To be worthy of protection a use must be "beneficial," that is to say, it must be economically or socially valuable, as opposed, for example, to a diversion of waters by one State merely for the purpose of harrassing another.

A "beneficial use" need not be *the* most productive use to which the water may be put, nor need it utilize the most efficient methods known in order to avoid waste and insure maximum utilization. As to the former, to provide otherwise would dislocate numerous productive and, indeed, essential portions of national economies; the latter, while a patently imperfect solution, reflects the financial limitations of many States; in its application, the present rule is not designed to foster waste but to hold States to a duty of efficiency which is commensurate with their financial resources. Of course, the ability of a State to obtain international financing will be considered in this context. Thus, State A, an economically advanced and prosperous State which utilizes the inundation method of irrigation, might be required to develop a more efficient and less wasteful system forthwith, while State B, an underdeveloped State using the same method, might be permitted additional time to obtain the means to make the required improvements.

ARTICLE V

(1) *What is a reasonable and equitable share within the meaning of Article IV is to be determined in the light of all the relevant factors in each particular case.*

(2) *Relevant factors which are to be considered include, but are not limited to:*

(a) *the geography of the basin, including in particular the extent of the drainage area in the territory of each basin State;*

(b) *the hydrology of the basin, including in particular the contribution of water by each basin State;*

(c) *the climate affecting the basin;*

(d) *the past utilization of the waters of the basin, including in particular existing utilization;*

(e) *the economic and social needs of each basin State;*

(f) *the population dependent on the waters of the basin in each basin State;*

(g) *the comparative costs of alternative means of satisfying the economic and social needs of each basin State;*

(h) *the availability of other resources;*

(i) *the avoidance of unnecessary waste in the utilization of waters of the basin;*

(j) *the practicability of compensation to one or more of the co-basin States as a means of adjusting conflicts among uses; and*

(k) *the degree to which the needs of a basin State may be satisfied, without causing substantial injury to a co-basin State.*

(3) *The weight to be given to each factor is to be determined by its importance in comparison with that of other relevant factors. In determining what is a reasonable and equitable share, all relevant factors are to be considered together and a conclusion reached on the basis of the whole.*

Comment:

GENERAL

This Article provides the express, but flexible guidelines essential to insuring the protection of the "equal right" of all basin States to share the waters. Under the rules set forth "all the relevant factors" must be considered. An exhaustive list of factors cannot readily be compiled, for there would likely be others applicable to particular cases.

This Article states some of the factors to be considered in determining what is a reasonable and equitable share.

Stated somewhat more generally, the factor-analysis approach seeks primarily to determine whether (i) the various uses are compatible; (ii) any of the uses is essential to human life, (iii) the uses are socially and economically valuable, (iv) other resources are available, (v) any of the uses is "existing" within the meaning of Article VIII, (vi) it is feasible to modify competing uses in order to accommodate all to some degree, (vii) financial contributions by one or more of the interested basin States for the construction of works could result in the accommodation of competing uses, (viii) the burden could be adjusted by the payment of compensation to one or more of the co-basin States, and (ix) overall efficiency of water utilization could be improved in order to increase the amount of available water.

In short, no factor has a fixed weight nor will all factors be relevant in all cases. Each factor is given such weight as it merits relative to all the other factors. And no factor occupies a position of preeminence per se with respect to any other factor. Further, to be relevant, a factor must aid in the determination or satisfaction of the social and economic needs of the co-basin states.

*   *   *

ARTICLE VI

A use or category of uses is not entitled to any inherent preference over any other use or category of uses.

Comment:

PREFERENTIAL USE

Historically, navigation was preferred over other uses of water, irrespective of the later needs of the particular drainage basin involved. In the past twenty-five years, however, the technological revolution and population explosion, which have led to the rapid growth of nonnavigational uses have resulted in the loss of the former pre-eminence accorded navigational uses. Today, neither navigation nor any other use enjoys such a preference. A drainage basin must be examined on an individual basis and a determination made as to which uses are most important in that basin or, in appropriate cases, in portions of the basin.

It has been said that domestic use has succeeded navigation as a preferential use. However, substantial authority supporting the proposition has not been found. Moreover, no artificial preference is necessary, and, indeed, the granting of such a preference would be inconsistent with a principle of equitable utilization which relies on an inductive process of determination. Granting domestic use an artificial preference can foster the very injustice in the uses of the waters of the basin which its proponents fear will arise by its absence. The purpose in insuring domestic uses a preference is to make certain that these uses—the basis of all life —are assured a first charge on the waters. . . .

*   *   *

Chapter 3

POLLUTION

Article IX

As used in this Chapter, the term "water pollution" refers to any detrimental change resulting from human conduct in the natural composition, content, or quality of the waters of an international drainage basin. . . .

* * *

Article X

1. Consistent with the principle of equitable utilization of the waters of an international drainage basin, a State
   (a) must prevent any new form of water pollution or any increase in the degree of existing water pollution in an international drainage basin which would cause substantial injury in the territory of a co-basin State, and
   (b) should take all reasonable measures to abate existing water pollution in an international drainage basin to such an extent that no substantial damage is caused in the territory of a co-basin State.
2. The Rule stated in paragraph 1 of this Article applies to water pollution originating
   (a) within the territory of the State, or
   (b) outside the territory of the State, if it is caused by the State's conduct.

Comment:

(a) GENERAL

International law imposes general limitations upon action that one State may take which would cause injury in the territory of another State. In the *Corfu Channel Case,* the International Court of Justice stated that international law obliges every State "not to allow knowingly its territory to be used for acts contrary to the rights of other states" [1949] I.C.J. Rep. 4, 22. The Secretary-General of the United Nations has expressed the view that "There has been general recognition of the rule that a State must not permit the use of its territory for purposes injurious to the interest of other States in a manner contrary to international law" [Survey of International Law 34 (U.N. Doc. A/CN4/1 Rev. 1) (1949)]. This statement is no more than a reflection of the principle *sic utere tuo ut alienum non laedas*—"one must so use his own as not to do injury to another." The same general thread of principle runs throughout the range of State-to-State relationships.

❖ ❖ ❖

Article XI

1. *In the case of a violation of the rule stated in paragraph 1 (a) of Article X of this Chapter, the State responsible shall be required to cease the wrongful conduct and compensate the injured co-basin State for the injury that has been caused to it.*

2. *In a case falling under the rule stated in paragraph 1 (b) of Article X, if a State fails to take reasonable measures, it shall be required promptly to enter into negotiations with the injured State with a view toward reaching a settlement equitable under the circumstances....*

❖ ❖ ❖

Suggested Reading List

Lipper, Jerome, "Equitable Utilization," in Garretson, A. H., Hayton, R. D., and Olmstead, C. J., eds., *The Law of International Drainage Basins* (1967), pp. 15–88.

Hayton, R. D., "The Formation of the Customary Rules of International Drainage Basins," *ibid.,* pp. 834–895.

Gutteridge, H. C., "Abuse of Rights," 5 *Camb. L. J.* 22 (1933).

Hutchins, W. A., and Steele, A. A., "Basic Water Rights Doctrines and Their Implications for River Basin Development," 22 *Law and Contemp. Probs.* 276 (1957).

Griffin, William L., "The Use of Waters of International Drainage Basins under Customary International Law," 53 *Amer. J. Int'l L.* 50 (1959).

Johnson, Ralph W., "Effect of Existing Uses on the Equitable Apportionment of International Rivers: An American View," *Univ. Brit. Colum.* L.R. 1: 389 (1960).

Jenks, C. W., "Liability for Ultra-Hazardous Activities in International Law," 117 *Acad. Droit Int.: Recueil des cours* (1966).

Goldie, L. F. E., "Liability for Damage and the Progressive Development of International Law," 14 *Int. and Comp. L.Q.* 1189 (1965).

Pollution of International Rivers and Lakes

NON-COASTAL BOUNDARY WATERS OF CANADA AND THE UNITED STATES: EVOLUTION OF THE INTERNATIONAL JOINT COMMISSION

▨ TREATY BETWEEN HIS MAJESTY AND THE UNITED STATES OF AMERICA RELATING TO BOUNDARY WATERS AND QUESTIONS ARISING ALONG THE BOUNDARY BETWEEN CANADA AND THE UNITED STATES

His Majesty the King of the United Kingdom of Great Britain and Ireland and of the British Dominions beyond the Seas, Emperor of India, and the United States of America, being equally desirous to prevent disputes regarding the use of boundary waters and to settle all questions which are now pending between the United States and the Dominion of Canada involving the rights, obligations, or interests of either in relation to the other or to the inhabitants of the other, along their common frontier, and to make provision for the adjustment and settlement of all such questions as may hereafter arise, have resolved to conclude a Treaty in furtherance of these ends, and for that purpose have appointed as their respective Plenipotentiaries.

His Britannic Majesty, the Right Honourable James Bryce, O.M., his Ambassador Extraordinary and Plenipotentiary at Washington; and

The President of the United States of America, Elihu Root, Secretary of State of the United States;

Who, after having communicated to one another their full powers, found in good and due form, have agreed upon the following articles:

Preliminary Article

For the purposes of this Treaty boundary waters are defined as the waters from main shore to main shore of the lakes and rivers and connecting waterways, or the portions thereof, along which the international boundary between the United States and the Dominion of Canada passes,

Signed at Washington, January 11, 1909; ratifications exchanged at Washington, May 5, 1910.

including all bays, arms and inlets thereof, but not including tributary waters which in their natural channels would flow into such lakes, rivers, and waterways, or waters flowing from such lakes, rivers, and waterways, or the waters of rivers flowing across the boundary.

* * *

Article IV.

The High Contracting Parties agree that, except in cases provided for by special agreement between them, they will not permit the construction or maintenance on their respective sides of the boundary of any remedial or protective works or any dams or other obstructions in waters flowing from boundary waters or in waters at a lower level than the boundary in rivers flowing across the boundary, the effect of which is to raise the natural level of waters on the other side of the boundary unless the construction or maintenance thereof is approved by the aforesaid International Joint Commission.

It is further agreed that the waters herein defined as boundary waters and waters flowing across the boundary shall not be polluted on either side to the injury of health or property on the other. [Emphasis added.]

Article VII.

The High Contracting Parties agree to establish and maintain an International Joint Commission of the United States and Canada composed of six commissioners, three on the part of the United States appointed by the President thereof, and three on the part of the United Kingdom appointed by His Majesty on the recommendation of the Governor in Council of the Dominion of Canada.

Article VIII.

This International Joint Commission shall have jurisdiction over and shall pass upon all cases involving the use or obstruction or diversion of the waters with respect to which under Articles III and IV of this treaty the approval of this Commission is required, and in passing upon such cases the Commission shall be governed by the following rules or principles which are adopted by the High Contracting Parties for this purpose:

The High Contracting Parties shall have, each on its own side of the boundary, equal and similar rights in the use of the waters hereinbefore defined as boundary waters.

The following order of precedence shall be observed among the various uses enumerated hereinafter for these waters, and no use shall be permitted which tends materially to conflict with or restrain any other use which is given preference over it in this order of precedence:

(1) Uses for domestic and sanitary purposes;

(2) Uses for navigation, including the service of canals for the purposes of navigation;

(3) Uses for power and for irrigation purposes.

The foregoing provisions shall not apply to or disturb any existing uses of boundary waters on either side of the boundary.

The requirement for an equal division may in the discretion of the Commission be suspended in cases of temporary diversions along boundary waters at points where such equal division can not be made advantageously on account of local conditions, and where such diversion does not diminish elsewhere the amount available for use on the other side.

The Commisssion in its discretion may make its approval in any case conditional upon the construction of remedial or protective works to compensate so far as possible for the particular use or diversion proposed, and in such cases may require that suitable and adequate provision, approved by the Commission, be made for the protection and indemnity against injury of any interests on either side of the boundary.

In cases involving the elevation of the natural level of waters on either side of the line as a result of the construction or maintenance on the other side of remedial or protective works or dams or other obstructions in boundary waters or in waters flowing therefrom or in waters below the boundary in rivers flowing across the boundary, the Commission shall require, as a condition of its approval thereof, that suitable and adequate provision, approved by it, be made for the protection and indemnity of all interests on the other side of the line which may be injured thereby.

The majority of the Commissioners shall have power to render a decision. In case the Commission is evenly divided upon any question or matter presented to it for decision, separate reports shall be made by the Commissioners on each side to their own Government. The High Contracting Parties shall thereupon endeavor to agree upon an adjustment of the question or matter of difference, and if an agreement is reached between them, it shall be reduced to writing in the form of a protocol, and shall be communicated to the Commissioners, who shall take such further proceedings as may be necessary to carry out such agreement.

Article IX.

The High Contracting Parties further agree that any other questions or matters of difference arising between them involving the rights, obligations, or interests of either in relation to the other or to the inhabitants of the other along the common frontier between the United States and the Dominion of Canada, shall be referred from time to time to the International Joint Commission for examination and report, whenever either the Government of the United States or the Government of the Dominion of Canada shall request that such questions or matters of difference be so referred.

The International Joint Commission is authorized in each case so referred to examine into and report upon the facts and circumstances of the particular questions and matters referred, together with such conclusions and recommendations as may be appropriate, subject, however, to any restrictions or exceptions which may be imposed with respect thereto by the terms of the reference.

Such reports of the Commission shall not be regarded as decisions of the questions or matters so submitted either on the facts or the law, and shall in no way have the character of an arbitral award.

The Commission shall make a joint report to both Governments in all cases in which all or a majority of the Commissioners agree, and in case of disagreement the minority may make a joint report to both Governments, or separate reports to their respective Governments.

In case the Commission is evenly divided upon any question or matter referred to it for report, separate reports shall be made by the Commissioners on each side to their own Government.

Article X.

Any questions or matters of difference arising between the High Contracting Parties involving the rights, obligations, or interests of the United States or of the Dominion of Canada either in relation to each other or to their respective inhabitants, may be referred for decision to the International Joint Commission by the consent of the two Parties, it being understood that on the part of the United States any such action will be by and with the advice and consent of the Senate, and on the part of His Majesty's Government with the consent of the Governor General in Council. In each case so referred, the said Commission is authorized to examine into and report upon the facts and circumstances of the particular questions and matters referred, together with such conclusions and recommendations as may be appropriate, subject, however, to any restrictions or exceptions which may be imposed with respect thereto by the terms of the reference.

A majority of the said Commission shall have power to render a decision or finding upon any of the questions or matters so referred.

If the said Commission is equally divided or otherwise unable to render a decision or finding as to any questions or matters so referred, it shall be the duty of the Commissioners to make a joint report to both Governments, or separate reports to their respective Governments, showing the different conclusions arrived at with regard to the matters or questions so referred, which questions or matters shall thereupon be referred for decision by the High Contracting parties to an umpire chosen in accordance with the procedure prescribed in the fourth, fifth, and sixth paragraphs of Article XLV of The Hague Convention for the pacific settlement of international disputes, dated October 18, 1907. Such umpire shall have power to render a final decision with respect to those matters and questions so referred on which the Commission failed to agree.

ARTICLE XI.

A duplicate original of all decisions rendered and joint reports made by the Commission shall be transmitted to and filed with the Secretary of State of the United States and the Governor General of the Dominion of Canada, and to them shall be addressed all communications of the Commission.

ARTICLE XII.

The International Joint Commission shall meet and organize at Washington promptly after the members thereof are appointed, and when organized the Commission may fix such times and places for its meetings as may be necessary, subject at all times to special call or direction by the two Governments. Each Commissioner, upon the first joint meeting of the Commission after his appointment, shall, before proceeding with the work of the Commission, make and subscribe a solemn declaration in writing that he will faithfully and impartially perform the duties imposed upon him under this treaty, and such declaration shall be entered on the records of the proceedings of the Commission.

The United States and Canadian sections of the Commission may each appoint a secretary, and these shall act as joint secretaries of the Commission at its joint sessions, and the Commission may employ engineers and clerical assistants from time to time as it may deem advisable. The salaries and personal expenses of the Commission and of the secretaries shall be paid by their respective Governments, and all reasonable and necessary joint expenses of the Commission, incurred by it, shall be paid in equal moieties by the High Contracting Parties.

The Commission shall have power to administer oaths to witnesses, and to take evidence on oath whenever deemed necessary in any proceeding, or inquiry, or matter within its jurisdiction under this treaty, and all parties interested therein shall be given convenient opportunity to be heard, and the High Contracting Parties agree to adopt such legislation as may be appropriate and necessary to give the Commission the powers above mentioned on each side of the boundary, and to provide for the issue of subpœnas and for compelling the attendance of witnesses in proceedings before the Commission. The Commission may adopt such rules of procedure as shall be in accordance with justice and equity, and may make such examination in person and through agents or employees as may be deemed advisable.

Article XIII.

In all cases where special agreements between the High Contracting Parties hereto are referred to in the foregoing articles, such agreements are understood and intended to include not only direct agreements between the High Contracting Parties, but also any mutual arrangement between the United States and the Dominion of Canada expressed by concurrent or reciprocal legislation on the part of Congress and the Parliament of the Dominion.

Article XIV.

The present treaty shall be ratified by the President of the United States of America, by and with the advice and consent of the Senate thereof, and by His Britannic Majesty. The ratifications shall be exchanged at Washington as soon as possible and the treaty shall take effect on the date of the exchange of its ratifications. It shall remain in force for five years, dating from the day of exchange of ratifications, and thereafter until terminated by twelve months' written notice given by either High Contracting Party to the other.

In faith whereof the respective plenipotentiaries have signed this treaty in duplicate and have hereunto affixed their seals.

Done at Washington the 11th day of January, in the year of our Lord one thousand nine hundred and nine.

(Signed)   Elihu Root   [seal]

(Signed)   James Bryce   [seal]

Protocol of Exchange.

(Treaty Series, No. 548; 36 Statutes at Large, 2455.)

On proceeding to the exchange of the ratifications of the treaty signed at Washington on January 11, 1909, between the United States and Great Britain, relating to boundary waters and questions arising along the boundary between the United States and the Dominion of Canada, the undersigned plenipotentiaries, duly authorized thereto by their respective Governments, hereby declare that nothing in this treaty shall be construed as affecting, or changing, any existing territorial, or riparian rights in the water, or rights of the owners of lands under water, on either side of the international boundary at the rapids of the St. Mary's River at Sault Ste. Marie, in the use of the waters flowing over such lands, subject to the requirements of navigation in boundary waters and of navigation canals, and without prejudice to the existing right of the United States and Canda, each to use the waters of the St. Mary's River, within its own territory; and further, that nothing in this treaty shall be construed to interfere with the drainage of wet, swamp, and overflowed lands into streams flowing into boundary waters, and also that this declaration shall be deemed to have equal force and effect as the treaty itself and to form an integral part thereto.

The exchange of ratifications then took place in the usual form.

In witness whereof, they have signed the present Protocol of Exchange and have affixed their seals thereto.

Done at Washington this 5th day of May, one thousand nine hundred and ten.

PHILANDER C KNOX   [SEAL]

JAMES BRYCE   [SEAL]

⚓ EXTRACT FROM EXCHANGE OF NOTES CONSTITUTING AN AGREEMENT BETWEEN THE UNITED STATES OF AMERICA AND CANADA RELATING TO A STUDY TO BE MADE BY THE INTERNATIONAL JOINT COMMISSION WITH RESPECT TO THE UPPER COLUMBIA RIVER BASIN

The American Ambassador to the Canadian Secretary of State for External Affairs

EMBASSY OF THE UNITED STATES OF AMERICA

Ottawa, Canada, February 25, 1944

*   *   *

2. It is desired that the Commission shall determine whether in its judgment further development of the water resources of the river basin would be practicable and in the public interest from the points of view

Ottawa, February 25 and March 3, 1944; came into force March 3, 1944, with the affirmative reply of the Canadian Government.

of the two Governments, having in mind (A) domestic water supply and sanitation, (B) navigation, (C) efficient development of water power, (D) the control of floods, (E) the needs of irrigation, (F) reclamation of wet lands, (G) conservation of fish and wildlife, and (H) other beneficial public purposes.

❊ ❊ ❊

⌘ TREATY BETWEEN THE UNITED STATES OF AMERICA AND CANADA RELATING TO THE USES OF THE WATERS OF THE NIAGARA RIVER

The United States of America and Canada, recognizing their primary obligation to preserve and enhance the scenic beauty of the Niagara Falls and River and, consistent with that obligation, their common interest in providing for the most beneficial use of the waters of that River,

❊ ❊ ❊

Article II

The United States of America and Canada agree to complete in accordance with the objectives envisaged in the final report submitted to the United States of America and Canada on December 11, 1929, by the Special International Niagara Board, the remedial works which are necessary to enhance the beauty of the Falls by distributing the waters so as to produce an unbroken crestline on the Falls. The United States of America and Canada shall request the International Joint Commission to make recommendations as to the nature and design of such remedial works and the allocation of the task of construction as between the United States of America and Canada. Upon approval by the United States of America and Canada of such recommendations the construction shall be undertaken pursuant thereto under the supervision of the International Joint Commission and shall be completed within four years after the date upon which the United States of America and Canada shall have approved the said recommendations. The total cost of the works shall be divided equally between the United States of America and Canada.

❊ ❊ ❊

Signed at Washington on February 27, 1950.

⚑ TREATY BETWEEN THE UNITED STATES OF AMERICA AND CANADA RELATING TO COOPERATIVE DEVELOPMENT OF THE WATER RESOURCES OF THE COLUMBIA RIVER BASIN AND ANNEXES

The Governments of the United States of America and Canada,

Recognizing that their peoples have, for many generations, lived together and cooperated with one another in many aspects of their national enterprises for the greater wealth and happiness of their respective nations, and

Recognizing that the Columbia River basin, as a part of the territory of both countries, contains water resources that are capable of contributing greatly to the economic growth and strength and to the general welfare of the two nations, and

Being desirous of achieving the development of those resources in a manner that will make the largest contribution to the economic progress of both countries and to the welfare of their peoples of which those resources are capable, and

Recognizing that the greatest benefit to each country can be secured by cooperative measures for hydroelectric power generation and flood control, which will make possible other benefits as well,

Have agreed as follows:

❈ ❈ ❈

ARTICLE XVI.

Settlement of differences

(1) Differences arising under the Treaty which the United States of America and Canada cannot resolve may be referred by either to the International Joint Commission for decision.

(2) If the International Joint Commission does not render a decision within three months of the referral or within such other period as may be agreed upon by the United States of America and Canada, either may then submit the difference to arbitration by written notice to the other.

(3) Arbitration shall be by a tribunal composed of a member appointed by Canada, a member appointed by the United States of America and a member appointed jointly by the United States of America and Canada who shall be Chairman. If within six weeks of the

Signed at Washington, January 17, 1961.

delivery of a notice under paragraph (2) either the United States of America or Canada has failed to appoint its member, or they are unable to agree upon the member who is to be Chairman, either the United States of America or Canada may request the President of the International Court of Justice to appoint the member or members. The decision of a majority of the members of an arbitration tribunal shall be the decision of the tribunal.

(4) The United States of America and Canada shall accept as definitive and binding and shall carry out any decision of the International Joint Commission or an arbitration tribunal.

(5) Provision for the administrative support of a tribunal and for remuneration and expenses of its members shall be as agreed in an exchange of notes between the United States of America and Canada.

(6) The United States of America and Canada may agree by an exchange of notes on alternative procedures for settling differences arising under the treaty including reference of any difference to the International Court of Justice for decision.

* * *

ARTICLE XVIII.

Liability for damage

(1) The United States of America and Canada shall be liable to the other and shall make appropriate compensation to the other in respect of any act, failure to act, omission or delay amounting to a breach of the Treaty or of any of its provisions other than an act, failure to act, omission or delay occurring by reason of war, strike, major calamity, act of God, uncontrollable force or maintenance curtailment.

(2) Except as provided in paragraph (1) neither the United States of America nor Canada shall be liable to the other or to any person in respect of any injury, damage or loss occurring in the territory of the other caused by any act, failure to act, omission or delay under the Treaty whether the injury, damage or loss results from negligence or otherwise.

(3) The United States of America and Canada, each to the extent possible within its territory, shall exercise due diligence to remove the cause of and to mitigate the effect of any injury, damage or loss occurring in the territory of the other as a result of any act, failure to act, omission or delay under the Treaty.

* * *

⚓ REPORT OF THE INTERNATIONAL JOINT COMMISSION ON THE POLLUTION OF RAINY RIVER AND LAKE OF THE WOODS (1965)

On May 30, 1959, the Prime Minister, for the Government of Canada, and the Secretary of State, for the Government of the United States, sent the following Reference to the International Joint Commission through identical letters addressed respectively to the Canadian and United States Sections of the Commission:

"I have the honour to advise you that the Governments of the United States and Canada have been informed that the waters of the Rainy River and the Lake of the Woods are being polluted by sewage and industrial wastes emptied into these waters. Having in mind the provisions of Article IV of the Boundary Waters Treaty signed January 11, 1909, that boundary waters and waters flowing across the boundary shall not be polluted on either side to the injury of health or property on the other side, the two Governments have agreed upon a joint Reference of the matter to the International Joint Commission, pursuant to the provisions of Article IX of said Treaty. The Commission is requested to inquire into and to report to the two Governments upon the following questions:

(1) Are the waters referred to in the preceding paragraph, or any of them, actually being polluted on either side of the boundary to the injury of health or property on the other side of the boundary?

(2) If the foregoing question is answered in the affirmative, to what extent, by what causes, and in what localities is such pollution taking place?

(3) If the Commission should find that pollution of the character just referred to is taking place, what measures for remedying the situation would, in its judgment, be most practicable from the economic, sanitary and other points of view?

(4) If the Commission should find that the construction or maintenance of remedial or preventive works is necessary to render the waters sanitary and suitable for domestic and other uses, it should indicate the nature, location, and extent of such works, and the probable cost thereof, and by whom and in what proportions such cost should be borne.

"For the purpose of assisting the Commission in making the investigation and recommendations provided for in this Reference, the two Governments will, upon request, make available to the Commission the services of engineers and other specially qualified personnel of their governmental agencies, and such information and technical data as may have been acquired by such agencies or as may be acquired by them during the course of the investigation.

"The Commission should submit its report and recommendations to the two Governments as soon as practicable."

❋   ❋   ❋

FINDINGS

After considering the results of the investigation, the evidence presented at the Public Hearing and subsequent briefs, the Commission arrived at the series of findings outlined below.

1. Multiple Uses of Rainy River

(a) *Domestic Water Supply:* Three communities obtain their domestic water supply from Rainy River. International Falls and South International Falls procure processed water from Minnesota and Ontario Paper Company's modern purification plant just above the International Bridge. The town of Rainy River obtains its domestic supply from the river. The only treatment given is chlorination. The estimated high cost of constructing and operating a suitable filtration plant forced Baudette to change its source of water supply from Rainy River to a "hard water" well.

(b) *Industrial Water Supply:* The pulp and paper mills at Fort Frances and International Falls use 83 million U.S. gallons (69 million Imperial gallons) per day, Minnesota and Ontario Paper Company has capacity to use up to 10,500 cfs for the generation of power at International Falls.

(c) *Domestic Sewage Disposal:* Sanitary sewage from four of the five sewered communities is discharged to Rainy River for final disposal. International Falls has secondary treatment facilities. Baudette provides primary treatment. The town of Rainy River has only sedimentation facilities. Fort Frances completed the construction of primary treatment works subsequent to the investigation. The fifth community, South International Falls, discharges its effluent into Rainy Lake.

(d) *Industrial Waste Disposal:* Industrial waste and sewage from the pulp and paper mills are discharged directly into Rainy River. Facilities to permit diversion of all domestic sewage from the paper mills to municipal systems are now under construction.

(e) *Recreation:* Most of the recreational developments are located in the section of Rainy River adjacent to Lake of the Woods. This resort area attracts those interested in fishing and boating. In 1959 vacationers spent an estimated $480,000 in this area.

2. Transboundary Movement

The currents of Rainy River cross and recross the international boundary. Observations on the movement of 72 floats released in the upper reaches of the river established the transboundary movement of these waters. Conductivity studies confirmed the results of the float tests. The constituents in these waters are thoroughly mixed at Manitou and Long Sault Rapids, about 30 miles downstream from International Falls.

3. Extent of Pollution

The quality of the waters under reference, after receiving domestic and industrial wastes, is discussed hereunder in relation to five indicators: coliform concentration, biochemical oxygen demand, dissolved oxygen, suspended solids and lignin. A detailed graphical presentation of the extent of pollution is found in Figures. . . .

(a) *Coliform Concentration:* The coliform group of bacteria is used as an indicator group because these bacteria are the normal inhabitants of the intestines. The coliform group when found in water indicates that the water may have been contaminated with human or animal excreta. Fecal material contains a large number of coliform bacteria which are usually associated with the pathogenic group, a class of bacteria harmful to man. It would be impracticable to examine each water sample for all known pathogens since each identification would require a separate analysis. Hence, if the coliform group is present, it is assumed that the pathogens which represent a public health hazard are also present.

Raw sewage contains 10 to 25 million coliform organisms per 100 ml (millilitres). The median coliform count was less than 35 per 100 ml in Rainy Lake above the known sources of pollution. The word median in the term "median coliform count" is used to designate that value which is so related to the other values in a given set of samples that exactly as many values exceed it as fall short of it. An average value is the arithmetic mean of a number of samples.

Three miles above the dam at International Falls at the outlet from Rainy Lake, the median coliform count in Rainy River varied from 8 to 44 per 100 ml. Immediately below Fort Frances near the Ontario shore the coliform count ranged up to 147,000 per 100 ml. The median count in 1960 was 47,000. About a mile below International Falls near the Minnesota shore the median coliform count was 66,000; near the Ontario shore, 3,900. The median coliform concentration remained high for the next twelve miles downstream. Twelve miles below International Falls it varied from 7,200 to 15,000 per 100 ml. This is at least four hundred times greater than the count above the dam. Ten miles below Long Sault Rapids the median coliform count ranged between 4,600 and 6,700 per 100 ml. The concentration of coliform bacteria gradually decreased as the water progressed downstream. Near Baudette, in 1961 the median coliform count was 2,000 per 100 ml. In Lake of the Woods the average coliform count was only 7 per 100 ml.

(b) *Biochemical Oxygen Demand:* Aerobic decomposition of organic matter requires oxygen. The amount of decomposible matter contained in the water can be estimated by determining the amount and rate of oxygen utilization. This determination is called the biochemical oxygen demand or BOD and is the amount of oxygen consumed over a 5-day period at a constant temperature of 20°C. A British Royal Commission on sewage disposal to river systems suggested with respect to BOD levels, the following river classification based on the standard 5-day BOD test: BOD-1 ppm "very clean", 2 ppm "clean", 5 ppm "doubtful", and 10 ppm "bad". One ppm (part per million) is equal to one mg/l (milligram per litre).

At the outlet from Rainy Lake the BOD varied from 0.9 to 2.6 mg/l. Near the Ontario Shore immediately below Fort Frances the BOD increased to 6.1 mg/l. About a mile below the mill at International Falls the average BOD near the Minnesota shore was 15.8 mg/l, in the middle of the river 3.5 mg/l, and near the Ontario shore 3.4 mg/l. Twelve miles below the pulp and paper plants the BOD varied from 4.0 to 7.4 mg/l— four times greater than the concentration above the dam. Ten miles below Long Sault Rapids biological stabilization reduced the BOD to 2.0 mg/l. In the Baudette-Rainy River area a slight increase in BOD was noted. In Lake of the Woods the average BOD was 1.7 mg/l.

(c) *Dissolved Oxygen:* A drop in the dissolved oxygen content indicates the presence of organic pollution. The point of maximum de-oxygenation may be some distance down river from the point of pollution, because the de-oxygenation of water by industrial wastes and sewage is a comparatively slow process. The oxygen deficiency is replaced by acquisition of oxygen from the atmosphere and by photosynthesis.

A substantial reduction in dissolved oxygen causes suffocation of fish. The second edition of Water Quality Criteria by the California State Water Quality Control Board cites the conclusions of M. M. Ellis that under average stream conditions, 3.0 mg/l of dissolved oxygen, or less, should be regarded as hazardous, and to maintain a varied fish fauna in good condition the dissolved oxygen concentration should remain at 5.0 mg/l or higher. The Aquatic Life Advisory Committee of the Ohio River Valley Water Sanitation Commission recommended that the minimum dissolved oxygen concentration for a well rounded warm water fish population should not be less than 5 mg/l during at least 16 hours of any 24 hour period and at no time should the dissolved oxygen content be less than 3 mg/l.

About a mile above the dam at International Falls the average DO (dissolved oxygen) concentration varied from 7.7 to 8.2 mg/l; the DO saturation varied from 85% to 90%. Twelve miles below the paper mills the average DO varied from 5.1 to 6.4 mg/l—a drop of 2.0 mg/l; the saturation varied from 58% to 73%—a drop of 25%. Ten miles below Long Sault Rapids the minimum DO value was 3.9 mg/l while the average value varied from 5.4 to 5.8. As the water progressed downstream the average DO dropped to 4.1 mg/l or 47% saturation near Baudette. In 1961 the minimum values in the reach of the river near Baudette varied from 0.9 to 1.1 mg/l or 10% saturation. Below Baudette the DO concentration began to recover due to algae in the slow moving water. In Lake of the Woods the average DO rose to 7.7 mg/l or 88% saturation.

(d) *Suspended Solids:* The concentration of suspended solids indicate the extent of pollution due to the discharge of solids into the river. All settleable solids are suspended solids until they have settled on the bottom of the water course. Dissolved or colloidal solids, such as sulphite waste liquors, may be synthesized by bacteria in the stream to form suspended and settleable sludge. Turbidity is attributable to suspended and colloidal matter. The analytical data on the concentration of suspended solids excludes floating masses and bottom deposits.

In general the standards for water quality for most States require substantially complete removal of suspended solids attributable to sewage, industrial or other wastes.

At the outlet of Rainy Lake the average suspended solids concentration for each of the four sampling points was relatively low, varying from 4.2 to 7.1 mg/l. Immediately below Fort Frances near the Ontario shore the concentration of suspended solids was as high as 87.0 mg/l with an average value of 31.9. About a mile below International Falls near the Minnesota shore the concentration was as high as 212.8 mg/l with an average value of 36.8. The concentration of suspended solids in the middle of the river was 14.2 mg/l and near the Ontario shore 12.3. Twelve miles below International Falls the average concentration varied from 11.0 to 20.8 mg/l—a threefold increase over the levels found at the outlet from Rainy Lake. Below Long Sault Rapids the average suspended solids varied from 9.9 to 15.1 mg/l. In this reach of the river about half of the suspended solids were of organic origin. Immediately below Baudette the average suspended solids varied from 7.9 to 15.7 mg/l. In Lake of the Woods the average was 10.0 mg/l.

(e) *Lignin:* Wood is made up of cellulose combined with lignin, a substance related to carbohydrates. Lignin degenerates very slowly. It is a common constituent of water flowing through wooded and swampy areas and is usually associated with a brown color in water. The pulping process liberates the lignin from the wood fibres. Thus the lignin concentrations identify the type of waste being discharged into the Rainy River.

At the outlet from Rainy Lake the average lignin concentration varied from 0.6 to 1.2 mg/l. Near the Ontario shore immediately below the Fort Frances plant the average lignin concentration was 2.2 in 1961. About a mile below the International Falls plant the average lignin concentration in 1961 was 9.5 mg/l near the Minnesota shore. The maximum concentration was 27.0. Twelve miles below the paper plants the average lignin concentration varied from 1.8 to 4.5 mg/l—a threefold increase over the values at the outlet from Rainy Lake. In the reach of Rainy River between Emo and Lake of the Woods lignin concentration was fairly uniform. Average values ranged from 1.4 to 3.1 mg/l. The average lignin concentration in Lake of the Woods was 1.5 mg/l.

Water of good quality entered Rainy River from Rainy Lake. Significant changes in water quality were found immediately below Fort Frances and International Falls. The strong wastes from the domestic and industrial sewer outlets were concentrated near each shore. Twelve miles downstream from International Falls the wastes had spread across the river. Essentially complete mixing of the wastes was attained by the time the water reached Long Sault Rapids about half way between the source of Rainy River in Rainy Lake and its outlet into Lake of the Woods. The effects of sedimentation and biological stabilization became more evident as the water progressed downstream. Serious pollution . . . existed throughout the Rainy River from Fort Frances to Lake of the Woods. The waters of Lake of the Woods showed a remarkable recovery when compared to the contaminated condition in the upper reaches of Rainy River. The water quality of Lake of the Woods is satisfactory.

4. Sources of Pollution

The water quality of the streams entering Rainy River below International Falls was determined. The median coliform count on the ten tributaries was relatively low, varying from 70 to 1,200; the average BOD ranged from 1.2 to 4.5 mg/l, a range from "clean" to nearly "doubtful"; the average dissolved oxygen varied from 4.4 to 6.9 mg/l; the average lignin concentration ranged from 1.4 to 3.9 mg/l; and the average suspended solids varied from 6.3 to 41.7 mg/l. Furthermore, since these ten tributaries contribute only fifteen percent of the total flow of the Rainy River, they cannot be regarded as a major source of pollution.

The estimated BOD load due to domestic wastes was 2,800 pounds per day. International Falls, with secondary treatment, contributed only 9 percent of the entire domestic waste load; Baudette, with primary treatment, contributed 18 percent; Rainy River, with only sedimentation, represented 5 percent; and Fort Frances, with no treatment at the time of the investigation, was responsible for 58 percent. The remaining 10 percent of the domestic BOD load was contributed by villages on the tributaries. The entire domestic BOD load discharged to Rainy River is about one percent of the combined domestic and industrial BOD load.

The major source of pollution was found to be the sewer outlets of the Minnesota and Ontario Paper Company's plants at Fort Frances and International Falls. All wastes from these plants, with the exception of 60 percent of the domestic sewage from the International Falls plant, were discharged to the Rainy River without treatment.

The sewer outlets at the International Falls plant discharged screened overflow from the pulp thickener, waste from the woodroom and bark recovery plant, overflow from the ash pond which receives the main boiler plant ashes, waste water from the sulphite screens and wet room, diluted spent sulphite liquor, bleach plant wastes, kraft mill wastes including lime sludge, wastes from the insulite mill, sewage wastes from the paper mill, backwash from the filtration plant and cooling water from the asphalt rodding mill. The Fort Frances plant discharged waste from the rotary bark screens, waste from the Tyler screens, waste from the sulphite deckers, lean white water overflow and sewage from the paper mill.

The mill surveys in 1960 and 1961 found the waste waters carried a high bacterial content. The BOD load contributed by the two plants was approximately 255,000 pounds per day. This is equivalent to the oxygen demand of the domestic wastes from a city of one and one half million people. Despite the effectiveness of the bark pond, before it washed out during the high water of 1962, the suspended solids load, including bark, fibre, chips and lime sludge, discharged to the Rainy River from the mill outlets exceeded 100 tons per day. Of this total the woody materials amounted to 61.5 tons per day. The lignin content of the waste was consistently high.

The Minnesota and Ontario Paper Company's brief of August 1964 confirmed the results of the Board's survey. The Company estimated that their overall daily discharge into the river included 57.2 tons of fibre and 60 tons of calcium carbonate (lime sludge).

5. Effects of Pollution

The discharge of untreated domestic wastes into Rainy River is a danger to health since the sewage contains organisms of diseases transmittable to humans. The coliform bacteria count in the first sixty miles below International Falls exceeded 6,000 per 100 ml. Thus, the river cannot be used safely as a source of drinking water unless there is auxiliary pre-treatment in addition to conventional purification. The waters of Rainy River, according to health authorities, are unsuitable for bathing.

The discharge of wastes from the pulp and paper mills has limited the development of river property between Fort Frances and Baudette. The unsightly and often odorous deposits along the shorelines and river bottom caused by suspended solids such as bark, fibre, chips and lime sludge has lessened the attractiveness of waterfront areas. The nutrients in the industrial wastes promoted the prolific growth of Sphaerotilus, a filamentous bacterium, in the upper reaches of the river. These slime masses attached to submerged or largely submerged obstructions and trapped fresh fibres have an objectionable appearance especially when the water level in the river recedes. The presence of suspended solids and slimes in the river has increased the cost of obtaining a satisfactory water supply at Baudette.

Biologically, Rainy River was most affected by wood fibres and associated wastes discharged from the pulp and paper mills. Benthos (the flora and fauna found at the bottom of streams, lakes and oceans) development was impeded. A number of the more desirable fish food organisms could not contend with the river environment during the summers with normal flows. In Four Mile Bay, at the outlet of Rainy River, the distribution of benthic animals was markedly affected by the pattern of sedimentation of wood waste materials. The condition of the river imposed limitations on the number of fish species in the upper eleven miles. Younger age groups of game fish were less numerous than normally anticipated. The fish population, according to witnesses at the Hearing, has been drastically reduced over the past twenty-five years.

The majority of organisms avoided fresh wood fibre deposits. Fresh wood fibres served as a nucleus for Sphaerotilus growth. The wood sugars (Xylose, Dextrose, and Fructose) from the pulping process not only have a high oxygen demand but also encourage the growth of Sphaerotilus which has a deleterious effect on fish propagation and fish food organisms.

Research studies established that survival conditions for Walleye eggs in Rainy River below International Falls were poor in 1961 and 1962.

Survival to fry (the first stage of a fish after the egg) was less than one percent in 1961 and varied from 0.02 to 6.0 percent in 1962. Survival in controls from the same lots at the Waskish State Hatchery were 69.6 percent in 1961 and 41.4 percent in 1962. The principal cause of low survival was Sphaerotilus, a bacterium slime, covering the eggs during incubation. This prevented successful emergence of the fry.

The sulphites in the mill wastes readily become oxidized by removing the dissolved oxygen from the receiving waters. The fish population was jeopardized by dissolved oxygen levels being below 4 mg/l for appreciable periods in the ten mile reach of the river above Baudette.

The waters of Rainy River are polluted to such a degree that they are unsatisfactory for recreation. Sludge banks and floating islands of bark, fibre and chips, floating scum from lime sludge wastes, and malodorous conditions caused by bottom deposits has adversely affected the aesthetic value of Rainy River. The deposits of woody materials are over three feet thick in some areas of its outlet in Four Mile Bay. The river is unsafe for recreational bathing due to its polluted condition. Fibre and slime entanglement on fish lines is so serious that sport fishing is limited to the fast waters of the Sioux and Manitou Rapids and the lower ten miles of the river. A witness testified at the hearing that outboard motors become so clogged with fibres that they have to be overhauled every two weeks. Fishermen who formerly used the resort facilities in the lower reach of the river have, in recent years, gone to other places because they did not like fishing under such conditions.

6. Effects of Weekend Flow Reduction

During periods of low inflow into Rainy Lake the weekend discharge from the dam at International Falls was reduced to less than half of the weekday average. This lowered the water level in the upper half of the river above Manitou Rapids, exposing unsightly banks and part of the river bed. As a result, bottom animals and fauna on the exposed areas were destroyed and malodorous conditions developed.

7. Remedial Measures Constructed or Planned

The Ontario Water Resources Commission in 1964 completed the construction of a pollution control plant with facilities for primary treatment of sewage from Fort Frances. It is operated by the Ontario Water Resources Commission under an agreement with the City of Fort Frances.

The pulp and paper companies are in the process of completing the connection of their sanitary sewers in the Fort Frances and International Falls mills with the respective municipal treatment plants. The companies have also announced that they plan to complete some of the necessary in-plant waste segregation and recovery projects by 1967. These projects include bark burning facilities in the new steam plant, improved bark and waste wood recovery facilities at the Fort Frances plant, better recovery of fibre at the insulite mill, and modification of the sulphite chemical-cooking plant to utilize half of the calcium cabonate now being wasted. These in-plant improvements will be an initial step towards reducing the pollutants in the mill wastes and as such will be helpful in improving the quality of the waters of Rainy River.

CONCLUSIONS

The conclusions of the Commission with regard to each of the questions contained in the Reference are as follows:

Question 1

Are the waters of the Rainy River and the Lake of the Woods, or any of them, actually being polluted on either side of the boundary to the injury of health or property on the other side of the boundary?

The Commission finds that the waters of Rainy River are being polluted on each side of the international boundary to an extent that is injurious to property and a hazard to health on the other side of the boundary. The water quality of Lake of the Woods appears to be satisfactory.

Question 2

If the foregoing question is answered in the affirmative, to what extent, by what causes, and in what localities is such pollution taking place?

The Commission finds that the Rainy River downstream from the Fort Frances-International Falls area is polluted to such an extent that it is a potential menace to health, unfit for bathing, discourages the development of water front property, is unsuitable for the growth of many forms of aquatic life and unattractive for recreation. The major cause of pollution is the discharge of untreated wastes from the two pulp and paper plants owned by Minnesota and Ontario Paper Company and its subsidiary company. The other sources of pollution at the time of the investigation were the discharge of domestic wastes from Fort Frances and to a lesser degree the effluents from the sewage treatment plants at Baudette, International Falls and Rainy River.

Question 3

If the Commission should find that pollution of the character just referred to is taking place, what measures for remedying the situation would, in its judgement, be most practicable from the economic, sanitary and other points of view?

In the judgment of the Commission the following measures are the most practicable for remedying the situation:

(a) adoption by Governments of the "Water Quality Objectives for the Rainy River" recommended hereunder;

(b) acceptance of these Objectives as the minimal criteria by the enforcement agencies in both countries;

(c) adoption and implementation by the paper companies and the municipalities of definite programmes for carrying out the remedial measures necessary to meet the Objectives; and,

(d) continuing surveillance by the Commission to ensure maximum practicable progress towards meeting the Objectives.

Question 4

If the Commission should find that the construction or maintenance of remedial or preventive works is necessary to render the waters sanitary and suitable for domestic and other uses, it should indicate the nature, location, and extent of such works, and the probable cost thereof, and by whom and in what proportions such cost should be borne.

The Commission considers that the remedial measures at the two pulp and paper plants should include an extension of the scheduled in-plant segregation and recovery projects to cover all processes, external treatment of all high-solids wastes, recovery or treatment of spent sulphite liquor, and continuous waste monitoring. Due to the complex nature of the two plants the companies were unable to supply a firm estimate of the costs of the necessary remedial works. A table indicating the costs for similar treatment works at other pulp and paper mills is attached as an appendix to the Advisory Board's report. The Commission considers that the cost of these pollution abatement measures should be borne by Minnesota and Ontario Paper Company. The cost is high for correction, but it is higher for the continuance of the defilement of these waters.

The Commission considers that the primary treatment plants at Fort Frances, Baudette and Rainy River should be extended to provide secondary treatment at the earliest practical date. A long term programme of separation of domestic sewage from storm water should be adopted. The estimated cost for secondary treatment of domestic wastes is $200,000 for the United States municipality and $508,000 for the Canadian municipalities. Such costs should be borne by the municipalities responsible. Federal, State or Provincial assistance is available under certain circumstances.

WATER QUALITY OBJECTIVES

Limitations on Waste Disposal

The Commission recognizes that the maximum beneficial use of available water resources should be permitted and unreasonable use of water should be prevented. The disposal of wastes into a river should be controlled so as to achieve the highest quality consistent with the maximum benefit to all users.

The Commission considers that discharging suitably treated domestic and industrial wastes into the river is a reasonable use of these waters provided that such use does not create a hazard to public health or cause undue interference with the rights of others to use these waters for legitimate purposes. In boundary waters as defined in the Boundary Waters Treaty of 1909, the wastes discharged into the river must be such as not to cause injury to health or property in the other country. Undue interference with the development of desirable types of aquatic life constitutes an injury to property even though it may be the property of the public at large.

The Commission recognizes that water quality requirements should not only safeguard public health and protect the beneficial uses of these waters but also permit legitimate use of these waters for the disposal of adequately prepared wastes. Water quality objectives should not exclude all impurities from the water course; nor should they tolerate the maximum quantity of domestic and industrial wastes that the stream can assimilate. Objectives designed to alleviate pollution in a specific stream or body of water are not necessarily applicable to other water courses where the conditions may be quite different.

The Objectives recommended hereunder are designed to permit the use of Rainy River for waste disposal only to such extent as would be compatible with the rights of others to enjoy the use of these waters for legitimate purposes. The pollution problem on the Rainy River was investigated on the basis of existing local conditions and current knowledge. If in the future there should be a substantial change in the uses to be made of the waters of Rainy River or in the quantity and nature of the wastes discharged into these waters, the Objectives recommended hereunder should be reviewed and amended as necessary to take into account the new factors so as to ensure that there will be no injury to health or property.

The Commission recognizes that the primary responsibility in the field of water pollution rests with the Provinces and the States. However, each Federal Government has an obligation to the other under Article IV of the Boundary Waters Treaty of 1909 which provides that "boundary waters and waters flowing across the boundary shall not be polluted on either side to the injury of health and property on the other." Thus the achievement of the water quality Objectives recommended hereunder will require the cooperation of the two levels of government in both countries.

Water Quality Objectives for the Rainy River

A. GENERAL OBJECTIVE

In general all wastes, including sanitary sewage, garbage, refuse, storm water and industrial effluents, should be in such a condition when discharged into the river that they do not create conditions which will adversely affect the use of these waters as a source of domestic or industrial water supply, or for navigation, fish and wildlife, bathing, recreation, agriculture and other riparian activities.

B. SANITARY SEWAGE, STORM WATER AND WASTES FROM WATERCRAFT

The coliform MPN (most probable number) median value should not exceed 2,400 per 100 ml at any point in the stream following initial dilution except in public recreational bathing areas where the median coliform values should not exceed 1,000 per 100 ml. The bacterial determinations used for this Objective include the presumptive and confirmed tests, or the MF (membrane filter) procedure for the coliform group of bacteria as given in "Standard Methods for the Examination of Water and Sewage," American Health Association, New York.

Solids and chemical constituents should be removed from all sanitary sewage, storm water and wastes from watercraft to such an extent that the effluents do not interfere with the above mentioned uses.

C. SUSPENDED SOLIDS

The discharge of suspended solids, including but not limited to floating materials such as bark, butts, sawdust, fibres and lime sludge, should be reduced to a point that they are not conducive to slime growths, formation of sludge islands and banks, and do not injure fish or wildlife or their habitats.

This objective will be met if facilities are provided to remove substantially all suspended solids from the pulp and paper mill's effluent.

D. DEOXYGENATING WASTES

The dissolved oxygen should not fall below 5 mg/l at the average monthly flow which is exceeded 95 percent of the time in the critical month, nor below 3 mg/l at the minimum daily flow that is exceeded 95 percent of the time in the critical month.

This Objective will be met if the treatment provided substantially removes the solids, bacteria, chemical constituents and other substances capable of reducing the dissolved oxygen in these waters to an unreasonable extent.

E. NUTRIENTS FOR SLIME BACTERIA

The discharge of nutrients, including but not limited to wood sugars, should be controlled to the extent that they do not promote the nuisance growths of Sphaerotilus and other slime bacteria in the river.

This Objective will be met if there is a marked reduction or complete removal of nutrients in the effluents.

F. PERIODIC REVIEW

Specific Objectives for water quality, including but not restricted to phenols, pH, odour, color, turbidity, oils and highly toxic wastes, will be added when the Commission after a review of new and existing uses and wastes, determines that such amendments are necessary to meet the General Objectives as set forth in A above.

RECOMMENDATIONS

1. The Commission recommends that the "Water Quality Objectives for the Rainy River" as set forth above be adopted by the two Governments as the criteria to be met in maintaining the waters of the Rainy River in satisfactory condition, as contemplated in Article IV of the Boundary Waters Treaty of 1909. Furthermore, the Commission recommends that the State of Minnesota and the Province of Ontario adopt these Objectives as the minimal criteria in formulating their respective State and Provincial water quality standards for the Rainy River.

2. The Commission recommends that the appropriate authorities require the industries and municipalities concerned to initiate, at the earliest possible date and pursuant to a definite time schedule, construc-

tion of the pollution abatement facilities necessary to achieve and maintain the said Objectives.

3. The Commission recommends that it be specifically authorized by the two Governments to establish and maintain continuing supervision over the waters of Rainy River in relation to pollution through a board to be appointed by the Commission. In carrying out this supervisory function, the Commission would notify those responsible for any pollution found objectionable in relation to the said Objectives and, in the event that assurance were not received that such pollution would be corrected within a reasonable time, would recommend to the appropriate authority or authorities having jurisdiction in respect thereof the action deemed necessary or advisable. The Commission would also, as the occasion required, review the quality of the waters of the Rainy River and recommend such amendments to the specific Objectives, B to F above, as may be necessary in order to conform with the General Objective, A above.

Signed this 24th day of February, 1965.

A. D. P. Heeney
Eugene W. Weber
D. M. Stephens
René Dupuis
Charles R. Ross

Report of International Joint Commission on Pollution of Lake Erie, Lake Ontario, and the International Section of the St. Lawrence River (1970)

CHAPTER I

Introduction

This is the report of the International Joint Commission on an intensive and extensive inquiry into the pollution of Lake Erie, Lake Ontario, and the International Section of the St. Lawrence River. It incorporates relevant excerpts from the three interim reports on this undertaking sent by the Commission to the Governments of Canada and the United States.

Lake Erie and Lake Ontario occupy the terminal position of the Great Lakes, the largest fresh water system in the world. They not only receive wastes passed on by the Upper Lakes but are also receptacles for wastes from the municipalities and industries they support. Also, being the smallest of the Great Lakes, they are more sensitive and responsive to the pollution pressures brought about by the activities of man.

Under Article IV of the Boundary Waters Treaty of 1909, Canada and the United States assumed a mutual obligation that "boundary waters and waters flowing across the boundary shall not be polluted on either side to the injury of health or property on the other." Lake Erie, Lake Ontario, and the International Section of the St. Lawrence River are boundary waters as defined by the Treaty. The current pollution problems in the Lower Great Lakes are now generally recognized as serious from the standpoint of international obligations and the viewpoint of the people, municipal officials, and industrial administrators on each side of the boundary.

In 1912 the lamentable prevalence of typhoid fever prompted the Governments of Canada and the United States to request the International Joint Commission to determine to what extent, by what causes and in what localities were the boundary waters between the two countries, including the Great Lakes, polluted so as to be injurious to public health and unfit for domestic and other uses. The Commission's subsequent investigation was essentially a bacteriological study. Regarding the major tributaries to Lake Erie and Lake Ontario, the Commission in its 1918 Report concluded that pollution was "very intense along the shores of the Detroit and Niagara Rivers" and that "conditions exist which imperil the health and welfare of the citizens of both countries in direct contravention of the Treaty."

The Commission in its 1918 Report stated that "it was feasible and practicable, without imposing an unreasonable burden upon the offending communities, to prevent or remedy pollution in boundary waters" and that "it is advisable to confer upon the International Joint Commission ample jurisdiction to regulate and prohibit this pollution." At the request of the two Governments, the Commission in 1920 drafted a "convention" which would accomplish this purpose. The Commission, in forwarding the draft convention, stated, "The Commission is firmly of the view that the best method to avoid the evils which the Treaty is designed to correct is to take proper steps to prevent dangerous pollution crossing the boundary line rather than to wait until it is manifest that such pollution has actually physically crossed, to the injury of health or property on the other side."

With the advent of chlorination of municipal water supplies and in the general belief that there was an inexhaustible supply of clean, fresh water to dilute all wastes, the expenditures of large sums of money on waste treatment facilities did not appear to be urgent. In any event, the proposed convention was not negotiated to a conclusion and the two

Governments did not give the Commission further direction or authority with respect to pollution of these waters.

Eventually, in 1946 the two Governments requested the Commission to examine the pollution problems of the Connecting Channels of the Great Lakes (the St. Marys, St. Clair, Detroit, and Niagara Rivers) resulting from the new types and greater volumes of wastes discharges by developing industrial complexes and accompanying growth and concentrations of population. This comprehensive study determined through physical, bacterial and chemical analysis the amount of domestic and industrial wastes in these four receiving streams. The Commission's 1950 Report set forth specific Water Quality Objectives designed to restore and maintain the waters of the Connecting Channels in a condition which would not impair the many uses desired of them. These Objectives, the first of their kind on an international basis, anticipated national action by both countries. The recommendations were approved by the two Governments to satisfy the requirements of the Treaty and subsequently were reflected in whole or in part in the pollution abatement programmes of enforcement agencies in both countries.

Progress in achieving the Objectives for the Connecting Channels in so far as individual communities and industries are concerned has been fairly good. For example, eight years after the Governments had approved the Objectives the total daily discharge of wastes from all industries had been reduced from 13,000 to 2,500 pounds of phenols, from 9,000 to 4,000 pounds of cyanides, from 18,000 to 2,500 gallons of oil, from 3.1 to 1.6 million pounds of suspended solids. However, the Commission's Water Quality Objectives are not being met currently in all reaches of the Connecting Channels because the responsible authorities and industries have not provided sufficient treatment facilities to keep pace with the population growth and with industrial expansion.

Pollution problems have changed materially over the last fifty years. The increased quantity and the different composition of municipal and industrial wastes in the last two decades as well as the residual characteristics of materials discharged into the Lakes have led to dramatic changes in the biological condition of the Lower Great Lakes System.

Finally, under provisions of the Boundary Waters Treaty the Governments of Canada and the United States in October 1964 requested the International Joint Commission to enquire into and report upon the following questions:

(1) Are the waters of Lake Erie, Lake Ontario, and the International Section of the St. Lawrence River being polluted on either side of the boundary to an extent which is causing or is likely to cause injury to health or property on the other side of the boundary?

(2) If the foregoing question is answered in the affirmative, to what extent, by what causes, and in what localities is such pollution taking place?

(3) If the Commission should find that pollution of the character just referred to is taking place, what remedial measures would, in its judgement, be most practicable from the economic, sanitary, and other points of view, and what would be the probable cost thereof?

*　*　*

Following a serious oil pollution incident off the California coast, the two Governments on March 21, 1969, requested the Commission as a matter of urgency and within the framework of the on-going pollution investigation, to make a special report on the adequacy of existing safety requirements applicable to underwater drilling and production operations in Lake Erie to prevent oil escaping into the Lake; the adequacy of known methods of confining and cleaning up any major oil spill that might occur in Lake Erie from any source; and the adequacy of existing contingency plans, and their implementation for dealing with such oil spills.

*　*　*

CHAPTER XIV

Conclusions

The Governments of Canada and the United States requested the International Joint Commission to inquire into and report on three questions.

1. In response to the question, *"Are the waters of Lake Erie, Lake Ontario, and the international section of the St. Lawrence River being polluted on either side of the boundary to an extent which is causing or is likely to cause injury to health or property on the other side of the boundary?"*

The Commission finds that the waters referred to in the question are being seriously polluted on both sides of the boundary to the detriment of both countries and to an extent which is causing injury to health and property on the other side of the boundary. On the basis of the transboundary movement described in Chapter VIII of this Report the Commission concludes that contaminants originating in one country do move across the boundary and degrade the quality of the waters in the other country.

2. In response to the question, *"If the foregoing question is answered*

in the affirmative, to what extent, by what causes, and in what localities is such pollution taking place?"

The Commission finds the polluted waters are lakewide in extent; that the two principal causes are wastes discharged by municipalities and industries into the above waters and their tributaries; and that pollution is taking place in all jurisdictions which share these boundary waters. The sources of pollution and their relative contributions are outlined in Chapter IX of this Report.

3. In response to the question, *"If the Commission should find that pollution of the character just referred to is taking place, what remedial measures would, in its judgment, be most practicable from the economic, sanitary, and other points of view and what would be the probable cost thereof?"*

The Commission finds that the remedial measures include the adoption of and adherence to this Commission's General and Specific Objectives as a matter of urgency; immediate reduction of the phosphorus content in detergents; the prompt implementation of a vigorous programme to provide the necessary municipal and industrial waste treatment facilities and to reduce the phosphorus inputs into the above waters and their tributaries; and making provision for continuous surveillance and monitoring. The estimated cost in terms of 1968 dollars for the required municipal and industrial treatment facilities located in Canada would be $211 million and for those facilities located in the United States would be $1,373 million. These and other remedial measures are described in Chapter XII of this Report.

The Governments of Canada and the United States also requested the International Joint Commission to report on the following matters pertaining to potential oil pollution in Lake Erie.

4. In response to, *"The adequacy of existing safety requirements and procedures in Canada and in the United States applicable to drilling and production operations in Lake Erie to prevent oil from escaping into the Lake so as to produce serious transboundary oil pollution conditions."*

The Commission concludes that the safety requirements and procedures applicable to drilling and production operations in Lake Erie of Pennsylvania, New York, and particularly those of Ontario, if effectively supervised and properly enforced, are adequate to prevent oil escaping into the Lake so as to produce serious transboundary oil pollution conditions. Drilling is prohibited in the Michigan portion of Lake Erie. The exact status of Ohio regulations is not clear. In the Ontario portion of Lake Erie, the only area where there are at present drilling and gas production operations, the enforcement of the regulations and the required operational procedures have been adequate to date.

5. In response to, *"The adequacy of existing mechanical, chemical and other methods of confining, removing, dispersing and cleaning up any major oil spill that may occur in Lake Erie from any source, bearing in mind the damage that such methods may cause to marine life, domestic water supplies or to other beneficial uses of the Lake in both countries."*

The Commission concludes that the current methods of confining, removing, dispersing, and cleaning up a major oil spill that may occur from any source are primitive and inadequate. Current methods can deal effectively with large spills only under the most ideal weather conditions. There is no one method that is a panacea. Each oil pollution mishap presents a unique situation in terms of water temperature, winds, currents, type of oil, and the ecology of the area. Very little is known on the residual effects on aquatic organisms of materials used to sink or disperse oil spills.

6. In response to, *"The adequacy of existing contingency plans and the action taken to implement them to confine and clean up transboundary pollution and to prevent or mitigate the destructive transboundary effects of any major oil spill from any source that may occur in Lake Erie."*

The Commission concludes that the United States contingency plan for the Lake Erie region is generally adequate although the roles of state and local agencies as well as private organizations require clarification. On the other hand, Canada does not yet have a detailed or coordinated contingency plan to marshal the capabilities of federal, provincial, and local agencies or private organizations. Such local plans as exist are relatively uncoordinated. Furthermore, the Commission notes that there is no formal plan for international cooperation on oil spills.

In addition to the above responses the International Joint Commission further concludes that:

7. There is a need for international contingency plans to cope with major spills of hazardous or radioactive materials.

8. The introduction and accumulation of untreated and partially treated wastes from municipalities, industries, and agricultural activities have been the causes of the pollution problems described in Chapter VI of this Report.

9. Lake Erie, particularly its Western Basin, is in an advanced state of eutrophication, and accelerated eutrophication is occurring in Lake Ontario. The accelerated eutrophication of these waters is due to the presence of nutrients which have been and are being added to these waters. The resultant biological productivity is proportional to the annual rate of input of these nutrients. Of the nutrients involved, phos-

phorus is the only one that is both growth-limiting in the lakes and controllable effectively by man with present technology.

10. The major source of phosphorus is municipal sewage. In the United States 70 percent of the phosphorus in sewage originates from detergents, most of the remainder from human excreta. In Canada approximately 50 percent originates from each sewage source. Apart from municipal sewage the other significant sources of phosphorus are agricultural runoff and some industrial wastes.

11. The input of phosphorus can be reduced by widespread improvement in the treatment in existing plants of municipal and industrial wastes containing phosphorus. An over-all programme to achieve this is essential if eutrophication is to be halted.

12. Because of the practical difficulties in implementing the municipal programme contemplated in the preceding conclusion within the reasonable future, it is essential that both countries reduce the phosphorus content of detergents to the maximum practicable extent at the earliest possible time.

13. The inputs to the waters of the basin of phosphorus, nitrogen, and other nutrients from agricultural operations are difficult to control but methods must be found to diminish them.

14. The contribution of very large quantities of polluting materials from heavily industrialized areas such as those along the St. Clair River, the Detroit River, the Maumee River, the Cuyahoga River, and the Buffalo-Niagara Falls, Rochester, and Hamilton-Toronto regions has: caused eutrophication of the Lower Great Lakes; depleted the dissolved oxygen in the hypolimnion of the Lakes, particularly the Central Basin of Lake Erie; induced adverse biological changes; been partially responsible for the dramatic changes in fish population; caused bacterial contamination along the shorelines; increased the accumulated dissolved solids and wastes in the Lakes; increased water treatment problems; impaired the recreational and aesthetic values of the Lakes and international section of the St. Lawrence River and destroyed wildlife. These and other effects are described in Chapter X of this Report.

15. Although commercial vessels and pleasure craft are not major sources of pollution when compared with urban centres, they are mobile sources that can discharge pathogenic organisms and petroleum wastes at or near sensitive areas such as water intakes, bathing beaches, and marinas.

16. Garbage, litter, bilge and ballast water discharged into the Lower Great Lakes System are not only aesthetically unattractive but also restrict recreational activities and interfere with the legitimate uses of these waters.

17. Unless the remedial measures outlined in Chapter XII of this Report, particularly waste treatment facilities and phosphorus control programmes, are undertaken as a matter of urgency the waters of Lake Erie, Lake Ontario, and the International Section of the St. Lawrence River will be further degraded.

18. The International Joint Commission should be assigned the tasks of coordinating continuous surveillance of water quality, of monitoring the implementation of pollution abatement programmes, of coordinating the exchange of information on all aspects of water pollution, and of reporting and publishing the results on the effectiveness of such governmental programmes.

19. The Upper Lakes and the Connecting Channels of the Great Lakes, particularly the Detroit and Niagara Rivers, have a profound effect on the water quality of the Lower Great Lakes. Thus, it is incumbent on both countries, as a matter of urgency, to take appropriate action to preserve and where necessary enhance the quality of all the boundary waters of the Great Lakes System and its tributaries.

CHAPTER XV

Proposed Water Quality Objectives
For Lake Erie, Lake Ontario,
the International Section of the
St. Lawrence River and the Connecting Channels
of the Great Lakes

GENERAL OBJECTIVES

The receiving waters of Lake Erie, Lake Ontario, the International Section of the St. Lawrence River, and the Connecting Channels of the Great Lakes at all places and at all times should be:

(a) free from substances attributable to municipal, industrial, or other discharges that will settle to form putrescent or otherwise objectionable sludge deposits, or that will adversely affect aquatic life or waterfowl.

(b) free from floating debris, oil, scum, and other floating materials attributable to municipal, industrial, or other discharges in amounts sufficient to be unsightly or deleterious.

(c) free from materials attributable to municipal, industrial, or other discharges producing colour, odour, or other conditions in such a degree as to create a nuisance.

(d) free from substances attributable to municipal, industrial, or other discharges in concentrations that are toxic or harmful to human, animal, or aquatic life.

(e) free from nutrients derived from municipal, industrial, and agricultural sources in concentrations that create nuisance growths of aquatic weeds and algae.

Furthermore, no substance should be introduced into these waters unless reasonable efforts have been made to ensure that it will not lead to the violation of any of the foregoing Objectives.

SPECIFIC OBJECTIVES

The Specific Objectives are for the receiving waters except in the restricted mixing zones at outfalls. (The periphery of the restricted mixing zones should be prescribed by water pollution control agencies.)

(a) *Microbiology (Coliform Group)*—The geometric mean of not less than five samples taken over not more than a 30-day period shall not exceed 1,000/100 ml total coliforms, nor 200/100 ml fecal coliforms in local waters. Waters used for body contact recreation activities should be free from bacteria, fungi, or viruses that may produce enteric disorders, or eye, ear, nose, throat, and skin infections.

(b) *Dissolved Oxygen*—In the Connecting Channels and in the upper waters of the Lakes not less than 6.0 mg/l at any time; in the hypolimnetic waters not less than the concentrations necessary for the support of fishlife, particularly cold water species.

(c) *Total Dissolved Solids*—Less than 200 mg/l in Lake Erie, Lake Ontario, and the International Section of the St. Lawrence River; in the St. Marys River, pending the results of a study of the Upper Great Lakes, a level of total dissolved solids not exceeding that of 1970; and in the other Connecting Channels a level consistent with maintaining the levels of total dissolved solids in Lake Erie and Lake Ontario less than 200 mg/l.

(d) *Temperature*—No change which would adversely affect any local or general use of these waters.

(e) *Taste and Odour*—No objectionable taste or odour. Phenols desirably absent but not to exceed a monthly average of 1.0 micrograms/l. Other taste and odour producing substances absent.

(f) *pH*—No change from the range of levels, 6.7 to 8.5, which now exist.

(g) *Iron*—Less than 0.3 mg/l.

(h) *Phosphorus**—Concentrations limited to the extent necessary to

---

* The term phosphorus in this Report refers to phosphorus as a constituent of various organic and inorganic complexes and compounds, not to elemental phosphorus as a chemical substance. The term phosphorus includes orthophosphates such as trisodiumphosphate, crystaline phosphates such as sodiumtripolyphosphate, and polyphosphates such as sodiumhexametaphosphate. However, in this Report concentrations and loads are given in terms of the element phosphorus as part of any compound to assure uniformity of expression.

prevent nuisance growths of algae, weeds and slimes which are or may become injurious to any beneficial water use. (Meeting this objective will require that the phosphorus loading to Lake Erie be limited to 0.39 g/m²/yr and the phosphorus loading to Lake Ontario be limited to 0.17 g/m²/yr.)

(i) *Radioactivity*—Elimination of radioactive materials to the extent necessary to prevent harmful effects on health. Pending the adoption of more stringent limits, in no event is gross beta activity to exceed 1,000 pCi/l, Radium-226 not to exceed 3 pCi/l and Strontium 90 not to exceed 10 pCi/l.

Additional Specific Objectives—When required, appropriate Specific Objectives will be established for water quality parameters including but not restricted to toxic materials, oils, and heavy metals.

CHAPTER XVI

Recommendations

In response to the Reference dated October 7, 1964, and to the letter dated March 21, 1969, from the Governments of Canada and the United States, and as the minimum basis for programmes to achieve and maintain waters in satisfactory condition as contemplated by Article IV of the Boundary Waters Treaty of 1909, the International Joint Commission recommends that:

1. The Water Quality Objectives for Lake Erie, Lake Ontario, the International Section of the St. Lawrence River, and the Connecting Channels of the Great Lakes as set forth in Chapter XV of this Report be adopted by the Governments of Canada and the United States and be recognized as the minimal basis for the establishment of standards for these waters by the States of Michigan, Ohio, and New York, the Commonwealth of Pennsylvania, and the Province of Ontario in the administration of their pollution control programmes.

2. The Governments of Canada and the United States enter into agreement on programmes and measures to achieve the said Objectives and the schedules for their implementation.

3. The Governments of Canada and the United States enter into agreement on an integrated programme of phosphorus control to include:

(a) the immediate reduction to a minimum practicable level of the phosphorus content of detergents and the total quantities of phosphorus-based detergents discharged into the Great Lakes System with the aim of complete replacement of all phosphorus in detergents with environmentally less harmful materials by December 31, 1972;

(b) further reduction, as a matter of urgency, of the remaining phosphorus in municipal and industrial waste effluents discharging to Lake Erie, Lake Ontario, and their tributaries and to the International Section of the St. Lawrence River, with a view to achieving at least an 80 percent reduction by 1975 and thereafter additional reduction to the maximum extent possible by economically feasible processes;

(c) the reduction of phosphorus discharged to these waters from agricultural activities.

4. The Governments of Canada and the United States agree to develop, as a matter of urgency, compatible and coordinated programmes in concert with provincial and state agencies to control effectively by 1972 the introduction of persistent organic contaminants such as herbicides and pesticides into these waters and that substitutes be found for such persistent substances.

5. The Governments of Canada and the United States agree to develop compatible and coordinated programmes, in concert with provincial and state agencies, to control effectively the introduction of toxic materials from municipal and industrial wastes into these waters.

6. The Governments of Canada and the United States agree to require a thorough investigation of the possible adverse health and ecological effects of substitutes proposed for use in lieu of organic contaminants, toxic materials, and any other substances now considered hazardous in these respects such as mercury and phosphorous.

7. Collection and treatment facilities for municipal and industrial wastes be, as a matter of urgency, built, enlarged, or improved to prevent pollution of these waters and be operated at all times at maximum capability; measures for handling storm water and combined sewage be so designed and operated as to avoid bypassing of untreated waste waters into these waters and their tributaries; all with a view of ensuring that all wastes receive adequate treatment at all times.

8. Federal, provincial, and state governments review and if necessary amend existing laws and regulations to control the disposal of solid waste materials in or on the shores of these waters so as to ensure maintenance of the Water Quality Objectives set forth herein and to prevent contaminants from entering these waters through seepage or runoff.

9. Dredged materials containing objectionable quantities of pollutants be disposed of in a manner to ensure maintenance of the Water Quality Objectives set forth herein.

10. The Government of Canada, as a matter of urgency, develop a detailed and fully coordinated contingency plan so that it can quickly and effectively respond to major accidental spills of oils, hazardous or

radioactive materials in the Canadian waters of the Great Lakes System; and the Government of the United States progressively improve its corresponding contingency plans so as to include all available response capabilities.

11. The Governments of Canada and the United States enter into agreement to develop coordinated international contingency plans so that both countries may quickly and effectively respond to major accidental spills of oils, hazardous or radioactive materials in the boundary waters of the Great Lakes System.

12. The two Governments in concert with provincial and state agencies and with industry accelerate and expand, as a matter of urgency, their applied research programmes on the containment and clean up of oil spills so that those responsible for the execution of contingency plans may have available the best possible technical advice, equipment, and support.

13. Until such time as each of the Governments is satisfied that the containment and clean-up methods and the contingency plans for oil spills applicable to the waters of Lake Erie within its jurisdiction are adequate:

(a) oil production and production of "wet gas" containing appreciable amounts of liquid hydrocarbons from wells in Lake Erie be prohibited,

(b) all wells in Lake Erie capable of oil production be adequately plugged,

(c) in the western basin of Lake Erie (west of a straight line drawn from the tip of Pele Point in Ontario to Marblehead in Ohio) all drilling be prohibited,

(d) in the remainder of Lake Erie drilling not be permitted unless the regulating agency having jurisdiction has determined in the light of known geologic conditions that there would be no reasonable likelihood of discovering oil or "wet gas" containing appreciable amounts of liquid hydrocarbons.

14. The two Governments take steps to exclude from the Great Lakes ships and masters likely to present an unreasonable risk of pollution by oils, hazardous or radioactive materials; and also make provision to alert appropriate officials in both countries when hazardous materials are in transit in these waters.

15. The federal, provincial, and state governments review and where necessary strengthen their existing laws and programmes relating to the reporting and control of spills and the disposal of oils, hazardous or radioactive materials, so as to prevent further pollution of these waters by oils, hazardous or radioactive materials.

16. The federal, provincial, and state governments in concert consider

and implement at the earliest possible date compatible regulations for the control of water pollution from all classes of commercial vessels and pleasure craft using the Great Lakes System.

17. Appropriate governmental agencies be involved in site selection and consulted in the design of all thermal power plants, both public and private, so as to minimize adverse effects on the receiving waters of temperature changes and input of radioactive materials into these waters.

18. The federal, provincial, and state governments give high priority to research including, but not restricted to, those problems enumerated in Chapter XII of this Report, with highest priority given to those problems related to human health, such as viral diseases.

19. The federal, provincial, and state governments support fully this Commission's water quality surveillance and monitoring programmes for these waters including the inputs from their tributaries.

20. The Governments of Canada and the United States extend, at the earliest practicable date, the Reference dated October 7, 1964 to include the remaining boundary waters of the Great Lakes System and the waters tributary thereto.

21. Until the Commission is in a position to recommend Water Quality Objectives for Lake Huron and Lake Superior, the States of Michigan, Wisconsin, and Minnesota and the Province of Ontario recognize the Water Quality Objectives as set forth herein as the minimal basis for the establishment of standards in the administration of their pollution control programmes for Lake Huron and Lake Superior.

22. The Governments of Canada and the United States specifically confer upon this Commission the authority, responsibility, and means for coordination, surveillance, monitoring, implementation, reporting, making recommendations to governments all as outlined in Chapter XIII of this Report, and such other duties related to preservation and improvement of the quality of the boundary waters of the Great Lakes–St. Lawrence System as may be agreed by the said Governments; the Commission to be authorized to establish, in consultation with the Governments, an international board or boards to assist it in carrying out these duties and to delegate to said board or boards such authority and responsibility as the Commission may deem appropriate.

✄ MEMORANDUM OF AGREEMENT

Made This 13th Day of August, 1971

BETWEEN

THE GOVERNMENT OF CANADA (hereinafter referred to as "Canada") represented by the Honourable Jack Davis, Minister of the

Environment of Canada, and the Honourable Robert Andras, Minister of State for Urban Affairs,

OF THE FIRST PART;

AND

THE GOVERNMENT OF THE PROVINCE OF ONTARIO (hereinafter referred to as "Ontario") represented by the Honourable George Kerr, Minister of the Environment of Ontario,

OF THE SECOND PART.

WHEREAS Canada and the United States are negotiating the conclusion of an international agreement on Great Lakes water quality that will establish for the Great Lakes general water quality objectives, specific water quality objectives, and programmes and mechanisms to achieve those objectives;

AND WHEREAS it is in the interest of both parties to this agreement to assure that the water quality of the Great Lakes is restored and protected and to that end to take all necessary steps to achieve the objectives to be established by the international agreement;

*   *   *

AND WHEREAS it is expedient to initiate immediately programmes by Canada and Ontario to meet the objectives that may be established by the international agreement and to establish the further obligations that will arise if that agreement is concluded;

AND WHEREAS the parties have agreed on other measures that should be taken to reduce pollution in the Great Lakes;

NOW THEREFORE THIS AGREEMENT WITNESSETH that the parties hereto, in consideration of the covenants and agreements hereinafter contained, covenant and agree with each other as follows:

General Water Quality Objectives

1. The boundary waters of the Great Lakes system should at all places and at all times be
   (a) free from substances attributable to municipal, industrial or other discharges that will settle to form putrescent or otherwise objectionable sludge deposits, or that will adversely affect aquatic life or waterfowl;
   (b) free from floating debris, oil, scum, and other floating materials

attributable to municipal, industrial, or other discharges in amounts sufficient to be unsightly or deleterious;

(c) free from materials attributable to municipal, industrial, or other discharges producing colour, odour, or other conditions in such a degree as to create a nuisance;

(d) free from substances attributable to municipal, industrial, or other discharges in concentrations that are toxic or harmful to human, animal, or aquatic life; and

(e) free from nutrients derived from municipal, industrial, and agricultural sources in concentrations that create nuisance growths of aquatic weeds and algae.

2. It is also agreed as a general water quality objective that no substance should be introduced into these waters unless reasonable efforts have been made to ensure that it will not lead to the violation of any of the foregoing objectives.

Specific Water Quality Objectives

3. (1) The specific water quality objectives listed in the Annex to this agreement are the minimal objectives to be used by the parties in establishing specific water quality standards in respect of the lower Great Lakes and are the basis for designing and assessing the programmes followed and the other measures taken pursuant to this agreement to restore the water quality of the lower Great Lakes.

(2) The specific water quality objectives listed in the Annex to this agreement shall be reviewed by the parties when comparable specific water quality objectives are established under the international agreement and when they are supplemented or amended pursuant to that agreement.

(3) Nothing in this section shall limit or restrict or be construed as limiting or restricting the adoption by the parties, either jointly or separately, of any specific water quality objective or of any standard established on the basis thereof that is more stringent than a specific water quality objective herein or that will cause it to be more stringent, as the case may be.

Term of the Agreement

4. (1) Subject to subsections (2) and (3), this agreement applies in respect of the period beginning on the 1st day of January, 1971, and ending on the 31st day of December, 1975.

(2) Sections 6, 7, 8, 10, subsections (2) and (3) of section 11, sections

12, 13, and 15 do not apply unless the international agreement is entered into by Canada.

(3) Where the international agreement is not entered into by Canada on or before the 31st day of March, 1972, sections 3 and 9 terminate on that date.

Initial Loans and Payment by Canada

5. (1) On or before the 31st day of December, 1971, Canada will, under Part VIII of the *National Housing Act,* make available for sewage treatment projects in the lower Great Lakes basin
   (a) that will contribute to the abatement of pollution in the lower Great Lakes, and
   (b) that have been considered by the Board of Review
loans in a total amount up to but not exceeding ten million dollars ($10,000,000), which loans shall be in addition to amounts already alloted for the same purpose under that Part on or after the 1st day of January, 1971, but prior to the execution of this agreement.

(2) On or before the 31st day of March, 1972, Canada will, under the *Canada Water Act,* pay to Ontario by way of matching grant for the conduct of research, as approved by the Board of Review, by or on behalf of the Commission or Canada, or both, in connection with the pollution of the waters of the lower Great Lakes, one-half the cost of such research up to but not exceeding the amount of three hundred thousand dollars ($300,000).

Covenants by Ontario

6. (1) During the term of the agreement Ontario will accelerate or cause to be accelerated the construction of sewage treatment projects in the lower Great Lakes basin for the abatement of pollution in the lower Great Lakes for the purpose of assisting, within its jurisdiction, in the implementation of the international agreement, and amounts advanced by way of loan pursuant to section 7 shall be used to that end.

(2) The acceleration referred to in subsection (1) shall be such as to bring the total estimated cost for sewage treatment projects undertaken in the lower Great Lakes basin during the term of the agreement to approximately two hundred fifty million dollars ($250,000,000), which amount includes the estimated cost of such projects undertaken during the term of the agreement but before it is entered into.

(3) Subject to section 8, Ontario, either alone or jointly with Canada, will conduct or provide for the conduct of research on a matching grant

basis with a view to reducing the cost of programmes to achieve the specific water quality objectives.

(4) Ontario further agrees that it will reasonably assist in the implementation in other respects of Canada's obligations under the international agreement that are within its legislative jurisdiction and will give due consideration to all proposals made by Canada during the term of the agreement with respect to such implementation.

(5) For the purposes of subsection (4) Ontario will carefully examine any findings by the International Joint Commission as to the effectiveness of programmes within Ontario to meet the specific water quality objectives and will give due consideration to any recommendations made in respect of those findings.

Covenants by Canada

7. (1) During the term of the agreement Canada will, under Part VIII of the *National Housing Act,* make available for sewage treatment projects in the lower Great Lakes basin that will contribute to the abatement of pollution in the lower Great Lakes, loans in a total amount up to but not exceeding one hundred and sixty-seven million dollars ($167,-000,000).

(2) The total amount of loans to be made available by Canada in accordance with subsection (1) in any year of the term of the agreement shall not exceed fifty million dollars ($50,000,000).

❋   ❋   ❋

Board of Review

9. (1) There shall be a Board of Review to be established by the parties for the purposes of this agreement composed of permanent officials of the parties and consisting of six members, three members appointed by Canada and three members appointed by Ontario.

❋   ❋   ❋

(5) The duties of the Board of Review are to monitor and report to the parties on the application of this agreement and, in particular,
   (a) to consider sewage treatment projects proposed pursuant to subsection (1) of section 5 and to section 7 and generally to review the sequence of projects proposed by the Commission and the progress of projects already undertaken;
   (b) to consider whether satisfactory arrangements have been made for the planning and construction of works auxiliary to sewage

treatment projects for which loans are committed pursuant to subsection (1) of section 5 and to section 7;

                                      *   *   *

(e) to consider any report by the International Joint Commission pursuant to the international agreement on the progress of the abatement of pollution in the Great Lakes that is transmitted to it by one of the parties and, following such consideration, to recommend to the parties the further steps, if any, that may be required in the Province of Ontario to meet the specific water quality objectives;

(f) to recommend to the parties any amendments to this agreement that will ensure the implementation in respect of the Great Lakes of the international agreement; and

(g) to discharge any other duties with respect to this agreement that the parties jointly may confer upon it.

Control of Industrial Pollution

10. The parties agree that an important aspect of the abatement of pollution in the Great Lakes and the meeting of the specific water quality objectives in the lower Great Lakes is the control of industrial pollution and they undertake to take all reasonable measures, within their respective jurisdictions, to effect such control.

Other Matters Relating to the International Agreement

11. (1) Prior to the execution of the international agreement or of any amendment thereto, Canada will consult Ontario with respect to any aspect of the international agreement or the amendment, as the case may be, that affects Ontario or the implementation of which may affect Ontario.

(2) Where, as a result of the execution of the international agreement or of any amendment thereto, Canada requests during the term of the agreement that Ontario undertake an acceleration of construction of sewage treatment projects, in excess of the acceleration provided in subsection (1) of section 6, consultations will be arranged to determine what amendments to this agreement may be desirable or required and are acceptable to both parties.

(3) In addition to any consultations that may be arranged pursuant to subsection (2), after the international agreement is executed and at any time thereafter during the term of the agreement, consultations will be arranged, at the request of either party, where, in the opinion of the

party making the request, an amendment to the international agreement may be desirable or required, or an amendment to this agreement may be desirable or required.

12.   The parties undertake to co-operate to the fullest extent with each other in the implementation of any contingency plans, including contingency plans of the United States or a state thereof, that are to operate, in accordance with the international agreement, in the event of the spilling of oil or hazardous materials in the basin of the Great Lakes.

13.   (1) Ontario will provide the International Joint Commission with any data that Ontario may from time to time have available or that Ontario may reasonably be expected to acquire concerning water quality in the basin of the Great Lakes that the International Joint Commission considers useful in the carrying out of any duty devolving upon it under the international agreement.

(2) In addition to the assistance to be accorded pursuant to subsection (1), Ontario will assist the International Joint Commission, its servants and agents, to carry out the duties of the International Joint Commission pursuant to the international agreement.

(3) The parties undertake to make available to each other data and other information relating to water quality in the Great Lakes.

General

14.   The parties agree that, where existing legislation does not enable them to discharge their obligations under this agreement, they will procure the enactment of legislation sufficient to enable them so to do.

15.   At any time before the end of the term of the agreement, at the request of either party, consultations will be held between their responsible officials with a view to extending the agreement and, in respect thereof, to proposing such amendments as may be required for the purposes of the extension.

ANNEX

Specific Water Quality Objectives

The specific water quality objectives are for the receiving waters of the lower Great Lakes except in the restricted mixing zones at outfalls; the periphery of the restricted mixing zones being as prescribed by appropriate water pollution control agencies.

(a) *Microbiology (Coliform Group)*—The geometric mean of not less than five samples taken over not more than a 30-day period shall not exceed 1,000/100 ml total coliforms, nor 200/100 ml fecal coliforms in local waters. Waters used for body contact recreation activities should be free from bacteria, fungi, or viruses that may produce enteric disorders, or eye, ear, nose, throat, and skin infections.

(b) *Dissolved Oxygen*—In the Connecting Channels and in the upper waters of the Lakes not less than 6.0 mg/l at any time; in the hypolimnetic waters not less than the concentrations necessary for the support of fishlife, particularly cold water species.

(c) *Total Dissolved Solids*—Less than 200 mg/l in Lake Erie, Lake Ontario, and the International Section of the St. Lawrence River; in the St. Marys River, pending the results of a study of the Upper Great Lakes, a level of total dissolved solids not exceeding that of 1970; and in the other Connecting Channels a level consistent with maintaining the levels of total dissolved solids in Lake Erie and Lake Ontario less than 200 mg/l.

(d) *Temperature*—No change which would adversely affect any local or general use of these waters.

(e) *Taste and Odour*—No objectionable taste or odour. Phenols desirably absent but not to exceed a monthly average of 1.0 micrograms/l. Other taste and odour producing substances absent.

(f) *pH*—No change from the range of levels, 6.7 to 8.5 which now exist.

(g) *Iron*—Less than 0.3 mg/l.

(h) *Phosphorus**—Concentrations limited to the extent necessary to prevent nuisance growths of algae, weeds, and slimes which are or may become injurious to any beneficial water use. (Meeting this objective will require that the phosphorous loading to Lake Erie be limited to 0.39 g/m²/yr and the phosphorous loading to Lake Ontario be limited to 0.17 g/m²/yr.)

(i) *Radioactivity*—Elimination of radioactive materials to the extent necessary to prevent harmful effects on health. Pending the adoption of more stringent limits, in no event is gross beta activity to exceed 1,000 pCi/l, Radium 226 not to exceed 3 pCi/l and Strontium 90 not to exceed 10 pCi/l.

---

* The term phosphorus in this Annex refers to phosphorus as a constituent of various organic and inorganic complexes and compounds, not to elemental phosphorus as a chemical substance. The term phosphorus includes orthophosphates such as trisodiumphosphate, crystaline phosphates such as sodiumtripolyphosphate, and polyphosphates such as sodiumhexametaphosphate. However, in this Annex concentrations and loads are given in terms of the element phosphorus as part of any compound to assure uniformity of expression.

✍ AGREEMENT BETWEEN CANADA AND THE UNITED STATES OF AMERICA ON GREAT LAKES WATER QUALITY

The Government of Canada and the Government of the United States of America,

Determined to restore and enhance water quality in the Great Lakes System;

Seriously concerned about the grave deterioration of water quality on each side of the boundary to an extent that is causing injury to health and property on the other side, as described in the 1970 report of the International Joint Commission on Pollution of Lake Erie, Lake Ontario, and the International Section of the St. Lawrence River;

Intent upon preventing further pollution of the Great Lakes System owing to continuing population growth, resource development, and increasing use of water;

Reaffirming in a spirit of friendship and cooperation the rights and obligations of both countries under the Boundary Waters Treaty signed on January 11, 1909, and in particular their obligation not to pollute boundary waters;

Recognizing the rights of each country in the use of its Great Lakes waters;

Satisfied that the 1970 report of the International Joint Commission provides a sound basis for new and more effective cooperative actions to restore and enhance water quality in the Great Lakes System;

Convinced that the best means to achieve improved water quality in the Great Lakes System is through the adoption of common objectives, the development and implementation of cooperative programs and other measures, and the assignment of special responsibilities and functions to the International Joint Commission;

Have agreed as follows:

ARTICLE I.

Definitions

As used in this Agreement:
(a) "Boundary waters of the Great Lakes System" or "boundary waters" means boundary waters, as defined in the Boundary Waters Treaty, that are within the Great Lakes System;

Signed at Ottawa, April 15, 1972; in force April 15, 1972.

(b) "Boundary Waters Treaty" means the Treaty between the United States and Great Britain Relating to Boundary Waters, and Questions Arising Between the United States and Canada, signed at Washington on January 11, 1909;

(c) "Compatible regulations" means regulations no less restrictive than agreed principles;

(d) "Great Lakes System" means all of the streams, rivers, lakes, and other bodies of water that are within the drainage basin of the St. Lawrence River at or upstream from the point at which this river becomes the international boundary between Canada and the United States;

(e) "Harmful quantity" means any quantity of a substance that if discharged into receiving waters would be inconsistent with the achievement of the water quality objectives;

(f) "Hazardous polluting substance" means any element or compound identified by the Parties which, when discharged in any quantity into or upon receiving waters or adjoining shorelines, presents an imminent and substantial danger to public health or welfare; for this purpose, "public health or welfare" encompasses all factors affecting the health and welfare of man including but not limited to human health, and the conservation and protection of fish, shellfish, wildlife, public and private property, shorelines, and beaches;

(g) "International Joint Commission" or "Commission" means the International Joint Commission established by the Boundary Waters Treaty;

(h) "Phosphorus" means the element phosphorus present as a constituent of various organic and inorganic complexes and compounds;

(i) "Specific water quality objective" means the level of a substance or physical effect that the Parties agree, after investigation, to recognize as a maximum or minimum desired limit for a defined body of water or portion thereof, taking into account the beneficial uses of the water that the Parties desire to secure and protect;

(j) "State and Provincial Governments" means the Governments of the States of Illinois, Indiana, Michigan, Minnesota, New York, Ohio, Pennsylvania, and Wisconsin, and the Government of the Province of Ontario;

(k) "Tributary waters of the Great Lakes System" or "tributary waters" means all the waters of the Great Lakes System that are not boundary waters;

(l) "Water quality objectives" means the general water quality objectives adopted pursuant to Article II of this Agreement and the specific water quality objectives adopted pursuant to Article III of this Agreement.

ARTICLE II.

General Water Quality Objectives

The following general water quality objectives for the boundary waters of the Great Lakes System are adopted. These waters should be:

(a) Free from substances that enter the waters as a result of human activity and that will settle to form putrescent or otherwise objectionable sludge deposits, or that will adversely affect aquatic life or waterfowl;

(b) Free from floating debris, oil, scum and other floating materials entering the waters as a result of human activity in amounts sufficient to be unsightly or deleterious;

(c) Free from materials entering the waters as a result of human activity producing colour, odour or other conditions in such a degree as to create a nuisance;

(d) Free from substances entering the waters as a result of human activity in concentrations that are toxic or harmful to human, animal or aquatic life;

(e) Free from nutrients entering the waters as a result of human activity in concentrations that create nuisance growths of aquatic weeds and algae.

ARTICLE III.

Specific Water Quality Objectives

1. The specific water quality objectives for the boundary waters of the Great Lakes System set forth in Annex 1 are adopted.

2. The specific water quality objectives may be modified and additional specific water quality objectives for the boundary waters of the Great Lakes System or for particular sections thereof may be adopted by the Parties in accordance with the provisions of Articles IX and XII of this Agreement.

3. The specific water quality objectives adopted pursuant to this Article represent the minimum desired levels of water quality in the boundary waters of the Great Lakes System and are not intended to preclude the establishment of more stringent requirements.

4. Notwithstanding the adoption of specific water quality objectives, all reasonable and practicable measures shall be taken to maintain the levels of water quality existing at the date of entry into force of this Agreement in those areas of the boundary waters of the Great Lakes System where such levels exceed the specific water quality objectives.

ARTICLE IV.

Standards and Other Regulatory Requirements

Water quality standards and other regulatory requirements of the Parties shall be consistent with the achievement of the water quality objectives. The Parties shall use their best efforts to ensure that water quality standards and other regulatory requirements of the State and Provincial Governments shall similarly be consistent with the achievement of the water quality objectives.

ARTICLE V.

Programs and Other Measures

1. Programs and other measures directed toward the achievement of the water quality objectives shall be developed and implemented as soon as practicable in accordance with legislation in the two countries. Unless otherwise agreed, such programs and other measures shall be either completed or in process of implementation by December 31, 1975. They shall include the following:

   (a) *Pollution from Municipal Sources.* Programs for the abatement and control of discharges of municipal sewage into the Great Lakes System including:

   (i) construction and operation in all municipalities having sewer systems of waste treatment facilities providing levels of treatment consistent with the achievement of the water quality objectives, taking into account the effects of waste from other sources;

   (ii) provision of financial resources to assist prompt construction of needed facilities;

   (iii) establishment of requirements for construction and operating standards for facilities;

   (iv) measures to find practical solutions for reducing pollution from overflows of combined storm and sanitary sewers;

   (v) monitoring, surveillance, and enforcement activities necessary to ensure compliance with the foregoing programs and measures.

(b) *Pollution from Industrial Sources.* Programs for the abatement and control of pollution from industrial sources, including:

   (i) establishment of waste treatment or control requirements for all industrial plants discharging waste into the Great Lakes System, to provide levels of treatment or reduction of inputs of substances and effects consistent with the achievement of the water quality objectives, taking into account the effects of waste from other sources;

   (ii) requirements for the substantial elimination of discharges into the Great Lakes System of mercury and other toxic heavy metals;

   (iii) requirements for the substantial elimination of discharges into the Great Lakes System of toxic persistent organic contaminants;

   (iv) requirements for the control of thermal discharges;

   (v) measures to control the discharges of radioactive materials into the Great Lakes System;

   (vi) monitoring, surveillance, and enforcement activities necessary to ensure compliance with the foregoing requirements and measures.

(c) *Eutrophication.* Measures for the control of inputs of phosphorus and other nutrients including programs to reduce phosphorus inputs, in accordance with the provisions of Annex 2.

(d) *Pollution from Agricultural, Forestry and Other Land Use Activities.* Measures for the abatement and control of pollution from agricultural, forestry, and other land use activities, including:

   (i) measures for the control of pest control products with a view to limiting inputs into the Great Lakes System, including regulations to ensure that pest control products judged to have long term deleterious effects on the quality of water or its biotic components shall be used only as authorized by the responsible regulatory agencies, and that pest control products shall not be applied directly to water except in accordance with the requirements of the responsible regulatory agencies;

   (ii) measures for the abatement and control of pollution from animal husbandry operations, including encouragement to appropriate regulatory agencies to adopt regulations governing site selection and disposal of liquid and solid wastes in order to minimize the loss of pollutants to receiving waters;

   (iii) measures governing the disposal of solid wastes and contributing to the achievement of the water quality objectives, including encouragement to appropriate regulatory agencies to ensure proper location of land fill and land dumping sites and regulations governing the disposal on land of hazardous polluting substances;

(iv) advisory programs and measures that serve to abate and control inputs of nutrients and sediments into receiving waters from agricultural, forestry and other land use activities.

(e) *Pollution from Shipping Activities.* Measures for the abatement and control of pollution from shipping sources, including:

(i) programs and compatible regulations for vessel design, construction and operation, to prevent discharges of harmful quantities of oil and hazardous polluting substances, in accordance with the principles set forth in Annex 3;

(ii) compatible regulations for the control of vessel waste discharges in accordance with the principles set forth in Annex 4;

(iii) such compatible regulations to abate and control pollution from shipping sources as may be deemed desirable in the light of studies to be undertaken in accordance with the terms of references set forth in Annex 5;

(iv) programs for the safe and efficient handling of shipboard generated wastes, including oil, hazardous polluting substances, garbage, waste water, and sewage, and their subsequent disposal, including any necessary compatible regulations relating to the type, quantity, and capacity of shore reception facilities;

(v) establishment of a coordinated system for the surveillance and enforcement of regulations dealing with the abatement and control of pollution from shipping activities.

(f) *Pollution from Dredging Activities.* Measures for the abatement and control of pollution from dredging activities, including the development of criteria for the identification of polluted dredged spoil and compatible programs for disposal of polluted dredged spoil, which shall be considered in the light of the review provided for in Annex 6; pending the development of compatible criteria and programs, dredging operations shall be conducted in a manner that will minimize adverse effects on the environment.

(g) *Pollution from Onshore and Offshore Facilities.* Measures for the abatement and control of pollution from onshore and offshore facilities, including programs and compatible regulations for the prevention of discharges of harmful quantities of oil and hazardous polluting substances, in accordance with the principles set forth in Annex 7.

(h) *Contingency Plan.* Maintenance of a joint contingency plan for use in the event of a discharge or the imminent threat of a discharge of oil or hazardous polluting substances, in accordance with the provisions of Annex 8.

(i) *Hazardous Polluting Substances.* Consultation within one year from the date of entry into force of this Agreement for the purpose of developing an Annex identifying hazardous polluting substances; the Parties shall further consult from time to time for the purpose of identifying harmful quantities of these substances and of reviewing the definition of "harmful quantity of oil" set forth in Annexes 3 and 7.

2. The Parties shall develop and implement such additional programs as they jointly decide are necessary and desirable for the achievement of the water quality objectives.

3. The programs and other measures provided for in this Article shall be designed to abate and control pollution of tributary waters where necessary or desirable for the achievement of the water quality objectives for the boundary waters of the Great Lakes System.

ARTICLE VI.

Powers, Responsibilities and Functions of the International Joint Commission

1. The International Joint Commission shall assist in the implementation of this Agreement. Accordingly, the Commission is hereby given, pursuant to Article IX of the Boundary Waters Treaty, the following responsibilities:

(a) Collation, analysis, and dissemination of data and information supplied by the Parties and State and Provincial Governments relating to the quality of the boundary waters of the Great Lakes System and to pollution that enters the boundary waters from tributary waters;

(b) Collection, analysis, and dissemination of data and information concerning the water quality objectives and the operation and effectiveness of the programs and other measures established pursuant to this Agreement;

(c) Tendering of advice and recommendations to the Parties and to the State and Provincial Governments on problems of the quality of the boundary waters of the Great Lakes System, including specific recommendations concerning the water quality objectives, legislation, standards, and other regulatory requirements, programs, and other measures, and intergovernmental agreements relating to the quality of these waters;

(d) Provision of assistance in the coordination of the joint activities envisaged by this Agreement, including such matters as contingency planning and consultation on special situations;

(e) Provision of assistance in the coordination of Great Lakes water quality research, including identification of objectives for research activities, tendering of advice and recommendations concerning research to the Parties and to the State and Provincial Governments, and dissemination of information concerning research to interested persons and agencies;

(f) Investigations of such subjects related to Great Lakes water quality as the Parties may from time to time refer to it. At the time of signature of this Agreement, the Parties are requesting the Commission to enquire into and report to them upon:

(i) pollution of the boundary waters of the Great Lakes System from agricultural, forestry, and other land use activities, in accordance with the terms of reference attached to this Agreement;

(ii) actions needed to preserve and enhance the quality of the waters of Lake Huron and Lake Superior in accordance with the terms of reference attached to this Agreement.

2. In the discharge of its responsibilities under this Agreement, the Commission may exercise all of the powers conferred upon it by the Boundary Waters Treaty and by any legislation passed pursuant thereto, including the power to conduct public hearings and to compel the testimony of witnesses and the production of documents.

3. The Commission shall make a report to the Parties and to the State and Provincial Governments no less frequently than annually concerning progress toward the achievement of the water quality objectives. This report shall include an assessment of the effectiveness of the programs and other measures undertaken pursuant to this Agreement, and advice and recommendations. The Commission may at any time make special reports to the Parties, to the State and Provincial Governments and to the public concerning any problem of water quality in the Great Lakes System.

4. The Commission may in its discretion publish any report, statement or other document prepared by it in the discharge of its functions under this Agreement.

5. The Commission shall have authority to verify independently the data and other information submitted by the Parties and by the State and Provincial Governments through such tests or other means as appear appropriate to it, consistent with the Boundary Waters Treaty and with applicable legislation.

ARTICLE VII.

Joint Institutions

1. The International Joint Commission shall establish a Great Lakes Water Quality Board to assist it in the exercise of the powers and re-sponsibilities assigned to it under this Agreement. Such Board shall be composed of an equal number of members from Canada and the United States, including representation from the Parties and from each of the State and Provincial Governments. The Commission shall also establish a Research Advisory Board in accordance with the terms of reference attached to this Agreement. The members of the Great Lakes Water Quality Board and the Research Advisory Board shall be appointed by the Commission after consultation with the appropriate government or governments concerned. In addition, the Commission shall have the authority to establish as it may deem appropriate such subordinate bodies as may be required to undertake specific tasks, as well as a regional office, which may be located in the basin of the Great Lakes System, to assist it in the discharge of its functions under this Agreement. The Commission shall also consult the Parties about the site and staffing of any regional office that might be established.

2. The Commission shall submit an annual budget of anticipated ex-penses to be incurred in carrying out its responsibilities under this Agreement to the Parties for approval. Each Party shall seek funds to pay one-half of the annual budget so approved, but neither Party shall be under an obligation to pay a larger amount than the other toward this budget.

ARTICLE VIII.

Submission and Exchange of Information

1. The International Joint Commission shall be given at its request any data or other information relating to the quality of the boundary waters of the Great Lakes System in accordance with procedures to be estab-lished, within three months of the entry into force of this Agreement or

as soon thereafter as possible, by the Commission in consultation with the Parties and with the State and Provincial Governments.

2. The Commission shall make available to the Parties and to the State and Provincial Governments upon request all data or other information furnished to it in accordance with this Article.

3. Each Party shall make available to the other at its request any data or other information in its control relating to the quality of the waters of the Great Lakes System.

4. Notwithstanding any other provision of this Agreement, the Commission shall not release without the consent of the owner any information identified as proprietary information under the law of the place where such information has been acquired.

ARTICLE IX.

Consultation and Review

1. Following the receipt of each report submitted to the Parties by the International Joint Commission in accordance with paragraph 3 of Article VI of this Agreement, the Parties shall consult on the recommendations contained in such report and shall consider such action as may be appropriate, including:
   (a) The modification of existing water quality objectives and the adoption of new objectives;
   (b) The modification or improvement of programs and joint measures;
   (c) The amendment of this Agreement or any annex thereto.
Additional consultations may be held at the request of either Party on any matter arising out of the implementation of this Agreement.

2. When a Party becomes aware of a special pollution problem that is of joint concern and requires an immediate response, it shall notify and consult the other Party forthwith about appropriate remedial action.

3. The Parties shall conduct a comprehensive review of the operation and effectiveness of this Agreement during the fifth year after its coming into force. Thereafter, further comprehensive reviews shall be conducted upon the request of either Party.

❊ ❊ ❊

ANNEX 1

Specific Water Quality Objectives

1. *Specific Objectives.* The specific water quality objectives for the boundary waters of the Great Lakes System are as follows:

(a) *Microbiology.* The geometric mean of not less than five samples taken over not more than a thirty-day period should not exceed 1,000/100 millilitres total coliforms, nor 200/100 millilitres fecal coliforms. Waters used for body contact recreation activities should be substantially free from bacteria, fungi, or viruses that may produce enteric disorders or eye, ear, nose, throat, and skin infections or other human diseases and infections.

(b) *Dissolved Oxygen.* In the Connecting Channels and in the upper waters of the Lakes, the dissolved oxygen level should be not less than 6.0 milligrams per litre at any time; in hypolimnetic waters, it should be not less than necessary for the support of fishlife, particularly cold water species.

(c) *Total Dissolved Solids.* In Lake Erie, Lake Ontario and the International Section of the St. Lawrence River, the level of total dissolved solids should not exceed 200 milligrams per litre. In the St. Clair River, Lake St. Clair, the Detroit River and the Niagara River, the level should be consistent with maintaining the levels of total dissolved solids in Lake Erie and Lake Ontario at not to exceed 200 milligrams per litre. In the remaining boundary waters, pending further study, the level of total dissolved solids should not exceed present levels.

(d) *Taste and Odour.* Phenols and other objectionable taste and odour producing substances should be substantially absent.

(e) *pH.* Values should not be outside the range of 6.7 to 8.5.

(f) *Iron (Fe).* Levels should not exceed 0.3 milligrams per litre.

(g) *Phosphorus (P).* Concentrations should be limited to the extent necessary to prevent nuisance growths of algae, weeds and slimes that are or may become injurious to any beneficial water use.

(h) *Radioactivity.* Radioactivity should be kept at the lowest practicable levels and in any event should be controlled to the extent necessary to prevent harmful effects on health.

2. *Interim Objectives.* Until objectives for particular substances and effects in the classes described in this paragraph are further refined, the objectives for them are as follows:

(a) *Temperature.* There should be no change that would adversely affect any local or general use of these waters.

(b) *Mercury and Other Toxic Heavy Metals.* The aquatic environment should be free from substances attributable to municipal, industrial, or other discharges in concentrations that are toxic or harmful to human, animal, or aquatic life.

(c) *Persistent Organic Contaminants.* Persistent pest control products and other persistent organic contaminants that are toxic or harmful to human, animal, or aquatic life should be substantially absent in the waters.

(d) *Settleable and Suspended Materials.* Waters should be free from substances attributable to municipal, industrial, or other discharges that will settle to form putrescent or otherwise objectionable sludge deposits, or that will adversely affect aquatic life or waterfowl.

(e) *Oil, Petrochemicals and Immiscible Substances.* Waters should be free from floating debris, oil, scum, and other floating materials attributable to municipal, industrial, or other discharges in amounts sufficient to be unsightly or deleterious.

3. *Non-degradation.* Notwithstanding the adoption of specific water quality objectives, all reasonable and practicable measures shall be taken in accordance with paragraph 4 of Article III of the Agreement to maintain the levels of water quality existing at the date of entry into force of the Agreement in those areas of the boundary waters of the Great Lakes System where such levels exceed the specific water quality objectives.

4. *Sampling Data.* The Parties agree that the determination of compliance with specific objectives shall be based on statistically valid sampling data.

5. *Mixing Zones.* The responsible regulatory agencies may designate restricted mixing zones in the vicinity of outfalls within which the specific water quality objectives shall not apply. Mixing zones shall not be considered a substitute for adequate treatment or control of discharges at their source.

6. *Localized Areas.* There will be other restricted, localized areas, such as harbours, where existing conditions such as land drainage and land use will prevent the objectives from being met at least over the short term; such areas, however, should be identified specifically and as early as possible by the responsible regulatory agencies and should be kept to a minimum. Pollution from such areas shall not contribute to the violation of the water quality objectives in the waters of the other Party. The International Joint Commission shall be notified of the identification of such localized areas, in accordance with Article VIII.

7. *Consultation.* The Parties agree to consult within one year from the date of entry into force of the Agreement, for the purpose of considering:

(a) Specific water quality objectives for the following substances:

Ammonia	Copper	Oil
Arsenic	Cyanide	Organic chemicals
Barium	Fluoride	Phenols
Cadmium	Lead	Selenium
Chloride	Mercury	Sulphate
Chromium	Nickel	Zinc

(b) Refined objectives for radioactivity and temperature; for radioactivity the objective shall be considered in the light of the recommendations of the International Commission on Radiation Protection.

8. *Amendment.*
(a) The objectives adopted herein shall be kept under review and may be amended by mutual agreement of the Parties.
(b) Whenever the International Joint Commission, acting pursuant to Article VI of the Agreement, shall recommend the establishment of new or modified specific water quality objectives, this Annex shall be amended in accordance with such recommendation on the receipt by the Commission of a letter from each Party indicating its agreement with the recommendation.

ANNEX 2

Control of Phosphorus

1. *Programs.* Programs shall be developed and implemented to reduce inputs of phosphorus to the Great Lakes System. These programs shall include:
(a) Construction and operation of waste treatment facilities to remove phosphorus from municipal sewage;
(b) Regulatory measures to require industrial dischargers to remove phosphorus from wastes to be discharged into the Great Lakes System;
(c) Regulatory and advisory measures to control inputs of phosphorus through reduction of waste discharges attributable to animal husbandry operations.

In addition, programs may include regulations limiting or eliminating phosphorus from detergents sold for use within the basin of the Great Lakes System.

2. *Effluent Requirements.* The phosphorus concentrations in effluent

from municipal waste treatment plants discharging in excess of one million gallons per day, and from smaller plants as required by regulatory agencies, shall not exceed a daily average of one milligram per litre into Lake Erie, Lake Ontario, and the International Section of the St. Lawrence River.

3. *Industrial Discharges.* Waste treatment or control requirements for all industrial plants discharging wastes into the Great Lakes System shall be designed to achieve maximum practicable reduction of phosphorus discharges to Lake Erie, Lake Ontario, and the International Section of the St. Lawrence River.

4. *Reductions for Lower Lakes.* These programs are designed to attain reductions in gross inputs of phosphorus to Lake Erie and Lake Ontario of the quantities indicated in the following tables for the years indicated. [Not reproduced here.]

5. *Reservation.* The amounts shown as "residual loads" in Tables 1 and 2 above do not constitute allocations to the two countries, but represent anticipated results of municipal and industrial waste reduction and detergent phosphorus control programs.

6. *Refinement of Data.* The residual loads are based upon best available data. The Parties, in cooperation with the State and Provincial Governments and with the International Joint Commission, shall continue to refine these estimates to ensure a comparable data base. These estimates are subject to revision upon agreement by the Parties to reflect future refinement of the data.

7. *Objective of Programs.* The objective of the foregoing programs is to minimize eutrophication problems in the Great Lakes System. It is anticipated that successful implementation of these programs will accomplish the following results, which are of critical importance to the success of the joint undertaking to preserve and enhance the quality of the waters of the Great Lakes System:
   (a) Restoration of year-round aerobic conditions in the bottom waters of the central basin of Lake Erie;
   (b) Reduction in present levels of algal growth in Lake Erie;
   (c) Reduction in present levels of algal growth in Lake Ontario, including the International Section of the St. Lawrence River;
   (d) Stabilization of Lake Superior and Lake Huron in their present oligotrophic state.
It is nevertheless recognized that additional measures and programs may be required to minimize eutrophication problems in the future. Available evidence suggests that reductions in phosphorus loadings to achieve a

net discharge to Lake Erie in the range of 8000 to 11,000 tons per year may be required to bring about mesotrophic conditions in this lake.

8. *Reductions for Upper Lakes.* The Parties, in consultation with the State and Provincial Governments and with the International Joint Commission, shall within one year from the entry into force of the Agreement determine the gross reductions in inputs of phosphorus that they agree to seek for Lake Superior and Lake Huron (including the St. Marys River). Pending such agreement, such limitations on municipal and industrial phosphorus discharges as may be required by regulatory agencies to meet loading objectives or to prevent and control eutrophication problems in Lake Superior and Lake Huron shall apply. Any more comprehensive findings resulting from the study by the International Joint Commission of water quality in these lakes shall be taken into account as soon as available.

9. *Commission Recommendations.* The Parties shall take into account, as soon as available, the recommendations of the International Joint Commission made pursuant to its study of pollution from agricultural, forestry and other land use activities, in order to develop and implement appropriate programs for control of inputs of phosphorus from these sources.

10. *Monitoring.* The Parties, in cooperation with the State and Provincial Governments and with the International Joint Commission, shall continue to monitor the extent of eutrophication in the Great Lakes System and the progress being made in reducing or preventing it. They shall consult periodically to exchange the results of research and to pursue proposals for additional programs to control eutrophication.

11. *Submission of Information.* The International Joint Commission shall be given information at least annually, in accordance with procedures established by the Commission in consultation with the Parties and with the State and Provincial Governments, concerning:
   (a) Total reductions in gross inputs of phorphorus achieved as a result of the programs implemented pursuant to this Annex;
   (b) Anticipated reductions in gross inputs of phorphorus for the succeeding twelve months.

12. *Review and Modification.* In connection with the first comprehensive joint review of the operation and effectiveness of the Agreement conducted in accordance with paragraph 3 of Article IX thereof, the effects of phosphorus control programs on the Great Lakes System shall be reviewed and further modifications in the programs undertaken pursuant to this Annex shall be considered.

ANNEX 3

Vessel Design, Construction and Operation

1. *Definitions.* As used in this Annex:
   (a) "Discharge" means the introduction of oil and hazardous polluting substances, including oily bilgewater, into receiving waters and includes, but is not limited to, any spilling, leaking, pumping, pouring, emitting, or dumping; it does not include unavoidable direct discharges of oil from a properly functioning vessel engine;
   (b) "Harmful quantity of oil" means any quantity of oil that, if discharged into receiving waters, would produce a film or sheen upon, or discoloration of, the surface of the water or adjoining shoreline, or that would cause a sludge or emulsion to be deposited beneath the surface of the water or upon the adjoining shoreline;
   (c) "Oily wastes" means oil and mixtures containing oil such as oily ballast, tank washing, and bilge slops;
   (d) "Tanker" means any vessel designed for the carriage of oil or liquid chemicals in bulk;
   (e) "Vessel" means any ship, barge or other floating craft, whether or not self-propelled.

2. *Oil.* As used in this Annex, "oil" refers to oil of any kind or in any form, including, but not limited to petroleum, fuel oil, oil sludge, oil refuse, and oil mixed with wastes, but does not include constituents of dredged spoil.

3. *General Principles.* Compatible regulations shall be adopted for the prevention of discharges into the Great Lakes System of harmful quantities of oil and hazardous polluting substances from vessels in accordance with the following principles:
   (a) Discharges of harmful quantities of oil or hazardous polluting substances shall be prohibited and made subject to appropriate penalties;
   (b) As soon as any person in charge has knowledge of any discharge of harmful quantities of oil or hazardous polluting substances, immediate notice of such discharge shall be given to the appropriate agency in the jurisdiction where the discharge occurs; failure to give this notice shall be made subject to appropriate penalties.

4. *Programs.* The programs and measures to be adopted for the prevention of discharges of harmful quantities of oil shall include the following:

(a) Compatible regulations for design and construction of vessels based on the following principles:
- (i)   each tanker shall have a suitable means of containing on board cargo oil spills caused by loading or transfer operations;
- (ii) each vessel shall have a suitable means of containing on board fuel oil spills caused by loading or transfer operations, including those from tank vents and overflow pipes;
- (iii) each vessel shall have a capability of retaining on board oily wastes accumulated during vessel operation;
- (iv) each vessel shall be capable of off-loading contained oily wastes to a shore facility.

(b) Compatible regulations for vessel operating procedures based on the following principles:
- (i)   tankers shall be provided with a means for rapidly and safely stopping the flow of cargo oil during transfer operations in the event of an emergency;
- (ii) suitable deck lighting shall be provided to illuminate all cargo and fuel handling areas if the transfer occurs at night;
- (iii) hose assemblies used aboard vessels for oil transfer shall be suitably designed, marked, and inspected to minimize the possibility of failure;
- (iv) oil transfer, loading and off-loading systems shall be designed to minimize the possibility of failure.

(c) Programs to train merchant vessel personnel in all functions involved in the use, handling, and stowage of oil and in procedures for abatement of oil pollution.

5. *Additional Measures.* The programs and measures to be adopted for the prevention of discharges of hazardous polluting substances shall use as a guide the Code for the Construction and Equipment of Ships Carrying Dangerous Chemicals in Bulk of the Intergovernmental Maritime Consultative Organization (IMCO). Such programs and measures shall include design and construction features, operating procedures, and merchant vessel personnel qualification standards with respect to handling hazardous polluting substances and pollution abatement. In addition, the programs shall establish compatible regulations for:

(a) Identification and placarding of vessels carrying hazardous polluting substances as well as containers and packages containing hazardous polluting substances when carried by vessels:

(b) Identification in vessel manifests of all hazardous polluting substances carried;

(c) Procedures for notification to responsible authorities of all hazardous polluting substances carried.

ANNEX 4

Vessel Wastes

1. *Definitions.* As used in this Annex:
   (a) "Garbage" means solid galley waste, paper, rags, plastics, glass, metal, bottles, crockery, junk, and similar refuse;
   (b) "Sewage" means human or animal waste generated on board ship and includes wastes from water closets, urinals, or hospital facilities handling fecal material;
   (c) "Vessel" means any ship, barge, or other floating craft, whether or not self-propelled;
   (d) "Waste water" means water in combination with other substances, including ballast water and water used for washing cargo holds, but excluding water in combination with oil, hazardous polluting substances, or sewage.

2. *Compatible Regulations.* The Parties shall adopt within one year from the entry into force of the Agreement regulations governing the disposal of vessel waste in the waters of the Great Lakes System in accordance with principles at least as stringent as the following:
   (a) Garbage shall not be discharged by a vessel into these waters;
   (b) Waste water shall not be discharged by a vessel into these waters in amounts or in concentrations that will be deleterious;
   (c) Every vessel operating in these waters with an installed toilet facility shall be equipped with a device or devices to contain the vessel's sewage, or to incinerate it, or to treat it to an adequate degree.

3. *Critical Use Areas.* Critical use areas of the Great Lakes System may be designated where the discharge of waste water or sewage shall be limited or prohibited.

4. *Containment Devices.* Regulations may be established requiring a device or devices to contain the sewage of pleasure craft or other classes of vessels operating in the Great Lakes System or designated areas thereof.

ANNEX 5

Studies of Pollution from Shipping Sources

1. *Studies.* The Parties agree that studies of pollution problems in the Great Lakes System that arise in relation to shipping activities shall be undertaken for the purpose of strengthening their programs and other

measures for the abatement and control of pollution from shipping sources. Responsibility for the coordination of these studies is assigned to the United States Coast Guard and the Canadian Ministry of Transport. Initially, these studies shall include the following subjects:

(a) *Navigational Equipment.* Determination of minimum safe standards respecting the fitting, maintenance, testing, and use of navigational equipment for both normal and ice operations.

(b) *Traffic Routes for Navigational Purposes.* Review of the existing informal system of traffic routes and determination of their adequacy and effectiveness; determination of the need for additional traffic routes; review of track widths, shifting of tracks, limited tracks, rules of passing, speeds, and similar matters for normal and ice operations; and identification of priorities for needed remedial measures.

(c) *Traffic Control.* Review of existing traffic control systems and determination of their adequacy and effectiveness; determination of the need for additional traffic control systems; review of operations with respect to open waters, harbours, and channels under normal and ice conditions; and identification of priorities for needed remedial measures.

(d) *Manning of Vessels.* Review of existing United States and Canadian competency standards to determine acceptable minimum standards; review of existing foreign competency standards to determine whether they are adequate and effective and equivalent to the United States and Canadian minimum standards; determination of the need for certificated pilots and other officers and for improvement of existing pilot certifications, for special manning regulations for towing vessels, for separate manning standards for ice operations, and for separate manning standards for vessels carrying oil and hazardous polluting substances in periods of adverse weather or in areas of high traffic density.

(e) *Aids to Navigation Systems.* Review of the adequacy and effectiveness of existing aids to navigation systems; determination of the need for additional aids to navigation; and identification of priorities for needed remedial measures.

(f) *Waste Water.* Review of problems arising from the discharge of waste waters, and recommendations for reducing the deleterious effects of such discharges.

(g) *Sewage Treatment Systems for Vessels.* Review of current research and development of systems for the treatment of vessel sewage.

(h) *Loading and Unloading of Grain and Ore.* Review of pollution problems arising from these operations.

2. *Consultation.* Representatives of the United States Coast Guard and Canadian Ministry of Transport together with representatives of other concerned agencies shall meet periodically in order to:

(a) Identify problems requiring further study;

(b) Apportion, as between Canada and the United States, responsibility for various aspects of the studies;

(c) Provide continuing interchange of information with respect to ongoing and proposed projects;

(d) Exchange results of completed projects.

3. *Additional Studies and Results.* The United States Coast Guard and the Canadian Ministry of Transport shall inform the International Joint Commission of any additional subjects that are being studied and of the results of all studies undertaken pursuant to this Annex as they become available.

ANNEX 6

Identification and Disposal of Polluted Dredged Spoil

1. *Definitions.* As used in this Annex:

(a) "Dredged spoil" means the solid materials removed from the bottom of water bodies generally for the purpose of improving waterways for navigation; these materials may include mud, silt, clay, sand, rock, and other solid materials that have been deposited from municipal and industrial discharges and from natural sources;

(b) "Confined area" means an area developed for the deposit of dredge spoil that precludes the return of the dredge spoil to open portions of the waterway; the area may be located in the waterway or on other upland sites and may consist of dikes, levees, bulkheads, cells, or any other type structure that will retain the material;

(c) "Open water" means any part of the boundary waters of the Great Lakes System other than a confined area;

(d) "Polluted dredged spoil" means dredged spoil containing harmful quantities of oil, hazardous polluting substances, or other deleterious substances as designated by the responsible regulatory agencies.

2. *Review.* Pursuant to arrangements to be made by the International Joint Commission in consultation with the Parties, a working group shall be established to undertake a Review of existing dredging practices, programs, laws, and regulations with the objective of developing compatible criteria for the characterization of polluted dredged spoil and recom-

mendations for compatible programs governing the disposal of polluted dredged spoil in open water. This review shall be completed within two years from the date of entry into force of the Agreement. The working group shall conduct its study and formulate its recommendations on the basis of the following principles:

(a) Dredging activities should be conducted in a manner that will minimize harmful environmental effects;

(b) All reasonable and practicable measures shall be taken to ensure that dredging activities do not cause a degradation of water quality and bottom sediments;

(c) As soon as practicable, the disposal of polluted dredged spoil in open water should be carried out in a manner consistent with the achievement of the water quality objectives, and should be phased out.

3. *Consultations.* Upon completion of the review provided for in paragraph 2 above, the Parties shall consult pursuant to Article IX of the Agreement to consider and act upon the recommendations of the working group.

4. *Interim Actions.* Pending the development of compatible criteria and programs:

(a) Dredged spoil found by the appropriate regulatory agencies to be polluted shall be disposed of in confined areas when they are available;

(b) The responsible agencies shall continue efforts to develop sites for confined areas.

ANNEX 7

Discharges from Onshore and Offshore Facilities

1. *Definitions.* As used in this Annex:

(a) "Discharge" means the introduction of oil or hazardous polluting substances into receiving waters and includes, but is not limited to, any spilling, leaking, pumping, pouring, emitting, or dumping; it does not include continuous effluent discharges from municipal or industrial treatment facilities;

(b) "Harmful quantity of oil" means any quantity of oil that, if discharged into receiving waters, would produce a film or sheen upon, or discoloration of the surface of the water or adjoining shoreline, or that would cause a sludge or emulsion to be deposited beneath the surface of the water or upon adjoining shoreline;

(c) "Offshore facility" means any facility of any kind located in, on, or under any water;

(d) "Onshore facility" means any facility of any kind located in, on, or under, any land other than submerged land.

2. *Facilities.* The term "facility" includes motor vehicles, rolling stock, pipelines, and any other facility that is used or capable of being used for the purpose of processing, producing, storing, transferring, or transporting oil or hazardous polluting substances, but excludes vessels.

3. *Oil.* As used in this Annex, "oil" refers to oil of any kind or in any form, including, but not limited to petroleum, fuel oil, oil sludge, oil refuse, and oil mixed with wastes, but does not include constituents of dredged spoil.

4. *Principles.* Regulations shall be adopted for the prevention of discharges into the Great Lakes System of harmful quantities of oil and hazardous polluting substances from onshore and offshore facilities in accordance with the following principles:

(a) Discharges of harmful quantities of oil or hazardous polluting substances shall be prohibited and made subject to appropriate penalties;

(b) As soon as any person in charge has knowledge of any discharge of harmful quantities of oil or hazardous polluting substances, immediate notice of such discharge shall be given to the appropriate agency in the jurisdiction where the discharge occurs; failure to give this notice shall be made subject to appropriate penalties.

ANNEX 8

Joint Contingency Plan

1. *The Plan.* The Parties agree that the "Joint U.S.–Canadian Oil and Hazardous Materials Pollution Contingency Plan for the Great Lakes Region" adopted on June 10, 1971, shall be maintained in force, as amended from time to time. It shall be the responsibility of the United States Coast Guard and the Canadian Ministry of Transport to coordinate and to maintain the plan, as so amended, in written form.

2. *Purpose.* The purpose of the Plan is to provide for coordinated and integrated response to pollution incidents in the Great Lakes System by responsible federal, state, provincial, and local agencies. The Plan supplements the national, provincial and regional plans of the Parties.

3. *Pollution Incidents.*

(a) A pollution incident is a discharge, or an imminent threat of a discharge, of oil or any other substance, of such magnitude or significance as to require immediate response to contain, clean up, or dispose of the material.

(b) The objectives of the plan in pollution incidents are:

    (i)   to develop appropriate preparedness measures and effective systems for discovery and reporting the existence of a pollution incident within the area covered by the plan;

    (ii) to institute prompt measures to restrict the further spread of the pollutant;

    (iii) to provide adequate equipment to respond to pollution incidents.

4. *Funding.* Unless otherwise agreed, the costs of operations of both Parties under the Plan shall be borne by the Party in whose waters the pollution incident occurred.

5. *Amendment.* The United States Coast Guard and the Canadian Ministry of Transport are empowered to amend the Plan subject to the requirement that such amendments shall be consistent with the purpose and objectives of this Annex.

Text of Reference to the International Joint Commission to Study Pollution in the Great Lakes System from Agricultural, Forestry and Other Land Use Activities

I have the honour to inform you that the Governments of Canada and the United States of America, pursuant to Article IX of the Boundary Waters Treaty of 1909, have agreed to request the International Joint Commission to conduct a study of pollution of the boundary waters of the Great Lakes System from agricultural, forestry and other land use activities, in the light of the provision of Article IV of the Treaty which provides that the boundary waters and waters flowing across the boundary shall not be polluted on either side to the injury of health and property on the other side, and in the light also of the Great Lakes Water Quality Agreement signed on this date.

The Commission is requested to enquire into and report to the two Governments upon the following questions:

(1) Are the boundary waters of the Great Lakes System being polluted by land drainage (including ground and surface runoff and sediments) from agriculture, forestry, urban and industrial land development, recreational and park land development, utility and transportation systems and natural sources?

(2) If the answer to the foregoing question is in the affirmative, to what extent, by what causes, and in what localities is the pollution taking place?

(3) If the Commission should find that pollution of the character just referred to is taking place, what remedial measures would, in its judgement, be most practicable and what would be the probable cost thereof?

The Commission is requested to consider the adequacy of existing programs and control measures, and the need for improvements thereto, relating to:

(a) inputs of nutrients, pest control products, sediments, and other pollutants from the sources referred to above;

(b) land use;

(c) and fills, land dumping, and deep well disposal practices;

(d) confined livestock feeding operations and other animal husbandry operations; and

(e) pollution from other agricultural, forestry and land use sources.

In carrying out its study the Commission should identify deficiencies in technology and recommend actions for their correction.

The Commission should submit its report and recommendations to the two Governments as soon as possible and should submit reports from time to time on the progress of its investigation.

In the conduct of its investigation and otherwise in the performance of its duties under this reference, the Commission may utilize the services of qualified persons and other resources made available by the concerned agencies in Canada and the United States and should as far as possible make use of information and technical data heretofore acquired or which may become available during the course of the investigation, including information and data acquired by the Commission in the course of its investigations and surveillance activities conducted on the lower Great Lakes and in the connecting channels.

In conducting its investigation, the Commission should utilize the services of the international board structure provided for in Article VII of the Great Lakes Water Quality Agreement.

Text of Reference to the International Joint Commission
to Study Pollution Problems of Lake Huron and Lake Superior

I have the honour to inform you that the Governments of Canada and the United States of America, pursuant to Article IX of the Boundary Waters Treaty of 1909, have agreed to request the International Joint Commission to conduct a study of water quality in Lake Huron and Lake Superior, in the light of the provision of Article IV of the Treaty which provides that the boundary waters and waters flowing across the boundary shall not be polluted on either side to the injury of health and property on the other side, and in the light also of the Great Lakes Water Quality Agreement signed on this date. This reference represents the response of the two Governments to recommendation No. 20 of the Commission in its final report dated December 9, 1970, on pollution of Lake Erie, Lake Ontario, and the International Section of the St. Lawrence River.

The Commission is requested to enquire into and to report to the two Governments upon the following questions:

(1) Are the waters of Lake Superior and Lake Huron being polluted on either side of the boundary to an extent (a) which is causing or is likely to cause injury to health or property on the other side of the boundary; or (b) which is causing, or likely to cause, a degradation of existing levels of water quality in these two lakes or in downstream portions of the Great Lakes System?

(2) If the foregoing questions are answered in the affirmative, to what extent, by what causes, and in what localities is such pollution taking place?

(3) If the Commission should find that pollution of the character just referred to is taking place, what remedial measures would, in its judgement, be most practicable to restore and protect the quality of the waters, and what would be the probable cost?

(4) In the event that the Commission should find that little or no pollution of the character referred to is taking place at the present time, what preventive measures would, in its judgement, be most practicable to ensure that such pollution does not occur in the future and what would be the probable cost?

The Governments would welcome the recommendations of the Commission with respect to the general and specific water quality objectives that should be established for these lakes, and the programs and measures that are required in the two countries in order to achieve and maintain these water quality objectives.

The Commission should submit its report and recommendations to the two Governments as soon as possible and should submit reports from time to time on the progress of its investigation.

In the conduct of its investigation, the Commission is requested to include consideration of pollution entering Lake Huron and Lake Superior from tributary waters, including Lake Michigan, which affects water quality in the two lakes, and to enquire into and report on the upstream sources of such pollution. The Commission may utilize the services of qualified persons and other resources made available by water management agencies in Canada and the United States and should as far as possible make use of information and technical data heretofore acquired or which may become available during the course of the investigation, including information and data acquired by the Commission in the course of its investigations and surveillance activities conducted on the lower Great Lakes and in the connecting channels.

In conducting its investigation, the Commission should utilize the services of the international board structure provided for in Article VII of the Great Lakes Water Quality Agreement.

Terms of Reference for the Establishment of a Research Advisory Board

1. As used herein, "research" includes development, demonstration, and research activities, but does not include regular monitoring and surveillance of water quality.

2. The functions and responsibilities of the Research Advisory Board relating to research activities in Canada and the United States concerning the quality of the waters of the Great Lakes System shall be as follows:

   (a) To review at regular intervals these research activities in order to:

      (i) examine the adequacy and reliability of research results, their dissemination, and the effectiveness of their application;

      (ii) identify deficiencies in their scope and inadequacies in their funding and in completion schedules;

      (iii) identify additional research projects that should be undertaken;

      (iv) identify specific research programs for which international cooperation will be productive;

   (b) To provide advice and consolidations of scientific opinion to the Commission and its boards on particular problems referred to the Advisory Board by the Commission or its boards;

   (c) To facilitate both formal and informal international cooperation and coordination of research;

   (d) To make recommendations to the Commission.

3. The Research Advisory Board on its own authority may seek analyses, assessments, and recommendations from other professional, academic, governmental, or intergovernmental groups about the problems of the Great Lakes water quality research and related research activities.

4. The International Joint Commission shall determine the size and composition of the Research Advisory Board. The Commission should appoint members to the Advisory Board from appropriate Federal, State, and Provincial Government agencies and from other agencies, organizations, and institutions involved in Great Lakes research activities. In making these appointments the Commission should consider individuals

from the academic, scientific, and industrial communities and the general public. Membership should be based primarily upon an individual's qualifications and potential contribution to the work of the Advisory Board.

5. The Research Advisory Board should work at all times in close cooperation with the Great Lakes Water Quality Board.

✍ CANADIAN REGULATIONS ON PHOSPHORUS IN DETERGENTS

Detergents are the source of as much as fifty per cent of the phosphorus in municipal sewage discharged into the Lower Lakes, according to the 1970 Report of the International Joint Commission. The immediate reduction "to a minimum practicable level of the phosphorus content of detergents . . . with the aim of complete replacement of all phosphorus in detergents with environmentally less harmful materials by December 31, 1972," was one of the Commission's major recommendations.

Recognizing that eutrophication was emerging as a problem which affects lakes in many parts of Canada, and in anticipation of the International Joint Commission's report, the Canadian Government included in the Canada Water Act of 1970 provisions for the regulation of nutrients in laundry detergents. Regulations established in August 1970 placed a maximum limit on phosphorus in detergents of 20 per cent as phosphorus pentoxide (P_2O_5) or 8.7 per cent as elemental phosphorus; and it was announced that further restrictions were intended which would reduce this limitation to not more than five per cent as P_2O_5 at the end of 1972.

Considerable research has been carried out by industry on suitable replacement substances for phosphorus. A number of promising substitutes have been identified, several of which are currently in use. Although the need for replacement is minimal at the 20 per cent level, further restrictions are likely to lead to the introduction of substantial quantities of replacement substances in detergent formulations. Extensive research studies have been carried out by both government and industry, on possible health and environmental effects arising from the use of such replacements.

One such substance is sodium nitrilotriacetate (NTA). Earlier fears about its adverse health effects have been shown to be exaggerated, and investigations carried out in Canada through the winter of 1971–72 have shown that NTA is readily broken down in rivers and lakes to harmless constituents. Another replacement for phosphorus in detergents

Department of the Environment (Canada), April 15, 1972.

is sodium citrate, which is currently used in a few laundry products. In the light of its occurrence in many foods, and its ready biodegradability, adverse health or environmental effects from the use of citrate in detergents are generally regarded as highly unlikely.

Canadian restrictions on phosphorous in detergents have already achieved a significant reduction in the quantity of phosphorus entering lakes and rivers across the country. By this action phosphorus from detergent sources have been reduced by about thirty per cent; this represents a reduction of about fifteen per cent in the total amount of phosphorus entering the Great Lakes from municipal sources on the Canadian side. The Canadian detergent industry has been able to comply readily with the August 1970 regulations, and the present limitation on phosphorous levels in detergents has not significantly affected their laundering performance.

Parallel restrictions on phosphorus in detergents have been imposed by the States of New York, Michigan, and Indiana, as well as several local authorities on the United States side of the Great Lakes. Thus, a significant reduction in phosphorus levels in detergents used on the United States side has been achieved, or is in sight.

Canada's regulations to restrict the phosphorus content of detergents is designed to complement Canada's longer-range program of phosphorus removal at treatment plants. In the Great Lakes region the Canadian Government has taken action jointly with the Government of Ontario to accelerate construction programs for phosphorus removal facilities at municipal sewage treatment plants and at sources of industrial waste.

OTHER INTERNATIONAL RIVERS AND LAKES

☙ TREATY BETWEEN THE UNITED STATES OF AMERICA AND MEXICO RELATING TO THE UTILIZATION OF THE WATERS OF THE COLORADO AND TIJUANA RIVERS, AND OF THE RIO GRANDE (RIO BRAVO) FROM FORT QUITMAN, TEXAS, TO THE GULF OF MEXICO

❋ ❋ ❋

Article 2

The International Boundary Commission established pursuant to the provisions of the Convention between the United States and Mexico signed in Washington March 1, 1889 to facilitate the carrying out of the principles contained in the Treaty of November 12, 1884 and to avoid

Signed at Washington on February 3, 1944, and supplementary protocol, signed at Washington on November 14, 1944.

difficulties occasioned by reason of the changes which take place in the beds of the Rio Grande (Rio Bravo) and the Colorado River shall hereafter be known as the International Boundary and Water Commission, United States and Mexico, which shall continue to function for the entire period during which the present Treaty shall continue in force. Accordingly, the term of the Convention of March 1, 1889 shall be considered to be indefinitely extended, and the Convention of November 21, 1900 between the United States and Mexico regarding that Convention shall be considered completely terminated.

The application of the present Treaty, the regulation and exercise of the rights and obligations which the two Governments assume thereunder, and the settlement of all disputes to which its observance and execution may give rise are hereby entrusted to the International Boundary and Water Commission, which shall function in conformity with the powers and limitations set forth in this Treaty.

Article 3

In matters in which the Commission may be called upon to make provision for the joint use of international waters, the following order of preference shall serve as a guide:

1. Domestic and municipal uses.
2. Agriculture and stock-raising.
3. Electric power.
4. Other industrial uses.
5. Navigation.
6. Fishing and hunting.
7. Any other beneficial uses which may be determined by the commission.

All of the foregoing uses shall be subject to any sanitary measures or works which shall be mutually agreed upon by the two Governments, which hereby agree to give preferential attention to the solution of all mutual sanitation problems.

❊　❊　❊

☙ PROTOCOL BETWEEN FRANCE, BELGIUM AND LUXEMBOURG TO ESTABLISH A TRIPARTITE STANDING COMMITTEE ON POLLUTED WATERS

The Tripartite Committee on classified establishments, which met at Brussels from 4 to 8 April 1950, under the auspices of the Minister of Foreign Affairs, noting, on the one hand, that its work has resulted in

Signed at Brussels, on April 8, 1950; came into force on April 8, 1950.

the conclusion of an arrangement with regard to the problems raised by the installation in the vicinity of the frontier or *storage depots of explosive materials for civil use*, and, on the other hand, that its work in connexion with the problem of *water pollution* requires detailed technical study, hereby assumes the title of "Tripartite Standing Committee on Polluted Waters."

The Committee hereby sets up a joint technical sub-committee for the Espierre, which shall consist of:

For *France*, the following authorities of the Nord Department:
The Prefect or his representative, head of delegation.
The Departmental Chief Engineer of Bridges and Highways.
The Chief Engineer of Mines, in charge of the Mineralogical Division.
The Inspector of Classified Establishments.
The Inspector of Waters and Forests.

For *Belgium:*
The Governor of West Flanders or his representative, head of delegation.
The Chief of the Service of the Office of Water Purification.
The Chief Engineer, Director of Bridges and Highways of the Escaut (Scheldt), riverain section, West Flanders.
The Inspector of Waters and Forests, delegated by the Ministry of Agriculture.
The Chief Inspector, Director of Public Health.

Each delegation may be assisted by experts of its own choosing.
It is understood that any member of the Tripartite Standing Committee on Polluted Waters is entitled to take part in the work of the joint technical sub-committee.
The joint technical sub-committee shall have the following terms of reference:
(a) to define the pollution factors (industrial or communal origin, degree of intensity, etc.), collect any appropriate technical opinions, assess each State's share of responsibility for the pollution;
(b) to draw up a report for submission to the Tripartite Standing Committee on Polluted Waters on the action to be recommended.
The joint technical sub-committee for the Espierre is empowered to deal in the same way with the problems raised by the pollution of the waters of the Haine, the Escaut (Scheldt) and the Lys canals.
The joint technical sub-committee shall hold its first meeting within two months of the date of signature of this Protocol.
The discussions of the joint technical sub-committee shall take place

at Lille and at Courtrai alternately, and shall be under the chairmanship of the head of the host delegation. The first meeting shall be held at Lille at the request of the Prefect of the Nord Department.

The joint technical sub-committee shall establish its own agenda and rules of procedure; notwithstanding, every six months it shall furnish a report on the progress of its work to the Tripartite Standing Committee on Polluted Waters.

The report shall be addressed to the heads of the French, Belgian, and Luxembourg delegations through their respective Ministers of Foreign Affairs.

The Tripartite Standing Committee on Polluted Waters shall be required to meet immediately upon receiving each half-yearly report from the sub-committee. Its meetings shall take place at Brussels and Paris alternately.

The chairman and secretariat of each meeting shall be provided by the host delegation.

The Tripartite Standing Committee on Polluted Waters reserves the right to set up further technical sub-committees when it takes up the study of the pollution of other waterways deemed to be the cause of unhealthy conditions in the territory of one of the three signatory States.

▶ Treaty between the Kingdom of the Netherlands and the Federal Republic of Germany Concerning the Course of the Common Frontier, the Boundary Waters, Real Property Situated Near the Frontier, Traffic Crossing the Frontier on Land and via Inland Waters, and Other Frontier Questions (Frontier Treaty)

The Kingdom of the Netherlands and the Federal Republic of Germany have agreed on the following provisions:

❖　❖　❖

CHAPTER 4

Boundary Waters

Article 56

1. Boundary waters within the meaning of this chapter are surface waters, including their banks, which cross or, in some of their sections, form the frontier between the Netherlands and Germany.

Signed at the Hague, on April 8, 1960; came into force on August 1, 1963.

2. The provisions of this chapter shall not apply to the Rhine, the Ems, and the Dollard.

3. Corporations within the meaning of this chapter are the provinces, municipalities and associations of public law which have jurisdiction *ratione loci* in matters relating to the boundary waters in the territories of the Contracting Parties.

Article 57

The Contracting Parties agree to conduct regular consultations on all questions relating to the use and management of water resources in so far as they effect the boundary waters within the territory of the neighbouring State, with a view to solving such questions in a manner satisfactory to both Contracting Parties. Such consultations shall be held in the Permanent Boundary Waters Commission referred to in article 64 and its sub-commissions.

Article 58

1. The Contracting Parties undertake to give due regard, in the performance of their tasks in the field of water management, to the neighbouring State's interests in the boundary waters. To that end, they agree to take or to support all measures required to establish and to maintain within the sections of the boundary waters situated in their respective territories such orderly conditions as will mutually safeguard their interests, and they shall neither take nor tolerate any measures causing substantial prejudice to the neighbouring State.

2. In performing the obligations undertaken in paragraph 1, the Contracting Parties shall in particular take or support, within an appropriate period of time, all measures required:

(a) To secure and maintain the adequate drainage of the boundary waters, to the extent required in the interest of the neighbouring State;

(b) To prevent inundations and other damage resulting from the inadequate servicing of sluices and weirs;

(c) To prevent such diversion of water as may cause substantial prejudice to the neighbouring State;

(d) To prevent the excessive extraction of sand and other solid substances liable to cause substantial prejudice to the neighbouring State;

(e) To prevent such excessive pollution of the boundary waters as may substantially impair the customary use of the waters by the neighbouring State.

3. In addition, the Contracting Parties shall endeavour, within the limits of their financial resources, to effect such improvements in the use and management of the boundary waters within their respective territories as will serve their mutual interests, and to participate financially, where such participation is equitable, in measures taken in respect of the boundary waters within the territory of the neighbouring State.

Article 59

1. For the purpose of implementing the provisions laid down in this chapter, the Contracting Parties agree to conclude such special agreements in respect of individual boundary waters as may be required. Agreements of this kind may also be concluded between the Kingdom of the Netherlands, on the one hand, and, subject to the approval of the Government of the Federal Republic of Germany, *Länder* Lower Saxony and North Rhine-Westphalia, on the other hand.

2. Agreements of the type designated in paragraph 1 may also be concluded, subject to the approval of the Governments of the Contracting Parties, by corporations.

3. Existing agreements, in so far as they concern boundary waters, shall continue in effect, until such time as they are amended or supplemented, even if they are at variance with the provisions of this chapter.

Article 60

1. If it is intended to carry into effect, within the territory of one of the Contracting Parties, any measures which may substantially affect the use and management of water resources in the territory of the other Contracting Party, or to allow such measures to be carried into effect, the Permanent Boundary Waters Commission shall be notified thereof as soon as possible.

2. The Contracting Parties shall notify each other of the authorities or corporations within its territory which are competent to make the notification referred to in paragraph 1.

Article 61

Each of the Contracting Parties may within a reasonable period of time present to the Permanent Boundary Waters Commission its objections to any measures, whether proposed or already under way, or to any cases of non-performance of an obligation on the part of the other Contracting Party which are liable to cause, or have already caused, substantial damage; such objections must be founded on the fact or the expectation of a violation of obligations entered into.

Article 62

1. Each of the Contracting Parties shall be obligated, pending the conclusion of the deliberations of the Permanent Boundary Waters Commission or, as the case may be, of the deliberations between the two Governments, to suspend the execution of any measures planned by it to which objections have been raised by the other Party, unless the other Contracting Party consents to some other arrangement.

2. Paragraph 1 shall not apply if a Party to this Treaty cannot suspend the execution of the measures objected to without seriously endangering its interests. The rights of the other Contracting Party shall not be affected thereby.

Article 63

1. If one of the Contracting Parties, notwithstanding the objections raised by the other Party under the terms of article 61, acts in violation of its obligations under this chapter or arising under any of the special agreements to be concluded as provided in article 59, thereby causing damage within the territory of the other Contracting Party, it shall be liable for damages.

2. Liability for damages shall arise in respect only of such damage as was sustained after the objections were raised.

Article 64

For the purpose of promoting good-neighbourly co-operation in matters relating to boundary waters, the Contracting Parties establish a Permanent Netherlands–German Boundary Waters Commission.

Article 65

1. Each Government shall appoint three expert members of the Commission, each group including one chairman, and their deputies. The first members of the Commission shall be appointed within a period of three months following the entry into force of this Treaty.

2. The Commission shall meet at least once every year and may, either at its discretion or upon the proposal of one of the two chairmen, hold additional meetings. The meetings shall be held in the two States alternately. Additional experts may be invited to attend the meetings of the Commission.

3. The two chairmen may communicate direct with each other on questions relating to the boundary waters.

4. The Commission may adopt rules of procedure to govern the conduct of its business.

Article 66

1. It shall be the function of the Commission to deliberate jointly on all questions which may arise in the application of the provisions of this chapter and thereby to promote the implementation of the provisions of this chapter through mutual information and exchange of experience.

2. The Commission shall receive the notifications provided for in article 60, paragraph 1.

3. It shall consider suggestions, complaints and objections under article 61. It shall direct its efforts towards bringing about the amicable settlement of disputes by the Parties concerned.

4. It shall consider forthwith how far existing agreements relating to matters within its jurisdictions are in need of amendment or supplementation and shall make recommendations for the modification of existing and the conclusion of new agreements.

5. It shall discuss the question of contributions by one Contracting Party towards the costs of measures carried out by the other Party.

6. It shall be authorized to inspect boundary waters. It shall, through the intermediary of its chairmen, receive from the authorities of both Contracting Parties such information as it may require in the exercise of its powers and the discharge of its functions.

7. It shall be authorized, within its terms of reference, to make recommendations to Governments and corporations.

8. It shall, in particular, seek to formulate recommendations in cases in which objections are submitted by the Contracting Parties in accordance with the provisions of article 61.

Article 67

1. If, in a case covered by article 66, paragraph 8, the commission fails to reach agreement on a recommendation, the two Governments shall endeavour to come to an agreement.

2. If such attempt fails, or if the Governments are unable to reach an agreement despite a recommendation of the Commission, either Government may bring the matter before the arbitral tribunal.

Article 68

1. The Commission shall decide to establish sub-commissions for individual boundary waters if the need therefor arises; the members of the sub-commission shall be appointed on a basis of parity.

2. The sub-commissions shall include representatives of the local authorities and corporations.

3. The sub-commissions shall, within their respective jurisdictions, exercise the same functions as the Commission; they shall report to the latter on their activities. The right to receive and to consider objections and the right of recommendation shall be reserved to the Commission.

Article 69

An arbitral tribunal having jurisdiction, to the exclusion of all other contractual provisions for the settlement of disputes, shall be established for the settlement of all disputes between the Contracting Parties which involve the interpretation or application of the provisions of this chapter and of the special agreements to be concluded pursuant to article 59.

Article 70

1. The arbitral tribunal shall be composed of a permanent umpire and two arbitrators appointed for each individual case. If the umpire ceases to discharge his functions or is prevented from discharging them, they shall be performed by a deputy.

2. Neither the umpire nor his deputy shall be a national of either Contracting Party. They shall not be persons having their ordinary residence in the territory of either Contracting Party or persons in the service of such Party.

3. The Governments of the Contracting Parties shall appoint the umpire and his deputy by mutual agreement, choosing them from among persons who possess the qualifications required in their respective countries for appointment to judicial offices or are otherwise qualified to discharge these functions by virtue of their special competence as jurisconsults.

4. The terms of office of the umpire and his deputy shall be five years, save in the case of the first deputy umpire to be appointed after the entry into force of this Treaty, who shall be so appointed for a term of six years. Thereafter, the terms of office shall be deemed extended successively by five-year periods unless the Government of one of the Contracting Parties notifies the Government of the other Party before the expiration of such term of office of its wish for the appointment of another umpire or deputy umpire.

5. If no agreement is reached by the Governments on the choice of an umpire or his deputy within three months after the entry into force of this Treaty, the President of the International Court of Justice at The Hague may be requested by the two Governments jointly, or by one of them, to appoint an umpire or his deputy. If the President is prevented from acting or if he is a national of one of the Contracting Parties, the appointment shall be made by the Vice-President, and if the latter is

also prevented or is a national of one of the Contracting Parties, the appointment shall be made by the senior member of the International Court of Justice not prevented from acting who is not a national of either Contracting Party. The same method shall be applied if, after the expiration of the terms of office, no agreement is reached by the Governments on the appointment of a new umpire or deputy umpire.

6. If, before the expiration of their terms of office, the umpire or his deputy cease to fulfil the conditions laid down in paragraph 2 above, or in the case of their separation for some other reason, a successor, who shall be a person fulfilling the conditions laid down in paragraphs 2 and 3, shall be appointed for the unexpired portion of the term. The appointment procedure shall be subject *mutatis mutandis* to paragraph 5; any extension of the successor's term of office shall be governed by the second sentence of paragraph 4.

7. As soon as the umpire addresses to the Governments the communication provided for in article 71, paragraph 3, each of the Governments shall appoint an arbitrator. If a Government fails to appoint an arbitrator within one month after the date of the communication provided for in article 71, paragraph 3, the other Government may request the President of the International Court of Justice to appoint an arbitrator for the vacant seat. The second sentence of paragraph 5 shall apply *mutatis mutandis*.

8. In the event of an arbitrator's separation from the arbitral tribunal, the vacancy shall be filled by the application *mutatis mutandis* of the procedure laid down in paragraph 7.

9. The arbitral tribunal shall itself determine the place of its meetings. It shall be assisted by two secretaries; each Government shall appoint one of these secretaries.

Article 71

1. If the Government of one of the Contracting Parties wishes to refer a dispute to the arbitral tribunal for adjudication, it shall submit to the umpire a statement of claim, at the same time sending a copy of such statement to the other Contracting Party.

2. If the Governments of the two Contracting Parties, availing themselves of the provisions of article 69, wish to refer a dispute to the arbitral tribunal by mutual agreement, they shall file with the umpire an arbitration agreement (*compromis*) in which they have formulated the point at issue.

3. The umpire shall first discuss the difference with the two Governments with a view to bringing about a settlement. If he considers his efforts to have failed he shall inform the two Governments accordingly.

Article 72

1. In deciding upon a case, the arbitral tribunal shall apply the provisions of this chapter and of the special agreements to be concluded pursuant to article 59, and the general principles of international law.

2. The procedure before the arbitral tribunal shall be governed by the provisions of articles 63 to 82 of the Hague Convention for the Pacific Settlement of International Disputes of 18 October 1907,* to the extent to which they are applicable.

3. In urgent cases, the umpire may, upon the motion of one of the two Governments, order interim measures to be taken even before the appointment of the arbitrators. Upon the motion of one of the two Governments, the arbitral tribunal shall decide whether the interim measure ordered by the umpire shall be revoked. The arbitral tribunal shall be authorized to order interim measures to be taken after hearing the Parties.

FINAL PROTOCOL TO THE TREATY

* * *

Article 10

All matters affected by the provisions of chapter 4 of the Treaty shall be adjudicated:
In the Federal Republic of Germany, in accordance with the water-conservancy laws of the Federation and the *Länder;*
In the Kingdom of the Netherlands, in accordance with the State and provincial water-conservancy laws, including the by-laws relating to drainage districts.

Article 11

The Governments of the Contracting Parties shall endeavour to ensure that the agreements provided for in article 59, paragraph 2, of the Treaty are concluded within a reasonable period of time.

Article 12

Under the terms of article 56, paragraph 2, of the Treaty, the Rhine does not form part of the frontier waters covered by the provisions of

---

* J. B. Scott, *The Hague Peace Conferences of 1899 and 1907,* Vol. 2, Documents, p. 309; and League of Nations, *Treaty Series,* Vol. LIV, p. 435, and Vol. CXXXIV, p. 453.

chapter 4 of the Treaty. The Governments of the Contracting Parties nevertheless declare that they will strive for the early conclusion of an arrangement between the riverain States to prevent pollution of the Rhine.

⚡ THE INDUS WATERS TREATY CONCLUDED BETWEEN INDIA AND PAKISTAN

PREAMBLE: The Government of India and the Government of Pakistan, being equally desirous of attaining the most complete and satisfactory utilisation of the waters of the Indus system of rivers and recognising the need, therefore, of fixing and delimiting, in a spirit of goodwill and friendship, the rights and obligations of each in relation to the other concerning the use of these waters and of making provision for the settlement, in a cooperative spirit, of all such questions as may hereafter arise in regard to the interpretation or application of the provisions agreed upon herein, have resolved to conclude a Treaty in furtherance of these objectives, ...

ARTICLE 1: *Definitions.* As used in this Treaty:

❀ ❀ ❀

(9) The term "Agricultural Use" means the use of water for irrigation, except for irrigation of household gardens and public recreational gardens.

(10) The term "Domestic Use" means the use of water for:
- (a) Drinking, washing, bathing, recreation, sanitation (including the conveyance and dilution of sewage and of industrial and other wastes), stock and poultry, and other like purposes;
- (b) Household and municipal purposes (including use for household gardens and public recreational gardens); and
- (c) Industrial purposes (including mining, milling and other like purposes);

but the term does not include Agricultural Use or use for the generation of hydro-electric power.

❀ ❀ ❀

(15) The term "interference with the waters" means:
- (a) Any act of withdrawal therefrom; or
- (b) Any man-made obstruction to their flow which causes a change in the volume (within the practical range of measurement) of the daily flow of the waters: Provided however that an obstruction

Signed at Karachi on September 19, 1960.

which involves only an insignificant and incidental change in the volume of the daily flow, for example, fluctuations due to afflux caused by bridge piers or a temporary by-pass, etc., shall not be deemed to be an interference with the waters.

(16) The term "Effective Date" means the date on which this Treaty takes effect in accordance with the provisions of Article XII, that is, the first of April 1960.

ARTICLE 2: *Provisions regarding Eastern Rivers*

(1) All the waters of the Eastern Rivers shall be available for the unrestricted use of India, except as otherwise expressly provided in this Article.

(2) Except for Domestic Use and Non-Consumptive Use, Pakistan shall be under an obligation to let flow, and shall not permit any interference with, the waters of the Sutlej Main and the Ravi Main in the reaches where these rivers flow in Pakistan and have not yet finally crossed into Pakistan.

* * *

(3) Except for Domestic Use, Non-Consumptive Use and Agricultural Use . . ., Pakistan shall be under an obligation to let flow, and shall not permit any interference with, the waters (while flowing in Pakistan) of any Tributary which in its natural course joins the Sutlej Main or the Ravi Main before these rivers have finally crossed into Pakistan.

* * *

ARTICLE 3: *Provisions regarding Western Rivers*

(1) Pakistan shall receive for unrestricted use all those waters of the Western Rivers which India is under obligation to let flow under the provisions of Paragraph (2).

(2) India shall be under an obligation to let flow all the waters of the Western Rivers, and shall not permit any interference with these waters, except for the following uses, restricted . . . in the case of each of the rivers, The Indus, the Jhelum and the Chenab, to the drainage basin thereof:
  (a) Domestic Use;
  (b) Non-Consumptive Use;
  (c) Agricultural Use, as set out in Annexure C [not reproduced here]; and
  (d) Generation of hydro-electric power, as set out in Annexure D [not reproduced here].

(3) Pakistan shall have the unrestricted use of all waters originating from sources other than the Eastern Rivers which are delivered by Pakistan into The Ravi or The Sutlej, and India shall not make use of these waters. Each Party agrees to establish such discharge observation stations and make such observations as may be considered necessary by the Commission for the determination of the component of water available for the use of Pakistan on account of the aforesaid deliveries by Pakistan.

❊   ❊   ❊

ARTICLE 4: *Provisions regarding Eastern Rivers and Western Rivers*

❊   ❊   ❊

(3) Nothing in this Treaty shall be construed as having the effect of preventing either Party from undertaking schemes of drainage, river training, conservation of soil against erosion and dredging, or from removal of stones, gravel or sand from the beds of the Rivers: Provided that

(a) In executing any of the schemes mentioned above, each Party will avoid, as far as practicable, any material damage to the other Party;

(b) Any such scheme carried out by India on the Western Rivers shall not involve any use of water or any storage in addition to that provided under Article III;

(c) Except as provided in Paragraph (5) and Article VII (1) (b), India shall not take any action to increase the catchment area, beyond the area on the Effective Date, of any natural or artificial drainage or drain which crosses into Pakistan, and shall not undertake such construction or remodeling of any drainage or drain which so crosses or falls into a drainage or drain as might cause material damage in Pakistan or entail the construction of a new drain or enlargement of an existing drainage or drain in Pakistan; and

(d) Should Pakistan desire to increase the catchment area, beyond the area on the Effective Date, of any natural or artificial drainage or drain, which receives drainage waters from India, or except in an emergency, to pour any waters into it in excess of the quantities received by it as on the Effective Date, Pakistan shall, before undertaking any work for these purposes, increase the capacity of that drainage or drain to the extent necessary so as not to impair its efficacy for dealing with drainage waters received from India as on the Effective Date.

❊   ❊   ❊

(8) The use of the natural channels of the Rivers for the discharge of flood or other excess waters shall be free and not subject to limitation by either Party, and neither Party shall have any claim against the other in respect of any damage caused by such use. Each Party agrees to communicate to the other Party, as far in advance as practicable, any information it may have in regard to such extraordinary discharges of water from reservoirs and flood flows as may affect the other Party.

(9) Each Party declares its intention to operate its storage dams, barrages and irrigation canals in such manner, consistent with the normal operations of its hydraulic systems, as to avoid, as far as feasible, material damage to the other Party.

(10) Each Party declares its intention to prevent, as far as practicable, undue pollution of the waters of the Rivers which might affect adversely uses similar in nature to those to which the waters were put on the Effective Date, and agrees to take all reasonable measures to ensure that, before any sewage or industrial waste is allowed to flow into the Rivers, it will be treated, where necessary, in such manner as not materially to affect those uses: Provided that the criterion of reasonableness shall be the customary practice in similar situations on the Rivers.

(11) The Parties agree to adopt, as far as feasible, appropriate measures for the recovery, and restoration to owners, of timber and other property floated or floating down the Rivers, subject to appropriate charges being paid by the owners.

(12) The use of water for industrial purposes under Articles II (2), II (3), and III (2) shall not exceed:
  (a) In the case of an industrial process known on the Effective Date, such quantum of use as was customary in that process on the Effective Date;
  (b) In the case of an industrial process not known on the Effective Date:
    (i) Such quantum of use as was customary on the Effective Date in similar or in any way comparable industrial processes; or
    (ii) If there was no industrial process on the Effective Date similar or in any way comparable to the new process, such quantum of use as would not have a substantially adverse effect on the other Party.

(13) Such part of any water withdrawn for Domestic Use under the provisions of Articles II (3) and III (2) as is subsequently applied to Agricultural Use shall be accounted for as part of the Agricultural Use spe-

cified in Annexure B [not reproduced here] and Annexure C [not reproduced here] respectively; each Party will use its best endeavours to return to the same river (directly or through one of its Tributaries) all water withdrawn therefrom for industrial purposes and not consumed either in the industrial processes for which it was withdrawn or in some other Domestic Use.

(14) In the event that either Party should develop a use of the waters of the Rivers which is not in accordance with the provisions of this Treaty, that Party shall not acquire by reason of such use any right, by prescription or otherwise, to a continuance of such use.

* * *

ARTICLE VIII: *Permanent Indus Commission*
(1) India and Pakistan shall each create a permanent post of Commissioner for Indus Waters, and shall appoint to this post, as often as a vacancy occurs, a person who should ordinarily be a high-ranking engineer competent in the field of hydrology and water-use. Unless either Government should decide to take up any particular question directly with the other Government, each Commissioner will be the representative of his Government for all matters arising out of this Treaty, and will serve as the regular channel of communication on all matters relating to the implementation of the Treaty, and, in particular, with respect to
   (a) The furnishing or exchange of information or data provided for in the Treaty; and
   (b) The giving of any notice or response to any notice provided for in the Treaty.
(2) The status of each Commissioner and his duties and responsibilities towards his Government will be determined by that Government.
(3) The two Commissioners shall together form the Permanent Indus Commission.

(4) The purpose and functions of the Commission shall be to establish and maintain co-operative arrangements for the implementation of this Treaty, to promote co-operation between the Parties in the development of the waters of the Rivers and, in particular,
   (a) To study and report to the two Governments on any problem relating to the development of the waters of the Rivers which may be jointly referred to the Commission by the Two Governments: in the event that a reference is made by one Government alone, the Commissioner of the other Government shall obtain the authorization of his Government before he proceeds to act on the reference;

(b) To make every effort to settle promptly, in accordance with the provisions of Article IX (1), any question arising thereunder;

(c) To undertake, once in every five years, a general tour of inspection of the Rivers for ascertaining the facts connected with various developments and works on the Rivers;

(d) To undertake promptly, at the request of either Commissioner, a tour of inspection of such works or sites on the Rivers as may be considered necessary by him for ascertaining the facts connected with those works or sites . . . .

* * *

ARTICLE 9: *Settlement of differences and disputes*
(1) Any question which arises between the Parties concerning the interpretation or application of this Treaty or the existence of any fact which, if established, might constitute a breach of this Treaty shall first be examined by the Commission, which will endeavour to resolve the question by agreement.

* * *

ARTICLE 11: *General provisions*
(1) It is expressly understood that
(a) This Treaty governs the rights and obligations of each Party in relation to the other with respect only to the use of the waters of the Rivers and matters incidental thereto; and

(b) Nothing contained in this Treaty, and nothing arising out of the execution thereof, shall be construed as constituting a recognition or waiver (whether tacit, by implication or otherwise) of any rights or claims whatsoever of either of the Parties other than those rights or claims which are expressly recognized or waived in this Treaty.

Each of the Parties agrees that it will not invoke this Treaty, anything contained therein, or anything arising out of the execution thereof, in support of any of its own rights or claims whatsoever or in disputing any of the rights or claims whatsoever of the other Party, other than those rights or claims which are expressly recognized or waived in this Treaty.

(2) Nothing in this Treaty shall be construed by the Parties as in any way establishing any general principle of law or any precedent.

(3) The rights and obligations of each Party under this Treaty shall remain unaffected by any provisions contained in, or by anything arising out of the execution of, any agreement establishing the Indus Basin Development Fund.

✍ CONVENTION ENTRE LE PAYS DE BADE-WURTEMBERG, L'ETAT LIBRE DE BAVIÈRE, LA RÉPUBLIQUE D'AUTRICHE ET LA CONFÉDÉRATION SUISSE, SUR LA PROTECTION DU LAC DE CONSTANCE CONTRE LA POLLUTION, CONCLUE À STECKBORN, LE 27 OCTOBRE 1960

Désireux de protéger, par des efforts communs, le lac de Constance contre la pollution, ont résolu de conclure une convention

✿ ✿ ✿

ARTICLE PREMIER. 1. Les Etats riverains du lac de Constance, à savoir le Pays de Bade-Wurtemberg, l'Etat libre de Bavière, la République d'Autriche et la Confédération suisse (cantons de Saint-Gall et de Thurgovie), s'engagent à collaborer dans le domaine de la protection des eaux du lac de Constance contre la pollution.

2. Les Etats riverains prendront sur leur territoire les mesures nécessaires en vue de prévenir une augmentation de la pollution du lac de Constance et d'améliorer autant que possible l'état sanitaire de ses eaux. A cet effet, ils appliqueront strictement, en ce qui concerne le lac de Constance et ses affluents, les dispositions sur la protection des eaux qui sont en vigueur sur leur territoire.

3. En particulier, les Etats riverains se communiqueront mutuellement, en temps opportun, les projets d'utilisation d'eau dont la réalisation pourrait porter atteinte aux intérêts d'un autre Etat riverain en ce qui concerne le maintien de la salubrité des eaux du lac de Constance. Ces projets ne seront realisés qu'après avoir été discutés commun par les Etats riverains, à moins qu'il n'y ait péril en la demeure ou que les autres Etats n'aient consenti expressément à leur exécution immédiate.

ARTICLE 2. Par lac de Constance au sens de la présente convention il faut entendre le lac Supérieur et le lac Inférieur.

ARTICLE 3. 1. La collaboration entre les Etats riverains est assurée par la commission internationale permanente pour la protection des eaux du lac de Constance (dénommée ci-après la commission) instituée par ces Etats.

2. Chaque Etat riverain est représenté au sein de la commission par une délégation qui dispose d'une voix.

3. Le gouvernement de la République fédérale d'Allemagne peut envoyer des observateurs aux séances de la commission.

4. Chaque délégation a le droit de s'adjoindre des experts.

5. La commission peut aussi confier à des experts des tâches particulières nettement définies.

Came into force on November 10, 1961.

ARTICLE 4. La commission a les tâches suivantes:

a. Elle détermine l'état sanitaire du lac de Constance et les causes de sa pollution.

b. Elle contrôle régulièrement l'état sanitaire des eaux du lac de Constance.

c. Elle discute de mesures propres à remédier à la pollution actuelle et à prévenir toute pollution future du lac de Constance et les recommande aux Etats riverains.

d. Elle discute des mesures que projette de prendre un Etat riverain conformément à l'article premier, paragraphe 3 ci-dessus.

e. Elle examine la possiblité de mettre sur pied une réglementation visant à maintenir le lac de Constance à l'abri de la pollution; elle discute du contenu éventuel d'une telle réglementation qui, le cas échéant, fera l'objet d'une autre convention entre les Etats riverains.

f. Elle s'occupe de toute autre question concernant la lutte contre la pollution du lac de Constance.

ARTICLE 5. 1. La commission prend ses décisions à l'unanimité en présence de toutes les délégatinstions. Pour les questions de procédure, la majorité simple suffit.

2. Un Etat riverain peut s'abstenir de voter dans des affaires qui ne le concernent pas, sans qu'il soit dérogé par là à la règle de l'unanimité. Les décisions se rapportant exclusivement au lac Inférieur exigent seulement l'accord des délégations de la Confédération suisse et du Pays de Bade-Wurtemberg.

3. La commission établit son règlement interne; il est adopté à l'unanimité.

4. Les chefs des délégations correspondent entre eux directement.

ARTICLE 6. 1. Les Etats riverains s'engagent à examiner avec soin les mesures de protection des eaux touchant leur territoire qui font l'objet de recommandations de la commission et à s'employer de leur mieux à faire appliquer ces mesures dans les limites de leur législation interne.

2. Les Etats riverains sur le territoire desquels des mesures de protection des eaux faisant l'objet de recommandations de la commission doivent être prises peuvent reconnaître comme obligatoire en ce qui les concerne une recommandation de la commission et charger leur délégation de faire une déclaration dans ce sens.

ARTICLE 7. Chaque Etat riverain assume les frais de sa délégation et de ses experts. Si des experts sont désignés par la commission, les frais qui en résultent seront répartis entre les Etats riverains selon une clé qui sera fixée dans chaque cas par la commission. Il en va de même des publications de la commission.

ARTICLE 8. 1. Les accords internationaux sur la navigation et la pêche ne sont pas touchés par la présente convention.

2. Dans son champ d'activité, la commission collabore avec les organes internationaux compétents en matière de navigation et de pêche ainsi qu'avec la commission internationale pour la protection du Rhin contre la pollution.

Suggested Reading List

Bloomfield, L. M., and Fitzgerald, G. F., *Boundary Waters Problems of Canada and the United States* (1958).

Berber, F. J., *Rivers in International Law* (1959).

Bédard, Charles, *Le Régime Juridique des Grands Lacs de l'Amérique du Nord et du Saint-Laurent* (1966).

Gorove, Stephen, *Law and Politics of the Danube: An Interdisciplinary Study* (1965).

Teclaff, Ludwik A., *The River Basin in History and Law* (1967).

Garretson, A. H., Hayton, R. D., and Olmstead, C. J., eds., *The Law of International Drainage Basins* (1967).

Piper, Don. C., *The International Law of the Great Lakes: A Study of Canadian–United States Co-operation* (1967).

Eagleton, Clyde, "The Use of the Waters of International Rivers," 33 *Can. Bar Rev.* 1018 (1955).

Austin, Jacob, "Canadian–United States Practice and Theory Respecting the International Law of International Rivers: A Study of the History and Influence of the Harmon Doctrine," 37 *Can. Bar Rev.* 393 (1959).

Adams, Milton P., "Water Pollution Control in the Great Lakes Region," 37 *Univ. Detroit L.J.* 96 (1959–1960).

Dobbert, J. P., "Water Pollution and International River Law," 35 *Y.B. of Amer. Arb. Assoc.* 60 (1965).

Wheeler, Virginia M., "Co-operation for Development in Lower Mekong Basin," 64 *Amer. J. Int'l. L.* 594 (1970).

Jordan, Fred J. E., "Great Lakes Pollution: A Framework for Action," 5 *Ottawa L. Rev.* 65 (1971).

Bourne, Charles, "International Law and Pollution of International Rivers and Lakes," 6 *Univ. Brit. Colum. L.R.* 115 (1971).

Bilder, Richard B., "Controlling Great Lakes Pollution: A Study in United States–Canadian Environmental Co-operation," 70 *Mich. L. Rev. 469 (1972).*

Air Pollution

⚡ TRAIL SMELTER CASE

PARTIES: United States of America, Canada.

SPECIAL AGREEMENT: Convention of Ottawa, April 15, 1935.

ARBITRATORS: Charles Warren (U.S.A.), Robert A. E. Greenshields (Canada), Jan Frans Hostie (Belgium).

AWARD: April 16, 1938, and March 11, 1941.

Special Agreement.

CONVENTION FOR SETTLEMENT OF DIFFICULTIES ARISING FROM OPERATION OF
SMELTER AT TRAIL, B.C.

The President of the United States of America, and His Majesty the King of Great Britain, Ireland and the British dominions beyond the Seas, Emperor of India, in respect of the Dominion of Canada,

Considering that the Government of the United States has complained to the Government of Canada that fumes discharged from the smelter of the Consolidated Mining and Smelting Company at Trail, British Columbia, have been causing damage in the State of Washington, and

Considering further that the International Joint Commission, established pursuant to the Boundary Waters Treaty of 1909, investigated problems arising from the operation of the smelter at Trail and rendered a report and recommendations thereon, dated February 28, 1931, and

Recognizing the desirability and necessity of effecting a permanent settlement

Have decided to conclude a convention for the purposes aforesaid. . . .

ARTICLE I.

The Government of Canada will cause to be paid to the Secretary of State of the United States, to be deposited in the United States Treasury,

Signed at Ottawa, April 15, 1935; ratifications exchanged Aug. 3, 1935.

within three months after ratifications of this convention have been exchanged, the sum of three hundred and fifty thousand dollars, United States currency, in payment of all damages which occurred in the United States, prior to the first day of January, 1932, as a result of the operation of the Trail Smelter.

ARTICLE II.

The Governments of the United States and of Canada, hereinafter referred to as "the Governments", mutually agree to constitute a tribunal hereinafter referred to as "the Tribunal", for the purpose of deciding the questions referred to it under the provisions of Article III. The Tribunal shall consist of a chairman and two national members.

The chairman shall be a jurist of repute who is neither a British subject nor a citizen of the United States. He shall be chosen by the Governments, or, in the event of failure to reach agreement within nine months after the exchange of ratifications of this convention, by the President of the Permanent Administrative Council of the Permanent Court of Arbitration at The Hague described in Article 49 of the Convention for the Pacific Settlement of International Disputes concluded at The Hague on October 18, 1907.

The two national members shall be jurists of repute who have not been associated, directly or indirectly, in the present controversy. One member shall be chosen by each of the Governments.

The Governments may each designate a scientist to assist the Tribunal.

ARTICLE III.

The Tribunal shall finally decide the questions, hereinafter referred to as "the Questions", set forth hereunder, namely:

(1) Whether damages caused by the Trail Smelter in the State of Washington has occurred since the first day of January, 1932, and, if so, what indemnity should be paid therefor?

(2) In the event of the answer to the first part of the preceding Question being in the affirmative, whether the Trail Smelter should be required to refrain from causing damage in the State of Washington in the future and, if so, to what extent?

(3) In the light of the answer to the preceding Question, what measures or régime, if any, should be adopted or maintained by the Trail Smelter?

(4) What indemnity or compensation, if any, should be paid on account of any decision or decisions rendered by the Tribunal pursuant to the next two preceding Questions?

ARTICLE IV.

The Tribunal shall apply the law and practice followed in dealing with cognate questions in the United States of America as well as international law and practice, and shall give consideration to the desire of the high contracting parties to reach a solution just to all parties concerned.

*   *   *

ARTICLE VIII.

The Tribunal shall hear such representations and shall receive and consider such evidence, oral or documentary, as may be presented by the Governments or by interested parties, and for that purpose shall have power to administer oaths. The Tribunal shall have authority to make such investigations as it may deem necessary and expedient, consistent with other provisions of this convention.

ARTICLE IX.

The Chairman shall preside at all hearings and other meetings of the Tribunal and shall rule upon all questions of evidence and procedure. In reaching a final determination of each or any of the Questions, the Chairman and the two members shall each have one vote, and, in the event of difference, the opinion of the majority shall prevail, and the dissent of the Chairman or member, as the case may be, shall be recorded. In the event that no two members of the Tribunal agree on a question, the Chairman shall make the decision.

*   *   *

ARTICLE XI.

The Tribunal shall report to the Governments its final decisions, together with the reasons on which they are based, as soon as it has reached its conclusions in respect to the Questions, and within a period of three months after the conclusions of proceedings. Proceedings shall be deemed to have been concluded when the Agents of the two Governments jointly inform the Tribunal that they have nothing additional to present. Such period may be extended by agreement of the two Governments.

Upon receiving such report, the Governments may make arrangements for the disposition of claims for indemnity for damage, if any, which may occur subsequently to the period of time covered by such report.

Article XII.

The Governments undertake to take such action as may be necessary in order to ensure due performance of the obligations undertaken hereunder, in compliance with the decision of the Tribunal.

Article XIII.

Each Government shall pay the expenses of the presentation and conduct of its case before the Tribunal and the expenses of its national member and scientific assistant.

All other expenses, which by their nature are a charge on both Governments, including the honorarium of the neutral member of the Tribunal, shall be borne by the two Governments in equal moieties.

* * *

TRAIL SMELTER ARBITRAL TRIBUNAL

Decision

REPORTED ON APRIL 16, 1938, TO THE GOVERNMENT OF THE UNITED STATES OF AMERICA AND TO THE GOVERNMENT OF THE DOMINION OF CANADA UNDER THE CONVENTION SIGNED APRIL 15, 1935.

* * *

In all the consideration which the Tribunal has given to the problems presented to it, and in all the conclusions which it has reached, it has been guided by that primary purpose of the Convention expressed in the words of Article IV, that the Tribunal "shall give consideration to the desire of the high contracting parties to reach a solution just to all parties concerned", and further expressed in the opening paragraph of the Convention as to the "desirability and necessity of effecting a permanent settlement" of the controversy.

The controversy is between two Governments involving damage occurring in the territory of one of them (the United States of America) and alleged to be due to an agency situated in the territory of the other (the Dominion of Canada), for which damage the latter has assumed by the Convention an international responsibility. In this controversy, the Tribunal is not sitting to pass upon claims presented by individuals or on behalf of one or more individuals by their Government, although individuals may come within the meaning of "parties concerned", in Article IV and of "interested parties", in Article VIII of the Convention and although the damage suffered by individuals may, in part, "afford a convenient scale for the calculation of the reparation due to the State" (see Judgment No. 13, Permanent Court of International Justice, Series A, No. 17, pp. 27, 28).

PART ONE.

By way of introduction to the Tribunal's decision, a brief statement, in general terms, of the topographic and climatic conditions and economic history of the locality involved in the controversy may be useful.

The Columbia River has its source in the Dominion of Canada. At a place in British Columbia named Trail, it flows past a smelter located in a gorge, where zinc and lead are smelted in large quantities. From Trail, its course is easterly and then it swings in a long curve to the International Boundary Line, at which point it is running in a southwesterly direction; and its course south of the boundary continues in that general direction. The distance from Trail to the boundary line is about seven miles as the crow flies or about eleven miles, following the course of the river (and possibly a slightly shorter distance by following the contour of the valley). At Trail and continuing down to the boundary and for a considerable distance below the boundary, mountains rise on either side of the river in slopes of various angles to heights ranging from 3,000 to 4,500 feet above sea-level, or between 1,500 to 3,000 feet above the river. The width of the valley proper is between one and two miles. On both sides of the river are a series of bench lands at various heights.

More or less half way between Trail and the boundary is a place, on the east side of the river, known as Columbia Gardens; at the boundary on the American side of the line and on the east side of the river, is a place known as Boundary; and four or five miles south of the boundary on the east bank of the river is a farm named after its owner, Stroh farm. These three places are specially noted since they are the locations of automatic sulphur dioxide recorders installed by one or other of the Governments. The town of Northport is located on the east bank of the river, about nineteen miles from Trail by the river, and about thirteen miles as the crow flies, and automatic sulphur dioxide recorders have been installed here and at a point on the west bank northerly of Northport. It is to be noted that mountains extending more or less in an easterly and westerly direction rise to the south between Trail and the boundary.

✿   ✿   ✿

In 1896, a smelter was started under American auspices near the locality known as Trail. In 1906, the Consolidated Mining and Smelting Company of Canada, Limited, obtained a charter of incorporation from the Canadian authorities, and that company acquired the smelter plant at Trail as it then existed. Since that time, the Canadian Company, without interruption, has operated the Smelter, and from time to time has greatly added to the plant until it has become one of the best and largest equipped smelting plants on this continent. In 1925 and 1927, two stacks of the plant were erected to 409 feet in height and the Smelter greatly increased its daily smelting of zinc and lead ores. This increased product resulted in more sulphur dioxide fumes and higher concentrations being emitted into the air; and it is claimed by one Government (though denied by the other) that the added height of the stacks increased the area of damage in the United States. In 1916, about 5,000 tons of sulphur per month were emitted; in 1924, about 4,700 tons; in 1926, about 9,000 tons —an amount which rose near to 10,000 tons per month in 1930. In other words, about 300-350 tons of sulphur were being emitted daily in 1930. (It is to be noted that one ton of sulphur is substantially the equivalent of two tons of sulphur dioxide or SO_2.)

From 1925, at least, to the end of 1931, damage occurred in the State of Washington, resulting from the sulphur dioxide emitted from the Trail Smelter.

❄   ❄   ❄

It has been contended that either by virtue of the Constitution of the State of Washington or of a statute of that State, the Trail Smelter (a Canadian corporation) was unable to acquire ownership or smoke easements over real estate, in the State of Washington, in any manner. In regard to this statement, either as to the fact or as to the law, the Tribunal expresses no opinion and makes no ruling.

The subject of fumigations and damage claimed to result from them was first taken up officially by the Government of the United States in June, 1927, in a communication from the Consul General of the United States at Ottawa, addressed to the Government of the Dominion of Canada.

In December, 1927, the United States Government proposed to the Canadian Government that problems growing out of the operation of the Smelter at Trail should be referred to the International Joint Commission, United States and Canada, for investigation and report, pursuant to Article IX of the Convention of January 11, 1909, between the United States and Great Britain. Following an extensive correspondence between the two Governments, they joined in a reference of the matter to that Commission under date of August 7, 1928. It may be noted that Article IX of the Convention of January 11, 1909, provides that the high contracting parties might agree that any other question or matters of difference arising between them involving the rights, obligations or interests of either in relation to the other, or to the inhabitants of the other, along the common frontier, between the United States and the Dominion of Canada shall be referred from time to time to the International Joint Commission for examination and report.... Such reports shall not be regarded as decisions of the question or matters so submitted either on the facts or on the law, and shall not, in any way, have the character of an arbitral award.

The questions referred to the International Joint Commission were five in number, the first two of which may be noted: First, the extent to which property in the State of Washington has been damaged by fumes from Smelter at Trail, B.C.; second, the amount of indemnity which would compensate United States interests in the State of Washington for past damages.

The International Joint Commission sat at Northport to take evidence and to hear interested parties in October, 1928; in Washington, D.C., in April, 1929; at Nelson in British Columbia in November, 1929; and final sittings were held in Washington, D.C., on January 22 and February 12, 1930. Witnesses were heard; reports of the investigations made by scientists were put in evidence; counsel for both the United States and Canada were heard, and briefs submitted; and the whole matter was taken under advisement by the Commission. On February 28, 1931, the Report of the Commission was signed and delivered to the proper authorities. The report was unanimous and need not be considered in detail.

Paragraph 2 of the report, in part, reads as follows:

In view of the anticipated reduction in sulphur fumes discharged from the Smelter at Trail during the present year, as hereinafter referred to, the Commission therefore has deemed it advisable to determine the amount of indemnity that will compensate United States interests in respect of such fumes, up to and including the first day of January, 1932. The Commission finds and determines that all past damages and all damages up to and including the first day of January next, is the sum of $350,000. Said sum, however, shall not include any damage occurring after January 1, 1932.

In paragraph 4 of the report, the Commission recommended a method of indemnifying persons in Washington State for damage which might be caused by operations of the Trail Smelter after the first of January, 1932, as follows:

Upon the complaint of any persons claiming to have suffered damage by the operations of the company after the first of January, 1932, it is recommended by the Commission that in the event of any such claim not being adjusted by the company within a reasonable time, the Governments of the United States and Canada shall determine the amount of such damage, if any, and the amount so fixed shall be paid by the company forthwith.

This recommendation, apparently, did not commend itself to the interested parties. In any event, it does not appear that any claims were made after the first of January, 1932, as contemplated in paragraph 4 of the report.

In paragraph 5 of the report, the Commission recommended that the Consolidated Mining and Smelting Company of Canada, Limited, should proceed to erect and put in operation certain sulphuric acid units for the purpose of reducing the amount of sulphur discharged from the stacks. It appears, from the evidence in the present case, that the General Manager of the company had made certain representations before the Commission as to the intentions of the company in this respect. There is a conflict of testimony as to the exact scope of these representations, but it is unnecessary now to consider the matter further, since, whatever they were, the company proceeded after 1930 to make certain changes and additions. With the intention and purpose of lessening the sulphur contents in the smoke emissions at the stacks, the following installations (amongst others) have been made in the plant since 1931; three 112 tons sulphuric acid plants in 1931; ammonia and ammonium sulphate plant in 1931; two units for reduction and absorption of sulphur in the zinc smelter, in 1936 and 1937, and an absorption plant for gases from the lead roasters in June, 1937. In addition, in an attempt to lessen injurious fumigations, a new system of control over the emission of fumes during the crop-growing season has been in operation, particularly since May, 1934. It is to be noted that the chief sulphur contents are in the gases from the lead smelter, but that there is still a certain amount of sulphur content in the fumes from the zinc smelter. As a result of the above, as well as of depressed business conditions, the tons of sulphur emitted into the air from the plants fell from about 10,000 tons per month in 1930 to about 7,200 tons in 1931, and to 3,400 tons in 1932. The emission of sulphur rose in 1933 to 4,000 tons, and in 1934 to nearly 6,300 tons, and in 1935 to 6,800 tons. In 1936, it fell to 5,600 tons; and in January to July, 1937 inclusive, it was 4,750 tons.

Two years after the signing of the International Joint Commission's Report of February 28, 1931, the United States Government on February 17, 1933, made representations to the Canadian Government that existing conditions were entirely unsatisfactory and that damage was still occurring, and diplomatic negotiations were renewed. Correspondence was exchanged between the two countries, and although that correspondence has its importance, it is sufficient here to say, that it resulted in the signing of the present Convention.

✿ ✿ ✿

PART TWO.

The first question under Article III of the Convention which the Tribunal is required to decide is as follows:

(1) Whether damage caused by the Trail Smelter in the State of Washington has occurred since the first day of January, 1932, and, if so, what indemnity should be paid therefor.

✿ ✿ ✿

On the basis of the evidence, the United States contended that damage had been caused by the emission of sulphur dioxide fumes at the Trail Smelter in British Columbia, which fumes, proceeding down the valley of the Columbia River and otherwise, entered the United States. The Dominion of Canada contended that even if such fumes had entered the United States, they had caused no damage after January 1, 1932. The witnesses for both Governments appeared to be definitely of the opinion that the gas was carried from the smelter by means of surface winds, and they based their views on this theory of the mechanism of gas distribution. The Tribunal finds itself unable to accept this theory. It has, therefore, looked for a more probable theory, and has adopted the following as permitting a more adequate correlation and interpretation of the facts which have been placed before it.

It appears from a careful study and comparison of recorder data furnished by the two Governments, that on numerous occasions fumigations occur practically simultaneously at points down the valley many miles apart—this being especially the fact during the growing season from April to October. It also appears from the data furnished by the different recorders, that the rate of gas attenuation down the river does not show a constant trend, but is more rapid in the first few miles below the boundary and more gradual further down the river. The Tribunal finds it impossible satisfactorily to account for the above conditions, on the basis of the theory presented to it. The Tribunal finds it further difficult to explain the times and durations of the fumigations on the basis of any probable surface-wind conditions.

The Tribunal is of opinion that the gases emerging from the stacks of the Trail Smelter find their way into the upper air currents, and are carried by these currents in a fairly continuous stream down the valley so long as the prevailing wind at that level is in that direction.

✿ ✿ ✿

(7) The United States in its Statement (p. 52) presents two further items of damages claimed by it, as follows: (Item e) which the United States terms "damages in respect of the wrong done the United States in violation of sovereignty"; . . .

With respect to (Item e), the Tribunal finds it unnecessary to decide whether the facts proven did or did not constitute an infringement or violation of sovereignty of the United States under international law independently of the Convention, for the following reason: By the Convention, the high contracting parties have submitted to this Tribunal the questions of the existence of damage caused by the Trail Smelter in the State of Washington, and of the indemnity to be paid therefor, and the Dominion of Canada has assumed under Article XII, such undertakings as will ensure due compliance with the decision of this Tribunal. The Tribunal finds that the only question to be decided on this point is the interpretation of the Convention itself. The United States in its Statement (p. 59) itemizes under the claim of damage for "violation of sovereignty" only money expended "for the investigation undertaken by the United States Government of the problems created in the United States by the operation of the Smelter at Trail". The Tribunal is of opinion that it was not within the intention of the parties, as expressed in the words "damage caused by the Trail Smelter" in Article III of the Convention, to include such moneys expended. This interpretation is confirmed by a consideration of the proceedings and of the diplomatic correspondence leading up to the making of the Convention. Since the United States has not specified any other damage based on an alleged violation of its sovereignty, the Tribunal does not feel that it is incumbent upon it to decide whether, in law and in fact, indemnity for such damage could have been awarded if specifically alleged. Certainly, the present controversy does not involve any such type of facts as the persons appointed under the Convention of January 23, 1934, between the United States of America and the Dominion of Canada felt to justify them in awarding to Canada damages for violation of sovereignty in the *I'm Alone* award of January 5, 1935. And in other cases of international arbitration cited by the United States, damages awarded for expenses were awarded, not as compensation for violation of national sovereignty, but as compensation for expenses incurred by individual claimants in prosecuting their claims for wrongful acts by the offending Government.

In his oral argument, the Agent for the United States, Mr. Sherley, claimed repayment of the aforesaid expense of investigations on a further and separate ground, *viz.*, as an incident to damages, saying (Transcript, p. 5157): "Costs and interest are incident to the damage, the proof of the damage which occurs through a given act complained of", and again (Transcript, p. 5158): "The point is this, that it goes as an incident to the award of damage." The Tribunal is unable to accept this view. While in cases involving merely the question of damage to individual claimants, it may be appropriate for an international tribunal to award costs and expenses as an incident to other damages proven (see cases cited by the Agent for the United States in the Answer and Argument, pp. 431, 437, 453–465, and at the oral argument in Transcript, p. 5153), the Tribunal is of opinion that such costs and expenses should not be allowed in a case of arbitration and final settlement of a long pending controversy between two independent Governments, such as this case, where each Government has incurred expenses and where it is to the mutual advantage of the two Governments that a just conclusion and permanent disposition of an international controversy should be reached.

The Agent for the United States also cited cases of litigation in courts of the United States (Answer and Argument, p. 439, and Transcript, p. 5152), in which expenses incurred were ordered by the court to be paid. Such cases, the Tribunal is of opinion, are inapplicable here.

The Tribunal is, therefore, of opinion that neither as a separable item of damage nor as an incident to other damages should any award be made for that which the United States terms "violation of sovereignty".

✻   ✻   ✻

In conclusion, the Tribunal answers Question 1 in Article III, as follows: Damage caused by the Trail Smelter in the State of Washington has occurred since the first day of January, 1932, and up to October 1, 1937, and the indemnity to be paid therefor is seventy-eight thousand dollars ($78,000), and is to be complete and final indemnity and compensation for all damage which occurred between such dates. Interest at the rate of six per centum per year will be allowed on the above sum of seventy-eight thousand dollars ($78,000) from the date of the filing of this report and decision until date of payment. This decision is not subject to alteration or modification by the Tribunal hereafter.

The fact of existence of damage, if any, occurring after October 1, 1937, and the indemnity to be paid therefor, if any, the Tribunal will determine in its final decision.

PART THREE.

As to Question No. 2, in Article III of the Convention, which is as follows:

(2) In the event of the answer to the first part of the preceding question being in the affirmative, whether the Trail Smelter should

be required to refrain from causing damage in the State of Washington in the future and, if so, to what extent?

the Tribunal decides that until the date of the final decision provided for in Part Four of this present decision, the Trail Smelter shall refrain from causing damage in the State of Washington in the future to the extent set forth in such Part Four until October 1, 1940, and thereafter to such extent as the Tribunal shall require in the final decision provided for in Part Four.

Part Four.

As to Question No. 3, in Article III of the Convention, which is as follows:

(3) In the light of the answer to the preceding question, what measures or régime, if any, should be adopted or maintained by the Trail Smelter?

the Tribunal is unable at the present time, with the information that has been placed before it, to determine upon a permanent régime, for the operation of the Trail Smelter. On the other hand, in view of the conclusions at which the Tribunal has arrived (as stated in an earlier part of this decision) with respect to the nature, the cause, and the course of the fumigations, and in view of the mass of data relative to sulphur emissions at the Trail Smelter, and relative to meteorological conditions and fumigations at various points down the Columbia River Valley, the Tribunal feels that the information now available does enable it to predict, with some degree of assurance, that a permanent régime based on a more adequate and intensive study and knowledge of meteorological conditions in the valley, and an extension and improvement of the methods of operation of the plant and its control in closer relation to such meteorological conditions, will effectively prevent future significant fumigations in the United States, without unreasonably restricting the output of the plant.

To enable it to establish a permanent régime based on the more adequate and intensive study and knowledge above referred to, the Tribunal establishes the following temporary régime. [Not reproduced here.]

*　*　*

Nothing in the above paragraphs of Part Four of this decision shall relieve the Dominion of Canada from any obligation now existing under the Convention with reference to indemnity or compensation, if any, which the Tribunal may find to be due for damage, if any, occurring during the period from October 1, 1937 (the date to which indemnity for damage is now awarded) to October 1, 1940, or to such earlier date at which the Tribunal may render its final decision.

Decision

REPORTED ON MARCH 11, 1941, TO THE GOVERNMENT OF THE UNITED STATES OF AMERICA AND TO THE GOVERNMENT OF THE DOMINION OF CANADA, UNDER THE CONVENTION SIGNED APRIL 15, 1935.

❁   ❁   ❁

The Tribunal herewith reports its final decisions.

❁   ❁   ❁

As between the two countries involved, each has an equal interest that if a nuisance is proved, the indemnity to damaged parties for proven damage shall be just and adequate and each has also an equal interest that unproven or unwarranted claims shall not be allowed. For, while the United States' interests may now be claimed to be injured by the operations of a Canadian corporation, it is equally possible that at some time in the future Canadian interests might be claimed to be injured by an American corporation. As has well been said: "It would not be to the advantage of the two countries concerned that industrial effort should be prevented by exaggerating the interests of the agricultural community. Equally, it would not be to the advantage of the two countries that the agricultural community should be oppressed to advance the interest of industry."

Considerations like the above are reflected in the provisions of the Convention in Article IV, that "the desire of the high contracting parties" is "to reach a solution just to all parties concerned". And the phraseology of the questions submitted to the Tribunal clearly evinces a desire and an intention that, to some extent, in making its answers to the questions, the Tribunal should endeavor to adjust the conflicting interests by some "just solution" which would allow the continuance of the operation of the Trail Smelter but under such restrictions and limitations as would, as far as foreseeable, prevent damage in the United States, and as would enable indemnity to be obtained, if in spite of such restrictions and limitations, damage should occur in the future in the United States.

In arriving at its decision, the Tribunal has had always to bear in mind the further fact that in the preamble to the Convention, it is stated that it is concluded with the recognition of "the desirability and necessity of effecting a permanent settlement".

The duty imposed upon the Tribunal by the Convention was to "finally decide" the following questions:

(1) Whether damage caused by the Trail Smelter in the State of Washington has occurred since the first day of January, 1932, and, if so, what indemnity should be paid therefor?

(2) In the event of the answer to the first part of the preceding question being in the affirmative, whether the Trail Smelter should be required to refrain from causing damage in the State of Washington in the future and, if so, to what extent?

(3) In the light of the answer to the preceding question, what measures or régime, if any, should be adopted or maintained by the Trail Smelter?

(4) What indemnity or compensation, if any, should be paid on account of any decision or decisions rendered by the Tribunal pursuant to the next two preceding questions?

* * *

On April 16, 1938, the Tribunal reported its "final decision" on Question No. 1, as well as its temporary decisions on Questions No. 2 and No. 3, and provided for a temporary régime thereunder. The decision reported on April 16, 1938, will be referred to hereinafter as the "previous decision".

* * *

PART TWO.

The first question under Article III of the Convention is:

(1) Whether damage caused by the Trail Smelter in the State of Washington has occurred since the first day of January, 1932, and, if so, what indemnity should be paid therefor.

This question has been answered by the Tribunal in its previous decision, as to the period from January 1, 1932 to October 1, 1937, as set forth above.

* * *

The Tribunal has examined carefully the records [for the period between October 1, 1937, and October 1, 1940] of all fumigations specifically alleged by the United States as having been caused or been likely to cause damage, as well as the records of all other fumigations which may be considered likely to have caused damage. In connection with each such instance, it has taken into detailed consideration, with a view of determining the fact or probability of damage, the length of the fumigation, the intensity of concentration, the combination of length and intensity, the frequency of fumigation, the time of day of occurrence, the conditions of humidity or drouth, the season of the year, the altitude and geographical locations of place subjected to fumigation, the reports as to personal surveys and investigations and all other pertinent factors.

As as result, it has come to the conclusion that the United States has failed to prove that any fumigation between October 1, 1937, and October 1, 1940, has caused injury to crops, trees or otherwise.

* * *

[The Tribunal was finally requested by the United States under Question I to provide indemnity with regard to expenditures incurred by it during the period July 1, 1936, to September 1, 1940.]

It is argued that where injury has been caused and the continuance of this injury is reasonably feared, investigation is needed and that the cost of this investigation is as much damageable consequence of the injury as damage to crops and trees. It is argued that the indemnity provided for in Question No. 1 necessarily comprises monies spent on such investigation.

There is a fundamental difference between expenditure incurred in mending the damageable consequences of an injury and monies spent in ascertaining the existence, the cause and the extent of the latter.

These are not part of the damage, any more than other costs involved in seeking and obtaining a judicial or arbitral remedy, such as the fees of counsel, the travelling expenses of witnesses, etc. In effect, it would be quite impossible to frame a logical distinction between the costs of preparing expert reports and the cost of preparing the statements and answers provided for in the procedure. Obviously, the fact that these expenditures may be incurred by different agencies of the same government does not constitute a basis for such a logical distinction.

The Convention does not warrant the inclusion of the cost of investigations under the heading of damage. On the contrary, apart from Article XIII, both the text of the Convention and the history of its conclusion disprove any intention of including them therein.

The damage for which indemnity should be paid is the damage caused by the Trail Smelter in the State of Washington. Investigations in the field took place there and it happens that experiments were conducted in that State. But these investigations were conducted by Federal agencies. The "damage"—assuming *ex hypothesi* that monies spent on the salaries and expenditures of the investigators should be so termed—was therefore caused, not in one State in particular, but in the entire territory of the Union.

* * *

If, under the Convention, the monies spent by the United States on investigations cannot be looked upon as damage, no indemnity can be claimed therefor, under the latter, even if such expenses could not properly be included in the "expenses of the presentation and conduct" of the case. If there were a gap in the Convention, the claim ought to be disallowed, as it is unsupported by international practice.

When a State espouses a private claim on behalf of one of its nationals, expenses which the latter may have incurred in prosecuting or endeavoring to establish his claim prior to the espousal are sometimes included and, under appropriate conditions, may legitimately be included in the claim. They are costs, incidental to damage, incurred by the national in seeking local remedy or redress, as it is, as a rule, his duty to do, if, on account of injury suffered abroad, he wants to avail himself of the diplomatic protection of his State. The Tribunal, however, has not been informed of any case in which a Government has sought before an international jurisdiction or been allowed by an international award or judgment indemnity for expenses by it in preparing the proof for presenting a national claim or private claims which it had espoused; and counsel for the United States, on being requested to cite any precedent for such an adjudication, have stated that they know of no precedent. Cases cited were instances in which expenses allowed had been incurred by the injured national, and all except one prior to the presentation of the claim by the Government.

In the absence of authority established by settled precedents, the Tribunal is of opinion that, where an arbitral tribunal is requested to award the expenses of a Government incurred in preparing proof to support its claim, particularly a claim for damage to the national territory, the intent to enable the Tribunal to do so should appear, either from the express language of the instrument which sets up the arbitral tribunal or as a necessary implication from its provision. Neither such express language nor implication is present in this case.

* * *

PART THREE.

The second question under Article III of the Convention is as follows:

> In the event of the answer to the first part of the preceding question being in the affirmative, whether the Trail Smelter should be required to refrain from causing damage in the State of Washington in the future and, if so, to what extent?

* * *

The first problem which arises is whether the question should be answered on the basis of the law followed in the United States or on the basis of international law. The Tribunal, however, finds that this problem need not be solved here as the law followed in the United States in dealing with the quasi-sovereign rights of the States of the Union, in the matter of air pollution, whilst more definite, is in conformity with the general rules of international law.

Particularly in reaching its conclusions as regards this question as well as the next, the Tribunal has given consideration to the desire of the high contracting parties "to reach a solution just to all parties concerned".

As Professor Eagleton puts in (Responsibility of States in International Law, 1928, p. 80): "A State owes at all times a duty to protect other States against injurious acts by individuals from within its jurisdiction." A great number of such general pronouncements by leading authorities concerning the duty of a State to respect other States and their territory have been presented to the Tribunal. These and many others have been carefully examined. International decisions, in various matters, from the Alabama case onward, and also earlier ones, are based on the same general principle, and, indeed, this principle, as such, has not been questioned by Canada. But the real difficulty often arises rather when it comes to determine what, pro subjecta materie, is deemed to constitute an injurious act.

A case concerning, as the present one does, territorial relations, decided by the Federal Court of Switzerland between the Cantons of Soleure and Argovia, may serve to illustrate the relativity of the rule. Soleure brought a suit against her sister State to enjoin use of a shooting establishment which endangered her territory. The court, in granting the injunction, said: "This right (sovereignty) excludes . . . . not only the usurpation and exercise of sovereign rights (of another State) . . . . but also an actual encroachment which might prejudice the natural use of the territory and the free movement of its inhabitants." As a result of the decision, Argovia made plans for the improvement of the existing installations. These, however, were considered as insufficient protection by Soleure. The Canton of Argovia then moved the Federal Court to decree that the shooting be again permitted after completion of the projected improvements. This motion was granted. "The demand of the Government of Soleure", said the court, "that all endangerment be absolutely abolished apparently goes too far." The court found that all risk whatever had not been eliminated, as the region was flat and absolutely safe shooting ranges were only found in mountain valleys; that there was a federal duty for the communes to provide facilities for military target practice and that "no more precautions may be demanded for shooting ranges near the boundaries of two Cantons than are required for shooting ranges in the interior of a Canton". (R. O. 26 I, p. 450, 451; R. O. 41, I, p. 137; see D. Schindler, "The Administration of Justice in the Swiss Federal Court in Intercantonal Disputes", *American Journal of International Law*, Vol. 15 (1921), pp. 172–174.)

No case of air pollution dealt with by an international tribunal has been brought to the attention of the Tribunal nor does the Tribunal know of any such case. The nearest analogy is that of water pollution. [Emphasis added.] But, here also, no decision of an international tribunal has been cited or has been found.

There are, however, as regards both air pollution and water pollution, certain decisions of the Supreme Court of the United States which may legitimately be taken as a guide in this field of international law, for it is reasonable to follow by analogy, in international cases, precedents established by that court in dealing with controversies between States of the Union or with other controversies concerning the quasi-sovereign rights of such States, where no contrary rule prevails in international law and no reason for rejecting such precedents can be adduced from the limitations of sovereignty inherent in the Constitution of the United States. [Emphasis added.]

In the suit of the State of Missouri *v.* the State of Illinois (200 U.S. 496, 521) concerning the pollution, within the boundaries of Illinois, of the Illinois River, and affluent of the Mississippi flowing into the latter where it forms the boundary between that State and Missouri, an injunction was refused. "Before this court ought to intervene", said the court, "the case should be of serious magnitude, clearly and fully proved, and the principle to be applied should be one which the court is prepared deliberately to maintain against all considerations on the other side. (See Kansas *v.* Colorado, 185 U.S. 125.)" The court found that the practice complained of was general along the shores of the Mississippi River at that time, that it was followed by Missouri itself and that thus a standard was set up by the defendant which the claimant was entitled to invoke.

As the claims of public health became more exacting and methods for removing impurities from the water were perfected, complaints ceased. It is significant that Missouri sided with Illinois when the other riparians of the Great Lakes' system sought to enjoin it to desist from diverting the waters of that system into that of the Illinois and Mississippi for the very purpose of disposing of the Chicago sewage.

In the more recent suit of the State of New York against the State of New Jersey (256 U.S. 296, 309), concerning the pollution of New York Bay, the injunction was also refused for lack of proof, some experts believing that the plans which were in dispute would result in the presence of "offensive odors and unsightly deposits", other equally reliable experts testifying that they were confidently of the opinion that the waters would be sufficiently purified. The court, referring to Missouri *v.* Illinois, said: ".... the burden upon the State of New York of sustaining the allegations of its bill is much greater than that imposed upon a complainant in an ordinary suit between private parties. Before this court can be moved to exercise its extraordinary power under the Constitution to control the conduct of one State at the suit of another, the threatened invasion of rights must be of serious magnitude and it must be established by clear and convincing evidence."

What the Supreme Court says there of its power under the Constitution equally applies to the extraordinary power granted this Tribunal under the Convention. What is true between States of the Union is, at least, equally true concerning the relations between the United States and the Dominion of Canada.

In another recent case concerning water pollution (283 U.S. 473), the complainant was successful. The City of New York was enjoined, at the request of the State of New Jersey, to desist, within a reasonable time limit, from the practice of disposing of sewage by dumping it into the sea, a practice which was injurious to the coastal waters of New Jersey in the vicinity of her bathing resorts.

In the matter of air pollution itself, the leading decisions are those of the Supreme Court in the State of Georgia v. Tennessee Copper Company and Ducktown Sulphur, Copper and Iron Company, Limited. Although dealing with a suit against private companies, the decisions were on questions cognate to those here at issue. Georgia stated that it had in vain sought relief from the State of Tennessee, on whose territory the smelters were located, and the court defined the nature of the suit by saying: "This is a suit by a State for an injury to it in its capacity of quasi-sovereign. In that capacity, the State has an interest independent of and behind the titles of its citizens, in all the earth and air within its domain."

On the question whether an injunction should be granted or not, the court said (206 U.S. 230):

It (the State) has the last word as to whether its mountains shall be stripped of their forests and its inhabitants shall breathe pure air .... It is not lightly to be presumed to give up quasi-sovereign rights for pay and .... if that be its choice, it may insist that an infraction of them shall be stopped. This court has not quite the same freedom to balance the harm that will be done by an injunction against that of which the plaintiff complains, that it would have in deciding between two subjects of a single political power. Without excluding the considerations that equity always takes into account .... it is a fair and reasonable demand on the part of a sovereign that the air over its territory should not be polluted on a great scale by sulphurous acid gas, that the forests on its mountains, be they better or worse, and whatever domestic destruction they may have suffered, should not be further destroyed or threatened by the act of persons beyond its control, that the crops and orchards on its hills should not be endangered from the same source.... Whether Georgia, by insisting upon this claim, is doing more harm than good to her own citizens, is for her to determine. The possible disaster to those outside the State must be accepted as a consequence of her standing upon her extreme rights.

Later on, however, when the court actually framed an injunction, in the case of the Ducktown Company (237 U.S. 474, 477) (an agreement on the basis of an annual compensation was reached with the most important of the two smelters, the Tennessee Copper Company), they did not go beyond a decree "adequate to diminish materially the present probability of damage to its (Georgia's) citizens".

Great progress in the control of fumes has been made by science in the last few years and this progress should be taken into account.

The Tribunal, therefore, finds that the above decisions, taken as a whole, constitute an adequate basis for its conclusions, namely, that, *under the principles of international law, as well as of the law of the United States, no State has the right to use or permit the use of its territory in such a manner as to cause injury by fumes in or to the territory of another or the properties or persons therein, when the case is of serious consequence and the injury is established by clear and convincing evidence.* [Emphasis added.]

The decisions of the Supreme Court of the United States which are the basis of these conclusions are decisions in equity and a solution inspired by them, together with the régime hereinafter prescribed, will, in the opinion of the Tribunal, be "just to all parties concerned", as long, at least, as the present conditions in the Columbia River Valley continue to prevail.

Considering the circumstances of the case, the Tribunal holds that the Dominion of Canada is responsible in international law for the conduct of the Trail Smelter. Apart from the undertakings in the Convention, it is, therefore, the duty of the Government of the Dominion of Canada to see to it that this conduct should be in conformity with the obligation of the Dominion under international law as herein determined.

The Tribunal, therefore, answers Question No. 2 as follows: (2) So long as the present conditions in the Columbia River Valley prevail, the Trail Smelter shall be required to refrain from causing any damage through fumes in the State of Washington; the damage herein referred to and its extent being such as would be recoverable under the decisions of the courts of the United States in suits between private individuals. The indemnity for such damage should be fixed in such manner as the Governments, acting under Article XI of the Convention, should agree upon.

PART FOUR.

The third question under Article III of the Convention is as follows:

In the light of the answer to the preceding question, what measures or régime, if any, should be adopted and maintained by the Trail Smelter?

Answering this question in the light of the preceding one, since the Tribunal has, in its previous decision, found that damage caused by the Trail Smelter has occurred in the State of Washington since January 1, 1932, and since the Tribunal is of opinion that damage may occur in the future unless the operations of the Smelter shall be subject to some control, in order to avoid damage occurring, The Tribunal now decides that a régime or measure of control shall be applied to the operations of the Smelter and shall remain in full force unless and until modified in accordance with the provisions hereinafter set forth in Section 3, Paragraph VI of the present part of this decision. [Not reproduced here.]

PART FIVE.

The fourth question under Article III of the Convention is as follows:

What indemnity or compensation, if any, should be paid on account of any decision or decisions rendered by the Tribunal pursuant to the next two preceding Questions?

The Tribunal is of opinion that the prescribed régime will probably remove the causes of the present controversy and, as said before, will probably result in preventing any damage of a material nature occurring in the State of Washington in the future.

But since the desirable and expected result of the régime or measure of control hereby required to be adopted and maintained by the Smelter may not occur, and since in its answer to Question No. 2, the Tribunal has required the Smelter to refrain from causing damage in the State of Washington in the future, as set forth therein, the Tribunal answers Question No. 4 and decides that on account of decisions rendered by the Tribunal in its answers to Question No. 2 and Question No. 3 there shall be paid as follows: (a) if any damage as defined under Question No. 2 shall have occurred since October 1, 1940, or shall occur in the future, whether through failure on the part of the Smelter to comply with the regulations herein prescribed or notwithstanding the maintenance of the régime, an indemnity shall be paid for such damage but only when and if the two Governments shall make arrangements for the disposition of claims for indemnity under the provisions of Article XI of the Convention; *(b)* if as a consequence of the decision of the Tribunal in its answers to Question No. 2 and Question No. 3, the United States shall find it necessary to maintain in the future an agent or agents in the area in order to ascertain whether damage shall have occurred in spite of the régime prescribed herein, the reasonable cost of such investigations not in excess of $7,500 in any one year shall be paid to the United States as a compensation, but only if and when the two Governments determine under Article XI of the Convention that damage has occurred in the year in question, due to the operation of the Smelter, and "disposition of claims for indemnity for damage" has been made by the two Governments; but in no case shall the aforesaid compensation be payable in excess of the indemnity for damage; and further it is understood that such payment is hereby directed by the Tribunal only as a compensation to be paid on account of the answers of the Tribunal to Question No. 2 and Question No. 3 (as provided for in Question No. 4) and *not* as any part of indemnity for the damage to be ascertained and to be determined upon by the two Governments under Article XI of the Convention.

Part Six.

Since further investigations in the future may be possible under the provisions of Part Four and of Part Five of this decision, the Tribunal finds it necessary to include in its report, the following provision:

Investigators appointed by or on behalf of either Government, whether jointly or severally, and the members of the Commission provided for in Paragraph VI of Section 3 of Part Four of this decision, shall be permitted at all reasonable times to inspect the operations of the Smelter and to enter upon and inspect any of the properties in the State of Washington which may be claimed to be affected by fumes. This provision shall also apply to any localities where instruments are operated under the present régime or under any amended régime. Wherever under the present régime or any amended régime, instruments have to be maintained and operated by the Smelter on the territory of the United States, the Government of the United States shall undertake to secure for the Government of the Dominion of Canada the facilities reasonably required to that effect.

The Tribunal expresses the strong hope that any investigations which the Governments may undertake in the future, in connection with the matters dealt with in this decision, shall be conducted jointly.

(Signed) JAN HOSTIE.
(Signed) CHARLES WARREN.
(Signed) R. A. E. GREENSHIELDS.

⚓ REPORT OF THE INTERNATIONAL JOINT COMMISSION ON AIR POLLUTION IN THE ST. CLAIR–DETROIT REGION (1971)

Summary: Investigations, Results and Conclusions, and Recommendations

Air pollution in the Detroit–Windsor area has been a cause of public concern for many years. As a result of this concern, the City of Windsor in 1964 requested of the Government of Canada, through the Province of Ontario, that action be taken to abate the flow of transboundary pollution emanating from the industrial complex in Wayne County, Michigan.

The Governments of Canada and the U. S., in considering this matter, decided to extend the geographical area of consideration because of complaints in the Port Huron, Michigan, area of a transboundary flow of air pollution emanating from the industrial complex in the Sarnia, Ontario, area.

Accordingly, the Governments referred this matter, in September 1966, to the International Joint Commission for investigation of the following questions:

1. Is the air in the vicinity of Port Huron–Sarnia and Detroit–Windsor being polluted on either side of the international boundary by quantities of contaminants that are detrimental to the public health, safety, or general welfare of citizens or that are detrimental to property on the other side of the international boundary?
2. If the first question or any part of it is answered in the affirmative, what sources contribute to this pollution and to what extent?
3. If the Commission should find that any sources on either side of the boundary in the vicinity of Port Huron–Sarnia and Detroit-Windsor contribute to air pollution on the other side of the boundary to an extent detrimental to the public health, safety, or general welfare of citizens or detrimental to property, what preventative or remedial measures would be most practical from economic, sanitary, and other points of view? The Commission should give an indication of the probable total cost of implementing the measures recommended.

Investigations

The Commission established in November 1966 the St. Clair–Detroit Air Pollution Board to conduct on its behalf an investigation to answer the questions referred to the Commission by Canada and the U. S.

In conducting this study, the Board utilized the facilities and manpower of the following participating agencies:

1. National Air Pollution Control Administration — Department of Health, Education, and Welfare — U. S.

2. Environmental Health Directorate — Department of National Health and Welfare — Canada

3. Air Management Branch — Department of Energy and Resources Management — Ontario, Canada

4. Division of Occupational Health — Department of Public Health — Michigan, U. S.

5. Air Pollution Control Division — Department of Health — Wayne County, Michigan, U. S.

Cooperation was obtained from municipalities in Ontario as well as from municipal agencies in Michigan.

During the 1968 study period the following work was undertaken:

1. Air quality measurements were made on both sides of the international boundary at approximately 80 locations. The following pollutants and effects were sampled:

Particulate matter	Fluorides	Hydrogen sulfide
Sulfur dioxide	Carbon monoxide	Nitrogen oxides
Hydrocarbons	Sulfation rates	Oxidants

In addition, samples of suspended particulates were analyzed quantitatively for 16 metals. Odorous pollutants were investigated in a special survey. An aircraft was instrumented and flown along the boundary to measure directly the flux of pollutants across the boundary.

2. Meteorological measurements were taken at 15 locations.
3. An inventory of atmospheric emissions was made of pollutants emanating from all sources.
4. A study of the effects of air pollutants in the area on selected vegetation and materials was conducted.

For the preparation of this report, the following methods of evaluation were used:

1. Production of pollution roses that show the frequency of wind directions along with selected pollution levels at measuring stations, thus indicating the frequency of the transboundary flow of pollutants.
2. Case studies of the wind direction that accompanied the occurrence

of levels of pollution in excess of concentrations that cause adverse effects.

3. Use of a mathematical dispersion model to compute the average concentrations on the opposite side of the boundary that result from transboundary flow.
4. Direct measurements of the transboundary flux of pollution by measurements taken on an instrumented aircraft.

Results and Conclusions

Because of the mass of information collected, all the data have not been analyzed; however, sufficient analysis has been performed to warrant the following conclusions:

1. A transboundary flow of air pollutants does occur across both the St. Clair and Detroit River international boundaries in the vicinities of Port Huron–Sarnia and Detroit–Windsor, producing pollution levels that are in excess of desirable air quality standards already established in Ontario and about to be established in Michigan. Although many pollutants were measured, particulates and SO_x only were used in this evaluation because of their magnitude and obvious relationship to area and point sources. It has been determined that SO_x and particulate pollution does exist and, in some regions of the study, pollution is being transported across the international boundary to an extent detrimental to the other country. In the Detroit–Windsor area, far more SO_x and particulate pollution is being transported from the U. S. into Canada than from Canada into the U. S. In the Port Huron–Sarnia area, transboundary pollution was also verified; however, the contributions from the respective countries were approximately equal.
2. In addition to pollution from transboundary flow of air pollutants, certain areas in both the U. S. and Canada are experiencing levels of air pollution in excess of their air quality standards because of sources located in their respective jurisdictions.
3. Transboundary and local pollution both exceed the level that is detrimental to the health, safety, and general welfare of citizens, and to property on the other side of the international boundary.

Air Quality Standards

In analyzing the data, the Board noted discrepancies between the established Ontario and the proposed Michigan ambient air quality standards as follows:

	Michigan (Proposed)	*Ontario*
SO_x, annual average	0.04 ppm	0.02 ppm
Suspended particulates, annual geometric mean	80 g/m^3	60 g/m^3

Although it is beyond the scope of this Board to resolve these discrepancies, it should be noted that the standards set by Ontario and proposed by Michigan have been used in the body of this report and in the summary to assess the air quality of the respective jurisdictions.

In addition, Ontario has set standards for ten other pollutants for which no comparable limits have yet been fixed in Michigan. Ontario figures, therefore, were used as a guide for evaluating the other pollutants measured.

Although Michigan has not officially promulgated its standards, Michigan officials have advised the National Air Pollution Control Administration that they intend to adopt standards equal to or more stringent than those used in this report. In this connection, it should be clearly stated that the U.S. National Air Pollution Control Administration has approved proposed air quality standards submitted to it by a number of states in various federally-designated Air Quality Control Regions; the approved standards are approximately equal to the Ontario standards for SO_2 and particulates.

It is apparent, then, that the agencies charged with the control of air pollution in the study area have the necessary power to achieve a decrease in air pollution emissions, as evidenced by the reductions of particulate emissions that have been accomplished during the period of study and since its completion.

* * *

Recommendations

1. That the responsible control agencies in both countries accelerate their abatement programs to bring all sources into compliance.
2. That the control agencies in both countries report semiannually to the Commission their progress in achieving compliance.
3. That the control agencies in both countries report annually to the Commission the ambient air quality existing in their jurisdictions.
4. That the Commission request the Governments of both countries and their respective air pollution control agencies to establish uniform air quality standards as soon as possible.

5. That the governments of the United States and Canada, together with the State of Michigan and the Province of Ontario, cooperate to control transboundary air pollution from existing sources and to prevent creation of new sources of transboundary air pollution.
6. That with the issuance of the Commission's report, the Board be terminated.

Suggested Reading List

Sproull, Wayne T., *Air Pollution and its Control* (1970). (Symposium), "Air Pollution," 33 *Law and Contemporary Problems* (Spring, 1968).

Rubin, A. P., "Pollution by Analogy: the Trail Smelter Arbitration," 50 *Ore. L. Rev.* 259 (1971).

Lee, E. G., "International Legal Aspects of Pollution of the Atmosphere," 21 *University of Toronto Law Journal* 2: 31 (1971).

Fitzgerald, Gerald F., "Aircraft Noise in the Vicinity of Aerodromes and Sonic Boom," *ibid.* 54.

Hassett, Charles M., "Air Pollution: Possible International Legal and Organizational Responses," 5 *N.Y.U.J. Int'l. L. and Politics* 1 (1972).

Marine Pollution

MULTILATERAL MEASURES

Pollution of the Sea by Oil

✠ INTERNATIONAL CONVENTION FOR THE PREVENTION OF POLLUTION OF THE SEA BY OIL, 1954

[The Governments represented at the International Conference on Pollution of the Sea by Oil held in London from 26th April, 1954, to 12th May, 1954,

As amended. The International Convention for the Prevention of Pollution of the Sea by Oil, 1954, was opened for signature at London, May 12, 1954, and entered into force July 26, 1958. Amendments to the 1954 Convention were adopted by the

Desiring to take action by common agreement to prevent pollution of the sea by oil discharged from ships, and considering that this end may best be achieved by the conclusion of a Convention,

Have accordingly appointed ... plenipotentiaries, who, having communicated their full powers, found in good and due form, have agreed as follows:-]

* * *

Article I

(1) For the purposes of the present Convention, the following expressions shall (unless the context otherwise requires) have the meanings hereby respectively assigned to them that is to say:

"The Bureau" has the meaning assigned to it by article XXI;

"Discharge" in relation to oil or to oily mixture means any discharge or escape howsoever caused;

"Heavy diesel oil" means diesel oil, other than those distillates of which more than 50 per cent by volume distils at a temperature not exceeding 340°C when tested by A.S.T.M. Standard Method D.86/59;

"Instantaneous rate of discharge of oil content" means the rate of discharge of oil in litres per hour at any instant divided by the speed of the ship in knots at the same instant.

"Mile" means a nautical mile of 6,080 feet or 1,852 metres;

"Nearest land." The term "from the nearest land" means "from the baseline from which the territorial sea of the territory in question is established in accordance with the Geneva Convention on the Territorial Sea and the Contiguous Zone, 1958";

"Oil" means crude oil, fuel oil, heavy diesel oil, and lubricating oil, and "oily" shall be construed accordingly;

"Oily mixture" means a mixture with any oil content;

"Organization" means the Inter-Governmental Maritime Consultative Organization;

"Ship" mean any sea-going vessel of any type whatsoever, including floating craft, whether self-propelled or towed by another vessel,

---

Conference of Contracting Governments, held at London, April 4–11, 1962. Amendments to Articles I–X, XVI, XVIII, and Annexes A and B entered into force May 18, 1967. The amendment to Article XIV entered into force June 28, 1967. Further amendments to the Convention were adopted by the Assembly of the Inter-Governmental Maritime Consultative Organization in London, on October 21, 1969. Article VI *bis* was added in 1971. These amendments will come into force twelve months after they have been ratified by two-thirds of the governments which are parties to the Convention.

Note: The text reproduced above is a composite of the original 1954 Convention and the amendments of 1962, 1969, and 1971. Portions of the original 1954 text are bracketed [ ]; the 1962 amendments are double-bracketed [[ ]]; the 1969 amendments are given no special treatment; and the 1971 amendment is braced { }.

making a sea voyage; and "tanker" means a ship in which the greater part of the cargo space is constructed or adapted for the carriage of liquid cargoes in bulk and which is not, for the time being, carrying a cargo other than oil in that part of its cargo space.

[[(2) For the purposes of the present Convention, the territories of a Contracting Government mean the territory of the country of which it is the Government and any other territory for the international relations of which it is responsible and to which the Convention shall have been extended under Article XVIII.]]

Article II

[[(1) The present Convention shall apply to ships registered in any of the territories of a Contracting Government and to unregistered ships having the nationality of a Contracting Party, except:

(a) tankers of under 150 tons gross tonnage and other ships of under 500 tons gross tonnage, provided that each Contracting Government will take the necessary steps, so far as is reasonable and practicable, to apply the requirements of the Convention to such ships also, having regard to their size, service and the type of fuel used for their propulsion.

(b) ships for the time being engaged in the whaling industry when actually employed on whaling operations;

(c) ships for the time being navigating the Great Lakes of North America and their connecting and tributary waters as far east as the lower exit of St. Lambert Lock at Montreal in the Province of Quebec, Canada;

(d) naval ships and ships for the time being used as naval auxiliaries.

(2) Each Contracting Government undertakes to adopt appropriate measures ensuring that requirements equivalent to those of the present Convention are, so far as is reasonable and practicable, applied to the ships referred to in subparagraph (d) of paragraph (1) of this Article.]]

Article III

Subject to the provisions of Articles IV and V:

(a) the discharge from a ship to which the present Convention applies, other than a tanker, of oil or oily mixture shall be prohibited except when the following conditions are all satisfied:

(i) the ship is proceeding en route;

(ii) the instantaneous rate of discharge of oil content does not exceed 60 litres per mile;

(iii) the oil content of the discharge is less than 100 parts per 1,000,000 parts of the mixture;

(iv) the discharge is made as far as practicable from land;

(b) the discharge from a tanker to which the present Convention applies of oil or oily mixture shall be prohibited except when the following conditions are all satisfied:

(i) the tanker is proceeding en route;

(ii) the instantaneous rate of discharge of oil content does not exceed 60 litres per mile;

(iii) the total quantity of oil discharged on a ballast voyage does not exceed 1/15,000 of the total cargo-carrying capacity;

(iv) the tanker is more than 50 miles from the nearest land;

(c) the provisions of sub-paragraph (b) of this Article shall not apply to:

(i) the discharge of ballast from a cargo tank which, since the cargo was last carried therein, has been so cleaned that any effluent therefrom, if it were discharged from a stationery tanker into clean calm water on a clear day, would produce no visible traces of oil on the surface of the water; or

(ii) the discharge of oil or oily mixture from machinery space bilges, which shall be governed by the provisions of sub-paragraph (a) of this Article.

Article IV

[[Article III shall not apply to:

(a) the discharge of oil or of oily mixture from a ship for the purpose of securing the safety of a ship, preventing damage to a ship or cargo, or saving life at sea;

(b) the escape of oil or of oily mixture resulting from damage to a ship or unavoidable leakage, if all reasonable precautions have been taken after the occurrence of the damage or discovery of the leakage for the purpose of preventing or minimizing the escape;]]

Article V

Article III shall not apply to the discharge of oily mixture from the bilges of a ship during the period of twelve months following the date on which the present Convention comes into force for the relevant territory in accordance with paragraph (1) of Article II.

Article VI

[[(1) Any contravention of Articles III and IX shall be an offense punishable under the law of the relevant territory in respect of the ship in accordance with paragraph (1) of Article II.

(2) The penalties which may be imposed under the law of any of the territories of a Contracting Government in respect of the unlawful discharge from a ship of oil or oily mixture outside the territorial sea of that territory shall be adequate in severity to discourage any such unlawful discharge and shall not be less than the penalties which may be imposed under the law of that territory in respect of the same infringements within the territorial sea.

(3) Each Contracting Government shall report to the Organization the penalties actually imposed for each infringement.]]

Article VI *bis*

{(1) Every tanker to which the present Convention applies and for which the building contract is placed on or after the date of coming into force of this Article shall be constructed in accordance with the provisions of Annex C [not reproduced here]. In addition, every tanker to which the present Convention applies and for which the building contract is placed, or in the absence of a building contract the keel of which is laid or which is at a similar state of construction, before the date of coming into force of this Article shall be required, within two years after that date, to comply with the Provisions of Annex C, where such a tanker falls into either of the following categories:

(a) a tanker, the delivery of which is after 1 January 1977; or
(b) a tanker to which both the following conditions apply:
   (i) delivery is not later than 1 January 1977; and
   (ii) the building contract is placed after 1 January 1972, or in cases where no building contract has previously been placed, the keel is laid or the tanker is at a similar stage of construction, after 30 June 1972.

(2) A tanker required under paragraph (1) of this Article to be constructed in accordance with Annex C and so constructed shall carry on board a certificate issued or authorized by the responsible Contracting Government attesting such compliance. A tanker which under paragraph (1) of this Article is not required to be constructed in accordance with Annex C shall carry on board a certificate to that effect issued or authorized by the responsible Contracting Government, or if the tanker

does comply with Annex C although not required to do so, it may carry on board a certificate issued or authorized by the responsible Contracting Government attesting such compliance. A Contracting Government shall not permit such tankers under its flag to trade unless the appropriate certificate has been issued.

(3) Certificates issued under the authority of a Contracting Government shall be accepted by the other Contracting Governments for all purposes covered by the present Convention. They shall be regarded by the other Contracting Governments as having the same force as certificates issued by them.

(4) If a Contracting Government has clear grounds for believing that a tanker required under paragraph (1) of this Article to be constructed in accordance with Annex C entering ports in its territory or using off-shore terminals under its control does not in fact comply with Annex C, such Contracting Government may request consultation with the Government with which the tanker is registered. If, after such consultation or otherwise, the Contracting Government is satisfied that the tanker does not comply with Annex C, such Contracting Government may for this reason deny such a tanker access to ports in its territorial waters or to off-shore terminals under its control until such time as the Contracting Government is satisfied that the tanker does comply.}

Article VII

(1) As from a date twelve months after the present Convention comes into force for the relevant territory in respect of a ship in accordance with paragraph (1) of Article II, such a ship shall be required to be so fitted as to prevent, as far as reasonable and practicable, the escape of oil into bilges, unless effective means are provided to ensure that the oil in the bilges is not discharged in contravention of this Convention.

(2) Carrying water ballast in oil fuel tanks shall be avoided if possible.

Article VIII

[[(1) Each Contracting Government shall take all appropriate steps to promote the provision of facilities as follows:
  (a) according to the needs of ships using them, ports shall be provided with facilities adequate for the reception, without causing undue delay to ships, of such residues and oily mixtures as would remain for disposal from ships other than tankers if the bulk of the water had been separated from the mixture;

(b) oil loading terminals shall be provided with facilities adequate for the reception of such residues and oily mixtures as would similarly remain for disposal by tankers;

(c) ship repair ports shall be provided with facilities adequate for the reception of such residues and oily mixtures as would similarly remain for disposal by all ships entering for repairs.

(2) Each Contracting Government shall determine which are the ports and oil loading terminals in its territories suitable for the purposes of sub-paragraphs (a), (b) and (c) of paragraph (1) of this Article.

(3) As regards paragraph (1) of this Article, each Contracting Government shall report to the Organization, for transmission to the Contracting Government concerned, all cases where the facilities are alleged to be inadequate.]]

Article IX

(1) Of the ships to which the present Convention applies, every ship which uses oil fuel and every tanker shall be provided with an oil record book, whether as part of the ship's official log book or otherwise, in the form specified in the Annex to the Convention.

(2) The oil record book shall be completed on each occasion, on a tank-to-tank basis, whenever any of the following operations take place in the ship:

(a) *for tankers:*
- (i) loading of oil cargo;
- (ii) transfer of oil cargo during voyage;
- (iii) discharge of oil cargo;
- (iv) ballasting of cargo tanks;
- (v) cleaning of cargo tanks;
- (vi) discharge of dirty ballast;
- (vii) discharge of water from slop-tanks;
- (viii) disposal of residues;
- (ix) discharge overboard of bilge water containing oil which has accumulated in machinery spaces whilst in port, and the routine discharge at sea of bilge water containing oil unless the latter has been entered in the appropriate log book.

(b) *for ships other than tankers;*
- (i) ballasting or cleaning of bunker fuel tanks;
- (ii) discharge of dirty ballast or cleaning water from tanks referred to under (i) of this sub-paragraph;

(iii) disposal of residues;

(iv) discharge overboard of bilge water containing oil which has accumulated in machinery spaces whilst in port, and the routine discharge at sea of bilge water containing oil unless the latter has been entered in the appropriate log book.

In the event of such discharge or escape of oil or oily mixture as is referred to in Article IV, a statement shall be made in the oil record book of the circumstances of, and the reason for, the discharge or escape.

[[(3) Each operation described in paragraph (2) of this Article shall be fully recorded without delay in the oil record book so that all the entries in the book appropriate to that operation are completed. Each page of the book shall be signed by the officer or officers in charge of the operations concerned and, when the ship is manned, by the master of the ship. The written entries in the oil record book shall be in an official language of the relevant territory in respect of the ship in accordance with paragraph (1) of Article II, or in English or French.

(4) Oil record books shall be kept in such a place as to be readily available for inspection at all reasonable times, and, except in the case of unmanned ships under tow, shall be kept on board the ship. They shall be preserved for a period of two years after the last entry has been made.

(5) The competent authorities of any of the territories of a Contracting Government may inspect on board any ship to which the present Convention applies, while within a port in that territory, the oil record book required to be carried in the ship in compliance with the provisions of this Article, and may make a true copy of any entry in that book and may require the master of the ship to certify that the copy is a true copy of such entry. Any copy so made which purports to have been certified by the master of the ship as a true copy of an entry in the ship's oil record book shall be made admissible in any judicial proceedings as evidence of the facts stated in the entry. Any action by the competent authorities under this paragraph shall be taken as expeditiously as possible and the ship shall not be delayed.]]

Article X

[[(1) Any Contracting Government may furnish to the Government of the relevant territory in respect of the ship in accordance with paragraph (1) of Article II particulars in writing of evidence that any provision of the present Convention has been contravened in respect of that ship, wheresoever the alleged contravention may have taken place. If it is practicable to do so, the competent authorities of the former Government shall notify the master of the ship of the alleged contravention.]]

(2) Upon receiving such particulars, the Government so informed shall investigate the matter, and may request the other Government to furnish further or better particulars of the alleged contravention. If the Government so informed is satisfied that sufficient evidence is available in the form required by its law to enable proceedings against the owner or master of the ship to be taken in respect of the alleged contravention, it shall cause such proceedings to be taken as soon as possible. That Government shall promptly inform the Government whose official has reported the alleged contravention, as well as the Organization, of the action taken as a consequence of the information communicated.

Article XI

[Nothing in the present Convention shall be construed as derogating from the powers of any Contracting Government to take measures within its jurisdiction in respect of any matter to which the Convention relates or as extending the jurisdiction of any Contracting Government.]

Article XII

[Each Contracting Government shall send to the Bureau and to the appropriate organ of the United Nations:–
  (a) the text of laws, decrees, orders and regulations in force in its territories which give effect to the present convention;
  (b) all official reports or summaries of official reports in so far as they show the results of the application of the provisions of the Convention, provided always that such reports or summaries are not, in the opinion of that Government, of a confidential nature.]

Article XIII

[Any dispute between Contracting Governments relating to the interpretation or application of the present Convention which cannot be settled by negotiation shall be referred at the request of either party to the International Court of Justice for decision unless the parties in dispute agree to submit it to arbitration.]

✍ AGREEMENT BETWEEN DENMARK, FINLAND, NORWAY AND SWEDEN CONCERNING CO-OPERATION TO ENSURE COMPLIANCE WITH THE REGULATIONS FOR PREVENTING THE POLLUTION OF THE SEA BY OIL

The Governments of Denmark, Finland, Norway and Sweden, desiring through co-operation with each other, to ensure compliance with the International Convention for the Prevention of Pollution of the Sea by Oil and with the national regulations in force in this matter, have agreed as follows:

Article 1

One Contracting State shall forthwith inform the competent authority of another Contracting State of the sighting of any considerable amount of oil on the sea which is apt to drift towards the territory of the latter State.

Article 2

One Contracting State shall inform the competent authority of another Contracting State of any case where a vessel registered in the latter State has been observed committing an offence, within the territorial or adjacent waters of the Contracting States, against the regulations concerning pollution by oil.

Article 3

The Contracting States shall furnish assistance to each other in the investigation of offences against the regulations concerning pollution by oil which are presumed to have been committed within the territorial or adjacent waters of the Contracting States.

Such assistance may include inspection of the oil record book, the ship's official log-book and the engine-room log, the taking of oil samples and so on.

Article 4

The Contracting States shall each year exchange information on the more important cases of oil pollution observed within the territorial

Signed at Copenhagen, on December 8, 1967.

waters of the respective States and on what measures were taken in each particular case.

Article 5

The Contracting States shall also exchange information concerning:
(a) the existence and the construction of facilities for the reception of oily residues from ships;
(b) national regulations and other circumstances which have a bearing on the prevention of oil pollution;
(c) the authorities of the respective Contracting States to which information in pursuance of this Agreement is to be transmitted.

✿ ✿ ✿

✉ AGREEMENT CONCERNING POLLUTION OF THE NORTH SEA BY OIL (BONN)

The Governments of

the Kingdom of Belgium
the Kingdom of Denmark
the French Republic
the Federal Republic of Germany
the Kingdom of the Netherlands
the Kingdom of Norway
the Kingdom of Sweden
the United Kingdom of Great Britain and Northern Ireland,

Recognising that grave pollution of the sea by oil in the North Sea area involves a danger to the coastal States,

Noting that the Council of the Intergovernmental Maritime Consultative Organisation at its third extraordinary session in May 1967 decided to include among the matters requiring study as a matter of urgency, inter alia,

procedures whereby States, regionally or inter-regionally where applicable, can co-operate at short notice to provide manpower, supplies, equipment and scientific advice to deal with discharge of oil or other noxious or hazardous substances including consideration of the possibility of patrols to ascertain the extent of the discharge and the manner of treating it both on sea and land,

Have agreed on the following:

Signed June 9, 1969; entered into force, August 9, 1969.

Article 1

This Agreement shall apply whenever the presence or the prospective presence of oil polluting the sea within the North Sea area, as defined in Article 2 of this Agreement, presents a grave and imminent danger to the coast or related interests of one or more Contracting Parties.

Article 2

For the purposes of this Agreement the North Sea area means the North Sea proper southwards of latitude 61° N, together with:

(a) the Skagerrak, the southern limit of which is determined by a line joining Skagen and Pater Noster Skären;

(b) the English Channel and its approaches eastwards of a line drawn fifty nautical miles to the west of a line joining the Scilly Isles and Ushant.

Article 3

The Contracting Parties consider that protection against pollution of the kind referred to in Article 1 of this Agreement is a matter which calls for active co-operation between the Contracting Parties.

Article 4

Contracting Parties undertake to inform the other Contracting Parties about:

(a) their national organisation for dealing with oil pollution;

(b) the competent authority responsible for receiving reports of oil pollution and for dealing with questions concerning measures of mutual assistance between Contracting Parties;

(c) new ways in which oil pollution may be avoided and about new effective measures to deal with oil pollution.

Article 5

1. Whenever a Contracting Party is aware of a casualty or the presence of oil slicks in the North Sea area likely to constitute a serious threat to the coast or related interests of any other Contracting Party, it shall inform that other Party without delay through its competent authority.

2. The Contracting Parties undertake to request the masters of all ships

flying their flags and pilots of aircraft registered in their countries to report without delay through the channels which may be most practicable and adequate in the circumstances:

(a) all casualties causing or likely to cause oil pollution of the sea;
(b) the presence, nature and extent of oil slicks on the sea likely to constitute a serious threat to the coast or related interests of one or more Contracting Parties.

Article 6

1. For the sole purposes of this Agreement the North Sea area is divided into the zones described in the Annex to this Agreement. [Not reproduced here.]

2. The Contracting Party within whose zone a situation of the kind described in Article 1 occurs, shall make the necessary assessments of the nature and extent of any casualty or, as the case may be, of the type and approximate quantity of oil floating on the sea, and the direction and speed of movement of the oil.

3. The Contracting Party concerned shall immediately inform all the other Contracting Parties through their competent authorities of its assessments and of any action which it has taken to deal with the floating oil and shall keep the oil under observation as long as it is drifting in its zone.

4. The obligations of the Contracting Parties under the provisions of this Article with respect to the zones of joint responsibility shall be the subject of special technical arrangements to be concluded between the Parties concerned. These arrangements shall be communicated to the other Contracting Parties.

5. In no case shall the division into zones referred to in this Article be invoked as a precedent or argument in any matter concerning sovereignty or jurisdiction.

Article 7

A Contracting Party requiring assistance to dispose of oil floating on the sea or polluting its coast may call on the help of the other Contracting Parties, starting with those which also seem likely to be affected by the floating oil. Contracting Parties called upon for help in accordance with this Article shall use their best endeavours to bring such assistance as is within their power.

Article 8

Any Contracting Party which has taken action in accordance with Article 7 of this Agreement shall submit a report thereon to the other Contracting Parties and to the Intergovernmental Maritime Consultative Organisation. . . .

⚓ INTERNATIONAL CONVENTION RELATING TO INTERVENTION ON THE HIGH SEAS IN CASES OF OIL POLLUTION CASUALTIES (BRUSSELS)

The States Parties to the present Convention,

CONSCIOUS of the need to protect the interests of their peoples against the grave consequences of a maritime casualty resulting in danger of oil pollution of sea and coastlines,

CONVINCED that under these circumstances measures of an exceptional character to protect such interests might be necessary on the high seas and that these measures do not affect the principle of freedom of the high seas,

HAVE AGREED as follows:

Article I

1. Parties to the present Convention may take such measures on the high seas as may be necessary to prevent, mitigate or eliminate grave and imminent danger to their coastline or related interests from pollution or threat of pollution of the sea by oil, following upon a maritime casualty or acts related to such a casualty, which may reasonably be expected to result in major harmful consequences.

2. However, no measures shall be taken under the present Convention against any warship or other ship owned or operated by a State and used, for the time being, only on government non-commercial service.

Article II

For the purposes of the present Convention:

1. "maritime casualty" means a collision of ships, stranding or other incident of navigation, or other occurrence on board a ship or external to

Adopted November 29, 1969.

it resulting in material damage or imminent threat of material damage to a ship or cargo;

2. "ship" means:

(a) any sea-going vessel of any type whatsoever, and

(b) any floating craft, with the exception of an installation or device engaged in the exploration and exploitation of the resources of the sea-bed and the ocean floor and the subsoil thereof;

3. "oil" means crude oil, fuel oil, diesel oil and lubricating oil;

4. "related interests" means the interests of a coastal State directly affected or threatened by the maritime casualty, such as:

(a) maritime coastal, port or estuarine activities, including fisheries activities, constituting an essential means of livelihood of the persons concerned;

(b) tourist attractions of the area concerned;

(c) the health of the coastal population and the well-being of the area concerned, including conservation of living marine resources and of wildlife;

5. "Organisation" means the Inter-Governmental Maritime Consultative Organisation.

Article III

When a Coastal State is exercising the right to take measures in accordance with Article I, the following provisions shall apply:

(a) before taking any measures, a coastal State shall proceed to consultations with other States affected by the maritime casualty, particularly with the flag State or States;

(b) the coastal State shall notify without delay the proposed measures to any persons physical or corporate known to the coastal State, or made known to it during the consultations, to have interests which can reasonably be expected to be affected by those measures. The coastal State shall take into account any views they may submit;

(c) before any measure is taken, the coastal State may proceed to a consultation with independent experts, whose names shall be chosen from a list maintained by the Organization;

(d) in cases of extreme urgency requiring measures to be taken immediately, the coastal State may take measures rendered necessary by the urgency of the situation, without prior notification or consultation or without continuing consultations already begun;

(e) a coastal State shall, before taking such measures and during their course, use its best endeavours to avoid any risk to human life, and to afford persons in distress any assistance of which they may stand in need, and in appropriate cases to facilitate the repatriation of ships' crews, and to raise no obstacle thereto;

(f) measures which have been taken in application of Article I shall be notified without delay to the States and to the known physical or corporate persons concerned, as well as to the Secretary-General of the Organization.

Article IV

1. Under the supervision of the Organization, there shall be set up and maintained the list of experts contemplated by Article III of the present Convention, and the Organization shall make necessary and appropriate regulations in connexion therewith, including the determination of the required qualifications.

2. Nominations to the list may be made by Member States of the Organization and by Parties to this Convention. The experts shall be paid on the basis of services rendered by the States utilizing those services.

Article V

1. Measures taken by the coastal State in accordance with Article I shall be proportionate to the damage actual or threatened to it.

2. Such measures shall not go beyond what is reasonably necessary to achieve the end mentioned in Article I and shall cease as soon as that end has been achieved; they shall not unnecessarily interfere with the rights and interests of the flag State, third States and of any persons, physical or corporate, concerned.

3. In considering whether the measures are proportionate to the damage, account shall be taken of:

(a) the extent and probability of imminent damage if those measures are not taken; and

(b) the likelihood of those measures being effective; and

(c) the extent of the damage which may be caused by such measures.

Article VI

Any Party which has taken measures in contravention of the provisions of the present Convention causing damage to others, shall be obliged to pay compensation to the extent of the damage caused by measures which exceed those reasonably necessary to achieve the end mentioned in Article I.

Article VII

Except as specifically provided, nothing in the present Convention shall prejudice any otherwise applicable right, duty, privilege or immunity or deprive any of the Parties or any interested physical or corporate person of any remedy otherwise applicable.

Article VIII

1. Any controversy between the Parties as to whether measures taken under Article I were in contravention of the provisions of the present Convention, to whether compensation is obliged to be paid under Article VI, and to the amount of such compensation shall, if settlement by negotiation between Parties involved or between the Party which took the measures and the physical or corporate claimants has not been possible, and if the Parties do not otherwise agree, be submitted upon request of any of the Parties concerned to conciliation or, if conciliation does not succeed, to arbitration, as set out in the Annex to the present Convention.

2. The Party which took the measure shall not be entitled to refuse a request for conciliation or arbitration under provisions of the preceding paragraph solely on the grounds that any remedies under municipal law in its own court have not been exhausted.

Annex

CHAPTER I

CONCILIATION

Article 1

Provided the Parties concerned do not decide otherwise, the procedure for conciliation shall be in accordance with the rules set out in this Chapter.

Article 2

1. A Conciliation Commission shall be established upon the request of one Party addressed to another in application of Article VIII of the Convention.

2. The request for conciliation submitted by a Party shall consist of a statement of the case together with any supporting documents.

3. If a procedure has been initiated between two Parties, any other Party the nationals or property of which have been affected by the same measures, or which is a coastal State having taken similar measures, may join in the conciliation procedure by giving written notice to the Parties which have originally initiated the procedure unless either of the latter Parties object to such joinder.

Article 3

1. The Conciliation Commission shall be composed of three members: one nominated by the coastal State which took the measures, one nominated by the State the nationals or property of which have been affected by those measures and a third, who shall preside over the Commission and shall be nominated by agreement between the two original members.

2. The Conciliators shall be selected from a list previously drawn up in accordance with the procedure set out in Article 4 below.

3. If within a period of 60 days from the date of receipt of the request for conciliation, the Party to which such request is made has not given notice to the other Party to the controversy of the nomination of the Conciliator for whose selection it is responsible, or if, within a period of 30 days from the date of nomination of the second of the members of the Commission to be designated by the Parties, the first two Conciliators have not been able to designate by common agreement the Chairmen of the Commission, the Secretary-General of the Organization shall upon request of either Party and within a period of 30 days, proceed to the required nomination. The members of the Commission thus nominated shall be selected from the list prescribed in the preceding paragraph.

4. In no case shall the Chairman of the Commission be or have been a national of one of the original Parties to the procedure, whatever the method of his nomination.

Article 4

1. The list prescribed in Article 3 above shall consist of qualified persons designated by the Parties and shall be kept up to date by the Organization. Each Party may designate for inclusion on the list four persons, who shall not necessarily be its nationals. The nominations shall be for periods of six years each and shall be renewable.

2. In the case of the decease or resignation of a person whose name appears on the list, the Party which nominated such person shall be permitted to nominate a replacement for the remainder of the term of office.

Article 5

1. Provided the Parties do not agree otherwise, the Conciliation Commission shall establish its own procedures, which shall in all cases permit a fair hearing. As regards examination, the Commission, unless it unanimously decides otherwise, shall conform with the provisions of Chapter III of The Hague Convention for the Peaceful Settlement of International Disputes of 18 October 1907.

2. The Parties shall be represented before the Conciliation Commission by agents whose duty shall be to act as intermediaries between the Parties and the Commission. Each of the Parties may seek also the assistance of advisers and experts nominated by it for this purpose and may request the hearing of all persons whose evidence the Party considers useful.

3. The Commission shall have the right to request explanations from agents, advisers and experts of the Parties as well as from any persons whom, with the consent of their Governments, it may deem useful to call.

Article 6

Provided the Parties do not agree otherwise, decisions of the Conciliation Commission shall be taken by a majority vote and the Commission shall not pronounce on the substance of the controversy unless all its members are present.

Article 7

The Parties shall facilitate the work of the Conciliation Commission and in particular, in accordance with their legislation, and using all means at their disposal:

(a) provide the Commission with the necessary documents and information;

(b) enable the Commission to enter their territory, to hear witnesses or experts, and to visit the scene.

Article 8

The task of the Conciliation Commission will be to clarify the matters under dispute, to assemble for this purpose all relevant information by means of examination or other means, and to endeavour to reconcile the Parties. After examining the case, the Commission shall communicate to the Parties a recommendation which appears to the Commission to be appropriate to the matter and shall fix a period of not more than 90 days within which the Parties are called upon to state whether or not they accept the recommendation.

Article 9

The recommendation shall be accompanied by a statement of reasons. If the recommendation does not represent in whole or in part the unanimous opinion of the Commission, any Conciliator shall be entitled to deliver a separate opinion.

Article 10

A conciliation shall be deemed unsuccessful if, 90 days after the Parties have been notified of the recommendation, either Party shall not have notified the other Party of its acceptance of the recommendation. Conciliation shall likewise be deemed unsuccessful if the Commission shall not have been established within the period prescribed in the third paragraph of Article 3 above, or provided the Parties have not agreed otherwise, if the Commission shall not have issued its recommendation within one year from the date on which the Chairman of the Commission was nominated.

Article 11

1. Each member of the Commission shall receive remuneration for his work, such remuneration to be fixed by agreement between the Parties which shall each contribute an equal proportion.
2. Contributions for miscellaneous expenditure incurred by the work of the Commission shall be apportioned in the same manner.

Article 12

The parties to the controversy may at any time during the conciliation procedure decide in agreement to have recourse to a different procedure for settlement of disputes.

CHAPTER II

ARBITRATION

Article 13

1. Arbitration procedure, unless the Parties decide otherwise, shall be in accordance with the rules set out in this Chapter.
2. Where conciliation is unsuccessful, a request for arbitration may only be made within a period of 180 days following the failure of conciliation.

Article 14

The Arbitration Tribunal shall consist of three members: one Arbitrator nominated by the coastal State which took the measures, one Arbitrator nominated by the State the nationals or property of which have been affected by those measures, and another Arbitrator who shall be nominated by agreement between the two first-named, and shall act as its Chairman.

Article 15

1. If, at the end of a period of 60 days from the nomination of the second Arbitrator, the Chairman of the Tribunal shall not have been nominated, the Secretary-General of the Organization upon request of either Party shall within a further period of 60 days proceed to such nomination, selecting from a list of qualified persons previously drawn up in accordance with the provisions of Article 4 above. This list shall be separate from the list of experts prescribed in Article IV of the Convention and from the list of Conciliators prescribed in Article 4 of the present Annex; the name of the same person may, however, appear both on the list of Conciliators and on the list of Arbitrators. A person who has acted as Conciliator in a dispute may not, however, be chosen to act as Arbitrator in the same matter.
2. If, within a period of 60 days from the date of receipt of the request, one of the Parties shall not have nominated the member of the Tribunal for whose designation it is responsible, the other Party may directly inform the Secretary-General of the Organization who shall nominate the Chairman of the Tribunal within a period of 60 days, selecting him from the list prescribed in paragraph 1 of the present Article.
3. The Chairman of the Tribunal shall, upon nomination, request the Party which has not provided an Arbitrator, to do so in the same manner and under the same conditions. If the Party does not make the required

nomination, the Chairman of the Tribunal shall request the Secretary-General of the Organization to make the nomination in the form and conditions prescribed in the preceding paragraph.

4. The Chairman of the Tribunal, if nominated under the provisions of the present Article, shall not be or have been a national of one of the Parties concerned, except with the consent of the other Party or Parties.

5. In the case of the decease or default of an Arbitrator for whose nomination one of the Parties is responsible, the said Party shall nominate a replacement within a period of 60 days from the date of decease or default. Should the said Party not make the nomination, the arbitration shall proceed under the remaining Arbitrators. In the case of decease or default of the Chairman of the Tribunal, a replacement shall be nominated in accordance with the provisions of Article 14 above, or in the absence of agreement between the members of the Tribunal within a period of 60 days of the decease or default, according to the provisions of the present Article.

Article 16

If a procedure has been initiated between two Parties, any other Party, the nationals or property of which have been affected by the same measures or which is a coastal State having taken similar measures, may join in the arbitration procedure by giving written notice to the Parties which have originally initiated the procedure unless either of the latter Parties object to such joinder.

Article 17

Any Arbitration Tribunal established under the provisions of the present Annex shall decide its own rules of procedure.

Article 18

1. Decisions of the Tribunal both as to its procedure and its place of meeting and as to any controversy laid before it, shall be taken by majority vote of its members; the absence or abstention of one of the members of the Tribunal for whose nomination the Parties were responsible shall not constitute an impediment to the Tribunal reaching a decision. In cases of equal voting, the Chairman shall cast the deciding vote.

2. The Parties shall facilitate the work of the Tribunal and in particular, in accordance with their legislation, and using all means at their disposal:

  (a) provide the Tribunal with the necessary documents and information;

(b) enable the Tribunal to enter their territory, to hear witnesses or experts, and to visit the scene.

3. Absence or default of one Party shall not constitute an impediment to the procedure.

Article 19

1. The award of the Tribunal shall be accompanied by a statement of reasons. It shall be final and without appeal. The Parties shall immediately comply with the award.

2. Any controversy which may arise between the Parties as regards interpretation and execution of the award may be submitted by either Party for judgment to the Tribunal which made the award, or, if it is not available, to another Tribunal constituted for this purpose in the same manner as the original Tribunal.

✌ INTERNATIONAL CONVENTION ON CIVIL LIABILITY FOR OIL POLLUTION DAMAGE (BRUSSELS)

The States Parties to the present Convention,

CONSCIOUS of the dangers of pollution posed by the worldwide maritime carriage of oil in bulk.

CONVINCED of the need to ensure that adequate compensation is available to persons who suffer damage caused by pollution resulting from the escape or discharge of oil from ships,

DESIRING to adopt uniform international rules and procedures for determining questions of liability and providing adequate compensation in such cases,

HAVE AGREED as follows:

Article I

For the purposes of this Convention:

1. "Ship" means any sea-going vessel and any seaborne craft of any type whatsoever, actually carrying oil in bulk as cargo.

2. "Person" means any individual or partnership or any public or private body, whether corporate or not, including a State or any of its constituent subdivisions.

Adopted November 29, 1969.

3. "Owner" means the person or persons registered as the owner of the ship or, in the absence of registration, the person or persons owning the ship. However in the case of a ship owned by a State and operated by a company which in that State is registered as the ship's operator, "owner" shall mean such company.

4. "State of the ship's registry" means in relation to registered ships the State of registration of the ship, and in relation to unregistered ships the State whose flag the ship is flying.

5. "Oil" means any persistent oil such as crude oil, fuel oil, heavy diesel oil, lubricating oil and whale oil, whether carried on board a ship as cargo or in the bunkers of such a ship.

6. "Pollution damage" means loss or damage caused outside the ship carrying oil by contamination resulting from the escape or discharge of oil from the ship, wherever such escape or discharge may occur, and includes the costs of preventive measures and further loss or damage caused by preventive measures.

7. "Preventive measures" means any reasonable measures taken by any person after an incident has occurred to prevent or minimize pollution damage.

8. "Incident" means any occurrence, or series of occurrences having the same origin, which causes pollution damage.

9. "Organization" means the Inter-Governmental Maritime Consultative Organization.

Article II

This Convention shall apply exclusively to pollution damage caused on the territory including the territorial sea of a Contracting State and to preventive measures taken to prevent or minimize such damage.

Article III

1. Except as provided in paragraphs 2 and 3 of this Article, the owner of a ship at the time of an incident, or where the incident consists of a series of occurrences at the time of the first such occurrence, shall be liable for any pollution damage caused by oil which has escaped or been discharged from the ship as a result of the incident.

2. No liability for pollution damage shall attach to the owner if he proves that the damage:

   (a) resulted from an act of war, hostilities, civil war, insurrection or a natural phenomenon of an exceptional, inevitable and irresistible character, or

   (b) was wholly caused by an act or omission done with intent to cause damage by a third party, or

(c) was wholly caused by the negligence or other wrongful act of any Government or other authority responsible for the maintenance of lights or other navigational aids in the exercise of that function.

3. If the owner proves that the pollution damage resulted wholly or partially either from an act or omission done with intent to cause damage by the person who suffered the damage or from the negligence of that person, the owner may be exonerated wholly or partially from his liability to such person.

4. No claim for compensation for pollution damage shall be made against the owner otherwise than in accordance with this Convention. No claim for pollution damage under this Convention or otherwise may be made against the servants or agents of the owner.

5. Nothing in this Convention shall prejudice any right of recourse of the owner against third parties.

Article IV

When oil has escaped or has been discharged from two or more ships, and pollution damage results therefrom, the owners of all the ships concerned, unless exonerated under Article III, shall be jointly and severally liable for all such damage which is not reasonably separable.

Article V

1. The owner of a ship shall be entitled to limit his liability under this Convention in respect of any one incident to an aggregate amount of 2,000 francs for each ton of the ship's tonnage. However, this aggregate amount shall not in any event exceed 210 million francs.

2. If the incident occurred as a result of the actual fault or privity of the owner, he shall not be entitled to avail himself of the limitation provided in paragraph 1 of this Article.

3. For the purpose of availing himself of the benefit of limitation provided for in paragraph 1 of this Article the owner shall constitute a fund for the total sum representing the limit of his liability with the Court or other competent authority of any one of the Contracting States in which action is brought under Article IX. The fund can be constituted either by depositing the sum or by producing a bank guarantee or other guarantee, acceptable under the legislation of the Contracting State where the fund is constituted, and considered to be adequate by the Court or another competent authority.

4. The fund shall be distributed among the claimants in proportion to the amounts of their established claims.

5. If before the fund is distributed the owner or any of his servants or

agents or any person providing him insurance or other financial security has as a result of the incident in question, paid compensation for pollution damage, such person shall, up to the amount he has paid, acquire by subrogation the rights which the person so compensated would have enjoyed under this Convention.

6. The right of subrogation provided for in paragraph 5 of this Article may also be exercised by a person other than those mentioned therein in respect of any amount of compensation for pollution damage which he may have paid but only to the extent that such subrogation is permitted under the applicable national law.

7. Where the owner or any other person establishes that he may be compelled to pay at a later date in whole or in part any such amount of compensation, with regard to which such person would have enjoyed a right of subrogation under paragraphs 5 or 6 of this Article, had the compensation been paid before the fund was distributed, the Court or other competent authority of the State where the fund has been constituted may order that a sufficient sum shall be provisionally set aside to enable such person at such later date to enforce his claim against the fund.

8. Claims in respect of expenses reasonably incurred or sacrifices reasonably made by the owner voluntarily to prevent or minimize pollution damage shall rank equally with other claims against the fund.

✿   ✿   ✿

11. The insurer or other person providing financial security shall be entitled to constitute a fund in accordance with this Article on the same conditions and having the same effect as if it were constituted by the owner. Such a fund may be constituted even in the event of the actual fault or privity of the owner but its constitution shall in that case not prejudice the rights of any claimant against the owner.

Article VI

1. Where the owner, after an incident, has constituted a fund in accordance with Article V, and is entitled to limit his liability,

   (a) no person having a claim for pollution damage arising out of that incident shall be entitled to exercise any right against any other assets of the owner in respect of such claim;

   (b) the Court or other competent authority of any Contracting State shall order the release of any ship or other property belonging to the owner which has been arrested in respect of a claim for pollution damage arising out of that incident, and shall similarly release any bail or other security furnished to avoid such arrest.

2. The foregoing shall, however, only apply if the claimant has access to the Court administering the fund and the fund is actually available in respect of his claim.

Article VII

1. The owner of a ship registered in a Contracting State and carrying more than 2,000 tons of oil in bulk as cargo shall be required to maintain insurance or other financial security, such as the guarantee of a bank or a certificate delivered by an international compensation fund, in the sums fixed by applying the limits of liability prescribed in Article V, paragraph 1 to cover his liability for pollution damage under this Convention.

2. A certificate attesting that insurance or other financial security is in force in accordance with the provisions of this Convention shall be issued to each ship. It shall be issued or certified by the appropriate authority of the State of the ship's registry after determining that the requirements of paragraph 1 of this Article have been complied with.

*　*　*

6. The State of Registry shall, subject to the provisions of this Article, determine the conditions of issue and validity of the certificate.

7. Certificates issued or certified under the authority of a Contracting State shall be accepted by other Contracting States for the purposes of this Convention and shall be regarded by other Contracting States as having the same force as certificates issued or certified by them. A Contracting State may at any time request consultation with the State of a ship's registry should it believe that the insurer or guarantor named in the certificate is not financially capable of meeting the obligations imposed by this Convention.

8. Any claim for compensation for pollution damage may be brought directly against the insurer or other person providing financial security for the owner's liability for pollution damage. In such case the defendant may, irrespective of the actual fault or privity of the owner, avail himself of the limits of liability prescribed in Article V, paragraph 1. He may further avail himself of the defences (other than the bankruptcy or winding up of the owner) which the owner himself would have been entitled to invoke. Furthermore, the defendant may avail himself of the defence that the pollution damage resulted from the wilful misconduct of the owner himself, but the defendant shall not avail himself of any other defence which he might have been entitled to invoke in proceedings brought by the owner against him. The defendant shall in any event have the right to require the owner to be joined in the proceedings.

9. Any sums provided by insurance or by other financial security maintained in accordance with paragraph 1 of this Article shall be available exclusively for the satisfaction of claims under this Convention.

10. A Contracting State shall not permit a ship under its flag to which this Article applies to trade unless a certificate has been issued under paragraph 2 or 12 of this Article.

11. Subject to the provisions of this Article, each Contracting State shall ensure, under its national legislation, that insurance or other security to the extent specified in paragraph 1 of this Article is in force in respect of any ship, wherever registered, entering or leaving a port in its territory, or arriving at or leaving an off-shore terminal in its territorial sea, if the ship actually carries more than 2,000 tons of oil in bulk as cargo.

12. If insurance or other financial security is not maintained in respect of a ship owned by a Contracting State, the provisions of this Article relating thereto shall not be applicable to such ship, but the ship shall carry a certificate issued by the appropriate authorities of the State of the ship's registry stating that the ship is owned by that State and that the ship's liability is covered within the limits prescribed by Article V, paragraph 1. Such a certificate shall follow as closely as practicable the model prescribed by paragraph 2 of this Article.

Article VIII

Rights of compensation under this Convention shall be extinguished unless an action is brought thereunder within three years from the date when the damage occurred. However, in no case shall an action be brought after six years from the date of the incident which caused the damage. Where this incident consists of a series of occurrences, the six years' period shall run from the date of the first such occurrence.

Article IX

1. Where an incident has caused pollution damage in the territory including the territorial sea of one or more Contracting States, or preventive measures have been taken to prevent or minimize pollution damage in such territory including the territorial sea, actions for compensation may only be brought in the Courts of any such Contracting State or States. Reasonable notice of any such action shall be given to the defendant.

2. Each Contracting State shall ensure that its Courts possess the necessary jurisdiction to entertain such actions for compensation.

3. After the fund has been constituted in accordance with Article V the Courts of the State in which the fund is constituted shall be exclusively competent to determine all matters relating to the apportionment and distribution of the fund.

Article X

1. Any judgment given by a Court with jurisdiction in accordance with Article IX which is enforceable in the State of origin where it is no longer subject to ordinary forms of review, shall be recognized in any Contracting State, except:
   (a) where the judgment was obtained by fraud; or
   (b) where the defendant was not given reasonable notice and a fair opportunity to present his case.
2. A judgment recognized under paragraph 1 of this Article shall be enforceable in each Contracting State as soon as the formalities required in that State have been complied with. The formalities shall not permit the merits of the case to be re-opened.

Article XI

1. The provisions of this Convention shall not apply to warships or other ships owned or operated by a State and used, for the time being, only on Government non-commercial service.
2. With respect to ships owned by a Contracting State and used for commercial purposes, each State shall be subject to suit in the jurisdictions set forth in Article IX and shall waive all defences based on its status as a sovereign State.

Article XII

This Convention shall supersede any International Conventions in force or open for signature, ratification or accession at the date on which the Convention is opened for signature, but only to the extent that such Conventions would be in conflict with it; however, nothing in this Article shall affect the obligations of Contracting States to non-Contracting States arising under such International Conventions.

✿ ✿ ✿

✍ Brussels Resolution on Establishment of an International Compensation Fund for Oil Pollution Damage (1969)

The International Legal Conference on Marine Pollution Damage, 1969,

NOTING that the International Convention on Civil Liability for Oil Pollution Damage 1969, although it lays down the principle of strict liability and provides for a system of compulsory insurance or other financial guarantee for ships carrying oil in bulk as cargo, does not afford full protection for victims in all cases,

RECOGNIZING the view having emerged during the Conference that some form of supplementary scheme in the nature of an international fund is necessary to ensure that adequate compensation will be available for victims of large scale oil pollution incidents,

TAKING ACCOUNT of the report submitted by the working party set up by the Committee of the Whole II to study the problems relating to the constitution of an international compensation fund,

REALISING, however, that the time available for the Conference has not made it possible to give full consideration to all aspects of such a compensation scheme,

REQUESTS the Inter-Governmental Maritime Consultative Organization to elaborate as soon as possible, through its Legal Committee and other Appropriate legal bodies, a draft for a compensation scheme based upon the existence of an International Fund,

CONSIDERS that such a compensation scheme should be elaborated taking into account as a foundation the following principles:
1. Victims should be fully and adequately compensated under a system based upon the principle of strict liability.
2. The fund should in principle relieve the shipowner of the additional financial burden imposed by the present Convention.

REQUESTS IMCO to convene, not later than the year 1971, an International Legal Conference for the consideration and adoption of such a new compensation scheme.

▨ INTERNATIONAL CONVENTION ON THE ESTABLISHMENT OF AN INTERNATIONAL FUND FOR COMPENSATION FOR OIL POLLUTION DAMAGE (BRUSSELS)

The States Parties to the present Convention,
BEING PARTIES to the International Convention on Civil Liability for Oil Pollution Damage, adopted at Brussels on 29 November 1969,
CONSCIOUS of the dangers of pollution posed by the world-wide maritime carriage of oil in bulk,

Adopted December 18, 1971.

CONVINCED of the need to ensure that adequate compensation is available to persons who suffer damage caused by pollution resulting from the escape or discharge of oil from ships,

CONSIDERING that the International Convention of 29 November 1969, on Civil Liability for Oil Pollution Damage, by providing a régime for compensation for pollution damage in Contracting States and for the costs of measures, wherever taken, to prevent or minimize such damage, represents a considerable progress towards the achievement of this aim,

CONSIDERING HOWEVER that this régime does not afford full compensation for victims of oil pollution damage in all cases while it imposes an additional financial burden on shipowners,

CONSIDERING FURTHER that the economic consequences of oil pollution damage resulting from the escape or discharge of oil carried in bulk at sea by ships should not exclusively be borne by the shipping industry but should in part be borne by the oil cargo interests,

CONVINCED of the need to elaborate a compensation and indemnification system supplementary to the International Convention on Civil Liability for Oil Pollution Damage with a view to ensuring that full compensation will be available to victims of oil pollution incidents and that the shipowners are at the same time given relief in respect of the additional financial burdens imposed on them by the said Convention,

TAKING NOTE of the Resolution on the Establishment of an International Compensation Fund for Oil Pollution Damage which was adopted on 29 November 1969 by the International Legal Conference on Maritime Pollution Damage,

HAVE AGREED as follows:

General Provisions

Article 1

For the purposes of this Convention—

1. "Liability Convention" means the International Convention on Civil Liability for Oil Pollution Damage, adopted at Brussels on 29 November 1969.

2. "Ship", "Person", "Owner", "Oil", "Pollution Damage", "Preventive Measures", "Incident" and "Organization", have the same meaning as in Article I of the Liability Convention, provided however that, for the purposes of these terms, "oil" shall be confined to persistent hydrocarbon mineral oils.

3. "Contributing Oil" means crude oil and fuel oil as defined in sub-paragraphs (a) and (b) below:

(a) "Crude Oil" means any liquid hydrocarbon mixture occurring naturally in the earth whether or not treated to render it suitable for transportation. It also includes crude oils from which certain distillate fractions have been removed (sometimes referred to as "topped crudes") or to which certain distillate fractions have been added (sometimes referred to as "spiked" or "reconstituted" crudes.

(b) "Fuel Oil" means heavy distillates or residues from crude oil or blends of such materials intended for use as a fuel for the production of heat or power of a quality equivalent to "American Society for Testing Materials Specification for Number Four Fuel Oil" (Designation D 396-69) or heavier.

4. "Franc" means the unit referred to in Article V, paragraph 9 of the Liability Convention.

5. "Ship's tonnage" has the same meaning as in Article V, paragraph 10 of the Liability Convention.

6. "Ton", in relation to oil, means a metric ton.

7. "Guarantor" means any person providing insurance or other financial security to cover an owner's liability in pursuance of Article VII, paragraph 1 of the Liability Convention.

8. "Terminal installation" means any site for the storage of oil in bulk which is capable of receiving oil from waterborne transportation, including any facility situated off-shore and linked to such site.

9. For the purposes of ascertaining the date of an incident where that incident consists of a series of occurrences, the incident shall be treated as having occurred on the date of the first such occurrence.

Article 2

1. An International Fund for compensation for pollution damage, to be named "The International Oil Pollution Compensation Fund" and hereinafter referred to as "The Fund", is hereby established with the following aims:

(a) to provide compensation for pollution damage to the extent that the protection afforded by the Liability Convention is inadequate;

(b) to give relief to shipowners in respect of the additional financial burden imposed on them by the Liability Convention, such relief being subject to conditions designed to insure compliance with safety at sea and other conventions;

(c) to give effect to the related purposes set out in this Convention.

2. The Fund shall in each Contracting State be recognized as a legal person capable under the laws of that State of assuming rights and obligations and of being a party in legal proceedings before the courts of

that State. Each Contracting State shall recognize the Director of the Fund (hereinafter referred to as "The Director") as the legal representative of the Fund.

Article 3

This Convention shall apply:–

1. with regard to compensation according to Article 4 exclusively to pollution damage caused on the territory including the territorial sea of a Contracting State, and to preventive measures taken to prevent or minimize such damage.

2. with regard to indemnification of shipowners and their guarantors according to Article 5, exclusively in respect of pollution damage caused on the territory including the territorial sea of a State party to the Liability Convention; by a ship registered in or flying the flag of a Contracting State and in respect of preventive measures taken to prevent or minimize such damage.

Compensation and indemnification

Article 4

1. For the purpose of fulfilling its function under Article 2, paragraph 1(a), the Fund shall pay compensation to any person suffering pollution damage if such person has been unable to obtain full and adequate compensation for the damage under the terms of the Liability Convention,

  (a) because no liability for the damage arises under the Liability Convention;

  (b) because the owner liable for the damage under the Liability Convention is financially incapable of meeting his obligations in full and any financial security that may be provided under Article VII of that Convention does not cover or is insufficient to satisfy the claims for compensation for the damage; an owner being treated as financially incapable of meeting his obligations and a financial security being treated as insufficient if the person suffering the damage has been unable to obtain full satisfaction of the amount of compensation due under the Liability Convention after having taken all reasonable steps to pursue the legal remedies available to him;

  (c) because the damage exceeds the owner's liability under the Liability Convention as limited pursuant to Article V, paragraph 1, of that Convention or under the terms of any other international

Convention in force or open for signature, ratification or accession at the date of this Convention. Expenses reasonably incurred or sacrifices reasonably made by the owner voluntarily to prevent or minimize pollution damage shall be treated as pollution damage for the purposes of this Article.

2. The Fund shall incur no obligation under the preceding paragraph if:

(a) it proves that the pollution damage resulted from an act of war, hostilities, civil war or insurrection or was caused by oil which has escaped or been discharged from a warship or other ship owned or operated by a State and used, at the time of the incident, only on Government noncommercial service; or

(b) the claimant cannot prove that the damage resulted from an incident involving one or more ships.

3. If the Fund proves that the pollution damage resulted wholly or partially either from an act or omission done with intent to cause damage by the person who suffered the damage or from the negligence of that person, the Fund may be exonerated wholly or partially from its obligation to pay compensation to such person provided, however, that there shall be no such exoneration with regard to such preventive measures which are compensated under paragraph 1. The Fund shall in any event be exonerated to the extent that the shipowner may have been exonerated under Article III, paragraph 3 of the Liability Convention.

4. (a) Except as otherwise provided in sub-paragraph (b) of this paragraph, the aggregate amount of compensation payable by the Fund under this Article shall in respect of any one incident be limited, so that the total sum of that amount and the amount of compensation actually paid under the Liability Convention for pollution damage caused in the territory of the Contracting States, including any sums in respect of which the Fund is under an obligation to indemnify the owner pursuant to Article 5, paragraph 1, of this Convention, shall not exceed 450 million francs.

(b) The aggregate amount of compensation payable by the Fund under this Article for the pollution damage resulting from a natural phenomenon of an exceptional, inevitable and irresistible character, shall not exceed 450 million francs.

5. Where the amount of established claims against the Fund exceeds the aggregate amount of compensation payable under paragraph 4, the amount available shall be distributed in such a manner that the proportion between any established claim and the amount of compensation actually recovered by the claimant under the Liability Convention and this Convention shall be the same for all claimants.

6. The Assembly of the Fund (hereinafter referred to as "the Assembly") may, having regard to the experience of incidents which have

occurred and in particular the amount of damage resulting therefrom and to changes in the monetary values, decide that the amount of 450 million francs referred to in paragraph 4, sub-paragraphs (a) and (b), shall be changed, provided however, that this amount shall in no case exceed 900 million francs or be lower than 450 million francs. The changed amount shall apply to incidents which occur after the date of the decision effecting the change.

7. The Fund shall, at the request of a Contracting State use its good offices as necessary to assist that State to secure promptly such personnel, material and services as are necessary to enable the State to take measures to prevent or mitigate pollution damage arising from an incident in respect of which the Fund may be called upon to pay compensation under this Convention.

8. The Fund may on conditions to be laid down in the Internal Regulations provide credit facilities with a view to the taking of preventive measures against pollution damage arising from a particular incident in respect of which the Fund may be called upon to pay compensation under this Convention.

Article 5

1. For the purpose of fulfilling its function under Article 2, paragraph 1 (b), the Fund shall indemnify the owner and his guarantor, for that portion of the aggregate amount of liability under the Liability Convention which:

- (a) is in excess of an amount equivalent to 1,500 francs for each ton of the ship's tonnage or of an amount of 125 million francs, whichever is the less, and
- (b) is not in excess of an amount equivalent to 2,000 francs for each ton of the said tonnage or an amount of 210 million francs whichever is the less, provided, however, that the Fund shall incur no obligation under this paragraph where the pollution damage resulted from the wilful misconduct of the owner himself.

2. The Assembly may decide that the Fund shall, on conditions to be laid down in the Internal Regulations, assume the obligations of a guarantor in respect of ships referred to in Article 3, paragraph 2, with regard to the portion of liability referred to in paragraph 1 of this Article. However, the Fund shall assume such obligations only if the owner so requests and if he maintains adequate insurance or other financial security covering the owner's liability under the Liability Convention up to an amount equivalent to 1,500 francs for each ton of the ship's tonnage or an amount of 125 million francs, whichever is the less. If the Fund

assumes such obligations, the owner shall in each Contracting State be considered to have complied with Article VII of the Liability Convention in respect of the portion of his liability mentioned above.

3. The Fund may be exonerated wholly or partially from its obligations under paragraph 1 towards the owner and his guarantor, if the Fund proves that as a result of the actual fault or privity of the owner:

(a) the ship from which the oil causing the pollution damage escaped, did not comply with the requirements laid down in:

   (i) the International Convention for the Prevention of Pollution of the Sea by Oil, 1954, as amended in 1962; or

   (ii) the International Convention for the Safety of Life at Sea, 1960; or

   (iii) the International Convention on Load Lines, 1966; or

   (iv) the International Regulations for Preventing Collisions at Sea, 1960; or

   (v) any amendments to the above-mentioned Conventions which have been determined as being of an important nature in accordance with Article XVI(5) of the Convention mentioned under (i), Article IX(e) of the Convention mentioned under (ii) or Article 29(3)(d) or (4)(d) of the Convention mentioned under (iii), provided, however, that such amendments had been in force for at least twelve months at the time of the incident;
and

(b) the incident or damage was caused wholly or partially by such non-compliance. The provisions of this paragraph shall apply irrespective of whether the Contracting State in which the ship was registered or whose flag it was flying, is a Party to the relevant Instrument.

4. Upon the entry into force of a new Convention designed to replace, in whole or in part, any of the Instruments specified in paragraph 3, the Assembly may decide at least six months in advance a date on which the new Convention will replace such Instrument or part thereof for the purpose of paragraph 3. However, any State Party to this Convention may declare to the Director of the Fund before that date that it does not accept such replacement; in which case the decision of the Assembly shall have no effect in respect of a ship registered in, or flying the flag of, that State at the time of the incident. Such a declaration may be withdrawn at any later date and shall in any event cease to have effect when the State in question becomes a party to such new Convention.

5. A ship complying with the requirements in an amendment to an Instrument, specified in paragraph 3, or with requirements in a new

Convention, where the amendment or Convention is designed to replace in whole or in part such Instrument, shall be considered as complying with the requirements in the said Instrument for the purposes of paragraph 3.

6. Where the Fund, acting as a guarantor, by virtue of paragraph 2, has paid compensation for pollution damage in accordance with the Liability Convention, it shall have a right of recovery from the owner, if and to the extent that the Fund would have been exonerated pursuant to paragraph 3 from its obligations under paragraph 1 to indemnify the owner.

7. Expenses reasonably incurred and sacrifices reasonably made by the owner voluntarily to prevent or minimize pollution damage shall be treated as included in the owner's liability for the purposes of this Article.

Article 6

1. Rights to compensation under Article 4 or indemnification under Article 5 shall be extinguished unless an action is brought thereunder or a notification has been made pursuant to Article 7, paragraph 6, within three years from the date when the damage occurred. However, in no case shall an action be brought after six years from the date of the incident which caused the damage.

2. Notwithstanding paragraph 1, the right of the owner or his guarantor to seek indemnification from the Fund pursuant to Article 5, paragraph 1, shall in no case be extinguished before the expiry of a period of six months as from the date on which the owner or his guarantor acquired knowledge of the bringing of an action against him under the Liability Convention.

Article 7

1. Subject to the subsequent provisions of this Article, any action against the Fund for compensation under Article 4 or indemnification under Article 5 of this Convention shall be brought only before a court competent under Article IX of the Liability Convention in respect of actions against the owner who is or who would, but for the provisions of Article III, paragraph 2, of that Convention, have been liable for pollution damage caused by the relevant incident.

2. Each Contracting State shall ensure that its courts possess the necessary jurisdiction to entertain such actions against the Fund as are referred to in paragraph 1.

3. Where an action for compensation for pollution damage has been

brought before a court competent under Article IX of the Liability Convention against the owner of a ship or his guarantor, such court shall have exclusive jurisdictional competence over any action against the Fund for compensation or indemnification under the provisions of Article 4 or 5 of this Convention in respect of the same damage. However, where an action for compensation for pollution damage under the Liability Convention has been brought before a court in a State Party to the Liability Convention but not to this Convention, any action against the Fund under Article 4 or Article 5, paragraph 1, of this Convention shall at the option of the claimant be brought either before a court of the State where the Fund has its headquarters or before any court of a State Party to this Convention competent under Article IX of the Liability Convention.

4. Each Contracting State shall ensure that the Fund shall have the right to intervene as a party to any legal proceedings instituted in accordance with Article IX of the Liability Convention before a competent court of that State against the owner of a ship or his guarantor.

5. Except as otherwise provided in paragraph 6, the Fund shall not be bound by any judgment or decision in proceedings to which it has not been a party or by any settlement to which it is not a party.

6. Without prejudice to the provisions of paragraph 4, where an action under Liability Convention for compensation for pollution damage has been brought against an owner or his guarantor, before a competent court in a Contracting State, each party to the proceedings shall be entitled under the national law of that State to notify the Fund of the proceedings. Where such notification has been made in accordance with the formalities required by the law of the court seized and in such time and in such a manner that the Fund has been in fact in a position effectively to intervene as a party to the proceedings, any judgment rendered by the court in such proceedings shall, after it has become final and enforceable in the State where the judgment was given, become binding upon the Fund in the sense that the facts and findings in that judgment may not be disputed by the Fund even if the Fund has not actually intervened in the proceedings.

Article 8

Subject to any decision concerning the distribution referred to in Article 4, paragraph 5, any judgment given against the Fund by a court having jurisdiction in accordance with Article 7, paragraphs 1 and 3, shall, when it has become enforceable in the State of origin and is in that State no longer subject to ordinary forms of review, be recognized and enforceable in each Contracting State on the same conditions as are prescribed in Article X of the Liability Convention.

Article 9

1. Subject to the provisions of Article 5, the Fund shall, in respect of any amount of compensation for pollution damage paid by the Fund in accordance with Article 4, paragraph 1, of this Convention, acquire by subrogation the rights that the person so compensated may enjoy under the Liability Convention against the owner or his guarantor.

2. Nothing in this Convention shall prejudice any right of recourse or subrogation of the Fund against persons other than those referred to in the preceding paragraph. In any event the right of the Fund to subrogation against such person shall be not less favourable than that of an insurer of the person to whom the compensation or indemnification has been paid.

3. Without prejudice to any other rights of subrogation or recourse against the Fund which may exist, a Contracting State, or agency thereof, which has paid compensation for pollution damage in accordance with provisions of national law shall acquire by subrogation the rights which the person so compensated would have enjoyed under this Convention.

Contributions

Article 10

1. Contributions to the Fund shall be made in respect of each Contracting State by any person who, in the calendar year referred to in Article 11, paragraph 1, as regards initial contributions and in Article 12, paragraphs 2 (a) or (b), as regards annual contributions, has received in total quantities exceeding 150,000 tons:

   (a) in the ports or terminal installations in the territory of that State contributing oil carried by sea to such ports or terminal installations; and

   (b) in any installations situated in the territory of that Contracting State contributing oil which has been carried by sea and discharged in a port or terminal installation of a non-Contracting State, provided that contributing oil shall only be taken into account by virtue of this sub-paragraph on first receipt in a Contracting State after its discharge in that non-Contracting State.

2. (a) For the purposes of paragraph 1, where the quantity of con-

tributing oil received in the territory of a Contracting State by
any person in a calendar year when aggregated with the quantity
of contributing oil received in the same Contracting State in that
year by any associated person or persons exceeds 150,000 tons,
such person shall pay contributions in respect of the actual quantity received by him notwithstanding that the quantity did not
exceed 150,000 tons.

(b) "Associated person" means any subsidiary or commonly controlled entity. The question whether a person comes within this
definition shall be determined by the national law of the State
concerned.

Article 11

1. In respect of each Contracting State initial contributions shall be
made of an amount which shall for each person referred to in Article
10 be calculated on the basis of a fixed sum for each ton of contributing
oil received by him during the calendar year preceding that in which
this Convention entered into force for that State.

2. The sum referred to in paragraph 1 shall be determined by the Assembly within two months after the entry into force of this Convention.
In performing this function the Assembly shall, to the extent possible,
fix the sum in such a way that the total amount of initial contributions
would, if contributions were to be made in respect of 90 per cent of
the quantities of contributing oil carried by sea in the world, equal
75 million francs.

3. The initial contributions shall in respect of each Contracting State be
paid within three months following the date at which the Convention
entered into force for that State.

Article 12

1. With a view to assessing for each person referred to in Article 10 the
amount of annual contributions due, if any, and taking account of the
necessity to maintain sufficient liquid funds, the Assembly shall for
each calendar year make an estimate in the form of a budget of:

(i) *Expenditure*
(a) costs and expenses of the administration of the Fund in the relevant year and any deficit from operations in preceding years;
(b) payments to be made by the Fund in the relevant year for the
satisfaction of claims against the Fund due under Article 4 or 5,

including repayment on loans previously taken by the Fund for the satisfaction of such claims, to the extent that the aggregate amount of such claims in respect of any one incident does not exceed 15 million francs;

(c) payments to be made by the Fund in the relevant year for the satisfaction of claims against the Fund due under Article 4 or 5, including repayment on loans previously taken by the Fund for the satisfaction of such claims, to the extent that the aggregate amount of such claims in respect of any one incident is in excess of 15 million francs;

(ii) *Income*

(a) surplus funds from operations in preceding years, including any interest;

(b) initial contributions to be paid in the course of the year;

(c) annual contributions, if required to balance the budget;

(d) any other income.

2. For each person referred to in Article 10 the amount of his annual contribution shall be determined by the Assembly and shall be calculated in respect of each Contracting State:

(a) in so far as the contribution is for the satisfaction of payments referred to in paragraph 1(i) (a) and (b) on the basis of a fixed sum for each ton of contributing oil received in the relevant State by such persons during the preceding calendar year; and

(b) in so far as the contribution is for the satisfaction of payments referred to in paragraph 1(i) (c) of this Article on the basis of a fixed sum for each ton of contributing oil received by such person during the calendar year preceding that in which the incident in question occurred, provided that State was a party to this Convention at the date of the incident.

3. The sums referred to in paragraph 2 above shall be arrived at by dividing the relevant total amount of contributions required by the total amount of contributing oil received in all Contracting States in the relevant year.

4. The Assembly shall decide the portion of the annual contribution which shall be immediately paid in cash and decide on the date of payment. The remaining part of each annual contribution shall be paid upon notification by the Director.

5. The Director may in cases and in accordance with conditions to be laid down in the Internal Regulations of the Fund, require a contributor to provide financial security for the sums due from him.

6. Any demand for payments made under paragraph 4 shall be called rateably from all individual contributors.

Article 13

1. The amount of any contribution due under Article 12 and which is in arrear shall bear interest at a rate which shall be determined by the Assembly for each calendar year provided that different rates may be fixed for different circumstances.

2. Each Contracting State shall ensure that any obligation to contribute to the Fund arising under this convention in respect of oil received within the territory of that State is fulfilled and shall take any appropriate measures under its law, including the imposing of such sanctions as it may deem necessary, with a view to the effective execution of any such obligation, provided however, that such measures shall only be directed against those persons who are under an obligation to contribute to the Fund.

3. Where a person who is liable in accordance with the provisions of Articles 10 and 11 to make contributions to the Fund does not fulfill his obligations in respect of any such contribution or any part thereof and is in arrears for a period exceeding three months, the Director shall take all appropriate action against such person on behalf of the Fund with a view to the recovery of the amount due. However, where the defaulting contributor is manifestly insolvent or the circumstances otherwise so warrant, the Assembly may, upon recommendation of the Director, decide that no action shall be taken or continued against the contributor.

Article 14

1. Each Contracting State may at the time when it deposits its instrument of ratification or accession or at any time thereafter declare that it assumes itself obligations that are incumbent under this Convention on any person who is liable to contribute to the Fund in accordance with Article 10, paragraph 1, in respect of oil received within the territory of that State. Such declaration shall be made in writing and shall specify which obligations are assumed.

* * *

Article 15

1. Each Contracting State shall ensure that any person, who receives contributing oil within its territory in such quantities that he is liable to contribute to the Fund, appears on a list to be established and kept up to date by the Director of the Fund in accordance with the subsequent provisions of this Article.

* * *

Dumping of Harmful Substances

⚹ BRUSSELS RESOLUTION ON INTERNATIONAL CO-OPERATION CONCERNING POLLUTANTS OTHER THAN OIL*

The States represented at the Conference,

IN ADOPTING the International Convention Relating to Intervention on the High Seas in Cases of Oil Pollution Casualties (hereinafter referred to as "the Convention");

NOTING that pollution may be caused by agents other than oil;

RECOGNIZING that the limitation of the Convention to oil is not intended to abridge any right of a coastal State to protect itself against pollution by any other agent;

PENDING the entry into force of an international Instrument concerning pollution by such other agents or that there should be an extension of the Convention to such pollution;

RECOMMEND that the Inter-Governmental Maritime Consultative Organization should intensify its work, in collaboration with all interested international organizations, on all aspects of pollution by agents other than oil;

FURTHER RECOMMEND that Contracting States which become involved in a case of pollution danger by agents other than oil co-operate as appropriate in applying wholly or partially the provisions of the Convention.

⚹ OSLO CONVENTION ON THE CONTROL OF MARINE POLLUTION BY DUMPING FROM SHIPS AND AIRCRAFT†

The Contracting Parties
RECOGNIZING that the marine environment and the living resources which it supports are of vital importance to all nations;

---

* Adopted at the International Legal Conference on Marine Pollution Damage held under IMCO auspices at Brussels in November 1969.

This resolution represented a minor concession to the position chiefly associated with Canada, namely, that it was necessary to adopt a comprehensive and preventive approach to the problem of marine pollution.

† Adopted at Oslo Conference on Marine Pollution held in October 1971; signed February 15, 1972.

MINDFUL that the ecological equilibrium and the legitimate uses of the sea are increasingly threatened by pollution;

RECOGNIZING that concerted action by Governments at national, regional and global levels is essential to prevent and combat marine pollution;

NOTING that this pollution has many sources, including dumping from ships and aircraft and discharges through rivers, estuaries, outfalls and pipelines within national jurisdiction, that it is important that states use the best practicable means to prevent such pollution, and that products and processes which will minimize the amount of harmful waste requiring disposal should be developed;

BEING CONVINCED that international action to control the pollution of the sea by the dumping of harmful substances from ships and aircraft can and should be taken without delay, but that this action should not preclude discussion of measures to control other sources of marine pollution as soon as possible;

CONSIDERING that the states bordering the North-East Atlantic have a particular responsibility to protect the waters of this region;

HAVE AGREED as follows:

Article 1.

The Contracting Parties pledge themselves to take all possible steps to prevent the pollution of the sea by substances that are liable to create hazards to human health, to harm living resources and marine life, to damage amenities or to interfere with other legitimate uses of the sea.

Article 2.

The area to which this Convention applies shall be the high seas and the territorial sea which are situated

a) within those parts of the Atlantic and Arctic Oceans and their dependent seas which lie north of 36° north latitude and between 42° west longitude and 51° east longitude, but excluding
   (i) the Baltic Sea and Belts lying to the south and east of lines drawn from Hasenore Head to Gniben Point, from Korshage to Spodsbierg and from Gilbierg Head to the Kullen, and
   (ii) the Mediterranean Sea and its dependent seas as far as the point of intersection of the parallel of 36° north latitude and the meridian of 5°36′ west longitude.
b) within that part of the Atlantic Ocean north of 59° north latitude and between 44° west longitude and 42° west longitude.

Article 3.

The Contracting Parties agree to apply the measures which they adopt in such a way as to prevent the diversion of dumping of harmful substances into seas outside the area to which this Convention applies.

Article 4.

The Contracting Parties shall harmonize their policies and introduce, individually and in common, measures to prevent the pollution of the sea by dumping by or from ships and aircraft.

Article 5.

The dumping of the substances listed in Annex I to this Convention is prohibited.

Article 6.

No waste containing such quantities of the substances and materials listed in Annex II to this Convention as the Commission established under the provisions of Article 16, hereinafter referred to as "the Commission", shall define as significant, shall be dumped without a specific permit in each case from the appropriate national authority or authorities. When such permits are issued, the provisions of Annexes II and III to this Convention shall be applied.

Article 7.

No substance or material shall be dumped without the approval of the appropriate national authority or authorities. When such approval is granted, the provisions of Annex III to this Convention shall be applied.

Article 8.

1) The provisions of Articles 5, 6 and 7 shall not apply in case of force majeure due to stress of weather or any other cause when the safety of human life or of a ship or aircraft is threatened. Such dumping shall be immediately reported to the Commission, together with full details of the circumstances and of the nature and quantities of the substances and materials dumped.

2) The provisions of Article 5 shall not apply where these substances occur as trace contaminants in waste to which they have not been added for the purpose of being dumped. However, such dumping shall remain subject to Articles 6 and 7.

Article 9.

If a Contracting Party in an emergency considers that a substance listed in Annex I to this Convention cannot be disposed of on land without unacceptable danger or damage, the Contracting Party concerned shall forthwith consult the Commission. The Commission shall recommend methods of storage or the most satisfactory means of destruction or disposal under the prevailing circumstances. The Contracting Party shall inform the Commission of the steps adopted in pursuance of its recommendation. The Contracting Parties pledge themselves to assist one another in such situations.

Article 10.

The composition of the waste shall be ascertained by the appropriate national authority or authorities in accordance with the provisions of Annex III to this Convention before any permit or approval for the dumping of waste at sea is issued.

Article 11.

Each Contracting Party shall keep, and transmit to the Commission, according to a standard procedure, records of the nature and the quantities of the substances and materials dumped under permits or approvals issued by that Contracting Party, and of the dates, places and methods of dumping.

Article 12.

The Contracting Parties agree to establish complementary or joint programmes of scientific and technical research, including research on alternative methods of disposal of harmful substances, and to transmit to each other information so obtained. In doing so they will have regard to the work carried out by the appropriate international organizations and agencies.

Article 13.

The Contracting Parties agree to institute, in co-operation with appropriate international organizations and agencies, complementary or joint programmes for monitoring the distribution and effects of pollutants in the area to which this convention applies.

Article 14.

The Contracting Parties pledge themselves to promote, within the competent specialized agencies and other international bodies, measures concerning the protection of the marine environment against pollution caused by oil and oily wastes, other noxious or hazardous cargoes, and radioactive materials.

Article 15.

1) Each Contracting Party undertakes to ensure compliance with the provisions of this Convention:
   a) by ships and aircraft registered in its territory;
   b) by ships and aircraft loading in its territory the substances and materials which are to be dumped;
   c) by ships and aircraft believed to be engaged in dumping within its territorial sea.

2) Each Contracting Party undertakes to issue instructions to its maritime inspection vessels and aircraft and to other appropriate services to report to its authorities any incidents or conditions on the high seas which give rise to suspicions that dumping in contravention of the provisions of the present Convention has occurred or is about to occur. That Contracting Party shall, if it considers it appropriate, report accordingly to any other Contracting Party concerned.

3) Each Contracting Party shall take in its territory appropriate measures to prevent and punish conduct in contravention of the provisions of this Convention.

4) The Contracting Parties undertake to assist one another as appropriate in dealing with pollution incidents involving dumping at sea, and to exchange information on methods of dealing with such incidents.

5) The Contracting Parties further agree to work together in the development of co-operative procedures for the application of the Convention, particularly on the high seas.

6) Nothing in this Convention shall abridge sovereign immunity to which certain vessels are entitled under international law.

Article 16.

A Commission, made up of representatives of each of the Contracting Parties, is hereby established. The Commission shall meet at regular intervals and at any time when, due to special circumstances, it is so decided in accordance with the Rules of Procedure.

Article 17.

It shall be the duty of the Commission:
a) To exercise overall supervision over the implementation of this Convention;
b) To receive and consider the records of permits and approvals issued and of dumping which has taken place, as provided for in Articles 8, 9 and 11 of this Convention, and to define the standard procedure to be adopted for this purpose;
c) To review generally the condition of the seas within the area to which this Convention applies, the efficacy of the control measures being adopted, and the need for any additional or different measures;
d) To keep under review the contents of the Annexes to this Convention, and to recommend such amendments, additions or deletions as may be agreed;
e) To discharge such other functions as may be appropriate under the terms of this Convention.

✻   ✻   ✻

Article 19.

For the purpose of this Convention:
1) "Dumping" means any deliberate disposal of substances and materials into the sea by or from ships or aircraft other than:
a) any discharge incidental to or derived from the normal operation of ships and aircraft and their equipment;
b) the placing of substances and materials for a purpose other than the mere disposal thereof, if not contrary to the aim of this Convention.
2) "Ships and aircraft" means sea-going vessels and air-borne craft of any type whatsoever. This expression includes air-cushion craft, floating craft whether self-propelled or not, and fixed or floating platforms.

✻   ✻   ✻

Article 24.

At any time after two years from the date on which this Convention has come into force with respect to a Contracting Party, that Party may withdraw from the Convention by means of a notice in writing addressed to the depositary Government. Any such withdrawal shall take effect twelve months after the date of its receipt.

* * *

Annex I.

The following substances are listed for the purposes of Article 5 of the Convention:

1. Organohalogen compounds and compounds which may form such substances in the marine environment, excluding those which are non-toxic, or which are rapidly converted in the sea into substances which are biologically harmless;

2. Organosilicon compounds and compounds which may form such substances in the marine environment, excluding those which are non-toxic, or which are rapidly converted in the sea into substances which are biologically harmless;

3. Substances which have been agreed between the Contracting Parties as likely to be carcinogenic under the conditions of disposal;

4. Mercury and mercury compounds;

5. Cadmium and cadmium compounds;

6. Persistent plastics and other persistent synthetic materials which may float or remain in suspension in the sea, and which may seriously interfere with fishing or navigation, reduce amenities, or interfere with other legitimate uses of the sea.

Annex II.

1. The following substances and materials requiring special care are listed for the purposes of Article 6:

a) Arsenic, lead, copper, zinc and their compounds, cyanides and fluorides, and pesticides and their by-products not covered by the provisions of Annex I;

b) Containers, scrap metal, tar-like substances liable to sink to the sea bottom and other bulky wastes which may present a serious obstacle to fishing or navigation;

c) Substances which, though of a non-toxic nature, may become harmful due to the quantities in which they are dumped, or which are liable to seriously reduce amenities.

2. The substances and materials listed under paragraph 1 (b) above should always be deposited in deep water.

3. In the issuance of permits or approvals for the dumping of large quantities of acids and alkalis, consideration should be given to the possible presence in such wastes of the substances listed in paragraph 1) above.

4. When, in the application of the provisions of Annexes II and III, it is considered necessary to deposit waste in deep water, this should be done only when the following two conditions are both fulfilled:

  a) that the depth is not less than 2000 metres,
  b) that the distance from the nearest land is not less than 150 nautical miles.

Annex III.

Provisions governing the issue of permits and approvals for the dumping of wastes at sea.

1. *Characteristics of the waste*
  a) Amount and composition;
  b) Amount of substances and materials to be deposited per day (per week, per month);
  c) Form in which it is presented for dumping, i.e. whether as a solid, sludge or liquid;
  d) Physical (especially solubility and specific gravity), chemical, biochemical (oxygen demand, nutrient production) and biological properties (presence of viruses, bacteria, yeasts, parasites, etc.);
  e) Toxicity;
  f) Persistence;
  g) Accumulation in biological materials or sediments;
  h) Chemical and physical changes of the waste after release, including possible formation of new compounds;
  i) Probability of production of taints reducing marketability of resources (fish, shellfish, etc.).

2. *Characteristics of dumping site and method of deposit*
  a) Geographical position, depth and distance from coast;
  b) Location in relation to living resources in adult or juvenile phases;
  c) Location in relation to amenity areas;
  d) Methods of packing, if any;
  e) Initial dilution achieved by proposed method of release;
  f) Dispersal, horizontal transport and vertical mixing characteristics;
  g) Existence and effects of current and previous discharges and dumping in the area (including accumulative effects).

3. *General considerations and conditions*

a) Interference with shipping, fishing, recreation, mineral extraction, desalination, fish and shellfish culture, areas of special scientific importance and other legitimate use of the sea;

b) In applying these principles the practical availability of alternative means of disposal or elimination will be taken into consideration.

✄ LONDON CONVENTION ON THE PREVENTION OF MARINE POLLUTION BY DUMPING OF WASTES AND OTHER MATTER

Preamble

The Contracting Parties to this Convention

Recognizing that the marine environment and the living organisms which it supports are of vital importance to humanity, and all people have an interest in assuring that it is so managed that its quality and resources are not impaired;

Recognizing that the capacity of the sea to assimilate wastes and render them harmless, and its ability to regenerate natural resources is not unlimited;

Recognizing that States have, in accordance with the Charter of the United Nations and the principles of international law, the sovereign right to exploit their own resources pursuant to their own environmental policies, and the responsibility to ensure that activities within their jurisdiction or control do not cause damage to the environment of other States or of areas beyond the limits of national jurisdiction;

Recalling Resolution 2749 (XXV) of the General Assembly of the United Nations on the principles governing the sea bed and the ocean floor and the subsoil thereof, beyond the limits of national jurisdiction;

Noting that marine pollution originates in many sources, such as dumping and discharges through the atmosphere, rivers, estuaries, outfalls and pipelines, and that it is important that States use the best practicable means to prevent such pollution and develop products and processes which will reduce the amount of harmful wastes to be disposed of;

Being convinced that international action to control the pollution of the sea by dumping can and must be taken without delay but that this action should not preclude discussion of measures to control other sources of marine pollution as soon as possible and;

Wishing to improve protection of the marine environment by encouraging States with a common interest in particular geographical areas to

Opened for signature in December 1972.

enter into appropriate agreements supplementary to this Convention:
Have agreed as follows:

Article I

Contracting Parties shall individually and collectively promote the effective control of all sources of pollution of the marine environment, and pledge themselves especially to take all practicable steps to prevent the pollution of the sea by the dumping of waste and other matter that is liable to create hazards to human health, to harm living resources and marine life, to damage amenities or to interfere with other legitimate uses of the sea.

Article II

Contracting Parties shall, as provided for in the following Articles, take effective measures individually, according to their scientific, technical and economic capabilities, and collectively, to prevent marine pollution caused by dumping and shall harmonize their policies in this regard.

Article III

For the purposes of this Convention:
1. (a) "Dumping" means:
    (i) any deliberate disposal at sea of wastes or other matter from vessels, aircraft, platforms or other man-made structures at sea;
    (ii) any deliberate disposal at sea of vessels, aircraft, platforms or other man-made structures at sea;
  (b) "Dumping" does not include:
    (i) the disposal at sea of wastes or other matter incidental to, or derived from the normal operations of vessels, aircraft, platforms or other man-made structures at sea and their equipment, other than wastes or other matter transported by or to vessels, aircraft, platforms or other man-made structures at sea, operating for the purpose of disposal of such matter or derived from the treatment of such wastes or other matter on such vessels, aircraft platforms or structures.
    (ii) placement of matter for a purpose other than the mere disposal thereof, provided that such placement is not contrary to the aims of this convention.
  (c) The disposal of wastes or other matter directly arising from, or related to the exploration, exploitation and associated off-shore

processing of seabed mineral resources will not be covered by the provisions of this Convention.

2. "Vessels and aircraft" means waterborne or airborne craft of any type whatsoever. This expression includes air cushioned craft and floating craft, whether self-propelled or not.

3. "Sea" means all marine waters other than the internal waters of States.

4. "Wastes or other matter" means material and substance of any kind, form or description.

5. "Special permit" means permission granted specifically on application in advance and in accordance with Annex II and Annex III.

6. "General permit" means permission granted in advance and in accordance with Annex III.

7. "The Organisation" means the organisation designated by the Contracting Parties in accordance with Article XIV2.

Article IV

1. In accordance with the provisions of this Convention Contracting Parties shall prohibit the dumping of any wastes or other matter in whatever form or condition except as otherwise specified below:

    a. The dumping of wastes or other matter listed in Annex I is prohibited;

    b. The dumping of wastes or other matter listed in Annex II requires a prior special permit;

    c. The dumping of all other wastes or matter requires a prior general permit.

2. Any permit shall be issued only after careful consideration of all the factors set forth in Annex III, including prior studies of the characteristics of the dumping site, as set forth in Sections B and C of that Annex.

3. No provision of this Convention is to be interpreted as preventing a Contracting Party from prohibiting, insofar as that Party is concerned, the dumping of wastes or other matter not mentioned in Annex I. That Party shall notify such measures to the Organisation.

Article V

1. The provisions of Article IV shall not apply when it is necessary to secure the safety of human life or of vessels, aircraft, platforms or other man-made structures at sea in cases of force majeure caused by stress of weather, or in any case which constitutes a danger to human life or a real threat to vessels, aircraft, platforms or other man-made structures at sea, if dumping appears to be the only way of averting the threat and

if there is every probability that the damage consequent upon such dumping will be less than would otherwise occur. Such dumping shall be so conducted as to minimise the likelihood of damage to human or marine life and shall be reported forthwith to the Organisation.

2. A Contracting Party may issue a special permit as an exception to Article IV1a, in emergencies posing unacceptable risk relating to human health and admitting no other feasible solution. Before doing so the Party shall consult any other country or countries that are likely to be affected and the Organisation which, after consulting other Parties, and international organisations as appropriate, shall, in accordance with Article XIV, promptly recommend to the Party the most appropriate procedures to adopt. The Party shall follow these recommendations to the maximum extent feasible consistent with the time within which action must be taken and with the general obligation to avoid damage to the marine environment and shall inform the Organisation of the action it takes. The Parties pledge themselves to assist one another in such situations.

3. Any Contracting Party may waive its rights under paragraph 2 at the time of, or subsequent to ratification of, or accession to this Convention.

Article VI

1. Each Contracting Party shall designate an appropriate authority or authorities to:
   a. issue special permits which shall be required prior to, and for, the dumping of matter listed in Annex II and in the circumstances provided for in Article V2;
   b. issue general permits which shall be required prior to and for the dumping of all other matter;
   c. keep records of the nature and quantities of all matter permitted to be dumped and the location, time and method of dumping;
   d. monitor individually, or in collaboration with other Parties and competent international organisations, the condition of the seas for the purposes of this Convention.

2. The appropriate authority or authorities of a Contracting Party shall issue special or general permits in accordance with paragraph 1 in respect of matter intended for dumping:
   a. loaded in its territory;
   b. loaded by a vessel or aircraft registered in its territory or flying its flag, when the loading occurs in the territory of a state not party to this Convention.

3. In issuing permits under sub-paragraphs 1a and b above, the appropriate authority or authorities shall comply with Annex III, together

with such additional criteria, measures and requirements as they may consider relevant.

4. Each Contracting Party, directly or through a Secretariat established under a regional agreement, shall report to the Organisation, and where appropriate to other Parties, the information specified in sub-paragraphs c and d of paragraph 1 above, and the criteria, measures and requirements it adopts in accordance with paragraph 3 above. The procedure to be followed and the nature of such reports shall be agreed by the Parties in consultation.

Article VII

1. Each Contracting Party shall apply the measures required to implement the present convention to all:
    a. vessels and aircraft registered in its territory or flying its flag;
    b. vessels and aircraft loading in its territory or territorial seas matter which is to be dumped;
    c. vessels and aircraft and fixed or floating platforms under its jurisdiction believed to be engaged in dumping.
2. Each Party shall take in its territory appropriate measures to prevent and punish conduct in contravention of the provisions of this Convention.
3. The Parties agree to co-operate in the development of procedures for the effective application of this Convention particularly on the high seas, including procedures for the reporting of vessels and aircraft observed dumping in contravention of the Convention.
4. This Convention shall not apply to those vessels and aircraft entitled to sovereign immunity under international law. However each party shall ensure by the adoption of appropriate measures that such vessels and aircraft owned or operated by it act in a manner consistent with the object and purpose of this Convention, and shall inform the Organisation accordingly.
5. Nothing in this Convention shall affect the right of each Party to adopt other measures, in accordance with the principles of international law, to prevent dumping at sea.

Article VIII

In order to further the objectives of this Convention, the Contracting Parties with common interests to protect in the marine environment in a given geographical area shall endeavour, taking into account characteristic regional features, to enter into regional agreements consistent with this Convention for the prevention of pollution, especially by dumping. The Contracting Parties to the present Convention shall endeavour to act consistently with the objectives and provisions of such regional agreements, which shall be notified to them by the Organisation. Contracting Parties shall seek to co-operate with the Parties to regional agreements in order to develop harmonized procedures to be followed by Contracting Parties to the different conventions concerned. Special attention shall be given to co-operation in the field of monitoring and scientific research.

Article IX

The Contracting Parties shall promote, through collaboration within the Organization and other international bodies, support for those Parties which request it for:

a. The training of scientific and technical personnel;
b. the supply of necessary equipment and facilities for research and monitoring;
c. the disposal and treatment of waste and other measures to prevent or mitigate pollution caused by dumping;

preferably within the countries concerned, so furthering the aims and purposes of this Convention.

Article X

In accordance with the principles of international law regarding state responsibility for damage to the environment of other States or to any other area of the environment, caused by dumping of wastes and other matter of all kinds, the Contracting Parties undertake to develop procedures for the assessment of liability and the settlement of disputes regarding dumping.

Article XI

The Contracting Parties shall at their first consultative meeting consider procedures for the settlement of disputes concerning the interpretation and application of this Convention.

Article XII

The Contracting Parties pledge themselves to promote, within the competent specialized agencies and other international bodies, measures to protect the marine environment against pollution caused by:

(a) hydrocarbons, including oil, and their wastes;

(b) other noxious or hazardous matter transported by vessels for purposes other than dumping;

(c) wastes generated in the course of operation of vessels, aircraft, platforms and other man-made structures at sea;

(d) radioactive pollutants from all sources, including vessels;

(e) agents of chemical and biological warfare;

(f) wastes or other matter directly arising from, or related to the exploration, exploitation and associated off-shore processing of seabed mineral resources.

The Parties will also promote, within the appropriate international organisation, the codification of signals to be used by vessels engaged in dumping.

Article XIII

Nothing in this Convention shall prejudice the codification and development of the law of the sea by the United Nations conference on the Law of the Sea convened pursuant to Resolution 2750C (XXV) of the General Assembly of the United Nations nor the present or future claims and legal views of any State concerning the law of the sea and the nature and extent of coastal and flag state jurisdiction. The Contracting Parties agree to consult at a meeting to be convened by the Organisation after the Law of the Sea Conference, and in any case not later than 1976, with a view to defining the nature and extent of the right and the responsibility of a coastal state to apply the Convention in a zone adjacent to its coast.

Article XIV

1. The Government of the United Kingdom of Great Britain and Northern Ireland as a depositary shall call a meeting of the Contracting Parties not later than three months after the entry into force of this Convention to decide on organisational matters.

2. The Contracting Parties shall designate a competent Organisation existing at the time of that meeting to be responsible for secretariat duties in relation to this Convention. Any Party to this Convention not being a member of this Organisation shall make an appropriate contribution to the expenses incurred by the Organisation in performing these duties.

3. The Secretariat duties of the Organisation shall include:

a. the convening of consultative meetings of the Contracting Parties not less frequently than once every two years and of special meetings of the Parties at any time on the request of two-thirds of the Parties;

b. preparing and assisting, in consultation with the Contracting Parties and appropriate International Organisations, in the development and implementation of procedures referred to in sub-paragraph 4e of this Article;

c. considering enquiries by, and information from the Contracting Parties, consulting with them and with the appropriate International Organisations, and providing recommendations to the Parties on questions related to, but not specifically covered by the Convention;

d. conveying to the Parties concerned all notifications received by the Organisations in accordance with Articles IV 3, V 1 and 2, VI 4, XIII, XX and XXI.

Prior to the designation of the Organisation these functions shall, as necessary, be performed by the depositary, who for this purpose shall be the Government of the United Kingdom of Great Britain and Northern Ireland.

4. Consultative or special meetings of the Contracting Parties shall keep under continuing review the implementation of this Convention and may, inter alia:

a. review and adopt amendments to this Convention and its Annexes in accordance with Article XV;

b. invite the appropriate scientific body or bodies to collaborate with and to advise the Parties or the Organisation on any scientific or technical aspect relevant to this Convention, including particularly the content of the Annexes;

c. receive and consider reports made pursuant to Article VI 4;

d. promote co-operation with and between regional organisations concerned with the prevention of marine pollution;

e. develop or adopt, in consultation with appropriate International Organisations, procedures referred to in Article V 2, including basic criteria for determining exceptional and emergency situations, and procedures for consultative advice and the safe disposal of matter in such circumstances, including the designation of appropriate dumping areas, and recommend accordingly;

f. consider any additional action that may be required.

5. The Contracting Parties at their first consultative meeting shall establish rules of procedure as necessary.

Article XV

1. a. At meetings of the Contracting Parties called in accordance with Article XIV amendments to this Convention may be adopted by a two-thirds majority of those present. An amendment shall enter

into force for the Parties which have accepted it on the sixtieth day after two-thirds of the Parties shall have deposited an instrument of acceptance of the amendment with the Organisation. Thereafter the amendment shall enter into force for any other Party 30 days after that Party deposits its instrument of acceptance of the amendment.

b. The Organisation shall inform all Contracting Parties of any requests made for a special meeting under Article XIV and of any amendments adopted at meetings of the Parties and of the date on which each such amendment enters into force for each Party.

2. Amendments to the Annexes will be based on scientific or technical considerations. Amendments to the Annexes approved by a two-thirds majority of those present at a meeting called in accordance with Article XIV shall enter into force for each Contracting Party immediately on notification of its acceptance to the Organisation and 100 days after approval by the meeting for all other Parties except for those which before the end of the 100 days make a declaration that they are not able to accept the amendment at that time. Parties should endeavour to signify their acceptance of an amendment to the Organisation as soon as possible after approval at a meeting. A Party may at any time substitute an acceptance for a previous declaration of objection and the amendment previously objected to shall thereupon enter into force for that Party.

3. An acceptance or declaration of objection under this Article shall be made by the deposit of an instrument with the Organisation. The organisation shall notify all Contracting Parties of the receipt of such instruments.

4. Prior to the designation of the Organisation, the Secretarial functions herein attributed to it shall be performed temporarily by the Government of the United Kingdom of Great Britain and Northern Ireland, as one of the depositaries of this Convention.

❖ ❖ ❖

Annex I

1. Organohalogen compounds.
2. Mercury and mercury compounds.
3. Cadmium and cadmium compounds.
4. Persistent plastics and other persistent synthetic materials, for example, netting and ropes, which may float or may remain in suspension in the sea in such a manner as to interfere materially with fishing, navigation or other legitimate uses of the sea.
5. Crude oil, fuel oil, heavy diesel oil, and lubricating oils, hydraulic

fluids, and any mixtures containing any of these, taken on board for the purpose of dumping.

6. High-level radioactive wastes or other high-level radioactive matter, defined on public health, biological or other grounds, by the competent international body in this field, at present the International Atomic Energy Agency, as unsuitable for dumping at sea.

7. Materials in whatever form (e.g. solids, liquids, semi-liquids, gases or in a living state) produced for biological and chemical warfare.

8. The preceding paragraphs of this Annex do not apply to substances which are rapidly rendered harmless by physical, chemical or biological processes in the sea provided they do not:

 (i) make edible marine organisms unpalatable, or

 (ii) endanger human health or that of domestic animals.

The consultative procedure provided for under Article XIV should be followed by a Party if there is doubt about the harmlessness of the substance.

9. This Annex does not apply to wastes or other materials (e.g. sewage sludges and dredged spoils) containing the matters referred to in paragraphs 1–5 above as trace contaminants. Such wastes shall be subject to the provisions of Annexes II and III as appropriate.

Annex II

The following substances and materials requiring special care are listed for the purposes of Article VI 1a.

A. Wastes containing significant amounts of the matters listed below:

arsenic
lead
copper   and their compounds
zinc
organosilicon compounds
cyanides
fluorides
pesticides and their by-products not covered in Annex I.

B. In the issue of permits for the dumping of large quantities of acids and alkalis, consideration shall be given to the possible presence in such wastes of the substances listed in paragraph A and to the following additional substances:

beryllium
chromium
nickel   and their compounds
vanadium

C. Containers, scrap metal and other bulky wastes liable to sink to the sea bottom which may present a serious obstacle to fishing or navigation.

D. Radioactive wastes or other radioactive matter not included in Annex I. In the issue of permits for the dumping of this matter, the Contracting Parties should take full account of the recommendations of the competent international body in this field, at present the International Atomic Energy Agency.

Annex III

Provisions to be considered in establishing criteria governing the issue of permits for the dumping of matter at sea, taking into account Article IV 2, include:

A. Characteristics and Composition of the Matter

1. Total amount and average composition of matter dumped (e.g., per year).
2. Form (e.g., solid, sludge, liquid, or gaseous).
3. Properties: physical (e.g., solubility and density), chemical and biochemical (e.g., oxygen demand, nutrients), and biological (e.g., presence of viruses, bacteria, yeasts, parasites).
4. Toxicity.
5. Persistence: physical, chemical and biological.
6. Accumulation and biotransformation in biological materials or sediments.
7. Susceptibility to physical, chemical and biochemical changes and interaction in the aquatic environment with other dissolved organic and inorganic materials.
8. Probability of production of taints or other changes reducing marketability of resources (fish, shellfish, etc.).

B. Characteristics of Dumping Site and Method of Deposit

1. Location (e.g., co-ordinates of the dumping area, depth and distance from the coast), location in relation to other areas (e.g., amenity areas, spawning, nursery and fishing areas and exploitable resources).
2. Rate of disposal per specific period (e.g., quantity per day, per week, per month).
3. Methods of packaging and containment, if any.
4. Initial dilution achieved by proposed method of release.

5. Dispersal characteristics (e.g., effects of currents, tides and wind on horizontal transport and vertical mixing).

6. Water characteristics (e.g., temperature, pH, salinity, stratification, oxygen indices of pollution—dissolved oxygen (DO), chemical oxygen demand (COD), biochemical oxygen demand (BOD)—nitrogen present in organic and mineral form including ammonia, suspended matter, other nutrients and productivity).

7. Bottom characteristics (e.g., topography, geochemical and geological characteristics and biological productivity).

8. Existence and effects of other dumpings which have been made in the dumping area (e.g., heavy metal background reading and organic carbon content).

9. In issuing a permit for dumping, Contracting Parties should consider whether an adequate scientific basis exists for assessing the consequences of such dumping, as outlined in this Annex, taking into account seasonal variations.

C. General Considerations and Conditions

1. Possible effects on amenities (e.g., presence of floating or stranded material, turbidity, objectionable odour, discolouration and foaming).

2. Possible effects on marine life, fish and shellfish culture, fish stocks and fisheries, seaweed harvesting and culture.

3. Possible effects on other uses of the sea (e.g., impairment of water quality for industrial use, underwater corrosion of structures, interference with ship operations from floating materials, interference with fishing or navigation through deposit of waste or solid objects on the sea floor and protection of areas of special importance for scientific or conservation purposes).

4. The practical availability of alternative land-based methods of treatment, disposal or elimination, or of treatment to render the matter less harmful for dumping at sea.

Technical Memorandum of Agreement of the Conference

The Conference agreed, on the advice of the Technical Working Party, that for a period of five years from the date when the present Convention comes into effect, wastes containing small quantities of inorganic compounds of mercury and cadmium, solidified by integration into concrete, may be approximately classified as wastes containing these substances as trace contaminants as mentioned in paragraph 9 of Annex I to the Convention, but in these circumstances such wastes may be dumped only in depths of not less than 3500 metres in conditions which would cause no harm to the marine environment and its living resources. When the Convention comes into effect, this method of disposal, which will be used for not longer than five years, will be subject to the relevant provisions of Article XIV 4.

UNILATERAL MEASURES

⚑ An Act to Prevent Pollution of Areas of the Arctic Waters Adjacent to the Mainland and Islands of the Canadian Arctic (1970)

Whereas Parliament recognizes that recent developments in relation to the exploitation of the natural resources of arctic areas, including the natural resources of the Canadian arctic, and the transportation of those resources to the markets of the world are of potentially great significance to international trade and commerce and to the economy of Canada in particular;

And whereas Parliament at the same time recognizes and is determined to fulfil its obligation to see that the natural resources of the Canadian arctic are developed and exploited and the arctic waters adjacent to the mainland and islands of the Canadian arctic are navigated only in a manner that takes cognizance of Canada's responsibility for the welfare of the Eskimo and other inhabitants of the Canadian arctic and the preservation of the peculiar ecological balance that now exists in the water, ice and land areas of the Canadian arctic;

Now therefore, Her Majesty, by and with the advice and consent of the Senate and House of Commons of Canada, enacts as follows:

SHORT TITLE

1. This Act may be cited as the *Arctic Waters Pollution Prevention Act.*

INTERPRETATION

2. In this Act,
   (a) "analyst" means a person designated as an analyst pursuant to the *Canada Water Act* or the *Northern Inland Waters Act;*

Came into effect on August 2, 1972.

(b) "icebreaker" means a ship specially designed and constructed for the purpose of assisting the passage of other ships through ice;

(c) "owner" in relation to a ship, includes any person having for the time being, either by law or by contract, the same rights as the owner of the ship as regards the possession and use thereof;

(d) "pilot" means a person licensed as a pilot pursuant to the *Canada Shipping Act;*

(e) "pollution prevention officer" means a person designated as a pollution prevention officer pursuant to section 14;

(f) "ship" includes any description of vessel or boat used or designed for use in navigation without regard to method or lack of propulsion;

(g) "shipping safety control zone" means an area of the arctic waters prescribed as a shipping safety control zone by order of the Governor in Council made under section 11; and

(h) "waste" means
  (i) any substance that, if added to any waters, would degrade or alter or form part of a process of degradation or alteration of the quality of those waters to an extent that is detrimental to their use by man or by any animal, fish or plant that is useful to man, and
  (ii) any water that contains a substance in such a quantity or concentration, or that has been so treated, processed or changed, by heat or other means, from a natural state that it would, if added to any waters, degrade or alter or form part of a process of degradation or alteration of the quality of those waters to an extent that is detrimental to their use by man or by any animal, fish or plant that is useful to man,

and without limiting the generality of the foregoing, includes anything that, for the purposes of the *Canada Water Act*, is deemed to be waste.

APPLICATION OF ACT

3. (1) Except where otherwise provided, this Act applies to the waters (in this Act referred to as the "arctic waters") adjacent to the mainland and islands of the Canadian arctic within the area enclosed by the sixtieth parallel of north latitude, the one hundred and forty-first meridian of longitude and a line measured seaward from the nearest Canadian land a distance of one hundred nautical miles; except that in the area between the islands of the Canadian arctic and Greenland, where the line of equidistance between the islands of the Canadian arctic and Greenland is

less than one hundred nautical miles from the nearest Canadian land, there shall be substituted for the line measured seaward one hundred nautical miles from the nearest Canadian land such line of equidistance.

(2) For greater certainty, the expression "arctic waters" in this Act includes all waters described in subsection (1) and, as this Act applies to or in respect of any person described in paragraph (a) of subsection (1) of section 6, all waters adjacent thereto lying north of the sixtieth parallel of north latitude, the natural resources of whose subjacent submarine areas Her Majesty in right of Canada has the right to dispose of or exploit, whether the waters so described or such adjacent waters are in a frozen or a liquid state, but does not include inland waters.

DEPOSIT OF WASTE

4. (1) Except as authorized by regulations made under this section, no person or ship shall deposit or permit the deposit of waste of any type in the arctic waters or in any place on the mainland or islands of the Canadian arctic under any conditions where such waste or any other waste that results from the deposit of such waste may enter the arctic waters.

* * *

(3) The Governor in Council may make regulations for the purposes of this section prescribing the type and quantity of waste, if any, that may be deposited by any person or ship in the arctic waters or in any place on the mainland or islands of the Canadian arctic under any conditions where such waste or any other waste that results from the deposit of such waste may enter the arctic waters, and prescribing the conditions under which any such waste may be so deposited.

5. (1) Any person who

(a) has deposited waste in violation of subsection (1) of section **4**, or

(b) carries on any undertaking on the mainland or islands of the Canadian arctic or in the arctic waters that, by reason of any accident or other occurrence, is in danger of causing any deposit of waste described in that subsection otherwise than of a type, in a quantity and under conditions prescribed by regulations made under that section,

shall forthwith report the deposit of waste or the accident or other occurrence to a pollution prevention officer at such location and in such manner as may be prescribed by the Governor in Council.

(2) The master of any ship that has deposited waste in violation of subsection (1) of section 4, or that is in distress and for that reason is

in danger of causing any deposit of waste described in that subsection otherwise than of a type, in a quantity and under conditions prescribed by regulations made under that section, shall forthwith report the deposit of waste or the condition of distress to a pollution prevention officer at such location and in such manner as may be prescribed by the Governor in Council.

6. (1) The following persons, namely:

(a) any person who is engaged in exploring for, developing or exploiting any natural resource on any land adjacent to the arctic waters or in any submarine area adjacent to the arctic waters,

(b) any person who carries on any undertaking on the mainland or islands of the Canadian arctic or in the arctic waters, and

(c) the owner of any ship that navigates within the arctic waters and the owner or owners of the cargo of any such ship,

are respectively liable and, in the case of the owner of a ship and the owner or owners of the cargo thereof, are jointly and severally liable, up to the amount determined in the manner provided by regulations made under section 9 in respect of the activity or undertaking so engaged in or carried on or in respect of that ship, as the case may be,

(d) for all costs and expenses of and incidental to the taking of action described in subsection (2) on the direction of the Governor in Council, and

(e) for all actual loss or damage incurred by other persons

resulting from any deposit of waste described in subsection (1) of section 4 that is caused by or is otherwise attributable to that activity or undertaking or that ship, as the case may be.

(2) Where the Governor in Council directs any action to be taken by or on behalf of Her Majesty in right of Canada to repair or remedy any condition that results from a deposit of waste described in subsection (1), or to reduce or mitigate any damage to or destruction of life or property that results or may reasonably be expected to result from such deposit of waste, the costs and expenses of and incidental to the taking of such action, to the extent that such costs and expenses can be established to have been reasonably incurred in the circumstances, are, subject to this section, recoverable by Her Majesty in right of Canada from the person or persons described in paragraph (a), (b) or (c) of that subsection, with costs, in proceedings brought or taken therefor in the name of Her Majesty.

* * *

7. (1) The liability of any person pursuant to section 6 is absolute and does not depend upon proof of fault or negligence, except that no person is liable pursuant to that section for any costs, expenses or actual loss

or damage incurred by another person whose conduct caused any deposit of waste described in subsection (1) of that section, or whose conduct contributed to any such deposit of waste, to the degree to which his conduct contributed thereto, and nothing in this Act shall be construed as limiting or restricting any right of recourse or indemnity that a person liable pursuant to section 6 may have against any other person.

*　*　*

(3) Notwithstanding anything in this Act, no person is liable pursuant to section 6, either alone or jointly and severally with any other person or persons, by reason only of his being the owner of all or any part of the cargo of a ship, if he can establish that the cargo or part thereof of which he is the owner is of such a nature, or is of such a nature and is carried in such a quantity that, if it and any other cargo of the same nature that is carried by that ship were deposited by that ship in the arctic waters, the deposit thereof would not constitute a violation of subsection (1) of section 4.

8. (1) The Governor in Council may require

  (a) any person who engages in exploring for, developing or exploiting any natural resource on any land adjacent to the arctic waters or in any submarine area subjacent to the arctic waters,

  (b) any person who carries on any undertaking on the mainland or islands of the Canadian arctic or in the arctic waters that will or is likely to result in the deposit of waste in the arctic waters or in any place under any conditions where such waste or any other waste that results from the deposit of such waste may enter the arctic waters,

  (c) any person, other than a person described in paragraph (a), who proposes to construct, alter or extend any work or works on the mainland or islands of the Canadian arctic or in the arctic waters that, upon completion thereof, will form all or part of an undertaking described in paragraph (b), or

  (d) the owner of any ship that proposes to navigate or that navigates within any shipping safety control zone specified by the Governor in Council and, subject to subsection (3) of section 7, the owner or owners of the cargo of any such ship,

to provide evidence of financial responsibility, in the form of insurance or an indemnity bond satisfactory to the Governor in Council, or in any other form satisfactory to him, in an amount determined in the manner provided by regulations made under section 9.

(2) Evidence of finanical responsibility in the form of insurance or an indemnity bond shall be in a form that will enable any person entitled pursuant to section 6 to claim against the person or persons giving such

evidence of financial responsibility to recover directly from the proceeds of such insurance or bond.

9. The Governor in Council may make regulations for the purposes of section 6 prescribing, in respect of any activity or undertaking engaged in or carried on by any person or persons described in paragraph (*a*), (*b*) or (*c*) of subsection (1) of section 6, or in respect of any ship of which any such person is the owner or of all or part of whose cargo any such person is the owner, the manner of determining the limit of liability of any such person or persons pursuant to that section, which prescribed manner shall, in the case of the owner of any ship and the owner or owners of the cargo thereof, take into account the size of such ship and the nature and quantity of the cargo carried or to be carried by it.

PLANS AND SPECIFICATIONS OF WORKS

10. (1) the Governor in Council may require any person who proposes to construct, alter or extend any work or works on the mainland or islands of the Canadian arctic or in the arctic waters that, upon completion thereof, will form all or part of an undertaking the operation of which will or is likely to result in the deposit of waste of any type in the arctic waters or in any place under any conditions where such waste or any other waste that results from the deposit of such waste may enter the arctic waters, to provide him with a copy of such plans and specifications relating to the work or works as will enable him to determine whether the deposit of waste that will or is likely to occur if the construction, alteration or extension is carried out in accordance therewith would constitute a violation of subsection (1) of section 4.

(2) If, after reviewing any plans and specifications provided to him under subsection (1) and affording to the person who provided those plans and specifications a reasonable opportunity to be heard, the Governor in Council is of the opinion that the deposit of waste that will or is likely to occur if the construction, alteration or extension is carried out in accordance with such plans and specifications would constitute a violation of subsection (1) of section 4, he may, by order, either

(*a*) require such modifications in those plans and specifications as he considers to be necessary, or

(*b*) prohibit the carrying out of the construction, alteration or extension.

SHIPPING SAFETY CONTROL ZONES

11. (1) Subject to subsection (2), the Governor in Council may, by order, prescribe as a shipping safety control zone any area of the arctic waters specified in the order, and may, as he deems necessary, amend any such area.

(2) A copy of each order that the Governor in Council proposes to make under subsection (1) shall be published in the *Canada Gazette;* and no order may be made by the Governor in Council under subsection (1) based upon any such proposal except after the expiration of sixty days following publication of the proposal in the *Canada Gazette.*

12. (1) The Governor in Council may make regulations applicable to ships of any class or classes specified therein, prohibiting any ship of that class or of any of those classes from navigating within any shipping safety control zone specified therein

  (*a*) unless the ship complies with standards prescribed by the regulations relating to

      (i) hull and fuel tank construction, including the strength of materials used therein, the use of double hulls and the subdivision thereof into watertight compartments,

     (ii) the construction of machinery and equipment and the electronic and other navigational aids and equipment and telecommunications equipment to be carried and the manner and frequency of maintenance thereof,

    (iii) the nature and construction of propelling power and appliances and fittings for steering and stabilizing,

    (iv) the manning of the ship, including the number of navigating and look-out personnel to be carried who are qualified in a manner prescribed by the regulations,

     (v) with respect to any type of cargo to be carried, the maximum quantity thereof that may be carried, the method of stowage thereof and the nature or type and quantity of supplies and equipment to be carried for use in repairing or remedying any condition that may result from the deposit of any such cargo in the arctic waters,

    (vi) the freeboard to be allowed and the marking of load lines,

   (vii) quantities of fuel, water and other supplies to be carried, and

  (viii) the maps, charts, tide tables and any other documents or publications relating to navigation in the arctic waters to be carried;

  (*b*) without the aid of a pilot, or of an ice navigator who is qualified in a manner prescribed by the regulations, at any time or during any period or periods of the year, if any, specified in the regulations, or without icebreaker assistance of a kind prescribed by the regulations; and

  (*c*) during any period or periods of the year, if any, specified in the regulations or when ice conditions of a kind specified in the regulations exist in that zone.

(2) The Governor in Council may by order exempt from the application of any regulations made under subsection (1) any ship or class of ship that is owned or operated by a sovereign power other than Canada where the Governor in Council is satisfied that appropriate measures have been taken by or under the authority of that sovereign power to ensure the compliance of such ship with, or with standards substantially equivalent to, standards prescribed by regulations made under paragraph (a) of subsection (1) that would otherwise be applicable to it within any shipping safety control zone, and that in all other respects all reasonable precautions have been or will be taken to reduce the danger of any deposit of waste resulting from the navigation of such ship within that shipping safety control zone.

(3) The Governor in Council may make regulations providing for the issue to the owner or master of any ship that proposes to navigate within any shipping safety control zone specified therein, of a certificate evidencing, in the absence of any evidence to the contrary, the compliance of such ship with standards prescribed by regulations made under paragraph (a) of subsection (1) that are or would be applicable to it within that shipping safety control zone, and governing the use that may be made of any such certificate and the effect that may be given thereto for the purposes of any provision of this Act.

13. (1) Where the Governor in Council has reasonable cause to believe that a ship that is within the arctic waters and is in distresss, stranded, wrecked, sunk or abandoned, is depositing waste or is likely to deposit waste in the arctic waters, he may cause the ship or any cargo or other material on board the ship to be destroyed, if necessary, or to be removed if possible to such place and sold in such manner as he may direct.

(2) The proceeds from the sale of a ship or any cargo or other material pursuant to subsection (1) shall be applied towards meeting the expenses incurred by the Government of Canada in removing and selling the ship, cargo or other material, and any surplus shall be paid to the owner of that ship, cargo or other material.

14. (1) The Governor in Council may designate any person as a pollution prevention officer with such of the powers set out in sections 15 and 23 as are specified in the certificate of designation of such person.

* * *

15. (1) A pollution prevention officer may, at any reasonable time,

(a) enter any area, place or premises (other than a ship, a private dwelling place or any part of any area, place or premises other than a ship that is designed to be used and is being used as a permanent or temporary private dwelling place) occupied by any person described in paragraph (a) or (b) of subsection (1) of section 8, in which he reasonably believes

(i) there is being or has been carried on any activity that may result in or has resulted in waste, or

(ii) there is any waste

that may be or has been deposited in the arctic waters or on the mainland or islands of the Canadian arctic under any conditions where such waste or any other waste that results from the deposit of such waste may enter the arctic waters in violation of subsection (1) of section 4;

(b) examine any waste found therein in bulk or open any container found therein that he has reason to believe contains any waste and take samples thereof; and

(c) require any person in such area, place or premises to produce for inspection or for the purpose of obtaining copies thereof or extracts therefrom, any books or other documents or papers concerning any matter relevant to the administration of this Act or the regulations.

(2) A pollution prevention officer may, at any reasonable time,

(a) enter any area, place or premises (other than a ship, a private dwelling place or any part of any area, place or premises other than a ship that is designed to be used and is being used as a permanent or temporary private dwelling place) in which any construction, alteration or extension of a work or works described in section 10 is being carried on; and

(b) conduct such inspections of the work or works being constructed, altered or extended as he deems necessary in order to determine whether any plans and specifications provided to the Governor in Council, and any modifications required by the Governor in Council, are being complied with.

(3) A pollution prevention officer may

(a) go on board any ship that is within a shipping safety control zone and conduct such inspections thereof as will enable him to determine whether the ship complies with standards prescribed by any regulations made under section 12 that are applicable to it within that shipping safety control zone;

(b) order any ship that is in or near a shipping safety control zone to proceed outside such zone in such manner as he may direct, to remain outside such zone or to anchor in a place selected by him,

(i) if he suspects, on reasonable grounds, that the ship fails to comply with standards prescribed by any regulations made under section 12 that are or would be applicable to it within that shipping safety control zone,

(ii) if such ship is within the shipping safety control zone or is about to enter the zone in contravention of a regulation made under paragraph (*b*) or (*c*) of subsection (1) of section 12, or

(iii) if, by reason of weather, visibility, ice or sea conditions, the condition of the ship or its equipment or the nature or condition of its cargo, he is satisfied that such an order is justified in the interests of safety; and

(*c*) where he is informed that a substantial quantity of waste has been deposited in the arctic waters or has entered the arctic waters, or where on reasonable grounds, he is satisfied that a grave and imminent danger of a substantial deposit of waste in the arctic waters exists,

(i) order all ships within a specified area of arctic waters to report their positions to him, and

(ii) order any ship to take part in the clean-up of such waste or in any action to control or contain the waste.

16. The owner or person in charge of any area, place or premises entered pursuant to subsection (1) or (2) of section 15, the master of any ship boarded pursuant to paragraph (*a*) of subsection (3) of that section and every person found in the area, place or premises or on board the ship shall give a pollution prevention officer all reasonable assistance in his power to enable the pollution prevention officer to carry out his duties and functions under this Act and shall furnish the pollution prevention officer with such information as he may reasonably require.

17. (1) No person shall obstruct or hinder a pollution prevention officer in the carrying out of his duties or functions under this Act.

(2) No person shall knowingly make a false or misleading statement, either verbally or in writing, to a pollution prevention officer engaged in carrying out his duties or functions under this Act.

OFFENCES

18. (1) Any person who violates subsection (1) of section 4 and any ship that violates that subsection is guilty of an offence and liable on summary conviction to a fine not exceeding, in the case of a person, five thousand dollars, and in the case of a ship, one hundred thousand dollars.

(2) Where an offence is committed by a person under subsection (1) on more than one day or is continued by him for more than one day, it shall be deemed to be a separate offence for each day on which the offence is committed or continued.

19. (1) Any person who

  (a) fails to make a report to a pollution prevention officer as and when required under subsection (1) of section 5,

  (b) fails to provide the Governor in Council with evidence of financial responsibility as and when required under subsection (1) of section 8,

  (c) fails to provide the Governor in Council with any plans and specifications required of him under subsection (1) of section 10, or

  (d) constructs, alters or extends any work described in subsection (1) of section 10

   (i) otherwise than in accordance with any plans and specifications provided to the Governor in Council in accordance with a requirement made under that subsection, or with any such plans and specifications as required to be modified by any order made under subsection (2) of that section, or

   (ii) contrary to any order made under subsection (2) of that section prohibiting the carrying out of such construction, alteration or extension,

  is guilty of an offence and is liable on summary conviction to a fine not exceeding twenty-five thousand dollars.

(2) Any ship

  (a) that navigates within a shipping safety control zone while not complying with standards prescribed by any regulations made under section 12 that are applicable to it within that shipping safety control zone,

  (b) that navigates within a shipping safety control zone in contravention of a regulation made under paragraph (b) or (c) of subsection (1) of section 12,

  (c) that, having taken on board a pilot in order to comply with a regulation made under paragraph (b) of subsection (1) of section 12, fails to comply with any reasonable direction given to it by the pilot in carrying out his duties,

  (d) that fails to comply with any order of a pollution prevention officer under paragraph (b) or (c) of subsection (3) of section 15 that is applicable to it,

  (e) the master of which fails to make a report to a pollution prevention officer as and when required under subsection (2) of section 5, or

(f) the master of which or any person on board which violates section 17,

is guilty of an offence and is liable on summary conviction to a fine not exceeding twenty-five thousand dollars.

(3) Any person, other than the master of a ship or any person on board a ship, who violates section 17 is guilty of an offence punishable on summary conviction.

20. (1) In a prosecution of a person for an offence under subsection (1) of section 18, it is sufficient proof of the offence to establish that it was committed by an employee or agent of the accused whether or not the employee or agent is identified or has been prosecuted for the offence, unless the accused establishes that the offence was committed without his knowledge or consent and that he exercised all due diligence to prevent its commission.

(2) In a prosecution of a ship for an offence under this Act, it is sufficient proof that the ship has committed the offence to establish that the act or neglect that constitutes the offence was committed by the master of or any person on board the ship, other than a pollution prevention officer or a pilot taken on board in compliance with a regulation made under paragraph (b) of subsection (1) of section 12, whether or not the person on board the ship has been identified; and for the purposes of any prosecution of a ship for failing to comply with any order or direction of a pollution prevention officer or a pilot, any order given by such pollution prevention officer or any direction given by such pilot to the master or any person on board the ship shall be deemed to have been given to the ship.

21. (1) Subject to this section, a certificate of an analyst stating that he has analysed or examined a sample submitted to him by a pollution prevention officer and stating the result of his analysis or examination is admissible in evidence in any prosecution for a violation of subsection (1) of section 4 and in the absence of evidence to the contrary is proof of the statements contained in the certificate without proof of the signature or the official character of the person appearing to have signed the certificate.

(2) The party against whom a certificate of an analyst is produced pursuant to subsection (1) may, with leave of the court, require the attendance of the analyst for the purposes of cross-examination.

(3) No certificate shall be received in evidence pursuant to subsection

(1) unless the party intending to produce it has given to the party against whom it is intended to be produced reasonable notice of such intention together with a copy of the certificate.

22. (1) Where any person or ship is charged with having committed an offence under this Act, any court in Canada that would have had cognizance of the offence if it had been committed by a person within the limits of its ordinary jurisdiction has jurisdiction to try the offence as if it had been so committed.

(2) Where a ship is charged with having committed an offence under this Act, the summons may be served by leaving the same with the master or any officer of the ship or by posting the summons on some conspicuous part of the ship, and the ship may appear by counsel or agent, but if it does not appear, a summary conviction court may, upon proof of service of the summons, proceed *ex parte* to hold the trial.

SEIZURE AND FORFEITURE

23. (1) Whenever a pollution prevention officer suspects on reasonable grounds that

 (*a*) any provision of this Act or the regulations has been contravened by a ship, or

 (*b*) the owner of a ship or the owner or owners of all or part of the cargo thereof has or have committed an offence under paragraph (*b*) of subsection (1) of section 19,

he may, with the consent of the Governor in Council, seize the ship and its cargo anywhere in the arctic waters or elsewhere in the territorial sea or internal or inland waters of Canada.

(2) Subject to subsection (3) and section 24, a ship and cargo seized under subsection (1) shall be retained in the custody of the pollution prevention officer making the seizure or shall be delivered into the custody of such person as the Governor in Council directs.

(3) Where all or any part of a cargo seized under subsection (1) is perishable, the pollution prevention officer or other person having custody thereof may sell the cargo or the portion thereof that is perishable, as the case may be, and the proceeds of the sale shall be paid to the Receiver General or shall be deposited in a chartered bank to the credit of the Receiver General.

24. (1) Where a ship is convicted of an offence under this Act, or where the owner of a ship or an owner of all or part of the cargo thereof has been convicted of an offence under paragraph (*b*) of subsection (1) of section 19, the convicting court may, if the ship and its cargo were seized under subsection (1) of section 23, in addition to any other penalty imposed, order that the ship and cargo or the ship or its cargo or any part thereof be forfeited, and upon the making of such order the ship and cargo or the ship or its cargo or part thereof is or are forfeited to Her Majesty in right of Canada.

(2) Where any cargo or part thereof that is ordered to be forfeited under subsection (1) has been sold under subsection (3) of section 23, the proceeds of such sale are, upon the making of such order, forfeited to Her Majesty in right of Canada.

(3) Where a ship and cargo have been seized under subsection (1) of section 23 and proceedings that could result in an order that the ship and cargo be forfeited have been instituted, the court in or before which the proceedings have been instituted may, with the consent of the Governor in Council, order redelivery thereof to the person from whom they were seized upon security by bond, with two sureties, in an amount and form satisfactory to the Governor in Council, being given to Her Majesty in right of Canada.

(4) Any ship and cargo seized under subsection (1) of section 23 or the proceeds realized from a sale of any perishable cargo under subsection (3) of that section shall be returned or paid to the person from whom the ship and cargo were seized within thirty days from the seizure thereof unless, prior to the expiration of the thirty days, proceedings are instituted in respect of an offence alleged to have been committed by the ship against this Act or in respect of an offence under paragraph (b) of subsection (1) of section 19 alleged to have been committed by the owner of the ship or an owner of all or part of the cargo thereof.

(5) Where proceedings referred to in subsection (4) are instituted and, at the final conclusion of those proceedings, a ship and cargo or ship or cargo or part thereof is or are ordered to be forfeited, they or it may, subject to section 25, be disposed of as the Governor in Council directs.

(6) Where a ship and cargo have been seized under subsection (1) of section 23 and proceedings referred to in subsection (4) have been instituted, but the ship and cargo or ship or cargo or part thereof or any proceeds realized from the sale of any part of the cargo are not at the final conclusion of the proceedings ordered to be forfeited, they or it shall be returned or the proceeds shall be paid to the person from whom the ship and cargo were seized, unless there has been a conviction and a fine imposed in which case the ship and cargo or proceeds may be detained until the fine is paid, or the ship and cargo may be sold under execution in satisfaction of the fine, or the proceeds realized from a sale of the cargo or any part thereof may be applied in payment of the fine.

* * *

26. (1) The Governor in Council may, by order, delegate to any member of the Queen's Privy Council for Canada designated in the order the power and authority to do any act or thing that the Governor in Council is directed or empowered to do under this Act; and upon the making of such an order, the provision or provisions of this Act that direct or empower the Governor in Council and to which the order relates shall be read as if the title of the member of the Queen's Privy Council for Canada designated in the order were substituted therein for the expression "the Governor in Council".

(2) This section does not apply to authorize the Governor in Council to delegate any power vested in him under this Act to make regulations, to prescribe shipping safety control zones or to designate pollution prevention officers and their powers, other than pollution prevention officers with only those powers set out in subsection (1) or (2) of section 15.

⚓ AN ACT TO CONSOLIDATE THE OIL IN NAVIGABLE WATERS ACTS 1955 TO 1971 AND SECTION 5 OF THE CONTINENTAL SHELF ACT 1964

Be it enacted by the Queen's most Excellent Majesty, by and with the advice and consent of the Lords Spiritual and Temporal, and Commons, in this present Parliament assembled, and by the authority of the same, as follows:—

General provisions for preventing oil pollution

1. (1) If any oil to which this section applies or any mixture containing such oil is discharged from a ship registered in the United Kingdom into any part of the sea outside the territorial waters of the United Kingdom, the owner or master of the ship shall, subject to the provisions of this Act, be guilty of an offence.

(2) This section applies—

(a) to crude oil, fuel oil and lubricating oil; and

(b) to heavy diesel oil, as defined by regulations made under this section by the Secretary of State;

and shall also apply to any other description of oil which may be specified by regulations made by the Secretary of State, having regard to the provisions of any Convention accepted by Her Majesty's Government in the United Kingdom in so far as it relates to the prevention of pollution of the sea by oil, or having regard to the persistent character of oil of that description and the likelihood that it would cause pollution if discharged from a ship into any part of the sea outside the territorial waters of the United Kingdom.

(3) Regulations made by the Secretary of State may make exceptions from the operation of subsection (1) of this section, either generally or with respect to particular classes of ships, particular descriptions of oil or mixtures containing oil or the discharge of oil or mixtures in particular circumstances or into particular areas of the sea, and may do so either absolutely or subject to any specified conditions.

(4) A person guilty of an offence under this section shall be liable on summary conviction to a fine not exceeding £50,000 or on conviction on indictment to a fine.

2. (1) If any oil or mixture containing oil is discharged as mentioned in the following paragraphs into waters to which this section applies, then, subject to the provisions of this Act, the following shall be guilty of an offence, that is to say—

(a) if the discharge is from a vessel, the owner or master of the vessel, unless he proves that the discharge took place and was caused as mentioned in paragraph (b) of this subsection;

(b) if the discharge is from a vessel but takes place in the course of a transfer of oil to or from another vessel or a place on land and is caused by the act or omission of any person in charge of any apparatus in that other vessel or that place, the owner or master of that other vessel or, as the case may be, the occupier of that place;

(c) if the discharge is from a place on land, the occupier of that place, unless he proves that the discharge was caused as mentioned in paragraph (d) of this subsection;

(d) if the discharge is from a place on land and is caused by the act of a person who is in that place without the permission (express or implied) of the occupier, that person;

(e) if the discharge takes place otherwise than as mentioned in the preceding paragraphs and is the result of any operations for the exploration of the sea-bed and subsoil or the exploitation of their natural resources, the person carrying on the operations.

(2) This section applies to the following waters, that is to say,

(a) the whole of the sea within the seaward limits of the territorial waters of the United Kingdom; and

(b) all other waters (including inland waters) which are within those limits and are navigable by sea-going ships.

(3) In this Act "place on land" includes anything resting on the bed or shore of the sea, or of any other waters to which this section applies,

and also includes anything afloat (other than a vessel) if it is anchored or attached to the bed or shore of the sea or of any such waters; and "occupier", in relation to any such thing as is mentioned in the preceding provisions of this subsection, if it has no occupier, means the owner thereof, and, in relation to a railway wagon or road vehicle, means the person in charge of the wagon or vehicle and not the occupier of the land on which the wagon or vehicle stands.

(4) A person guilty of an offence under this section shall be liable on summary conviction to a fine not exceeding £50,000 or on conviction on indictment to a fine.

3. (1) If any oil to which section 1 of this Act applies, or any mixture containing such oil, is discharged into any part of the sea—

(a) from a pipe-line; or

(b) (otherwise than from a ship) as the result of any operation for the exploration of the sea-bed and subsoil or the exploitation of their natural resources in a designated area,

then, subject to the following provisions of this Act, the owner of the pipe-line or, as the case may be, the person carrying on the operations shall be guilty of an offence unless the discharge was from a place of his occupation and he proves that it was due to the act of a person who was there without his permission (express or implied).

(2) In this section "designated area" means an area for the time being designated by an Order made under section 1 of the Continental Shelf Act 1964.

(3) A person guilty of an offence under this section shall be liable on summary conviction to a fine not exceeding £50,000 or on conviction on indictment to a fine.

4. (1) For the purpose of preventing or reducing discharges of oil and mixtures containing oil into the sea, the Secretary of State may make regulations requiring ships registered in the United Kingdom to be fitted with such equipment and to comply with such other requirements as may be specified in the regulations.

(2) Without prejudice to the generality of subsection (1) of this section, where any regulations made thereunder require ships to be fitted with equipment of a specified description, the regulations may provide that equipment of that description—

(a) shall not be installed in a ship to which the regulations apply unless it is of a type tested and approved by a person appointed by the Secretary of State;

(b) while installed in such a ship, shall not be treated as satisfying the requirements of the regulations unless, at such times as may be specified in the regulations, it is submitted for testing and approval by a person so appointed.

(3) The Secretary of State may appoint persons to carry out tests for the purposes of any regulations made under this section, and, in respect of the carrying out of such tests, may charge such fees as, with the approval of the Treasury, may be prescribed by the regulations.

(4) Every surveyor of ships shall be taken to be a person appointed by the Secretary of State to carry out tests for the purposes of any regulations made under this section, in so far as they relate to tests required in accordance with paragraph (b) of subsection (2) of this section.

(5) If, in the case of any ship, the provisions of any regulations made under this section which apply to that ship are contravened, the owner or master of the ship shall be guilty of an offence.

(6) A person guilty of an offence under this section shall be liable on summary conviction to a fine not exceeding £1,000 or on conviction on indictment to a fine.

5. (1) Where a person is charged with an offence under section 1 of this Act, or is charged with an offence under section 2 of this Act as the owner or master of a vessel, it shall be a defence to prove that the oil or mixture was discharged for the purpose of securing the safety of any vessel, or of preventing damage to any vessel or cargo, or of saving life, unless the court is satisfied that the discharge of the oil or mixture was not necessary for that purpose or was not a reasonable step to take in the circumstances.

(2) Where a person is charged as mentioned in subsection (1) of this section, it shall also be a defence to prove—

(a) that the oil or mixture escaped in consequence of damage to the vessel, and that as soon as practicable after the damage occurred all reasonable steps were taken for preventing, or (if it could not be prevented) for stopping or reducing the escape of the oil or mixture, or

(b) that the oil or mixture escaped by reason of leakage, that neither the leakage nor any delay in discovering it was due to any want of reasonable care, and that as soon as practicable after the escape was discovered all reasonable steps were taken for stopping or reducing it.

6. (1) Where a person is charged, in respect of the escape of any oil or mixture containing oil, with an offence under section 2 or 3 of this Act—

(a) as the occupier of a place on land; or

(b) as a person carrying on operations for the exploration of the sea-bed and subsoil or the exploitation of their natural resources; or

(*c*) as the owner of a pipe-line,

it shall be a defence to prove that neither the escape nor any delay in discovering it was due to any want of reasonable care and that as soon as practicable after it was discovered all reasonable steps were taken for stopping or reducing it.

(2) Where a person is charged with an offence under section 2 of this Act in respect of the discharge of a mixture containing oil from a place on land, it shall also, subject to subsection (3) of this section, be a defence to prove—

(*a*) that the oil was contained in an effluent produced by operations for the refining of oil;

(*b*) that it was not reasonably practicable to dispose of the effluent otherwise than by discharging it into waters to which that section applies; and

(*c*) that all reasonably practicable steps had been taken for eliminating oil from the effluent.

(3) If it is proved that, at a time to which the charge relates, the surface of the waters into which the mixture was discharged from the place on land, or land adjacent to those waters, was fouled by oil, subsection (2) of this section shall not apply unless the court is satisfied that the fouling was not caused, or contributed to, by oil contained in any effluent discharged at or before that time from that place.

7. (1) Where any oil, or mixture containing oil, is discharged in consequence of—

(*a*) the exercise of any power conferred by sections 530 to 532 of the Merchant Shipping Act 1894 (which relate to the removal of wrecks by harbour, conservancy and lighthouse authorities); or

(*b*) the exercise, for the purpose of preventing an obstruction or danger to navigation, of any power to dispose of sunk, stranded or abandoned vessels which is exercisable by a harbour authority under any local enactment;

and apart from this subsection the authority exercising the power, or a person employed by or acting on behalf of the authority, would be guilty of an offence under section 1 or section 2 of this Act in respect of that discharge, the authority or person shall not be convicted of that offence unless it is shown that they or he failed to take such steps (if any) as were reasonable in the circumstances for preventing, stopping or reducing the discharge.

(2) Subsection (1) of this section shall apply to the exercise of any power conferred by section 13 of the Dockyard Ports Regulation Act

1865 (which relates to the removal of obstructions to dockyard ports) as it applies to the exercise of any such power as is mentioned in paragraph (*a*) of that subsection, and shall, as so applying, have effect as if references to the authority exercising the power were references to the Queen's harbour master for the port in question.

8. (1) A harbour authority may appoint a place within their jurisdiction where the ballast water of vessels in which a cargo of petroleum-spirit has been carried may be discharged into the waters of the harbour, at such times, and subject to such conditions, as the authority may determine; and, where a place is so appointed, the discharge of ballast water from such a vessel shall not constitute an offence under section 2 of this Act, if the ballast water is discharged at that place, and at a time and in accordance with the conditions so determined, and the ballast water contains no oil other than petroleum-spirit.

*   *   *

10. (1) No oil shall be transferred between sunset and sunrise to or from a vessel in any harbour in the United Kingdom unless the requisite notice has been given in accordance with this section or the transfer is for the purposes of a fire brigade.

(2) A general notice may be given to the harbour master of a harbour that transfers of oil between sunset and sunrise will be frequently carried out at a place in the harbour within such period, not ending later than twelve months after the date on which the notice is given, as is specified in the notice; and if such a notice is given it shall be the requisite notice for the purposes of this section as regards transfers of oil at that place within the period specified in the notice.

(3) Subject to subsection (2) of this section, the requisite notice for the purposes of this section shall be a notice given to the harbour master not less than three hours nor more than ninety-six hours before the transfer of oil begins.

(4) In the case of a harbour which has no harbour master, references in this section to the harbour master shall be construed as references to the harbour authority.

(5) If any oil is transferred to or from a vessel in contravention of this section, the master of the vessel, and, if the oil is transferred from or to a place on land, the occupier of that place, shall be liable on summary conviction to a fine not exceeding £100.

11. (1) If any oil or mixture containing oil—
   (*a*) is discharged from a vessel into the waters of a harbour in the United Kingdom; or

(*b*) is found to be escaping or to have escaped from a vessel into any such waters; or

(*c*) is found to be escaping or to have escaped into any such waters from a place on land;

the owner or master of the vessel, or the occupier of the place on land, as the case may be, shall forthwith report the occurrence to the harbour master, or, if the harbour has no harbour master, to the harbour authority.

*   *   *

Shipping Casualties

12. (1) The powers conferred by this section shall be exercisable where—

(*a*) an accident has occurred to or in a ship; and

(*b*) in the opinion of the Secretary of State oil from the ship will or may cause pollution on a large scale in the United Kingdom or in the waters in or adjacent to the United Kingdom up to the seaward limits of territorial waters; and

(*c*) in the opinion of the Secretary of State the use of the powers conferred by this section is urgently needed.

(2) For the purpose of preventing or reducing oil pollution, or the risk of oil pollution, the Secretary of State may give directions as respects the ship or its cargo—

(*a*) to the owner of the ship, or to any person in possession of the ship; or

(*b*) to the master of the ship; or

(*c*) to any salvor in possession of the ship, or to any person who is the servant or agent of any salvor in possession of the ship, and who is in charge of the salvage operation.

(3) Directions under subsection (2) of this section may require the person to whom they are given to take, or refrain from taking any action of any kind whatsoever, and without prejudice to the generality of the preceding provisions of this subsection the directions may require—

(*a*) that the ship is to be, or is not to be, moved, or is to be moved to a specified place, or is to be removed from a specified area or locality; or

(*b*) that the ship is not to be moved to a specified place or area, or over a specified route; or

(*c*) that any oil or other cargo is to be, or is not to be, unloaded or discharged; or

(*d*) that specified salvage measures are to be, or are not to be, taken.

(4) If in the opinion of the Secretary of State the powers conferred by subsection (2) of this section are, or have proved to be, inadequate for

the purpose, the Secretary of State may, for the purpose of preventing or reducing oil pollution, or the risk of oil pollution, take, as respects the ship or its cargo, any action of any kind whatsoever, and without prejudice to the generality of the preceding provisions of this subsection the Secretary of State may—

(a) take any such action as he has power to require to be taken by a direction under this section;

(b) undertake operations for the sinking or destruction of the ship, or any part of it, of a kind which is not within the means of any person to whom he can give directions;

(c) undertake operations which involve the taking over of control of the ship.

(5) The powers of the Secretary of State under subsection (4) of this section shall also be exercisable by such persons as may be authorised in that behalf by the Secretary of State.

(6) Every person concerned with compliance with directions given, or with action taken, under this section shall use his best endeavours to avoid any risk to human life.

(7) The provisions of this section and of section 16 of this Act are without prejudice to any rights or powers of Her Majesty's Government in the United Kingdom exercisable apart from those sections whether under international law or otherwise.

(8) It is hereby declared that any action taken as respects a ship which is under arrest or as respects the cargo of such a ship, being action duly taken in pursuance of a direction given under this section, or being any action taken under subsection (4) or (5) of this section—

(a) does not constitute contempt of court; and

(b) does not in any circumstances make the Admiralty Marshal liable in any civil proceedings.

(9) In this section, unless the context otherwise requires—

"accident" includes the loss, stranding, abandonment of or damage to a ship; and

"specified", in relation to a direction under this section, means specified by the direction;

and the reference in subsection (8) of this section to the Admiralty Marshal includes a reference to the Admiralty Marshal of the Supreme Court of Northern Ireland.

13. (1) If any action duly taken by a person in pursuance of a direction given to him under section 12 of this Act, or any action taken under subsection (4) or (5) of that section—

(a) was not reasonably necessary to prevent or reduce oil pollution, or risk of oil pollution; or

(b) was such that the good it did or was likely to do was dispropor-
tionately less than the expense incurred, or damage suffered, as
a result of the action,

a person incurring expense or suffering damage as a result of, or by himself taking, the action shall be entitled to recover compensation from
the Secretary of State.

(2) In considering whether subsection (1) of this section applies,
account shall be taken of—

(a) the extent and risk of oil pollution if the action had not been
taken;

(b) the likelihood of the action being effective; and

(c) the extent of the damage which has been caused by the action.

(3) Any reference in this section to the taking of any action includes
a reference to a compliance with a direction not to take some specified
action.

(4) The Admiralty jurisdiction of the High Court, of the Court of
Session and of the Supreme Court of Northern Ireland shall include
jurisdiction to hear and determine any claim arising under this section.

14. (1) If the person to whom a direction is duly given under section 12
of this Act contravenes, or fails to comply with, any requirement of the
direction, he shall be guilty of an offence.

(2) If a person wilfully obstructs any person who is—

(a) acting on behalf of the Secretary of State in connection with the
giving or service of a direction under section 12 of this Act;

(b) acting in compliance with a direction under that section; or

(c) acting under subsection (4) or (5) of that section;

he shall be guilty of an offence.

(3) In proceedings for an offence under subsection (1) of this section,
it shall be a defence for the accused to prove that he has used all due
diligence to ensure compliance with the direction, or that he had reasonable cause for believing that compliance with the direction would have
involved a serious risk to human life.

(4) A person guilty of an offence under this section shall be liable
on summary conviction to a fine not exceeding £50,000, or on conviction
on indictment to a fine.

15. (1) If the Secretary of State is satisfied that a company or other
body is not one to whom section 412 or section 437 of the Companies
Act 1948 (service of notices) applies so as to authorise the service of a
direction on that body under either of those sections, he may give a
direction under section 12 of this Act—

(*a*) to that body, as the owner of, or the person in possession of, a ship, by serving the direction on the master of the ship; or

(*b*) to that body, as a salvor, by serving the direction on the person in charge of the salvage operations.

(2) For the purpose of giving or serving a direction under section 12 of this Act to or on any person on a ship, a person acting on behalf of the Secretary of State shall have the right to go on board the ship.

(3) In the application of subsection (1) of this section to Northern Ireland, for references to sections 412 and 437 of the Companies Act 1948 there shall be substituted references to sections 361 and 385 of the Companies Act (Northern Ireland) 1960.

16. (1) Her Majesty may by Order in Council provide that sections 12 to 15 of this Act, together with any other provisions of this Act, shall apply to a ship—

(*a*) which is not a ship registered in the United Kingdom; and

(*b*) which is for the time being outside the territorial waters of the United Kingdom;

in such cases and circumstances as may be specified in the Order, and subject to such exceptions, adaptations and modifications, if any, as may be so specified.

(2) An Order in Council under subsection (1) of this section may contain such transitional and other consequential provisions as appear to Her Majesty to be expedient.

(3) Except as provided by an Order in Council under subsection (1) of this section, no direction under section 12 of this Act shall apply to a ship which is not registered in the United Kingdom and which is for the time being outside the territorial waters of the United Kingdom, and no action shall be taken under subsection (4) or (5) of section 12 of this Act as respects any such ship.

(4) No direction under section 12 of this Act shall apply to any vessel of Her Majesty's navy or to any Government ship (within the meaning of section 80 of the Merchant Shipping Act 1906) and no action shall be taken under subsection (4) or (5) of that section as respects any such vessel or ship.

Enforcement

17. (1) The Secretary of State may make regulations requiring oil record books to be carried in ships registered in the United Kingdom and requiring the master of any such ship to record in the oil record book carried by it—

(a) the carrying out, on board or in connection with the ship, of such of the following operations as may be prescribed, that is to say, operations relating to—

    (i) the loading of oil cargo, or

    (ii) the transfer of oil cargo during a voyage, or

    (iii) the discharge of oil cargo, or

    (iv) the ballasting of oil tanks (whether cargo or bunker fuel tanks) and the discharge of ballast from, and cleaning of, such tanks, or

    (v) the separation of oil from water, or from other substances, in any mixture containing oil, or

    (vi) the disposal of any oil or water, or any other substance, arising from operations relating to any of the matters specified in the preceding sub-paragraphs, or

    (vii) the disposal of any other oil residues;

(b) any occasion on which oil or a mixture containing oil is discharged from the ship for the purpose of securing the safety of any vessel, or of preventing damage to any vessel or cargo, or of saving life;

(c) any occasion on which oil or a mixture containing oil is found to be escaping, or to have escaped, from the ship in consequence of damage to the ship, or by reason of leakage.

(2) The Secretary of State may make regulations requiring the keeping of records relating to the transfer of oil to and from vessels while they are within the seaward limits of the territorial waters of the United Kingdom; and the requirements of any regulations made under this subsection shall be in addition to the requirements of any regulations made under subsection (1) of this section.

(3) Any records required to be kept by regulations made under subsection (2) of this section shall, unless the vessel is a barge, be kept by the master of the vessel, and shall, if the vessel is a barge, be kept, in so far as they relate to the transfer of oil to the barge, by the person supplying the oil and, in so far as they relate to the transfer of oil from the barge, by the person to whom the oil is delivered.

(4) Regulations under this section requiring the carrying of oil record books or the keeping of records may—

(a) prescribe the form of the oil record books or records and the nature of the entries to be made in them;

(b) require the person providing or keeping the books or records to retain them for a prescribed period;

(c) require that person, at the end of the prescribed period, to transmit the books or records to a place or person determined by or under the regulations;

(*d*) provide for the custody or disposal of the books or records after their transmission to such a place or person.

(5) If any ship fails to carry such an oil record book as it is required to carry under this section the owner or master shall be liable on summary conviction to a fine not exceeding £500; if any person fails to comply with any requirements imposed on him by or under this section, he shall be liable on summary conviction to a fine not exceeding £500; and if any person makes an entry in any oil record book carried or record kept under this section which is to his knowledge false or misleading in any material particular, he shall be liable on summary conviction to a fine not exceeding £500, or imprisonment for a term not exceeding six months, or both, or on conviction on indictment to a fine or to imprisonment for a term not exceeding two years or both.

(6) in any proceedings under this Act—

(*a*) any oil record book carried or record kept in pursuance of regulations made under this section shall be admissible as evidence, and in Scotland shall be sufficient evidence, of the facts stated in it;

(*b*) any copy of an entry in such an oil record book or record which is certified by the master of the ship in which the book is carried or by the person by whom the record is required to be kept to be a true copy of the entry shall be admissible as evidence, and in Scotland shall be sufficient evidence, of the facts stated in the entry;

(*c*) any document purporting to be an oil record book carried or record kept in pursuance of regulations made under this section, or purporting to be such a certified copy as is mentioned in the preceding paragraph, shall, unless the contrary is proved, be presumed to be such a book, record or copy, as the case may be.

18. (1) The Secretary of State may appoint any person as an inspector to report to him—

(*a*) whether the prohibitions, restrictions and obligations imposed by virtue of this Act (including prohibitions so imposed by the creation of offences under any provision of this Act other than section 3) have been complied with;

(*b*) what measures (other than measures made obligatory by regulations made under section 4 of this Act) have been taken to prevent the escape of oil and mixtures containing oil;

(c) whether the oil reception facilities provided in harbours are adequate;

and any such inspector may be so appointed to report either in a particular case or in a class of cases specified in his appointment.

(2) Every surveyor of ships shall be taken to be a person appointed generally under the preceding subsection to report to the Secretary of State in every kind of case falling within that subsection.

(3) Section 729 of the Merchant Shipping Act 1894 (powers of inspectors) shall apply to persons appointed or taken to be appointed under subsection (1) of this section as it applies to the inspectors referred to in that section and shall, as so applying, have effect as if—

(a) in paragraph (a) of subsection (1) of that section, the reference to a ship included any vessel, and the reference to that Act were a reference to this Act and any regulations made under this Act; and

(b) any power under that section to inspect premises included power to inspect any apparatus used for transferring oil.

(4) Any power of an inspector, under section 729 as applied by the preceding subsection, to inspect a vessel shall include power to test any equipment with which the vessel is required to be fitted in pursuance of regulations made under section 4 of this Act.

(5) Any power of an inspector, under section 729 as so applied, to require the production of any oil record book required to be carried or records required to be kept in pursuance of regulations made under section 17 of this Act shall include power to copy any entry therein and require the master to certify the copy as a true copy of the entry; and in subsection (3) of section 729, as so applied, the reference to making a declaration shall be construed as a reference to the certification of such a copy.

(6) Without prejudice to any powers exercisable by virtue of the preceding provisions of this section, in the case of a vessel which is for the time being in a harbour in the United Kingdom, the harbour master, and any other person appointed by the Secretary of State under this subsection (either generally or in relation to a particular vessel), shall have power—

(a) to go on board and inspect the vessel or any part thereof, or any of the machinery, boats, equipment or articles on board the vessel, for the purpose of ascertaining the circumstances relating to an alleged discharge of oil or a mixture containing oil from the vessel into the waters of the harbour;

(b) to require the production of any oil record book required to be carried or records required to be kept in pursuance of regulations made under section 17 of this Act; and

(c) to copy any entry in any such book or record and require the master to certify the copy as a true copy of the entry.

(7) A person exercising any powers conferred by subsection (6) of

this section shall not unnecessarily detain or delay the vessel from proceeding on any voyage.

(8) If any person fails to comply with any requirement duly made in pursuance of paragraph (*b*) or paragraph (*c*) of subsection (6) of this section, he shall be liable on summary conviction to a fine not exceeding £10; and if any person wilfully obstructs a person acting in the exercise of any power conferred by virtue of this section, he shall be liable on summary conviction to a fine not exceeding £100.

*　*　*

21. (1) Her Majesty may by Order in Council empower such persons as may be designated by or under the Order to go on board any Convention ship while the ship is within a harbour in the United Kingdom, and to require production of any oil record book required to be carried in accordance with the Convention.

(2) An Order in Council under this section may, for the purposes of the Order, and with any necessary modifications, apply any of the provisions of this Act relating to the production and inspection of oil record books and the taking of copies of entries therein, and to the admissibility in evidence of such oil record books and copies, including any provisions of the Merchant Shipping Act 1894 applied by those provisions, and including any penal provisions of this Act in so far as they relate to those matters.

(3) Her Majesty, if satisfied that the government of any country has accepted, or denounced, the Convention, or that the Convention extends, or has ceased to extend, to any territory, may by Order in Council make a declaration to that effect.

(4) In this section "the Convention" means any Convention accepted by Her Majesty's Government in the United Kingdom in so far as it relates to the prevention of pollution of the sea by oil; and "Convention ship" means a ship registered in—

  (*a*) a country the government of which has been declared by an Order in Council under the preceding subsection to have accepted the Convention, and has not been so declared to have denounced it; or

  (*b*) a territory to which it has been so declared that the Convention extends, not being a territory to which it has been so declared that the Convention has ceased to extend.

Miscellaneous and Supplementary

22. (1) Her Majesty may by Order in Council direct that, subject to such exceptions and modifications as may be specified in the Order, any regulations made under section 4 or section 17(1) of this Act shall apply to ships registered in countries and territories other than the United Kingdom at any time when they are in a harbour in the United Kingdom, or are within the seaward limits of the territorial waters of the United Kingdom while on their way to or from a harbour in the United Kingdom.

(2) An Order in Council under subsection (1) of this section shall not be made so as to impose different requirements in respect of ships of different countries or territories; but if Her Majesty is satisfied, as respects any country or territory, that ships registered there are required, by the law of that country or territory, to comply with provisions which are substantially the same as, or equally effective with, the requirements imposed by virtue of the Order, Her Majesty may by Order in Council direct that those requirements shall not apply to any ship registered in that country or territory if the ship complies with such of those provisions as are applicable thereto under the law of that country or territory.

(3) No regulation shall by virtue of an Order in Council under this section apply to any ship as being within a harbour in the United Kingdom, or on her way to or from such a harbour, if the ship would not have been within the harbour, or, as the case may be, on her way to or from the harbour, but for stress of weather or any other circumstances which neither the master nor the owner nor the charterer (if any) of the ship could have prevented or forestalled.

23. The Secretary of State may exempt any vessels or classes of vessels from any of the provisions of this Act or of any regulations made thereunder, either absolutely or subject to such conditions as he thinks fit.

24. (1) The Provisions of this Act do not apply to vessels of Her Majesty's navy, nor to Government ships in the service of the Secretary of State while employed for the purposes of Her Majesty's navy.

(2) Subject to subsection (1) of this section and subsection (4) of section 16 of this Act—

    (a) provisions of this Act which are expressed to apply only to ships registered in the United Kingdom apply to Government ships so registered and also to Government ships not so registered but held for the purposes of Her Majesty's Government in the United Kingdom;

    (b) provisions of this Act which are expressed to apply to vessels generally apply to Government ships.

(3) In this section "Government ships" has the same meaning as in section 80 of the Merchant Shipping Act 1906.

*　*　*

26. The Secretary of State shall, as soon as possible after the end of each calendar year, make a report on the exercise and performance of his functions under this Act during that year, which shall include such observations as he may think fit to make on the operation during that year of this Act and of any Convention accepted by Her Majesty's Government in the United Kingdom in so far as it relates to the prevention of pollution of the sea by oil, and the Secretary of State shall lay a copy of every such report before each House of Parliament.

＊　＊　＊

29. (1) In this Act—
"barge" includes a lighter and any similar vessel;
"harbour authority" and "harbour in the United Kingdom" have the meanings assigned to them by section 8(2) of this Act;
"harbour master" includes a dock master or pier master, and any person specially appointed by a harbour authority for the purpose of enforcing the provisions of this Act in relation to the harbour;
"local enactment" means a local or private Act, or an order confirmed by Parliament or brought into operation in accordance with special parliamentary procedure;
"oil" means oil of any description and includes spirit produced from oil of any description, and also includes coal tar;
"oil reception facilities" has the meaning assigned to it by section 9(1) of this Act;
"oil residues" means any waste consisting of, or arising from, oil or a mixture containing oil;
"outside the territorial waters of the United Kingdom" means outside the seaward limits of those waters;
"petroleum-spirit" has the same meaning as in the Petroleum (Consolidation) Act 1928;
"place on land" has the meaning assigned to it by section 2(3) of this Act;
"sea" includes any estuary or arm of the sea;
"transfer", in relation to oil, means transfer in bulk.

＊　＊　＊

31. The enactments and instruments with respect to which provision may be made by an Order in Council under section 1(1)(h) of the Hovercraft Act 1968 shall include this Act and any instrument made under it.

Suggested Reading List

Brown, E. D., *The Legal Regime of Hydrospace* (1971).

Sweeney, Joseph C., "Oil Pollution of the Oceans," 37 *Ford. L. Rev.* 155 (1968–69).

Mendelsohn, Allan I., "Maritime Liability for Oil Pollution—Domestic and International Law," 38 *Geo. Washington L. Rev.* 1 (1969).

LeGault, Leonard, "Canadian Arctic Waters Pollution Prevention Legislation," *Proceedings of Fifth Annual Conference of the Law of the Sea Institute* (University of Rhode Island), at 294–300 (1970).

Johnston, Douglas M., "The Arctic Marine Environment: A Managerial Perspective," *ibid.* 312–318.

(Note), "Ocean Pollution: An Examination of the Problem and an Appeal for International Co-operation," 7 *San Diego L. Rev.* 574 (1970).

Bilder, Richard R., "The Canadian Arctic Waters Pollution Prevention Act: New Stresses on the Law of the Sea," 69 *Mich. L. Rev.* 1 (1970).

Neuman, Robert H., "Oil on Troubled Waters: The International Control of Marine Pollution," 2 *J. Mar. L. and Comm.* 349 (1970–71).

Wilkes, Daniel, "International Administrative Due Process and the Control of Pollution: The Canadian Arctic Waters Example," *ibid.* 499.

Beesley, J. A., "Rights and Responsibilities of Arctic Coastal States: The Canadian View," 3 *J. Mar. L. and Comm.* 1 (1971–72).

Gold, Edgar, "Pollution of the Sea and International Law: A Canadian Perspective," *ibid.* 13.

Wulf, Norman A., "Contiguous Zones for Pollution Control," *ibid.* 537.

Dinstein, Y., "Oil Pollution by Ships and the Freedom of the High Seas," *ibid.* 363.

Green, L. C., "International Law and Canada's Anti-Pollution Legislation," 50 *Ore. L. Rev.* 462 (1971).

Swan, Peter N., "International and National Approaches to Oil Pollution Responsibility: An Emerging Regime for a Global Problem," *ibid.* 506.

Henkin, Louis, "Arctic Anti-Pollution: Does Canada Make or Break International Law," 65 *Amer. J. Int'l L.* 131 (1971).

Schachter, Oscar, and Serwer, Daniel, "Marine Pollution Problems and Remedies," 65 *Amer. J. Int'l L.* 84 (1971).

Hardy, Michael, "International Control of Marine Pollution," 11 *Nat. Res. J.* 296 (1971).

Brown, E. D., "International Law and Marine Pollution: Radioactive Waste and Other Hazardous Substances," *ibid.* 221.

Macdonald, R. St. J., Morris, G., and Johnston, D. M., "The Canadian Initiative to Establish a Maritime Zone for Environmental Protection: Its Significance for Multilateral Development of International Law," 21 *Univ. Toronto L.J.* 247 (1971).

Legault, L. J. H., "The Freedom of the Seas: A Licence to Pollute?" *ibid.* 39.

Scheffer, H. E., "Pollution of the Sea by Oil: The Brussels Convention of 1969 Relating to Oil Pollution Casualties," 18 *Netherlands Int'l L. Rev.* 2 (1971).

Pharand, Donat, "Oil Pollution Control in the Canadian Arctic," 7 *Texas Int'l L.J.* 45 (1971).

Hunter, L. A. W., "Proposed International Compensation Fund for Oil Pollution Damage," 4 *J. Mar. L. and Comm.* 117 (1972).

Marks, Ronald A., "Pollution of the Seas by Crude Oil—A Proposal for Effective Remedial Action," 33 *Ohio State L.J.* 80 (1972).

Goldie, L. F. E., "Pollution and Liability Problems Connected with Deep-Sea Mining," 12 *Nat. Res. J.* 172 (1972).

Teclaff, Ludwik A., "International Law and the Protection of Oceans from Pollution," 40 *Ford. L. Rev.* 529 (1972).

Petaccio, V., "Water Pollution and the Future Law of the Sea," 21 *Int'l and Comp. L.Q.* 15 (1972).

Caflisch, L. C., "International Law and Ocean Pollution: The Present and the Future," 8 *Rev. belge de droit int'l* 7 (1972).

Johnston, Douglas M., "Marine Pollution: Law, Science and Politics," 28 *Int'l J.* 69 (1972–1973).

Britton, M. E., "Special Problems of the Arctic Environment," in Alexander and Hawkins, eds., *Canadian–U.S. Maritime Problems,* at 9–28 (1972). (Papers presented at the Toronto Workshop held in June 1971 under auspices of the Law of the Sea Institute, Rhode Island, the Canadian Institute of International Affairs, and the Faculty of Law, University of Toronto).

Johnston, Douglas M., "Recent Canadian Marine Legislation: An Historical Perspective," *ibid.* 63–67.

Clingan, Thomas A., "Third-Party Imitations of Canadian Legislation and the Implications for International Law Development," *ibid.* 68–74.

Pharand, Donat, "The Implications of Canadian Marine and Arctic Legislation for the Development of International Law," *ibid.* 75–81.

International Environmental Co-operation and Regulation

GLOBAL: THE UNITED NATIONS CONFERENCE ON THE HUMAN ENVIRONMENT (1972)

◪ TEXT OF THE U.N. GENERAL ASSEMBLY RESOLUTION ON PROBLEMS OF THE HUMAN ENVIRONMENT

The General Assembly,

Noting that the relationship between man and his environment is undergoing profound changes in the wake of modern scientific and technological developments,

Aware that these developments, while offering unprecedented opportunities to change and shape the environment of man to meet his needs and aspirations, also involve grave dangers if not properly controlled,

Noting, in particular, the continuing and accelerating impairment of the quality of the human environment caused by such factors as air and water pollution, erosion and other forms of soil deterioration, waste, noise and the secondary effects of biocides, which are accentuated by rapidly increasing population and accelerating urbanization,

Concerned about the consequent effects on the condition of man, his physical, mental and social well-being, his dignity and his enjoyment of basic human rights, in developing as well as developed countries,

Convinced that increased attention to the problems of the human environment is essential for sound economic and social development,

Expressing the strong hope that the developing countries will, through appropriate international co-operation, derive particular benefit from the mobilization of knowledge and experience about the problems of the human environment, enabling them, *inter alia,* to forestall the occurrence of many such problems,

Having considered Economic and Social Council resolution 1346 (XLV) of 30 July 1968 on the question of convening an international conference on the problems of the human environment,

Bearing in mind the important work on some problems of the human environment at present being undertaken by organizations in the United

Resolution No. 2398 (XXIII), December 3, 1968; passed at the Twenty-Third Regular Session of the General Assembly.

Nations system, in particular the United Nations (including the Economic Commission for Europe), the International Labour Organisation, the Food and Agriculture Organization of the United Nations, the United Nations Educational, Scientific and Cultural Organization, the World Health Organization, the World Meteorological Organization, the Inter-Governmental Maritime Consultative Organization and the International Atomic Energy Agency, as referred to in the report of the Secretary-General on activities of United Nations organizations and programmes relevant to the human environment,

Aware of the important work being done on the problems of the human environment by Governments as well as by intergovernmental organizations such as the Organization of African Unity and non-governmental organizations such as the International Union for Conservation of Nature and Natural Resources, the International Council of Scientific Unions and the International Biological Programme,

Bearing in mind the recommendations of the Intergovernmental Conference of Experts on the Scientific Basis for Rational Use and Conservation of the Resources of the Biosphere, convened by the United Nations Educational, Scientific and Cultural Organization with the participation of the United Nations, the Food and Agriculture Organization of the United Nations and the World Health Organization,

Convinced of the need for intensified action at the national, regional and international level in order to limit and, where possible, eliminate the impairment of the human environment and in order to protect and improve the natural surroundings in the interest of man,

Desiring to encourage further work in this field and to give it a common outlook and direction,

Believing it desirable to provide a framework for comprehensive consideration within the United Nations of the problems of the human environment in order to focus the attention of Governments and public opinion on the importance and urgency of this question and also to identify those aspects of it that can only or best be solved through international co-operation and agreement,

1. *Decides,* in furtherance of the objectives set out above, to convene in 1972 a United Nations Conference on the Human Environment;

2. *Requests* the Secretary-General, in consultation with the Advisory Committee on the Application of Science and Technology to Development, to submit to the General Assembly at its twenty-fourth session, through the Economic and Social Council at its forty-seventh session, a report concerning:

(*a*) The nature, scope and progress of work at present being done in the field of the human environment;

(*b*) The main problems facing developed and developing countries in this area, which might with particular advantage be considered at such a conference, including the possibilities for increased international co-operation, especially as they relate to economic and social development, in particular of the developing countries;

(c) Possible methods of preparing for the Conference and the time necessary for such preparations;

(d) A possible time and place for the Conference;

(e) The range of financial implications for the United Nations of the holding of the Conference;

3. *Further requests* the Secretary-General, in preparing the report, to consult Governments of States Members of the United Nations and members of the specialized agencies and of the International Atomic Energy Agency and appropriate organizations of the United Nations system, and to draw on contributions from appropriate intergovernmental and non-governmental organizations.

⚓ TEXT OF U.N. GENERAL ASSEMBLY RESOLUTION CALLING FOR A 1972 CONFERENCE ON THE HUMAN ENVIRONMENT

The General Assembly,

In pursuance of its decision in resolution 2398 (XXIII) of 3 December 1968 to convene in 1972 a United Nations Conference on the Human Environment and to begin immediately preparations for the Conference,

Having considered with appreciation the report of the Secretary-General called for in the above-mentioned resolution,

Having considered the relevant chapter of the report of the Economic and Social Council,

Taking into account the recommendations of the Economic and Social Council in the matter,

Having taken cognizance of the note by the Secretary-General of 21 October 1969,

Reaffirming the importance and urgency of the problems of the human environment and underlining the necessity for complete preparatory arrangements for the 1972 United Nations Conference on the Human Environment to become operative as soon as possible,

Recognizing the important work on the problems of the human environment that is at present being undertaken and planned by the organizations in the United Nations system, other intergovernmental organizations, non-governmental organizations and national Governments,

Resolution No. 2581 (XXIV), December 15, 1969; passed at the Twenty-Fourth Regular Session of the General Assembly.

1. *Endorses* in general the proposals contained in the report of the Secretary-General regarding the purposes and objectives of the United Nations Conference on the Human Environment;

2. *Affirms* that it should be the main purpose of the Conference to serve as a practical means to encourage, and to provide guidelines for, action by Governments and international organizations designed to protect and improve the human environment, and to remedy and prevent its impairment, by means of international co-operation, bearing in mind the particular importance of enabling developing countries to forestall the occurrence of such problems;

3. *Entrusts* to the Secretary-General the over-all responsibility for organizing and preparing for the Conference, bearing in mind the views expressed during the debates of the forty-seventh session of the Economic and Social Council and the twenty-fourth session of the General Assembly;

4. *Establishes* a Preparatory Committee for the United Nations Conference on the Human Environment—consisting of highly qualified representatives nominated by the Governments of Argentina, Brazil, Canada, Costa Rica, Cyprus, Czechoslovakia, France, Ghana, Guinea, India, Iran, Italy, Jamaica, Japan, Mauritius, Mexico, the Netherlands, Nigeria, Singapore, Sweden, Togo, the Union of Soviet Socialist Republics, the United Arab Republic, the United Kingdom of Great Britain and Northern Ireland, the United States of America, Yugoslavia, and Zambia—to advise the Secretary-General;

5. *Requests* the Secretary-General to set up immediately a small conference secretariat, by drawing, with the agreement of the specialized agencies concerned, particularly upon regular staff of the United Nations system, and to appoint, at the appropriate time, a Secretary-General of the Conference;

6. *Further requests* the Secretary-General to pursue the consultations on the preparations for the Conference, undertaken by him in accordance with the General Assembly resolution 2398 (XXIII), to take account of the results of other international conferences such as the Conference on the Problems of Environment organized by the Economic Commission for Europe and scheduled to take place at Prague in 1971, and to draw on contributions from appropriate intergovernmental and non-governmental organizations;

7. *Invites* the specialized agencies, the International Atomic Energy Agency and the Advisory Committee on the Application of Science and Technology to Development to collaborate closely with the Secretary-General in the preparations for the Conference and to assist, as appropriate, in the work of the Preparatory Committee;

8. *Invites* the intergovernmental and non-governmental organizations concerned to lend every possible assistance in the preparations for the Conference;

9. *Requests* the Secretary-General, in collaboration with the Preparatory Committee, to take the necessary steps, as part of the preparations for the Conference, to bring to public attention the nature and importance of the problems of the human environment;

10. *Believes it essential* that all participating countries be enabled to take an active part in the preparations for the Conference and the Conference itself, and requests the Secretary-General to investigate what concrete steps could be taken to this end;

11. *Notes* the outline of the range of the possible financial implications for the United Nations of the holding of the Conference presented in the Secretary-General's reports and requests the Secretary-General, in the light of the views expressed during the debates of the forty-seventh session of the Economic and Social Council and the twenty-fourth session of the General Assembly, to make all efforts to reduce the costs of the Conference;

12. *Decides* that the Conference should be of two weeks' duration and requests the Secretary-General to take full account of this fact in preparing for the Conference;

13. *Believes* that, in order for the Conference to achieve its objectives, it is essential that its agenda be selective, its organizational structure be simple and efficient, and that the documentation be kept reasonably limited;

14. *Accepts with appreciation* the invitation of the Government of Sweden to hold the Conference in Sweden in June 1972;

15. *Requests* the Secretary-General to submit a brief progress report to the General Assembly at its twenty-fifth session through the Economic and Social Council at its forty-ninth session;

16. *Decides* to consider the progress of the preparatory work and to take the necessary further decisions at its twenty-fifth and twenty-sixth sessions.

Also on 15 December 1969 at the 1834th plenary meeting, the General Assembly, without objection, adopted the following decision on the recommendation of the Second Committee (A/7866):

The General Assembly decides that any interested Member State not appointed to the Preparatory Committee for the United Nations Conference on the Human Environment may designate highly qualified representatives to act as accredited observers at sessions of the Committee, with the right to participate in its discussions.

◪ STOCKHOLM DECLARATION ON THE HUMAN ENVIRONMENT (1972)

The United Nations Conference on the Human Environment,
Having met at Stockholm from 5 to 16 June 1972, and
Having considered the need for a common outlook and for common principles to inspire and guide the peoples of the world in the preservation and enhancement of the human environment,

PROCLAIMS

1. Man is both creature and moulder of his environment which gives him physical sustenance and affords him the opportunity for intellectual, moral, social and spiritual growth. In the long and tortuous evolution of the human race on this planet a stage has been reached when through the rapid acceleration of science and technology, man has acquired the power to transform his environment in countless ways and on an unprecedented scale. Both aspects of man's environment, the natural and the man-made, are essential to his well-being and to the enjoyment of basic human rights—even the right to life itself.

2. The protection and improvement of the human environment is a major issue which affects the well-being of peoples and economic development throughout the world; it is the urgent desire of the peoples of the whole world and the duty of all governments.

3. Man has constantly to sum up experience and go on discovering, inventing, creating and advancing. In our time man's capability to transform his surroundings, if used wisely, can bring to all peoples the benefits of development and the opportunity to enhance the quality of life. Wrongly or heedlessly applied, the same power can do incalculable harm to human beings and the human environment. We see around us growing evidence of man-made harm in many regions of the earth: dangerous levels of pollution in water, air, earth and living beings; major and undesirable disturbances to the ecological balance of the biosphere; destruction and depletion of irreplaceable resources; and gross deficiencies harmful to the physical, mental and social health of man, in the man-made environment; particularly in the living and working environment.

* * *

6. A point has been reached in history when we must shape our actions throughout the world with a more prudent care for their environmental

Adopted by consensus at the United Nations Conference on the Human Environment held at Stockholm in June 1972.

consequences. Through ignorance or indifference we can do massive and irreversible harm to the earthly environment on which our life and well-being depend. Conversely, through fuller knowledge and wiser action, we can achieve for ourselves and our posterity a better life in an environment more in keeping with human needs and hopes. There are broad vistas for the enhancement of environmental quality and the creation of a good life. What is needed is an enthusiastic but calm state of mind and intense but orderly work. For the purpose of attaining freedom in the world of nature, man must use knowledge to build in collaboration with nature a better environment. To defend and improve the human environment for present and future generations has become an imperative goal for mankind—a goal to be pursued together with, and in harmony with, the established and fundamental goals of peace and of world-wide economic and social development.

7. To achieve this environmental goal will demand the acceptance of responsibility by citizens and communities and by enterprises and institutions at every level, all sharing equitably in common efforts. Individuals in all walks of life as well as organizations in many fields, by their values and the sum of their actions, will shape the world environment of the future. Local and national governments will bear the greatest burden for large-scale environmental policy and action within their jurisdictions. International co-operation is also needed in order to raise resources to support the developing countries in carrying out their responsibilities in this field. A growing class of environmental problems, because they are regional or global in extent or because they affect the common international realm, will require extensive co-operation among nations and action by international organizations in the common interest. The Conference calls upon the Governments and peoples to exert common efforts for the preservation and improvement of the human environment, for the benefit of all the people and for their posterity.

Principles

STATES THE COMMON CONVICTION THAT

✿   ✿   ✿

Principle 6

The discharge of toxic substances or of other substances and the release of heat, in such quantities or concentrations as to exceed the capacity of the environment to render them harmless, must be halted in order to ensure that serious or irreversible damage is not inflicted upon ecosystems. The just struggle of the peoples of all countries against pollution should be supported.

Principle 7

States shall take all possible steps to prevent pollution of the seas by substances that are liable to create hazards to human health, to harm living resources and marine life, to damage amenities or to interfere with other legitimate uses of the sea.

* * *

Principle 11

The environmental policies of all States should enhance and not adversely affect the present or future development potential of developing countries, nor should they hamper the attainment of better living conditions for all, and appropriate steps should be taken by States and international organizations with a view to reaching agreement on meeting the possible national and international economic consequences resulting from the application of environmental measures.

* * *

Principle 18

Science and technology, as part of their contribution to economic and social development, must be applied to the identification, avoidance and control of environmental risks and the solution of environmental problems and for the common good of mankind.

* * *

Principle 21

States have, in accordance with the Charter of the United Nations and the principles of international law, the sovereign right to exploit their own resources pursuant to their own environmental policies, and the responsibility to ensure that activities within their jurisdiction or control do not cause damage to the environment of other States or of areas beyond the limits of national jurisdiction.

Principle 22

States shall co-operate to develop further the international law regarding liability and compensation for the victims of pollution and other environmental damage caused by activities within the jurisdiction or control of such States to areas beyond their jurisdiction.

Principle 23

Without prejudice to such criteria as may be agreed upon by the international community, or to standards which will have to be determined nationally, it will be essential in all cases to consider the systems of values prevailing in each country, and the extent of the applicability of standards which are valid for the most advanced countries but which may be inappropriate and of unwarranted social cost for the developing countries.

Principle 24

International matters concerning the protection and improvement of the environment should be handled in a co-operative spirit by all countries, big or small, on an equal footing. Co-operation through multilateral or bilateral arrangements or other appropriate means is essential to prevent, reduce or eliminate adverse environmental effects resulting from activities conducted in all spheres, in such a way that due account is taken of the sovereignty and interests of all States.

Principle 25

States shall ensure that international organizations play a co-ordinated, efficient and dynamic role for the protection and improvement of the environment.

Note: The Conference forwarded principle 26 for consideration by the U.N. General Assembly in the autumn of 1972:

Principle 26

Man and his environment must be spared the effects of nuclear weapons and all other means of mass destruction. States must strive to reach prompt agreement, in the relevant international organs, on the elimination and complete destruction of such weapons.

Note: The Chinese delegation rejected this principle and proposed the following language in its place:

In order to protect mankind and the human environment, it is imperative to firmly prohibit the use of and thoroughly destroy the inhuman biological and chemical weapons which seriously pollute and damage the environment; to completely prohibit and thoroughly destroy nuclear weapons and, as the first step, to reach an agreement by the nuclear states on the non-use of nuclear weapons at no time and under no circumstances.

✍ STOCKHOLM RECOMMENDATIONS ON DEVELOPMENT AND ENVIRONMENT

Recommendation 102

It is recommended that the appropriate regional organizations give full consideration to the following steps:

(a) Preparing short-term and long-term plans at regional, subregional and sectoral levels for the study and identification of the major environmental problems faced by the countries of the region concerned as well as the special problems of the least developed countries of the region and of countries with coastlines and inland lakes and rivers exposed to the risk of marine and other forms of pollution;

(b) Evaluating the administrative, technical and legal solutions to various environmental problems in terms of both preventive and remedial measures, taking into account possible alternative and/or multidisciplinary approaches to development;

(c) Preparation, within the framework of international agreements, of legislative measures designed to protect marine (and fresh-water) fisheries resources within the limits of their national jurisdiction;

❊ ❊ ❊

Recommendation 103

It is recommended that Governments take the necessary steps to ensure:

(a) That all countries present at the Conference agree not to invoke environmental concerns as a pretext for discriminatory trade policies or for reduced access to markets and recognize further that the burdens of the environmental policies of the industrialized countries should not be transferred, either directly or indirectly, to the developing countries. As a general rule, no country should solve or disregard its environmental problems at the expense of other countries;

(b) That where environmental concerns lead to restrictions on trade, or to stricter environmental standards with negative effects on exports, particularly from developing countries, appropriate measures for com-

Approved at the United Nations Conference on the Human Environment held at Stockholm in June 1972.

pensation should be worked out within the framework of existing contractual and institutional arrangements and any new such arrangements that can be worked out in the future;

(c) That the General Agreement of Tariffs and Trade, among other international organizations, could be used for the examination of the problems, specifically through the recently established Group on Environmental Measures and International Trade and through its general procedures for bilateral and multilateral adjustment of differences;

(d) That whenever possible (that is, in cases which do not require immediate discontinuation of imports), countries should inform their trading partners in advance about the intended action in order that there might be an opportunity to consult within the GATT Group on Environmental Measures and International Trade, among other international organizations. Assistance in meeting the consequences of stricter environmental standards ought to be given in the form of financial or technical assistance for research with a view to removing the obstacles that the products of developing countries have encountered;

(e) That all countries agree that uniform environmental standards should not be expected to be applied universally by all countries with respect to given industrial processes or products except in those cases where environmental disruption may constitute a concern to other countries. In addition, in order to avoid an impairment of the access of the developing countries to the markets of the industrialized countries because of differential product standards, Governments should aim at world-wide harmonization of such standards. Environmental standards should be established, at whatever levels are necessary, to safeguard the environment, and should not be directed towards gaining trade advantages;

(f) That the Governments and the competent international organizations keep a close watch on medium- and long-term trends in international trade and take measures with a view to promoting:

(i) The exchange of environmental protection technologies;

(ii) International trade in natural products and commodities which compete with synthetic products that have a greater capacity for pollution.

Recommendation 104

It is recommended that the Secretary-General ensure:

(a) That appropriate steps shall be taken by the existing United Nations organizations to identify the major threats to exports, particularly those of developing countries, that arise from environmental concerns, their character and severity, and the remedial action that may be envisaged;

(b) That the United Nations system, in co-operation with other governmental and non-governmental agencies working in this field, should assist Governments to develop mutually acceptable common international environmental standards on products which are considered by Governments to be of significance in foreign trade. Testing and certification procedures designed to ensure that the products conform to these standards should be such as to avoid arbitrary and discriminatory actions that might affect the trade of developing countries.

Recommendation 105

It is recommended that the General Agreement of Tariffs and Trade, the United Nations Conference on Trade and Development and other international bodies, as appropriate, should, within their respective fields of competence, consider undertaking to monitor, assess, and regularly report the emergence of tariff and non-tariff barriers to trade as a result of environmental policies.

Recommendation 106

It is recommended:

(a) That the Secretary-General, in co-operation with other international bodies as appropriate, should examine the extent to which the problems of pollution could be ameliorated by a reduction in the current levels of production and in the future rate of growth of the production of synthetic products and substitutes which, in their natural form, could be produced by developing countries; and make recommendations for national and international action;

(b) That Governments of the developing countries consider fully the new opportunities that may be offered to them to establish industries and/or expand existing industries in which they may have comparative advantages because of environmental considerations, and that special care be taken to apply the appropriate international standards on environment in order to avoid the creation of pollution problems in developing countries;

(c) That the Secretary-General, in consultation with appropriate international agencies, undertake a full review of the practical implications of environmental concerns in relation to distribution of future industrial capacity and, in particular, to ways in which the developing countries may be assisted to take advantage of opportunities and to minimize risks in this area.

Recommendation 107

It is recommended that the Secretary-General, in collaboration with appropriate international agencies, ensure that a study be conducted of appropriate mechanisms for financing international environmental action, taking into account General Assembly resolution 2849 (XXVI).

Recommendation 108

It being recognized that it is in the interest of mankind that the technologies for protecting and improving the environment be employed universally, *it is recommended* that the Secretary-General be asked to undertake studies, in consultation with Governments and appropriate international agencies, to find means by which environmental technologies may be made available for adoption by developing countries under terms and conditions that encourage their wide distribution without constituting an unacceptable burden to developing countries.

Recommendation 109

It is recommended that the Secretary-General, in collaboration with appropriate international agencies, take steps to ensure that the environmental considerations of an international nature related to the foregoing recommendations be integrated into the review and appraisal of the International Development Strategy for the Second Development Decade in such a way that the flow of international aid to developing countries is not hampered. Recommendations for national action, proposed by the Secretary-General of the Conference, shall be referred to Governments for their consideration and, when deemed appropriate, should be taken into account in the review and appraisal process during the consideration of matters for national action as included in the International Development Strategy. It should further be ensured that the preoccupation of developed countries with their own environmental problems should not effect the flow of assistance to developing countries, and that this flow should be adequate to meet the additional environmental requirements of such countries.

⚡ STOCKHOLM RECOMMENDATIONS ON THE PLANNING AND MANAGEMENT OF HUMAN SETTLEMENTS FOR ENVIRONMENTAL QUALITY

Recommendation 3

Certain aspects of human settlements can have international implications, for example, the "export" of pollution from urban and industrial areas, and the effects of seaports on international hinterlands. Accordingly, *it is recommended* that the attention of Governments be drawn to the need to consult bilaterally or regionally whenever environmental conditions or development plans in one country could have repercussions in one or more neighbouring countries.

Recommendation 4

1. *It is recommended* that Governments and the Secretary-General, the latter in consultation with the appropriate United Nations agencies, take the following steps:

(a) Entrust the over-all responsibility for an agreed programme of environmental research at the international level to any central body that may be given the co-ordinating authority in the field of the environment, taking into account the co-ordination work already being provided on the regional level, especially by the Economic Commission for Europe;

(b) Identify, wherever possible, an existing agency within the United Nations system as the principal focal point for initiating and co-ordinating research in each principal area and, where there are competing claims, establish appropriate priorities;

(c) Designate the following as priority areas for research:

❖ ❖ ❖

(vi) Water supply, sewerage and waste-disposal systems adapted to local conditions, particularly in semi-tropical, tropical, Arctic and sub-Arctic areas (principal body responsible: World Health Organization);

❖ ❖ ❖

Approved at the United Nations Conference on the Human Environment held at Stockholm in June 1972.

Recommendation 9

It is recommended that the World Health Organization increase its efforts to support Governments in planning for improving water supply and sewerage services through its community water supply programme, taking account, as far as possible, of the framework of total environment programmes for communities.

Recommendation 10

It is recommended that development assistance agencies should give higher priority, where justified in the light of the social benefits, to supporting Governments in financing and setting up services for water supply, disposal of water from all sources, and liquid-waste and solid-waste disposal and treatment as part of the objectives of the Second United Nations Development Decade.

✍ STOCKHOLM RECOMMENDATIONS ON ENVIRONMENTAL ASPECTS OF NATURAL RESOURCES MANAGEMENT

Recommendation 21

It is recommended that Governments, the Food and Agriculture Organization of the United Nations and the World Health Organization, in co-operation with the United Nations Educational, Scientific and Cultural Organization and the International Atomic Energy Agency, strengthen and co-ordinate international programmes for integrated pest control and reduction of the harmful effects of agro-chemicals:

(a) Existing international activities for the exchange of information and co-operative research and technical assistance to developing countries should be strengthened to support the national programmes described above, with particular reference to:

    (i) Basic research on ecological effects of pesticides and fertilizers (MAB);

    (ii) Use of radio-isotope and radiation techniques in studying the fate of pesticides in the environment (joint IAEA/FAO Division);

    (iii) Evaluation of the possibility of using pesticides of biological

Approved at the United Nations Conference on the Human Environment held at Stockholm in June 1972.

origin in substitution for certain chemical insecticides which cause serious disturbances in the environment;

(iv) Dose and timing of fertilizers' application and their effects on soil productivity and the environment (Food and Agriculture Organization of the United Nations);

(v) Management practices and techniques for integrated pest control, including biological control (Food and Agriculture Organization of the United Nations and World Health Organization);

(vi) Establishment and/or strengthening of national and regional centres for integrated pest control, particularly in developing countries (Food and Agriculture Organization of the United Nations and World Health Organization);

(b) Existing expert committees of the Food and Agriculture Organization of the United Nations and the World Health Organization on various aspects of pest control should be convened periodically:

(i) To assess recent advances in the relevant fields of research mentioned above;

(ii) To review and further develop international guidelines and standards with special reference to national and ecological conditions in relation to the use of chlorinated hydrocarbons, pesticides containing heavy metals, and the use and experimentation of biological controls;

(c) In addition, *ad hoc* panels of experts should be convened, by the Food and Agriculture Organization of the United Nations, the World Health Organization and, where appropriate, the International Atomic Energy Agency, in order to study specific problems, and facilitate the work of the above-mentioned committees.

Recommendation 22

It is recommended that the Food and Agriculture Organization of the United Nations, under its "War on Waste" programme, place increased emphasis on control and recycling of wastes in agriculture:

(a) This programme should assist the national activities relating to:

(i) Control and recycling of crop residues and animal wastes;

(ii) Control and recycling of agro-industrial waste;

(iii) Use of municipal wastes as fertilizers;

(b) The programme should also include measures to avoid wasteful use of natural resources through the destruction of unmarketable agricultural products or their use for improper purposes.

* * *

Recommendation 29

It is recommended that the Secretary-General ensure that the effect of pollutants upon wildlife shall be considered, where appropriate, within environmental monitoring systems. Particular attention should be paid to those species of wildlife that may serve as indicators for future wide environmental disturbances, and an ultimate impact upon human populations.

✤   ✤   ✤

Recommendation 47

It is recommended that Governments, and the Secretary-General of the United Nations in co-operation with the Food and Agriculture Organization of the United Nations and other United Nations organizations concerned, as well as development assistance agencies, take steps to ensure clóse participation of fishery agencies and interests in the preparations for the United Nations Conference on the Law of the Sea. In order to safeguard the marine environment and its resources through the development of effective and workable principles and laws, the information and insight of international and regional fishery bodies, as well as the national fishery agencies, are essential.

Recommendation 48

It is recommended that Governments, and the Secretary-General in co-operation with the Food and Agriculture Organization of the United Nations and other United Nations organizations concerned, as well as development assistance agencies, take steps to ensure international co-operation in the research, control and regulation of the side effects of national activities in resource utilization where these affect the aquatic resources of other nations:

(a) Estuaries, intertidal marshes, and other near-shore and in-shore environments play a crucial role in the maintenance of several marine fish stocks. Similar problems exist in those fresh-water fisheries that occur in shared waters;

(b) Discharge of toxic chemicals, heavy metals, and other wastes may affect even high-seas resources;

(c) Certain exotic species, notably the carp, lamprey and alewife, have invaded international waters with deleterious effects as a result of unregulated unilateral action.

✤   ✤   ✤

Recommendation 51

It is recommended that Governments concerned consider the creation of river-basin commissions or other appropriate machinery for co-operation between interested States for water resources common to more than one jurisdiction.

(a) In accordance with the Charter of the United Nations and the principles of international law full consideration must be given to the right of permanent sovereignty of each country concerned to develop its own resources;

(b) The following principles should be considered by the States concerned when appropriate:

>(i) Nations agree that when major water resource activities are contemplated that may have a significant environmental effect on another country, the other country should be notified well in advance of the activity envisaged;

>(ii) The basic objective of all water resource use and development activities from the environmental point of view is to ensure the best use of water and to avoid its pollution in each country;

>(iii) The net benefits of hydrologic regions common to more than one national jurisdiction are to be shared equitably by the nations affected;

(c) Such arrangements, when deemed appropriate by the States concerned, will permit undertaking on a regional basis:

>(i) Collection, analysis, and exchanges of hydrologic data through some international mechanism agreed upon by the States concerned;

>(ii) Joint data-collection programmes to serve planning needs;

>(iii) Assessment of environmental effects of existing water uses;

>(iv) Joint study of the causes and symptoms of problems related to water resources, taking into account the technical, economic, and social considerations of water quality control;

>(v) Rational use, including a programme of quality control, of the water resource as an environmental asset;

>(vi) Provision for the judicial and administrative protection of water rights and claims;

>(vii) Prevention and settlement of disputes with reference to the management and conservation of water resources;

>(viii) Financial and technical co-operation of a shared resource;

(d) Regional conferences should be organized to promote the above considerations.

✿　✿　✿

Recommendation 55

It is recommended that the Secretary-General take steps to conduct an exploratory programme to assess the actual and potential environmental effects of water management upon the oceans, define terms and estimate the costs for a comprehensive programme of action, and establish and maintain as far as possible:

(a) A world registry of major or otherwise important rivers arranged regionally and classified according to their discharge of water and pollutants;

(b) A world registry of clean rivers which would be defined in accordance with internationally agreed quality criteria and to which nations would contribute on a voluntary basis:

    (i) The oceans are the ultimate recipient for the natural and man-made wastes discharged into the river systems of the continents;

    (ii) Changes in the amount of river-flow into the oceans, as well as in its distribution in space and time, may considerably affect the physical, chemical and biological régime of the estuary regions and influence the oceanic water systems;

    (iii) It would be desirable for nations to declare their intention to have admitted to the world registry of clean rivers those rivers within their jurisdiction that meet the quality criteria as defined and to declare their further intention to ensure that certain other rivers shall meet those quality criteria by some target date.

* * *

Recommendation 57

It is recommended that the Secretary-General take steps to ensure proper collection, measurement and analysis of data relating to the environmental effects of energy use and production within appropriate monitoring systems.

(a) The design and operation of such networks should include, in particular, monitoring the environmental levels resulting from emission of carbon dioxide, sulphur dioxide, oxidants, nitrogen oxides (NO_x), heat and particulates, as well as those from releases of oil and radioactivity;

(b) In each case the objective is to learn more about the relationships between such levels and the effects on weather, human health, plant and animal life, and amenity values.

✍ STOCKHOLM RECOMMENDATIONS ON IDENTIFICATION AND CONTROL OF POLLUTANTS OF BROAD INTERNATIONAL SIGNIFICANCE

A. Pollution Generally

Recommendation 70

It is recommended that Governments be mindful of activities in which there is an appreciable risk of effects on climate, and to this end:

(a) Carefully evaluate the likelihood and magnitude of climatic effects and disseminate their findings to the maximum extent feasible before embarking on such activities;

(b) Consult fully other interested States when activities carrying a risk of such effects are being contemplated or implemented.

Recommendation 71

It is recommended that Governments use the best practicable means available to minimize the release to the environment of toxic or dangerous substances, especially if they are persistent substances such as heavy metals and organochlorine compounds, until it has been demonstrated that their release will not give rise to unacceptable risks or unless their use is essential to human health or food production, in which case appropriate control measures should be applied.

Recommendation 72

It is recommended that in establishing standards for pollutants of international significance, Governments take into account the relevant standards proposed by competent international organizations, and concert with other concerned Governments and the competent international organizations in planning and carrying out control programmes for pollutants distributed beyond the national jurisdiction from which they are released.

Recommendation 73

It is recommended that Governments actively support, and contribute to, international programmes to acquire knowledge for the assessment of

Approved at the United Nations Conference on the Human Environment held at Stockholm in June 1972.

pollutant sources, pathways, exposures and risks and that those Governments in a position to do so provide educational, technical and other forms of assistance to facilitate broad participation by countries regardless of their economic or technical advancement.

Recommendation 74

It is recommended that the Secretary-General, drawing on the resources of the entire United Nations system, and with the active support of Governments and appropriate scientific and other international bodies:

(a) Increase the capability of the United Nations system to provide awareness and advance warning of deleterious effects to human health and well-being from man-made pollutants;

(b) Provide this information in a form which is useful to policy-makers at the national level;

(c) Assist those Governments which desire to incorporate these and other environmental factors into national planning processes;

(d) Improve the international acceptability of procedures for testing pollutants and contaminants by:

   (i) International division of labour in carrying out the large-scale testing programmes needed;

   (ii) Development of international schedules of tests for evaluation of the environmental impact potential of specific contaminants or products. Such a schedule of tests should include consideration of both short-term and long-term effects of all kinds, and should be reviewed and brought up to date from time to time to take into account new knowledge and techniques;

   (iii) Development and implementation of an international inter-calibration programme for sampling and analytical techniques to permit more meaningful comparisons of national data;

   (iv) Develop plans for an International Registry of Data on Chemicals in the Environment based on a collection of available scientific data on the environmental behaviour of the most important man-made chemicals and containing production figures of the potentially most harmful chemicals, together with their pathways from factory *via* utilization to ultimate disposal or recirculation.

Recommendation 75

It is recommended that, without reducing in any way their attention to non-radioactive pollutants, Governments should:

(a) Explore with the International Atomic Energy Agency and the World Health Organization the feasibility of developing a registry of releases to the biosphere of significant quantities of radioactive materials;

(b) Support and expand, under the International Atomic Energy Agency and appropriate international organizations, international co-operation on radioactive waste problems, including problems of mining and tailings and also including co-ordination of plans for the siting of fuel-reprocessing plants in relation to the siting of the ultimate storage areas, considering also the transportation problems.

Recommendation 76

It is recommended:

(a) That a major effort be undertaken to develop monitoring and both epidemiological and experimental research programmes providing data for early warning and prevention of the deleterious effects of the various environmental agents, acting singly or in combination, to which man is increasingly exposed, directly or indirectly, and for the assessment of their potential risks to human health, with particular regard to the risks of mutagenicity, teratogenicity and carcinogenicity. Such programmes should be guided and co-ordinated by the World Health Organization;

(b) That the World Health Organization co-ordinate the development and implementation of an appropriate international collection and dissemination system to correlate medical, environmental and family-history data;

(c) That Governments actively support and contribute to international programmes for research and development of guidelines concerning environmental factors in the work environment.

Recommendation 77

It is recommended that the World Health Organization, in collaboration with the relevant agencies, in the context of an approved programme, and with a view to suggesting necessary action, assist Governments, particularly those of developing countries, in undertaking co-ordinated programmes of monitoring of air and water and in establishing monitoring systems in areas where there may be a risk to health from pollution.

Recommendation 78

It is recommended that internationally co-ordinated programmes of research and monitoring of food contamination by chemical and biological agents be established and developed jointly by the Food and Agriculture Organization of the United Nations and the World Health Organization, taking into account national programmes, and that the results of monitoring be expeditiously assembled, evaluated and made available so as to provide early information on rising trends of contamination and on levels that may be considered undesirable or may lead to unsafe human intakes.

Recommendation 79

It is recommended:

(a) That approximately 10 baseline stations be set up, with the consent of the States involved, in areas remote from all sources of pollution in order to monitor long-term global trends in atmospheric constituents and properties which may cause changes in meteorological properties, including climatic changes;

(b) That a much larger network of not less than 100 stations be set up, with the consent of the States involved, for monitoring properties and constituents of the atmosphere on a regional basis and especially changes in the distribution and concentration of contaminants;

(c) That these programmes be guided and co-ordinated by the World Meteorological Organization;

(d) That the World Meteorological Organization, in co-operation with the International Council of Scientific Unions (ICSU), continue to carry out the Global Atmospheric Research Programme (GARP), and if necessary establish new programmes to understand better the general circulation of the atmosphere and the causes of climatic changes whether these causes are natural or the result of man's activities.

Recommendation 80

It is recommended that the Secretary-General ensure:

(a) That research activities in terrestrial ecology be encouraged, supported and co-ordinated through the appropriate agencies, so as to provide adequate knowledge of the inputs, movements, residence times and ecological effects of pollutants identified as critical;

(b) That regional and global networks of existing and, where necessary, new research stations, research centres, and biological reserves be designated or established within the framework of the Man and the Biosphere Programme (MAB) in all major ecological regions, to facilitate intensive analysis of the structure and functioning of ecosystems under natural or managed conditions;

(c) That the feasibility of using stations participating in this programme for surveillance of the effects of pollutants on ecosystems be investigated;

(d) That programmes such as the Man and the Biosphere Programme be used to the extent possible to monitor:

(i) the accumulation of hazardous compounds in biological and abiotic material at representative sites;

(ii) the effect of such accumulation on the reproductive success and population size of selected species.

Recommendation 81

It is recommended that the World Health Organization, together with the international organizations concerned, continue to study, and establish, primary standards for the protection of the human organism, especially from pollutants that are common to air, water and food, as a basis for the establishment of derived working limits.

Recommendation 82

It is recommended that increased support be given to the Codex Alimentarius Commission to develop international standards for pollutants in food and a code of ethics for international food trade, and that the capabilities of the Food and Agriculture Organization of the United Nations and the World Health Organization to assist materially and to guide developing countries in the field of food control be increased.

Recommendation 83

It is recommended that the appropriate United Nations agencies develop agreed procedures for setting derived working limits for common air and water contaminants.

Recommendation 84

It is recommended that Governments make available, through the International Referral System established in pursuance of recommendation 101 of this Conference, such information as may be requested on their pollution research and pollution control activities, including legislative and administrative arrangements, research on more efficient pollution control technology, and cost-benefit methodology.

Recommendation 85

It is recommended that any mechanism for co-ordinating and stimulating the actions of the different United Nations organs in connexion with environmental problems include among its functions:

(a) Development of an internationally accepted procedure for the identification of pollutants of international significance and for the definition of the degree and scope of international concern;

(b) Consideration of the appointment of appropriate intergovernmental, expert bodies to assess quantitatively the exposures, risks, pathways and sources of pollutants of international significance;

(c) Review and co-ordination of international co-operation for pollution control, ensuring in particular that needed measures shall be taken and that measures taken in regard to various media and sources shall be consistent with one another;

(d) Examination of the needs for technical assistance to Governments in the study of pollution problems, in particular those involving international distribution of pollutants;

(e) Encouragement of the establishment of consultation mechanisms for speedy implementation of concerted abatement programmes with particular emphasis on regional activities.

B. Marine Pollution

Recommendation 86

It is recommended that Governments, with the assistance and guidance of appropriate United Nations bodies, in particular the Joint Group of Experts on the Scientific Aspects of Marine Pollution (GESAMP):

(a) Accept and implement available instruments on the control of the maritime sources of marine pollution;

(b) Ensure that the provisions of such instruments are complied with by ships flying their flags and by ships operating in areas under their jurisdiction and that adequate provisions are made for reviewing the effectiveness of, and revising, existing and proposed international measures for control of marine pollution;

(c) Ensure that ocean dumping by their nationals anywhere, or by any person in areas under their jurisdiction, is controlled and that Governments shall continue to work towards the completion of, and bringing into force as soon as possible of, an over-all instrument for the control of ocean dumping as well as needed regional agreements within the framework of this instrument, in particular for enclosed and semi-enclosed seas, which are more at risk from pollution;

(d) Refer the draft articles and annexes contained in the report of the intergovernmental meetings at Reykjavik, Iceland, in April 1972 and in London in May 1972 to the United Nations Committee on the Peaceful Uses of the Seabed and the Ocean Floor beyond the Limits of National Jurisdiction at its session in July/August 1972 for information and comments and to a conference of Governments to be convened by the Government of the United Kingdom of Great Britain and Northern Ireland in consultation with the Secretary-General of the United Nations before November 1972 for further consideration, with a view to opening the proposed convention for signature at a place to be decided by that Conference, preferably before the end of 1972;

(e) Participate fully in the 1973 Inter-Governmental Maritime Consultative Organization (IMCO) Conference on Marine Pollution and the Conference on the Law of the Sea scheduled to begin in 1973, as well as in regional efforts, with a view to bringing all significant sources of pollution within the marine environment, including radioactive pollution from nuclear surface ships and submarines, and in particular in enclosed and semi-enclosed seas, under appropriate controls and particularly to complete elimination of deliberate pollution by oil from ships, with the goal of achieving this by the middle of the present decade;

(f) Strengthen national controls over land-based sources of marine pollution, in particular in enclosed and semi-enclosed seas, and recognize that, in some circumstances, the discharge of residual heat from nuclear and other power-stations may constitute a potential hazard to marine ecosystems.

Recommendation 87

It is recommended that Governments:

(a) Support national research and monitoring efforts that contribute to agreed international programmes for research and monitoring in the marine environment, in particular the Global Investigation of Pollution in the Marine Environment (GIPME) and the Integrated Global Ocean Station System (IGOSS);

(b) Provide to the United Nations, the Food and Agriculture Organization of the United Nations and the United Nations Conference on Trade and Development, as appropriate to the data-gathering activities of each, statistics on the production and use of toxic or dangerous substances that are potential marine pollutants, especially if they are persistent;

(c) Expand their support to components of the United Nations system concerned with research and monitoring in the marine environment and adopt the measures required to improve the constitutional, financial and operational basis under which the Inter-governmental Oceanographic Commission is at present operating so as to make it an effective joint mechanism for the Governments and United Nations organizations concerned (United Nations Educational, Scientific and Cultural Organization, Food and Agriculture Organization of the United Nations, World Meteorological Organization, Inter-Governmental Maritime Consultative

Organization, United Nations) and in order that it may be able to take on additional responsibilities for the promotion and co-ordination of scientific programmes and services.

Recommendation 88

It is recommended that the Secretary-General, together with the sponsoring agencies, make it possible for the Joint Group of Experts on the Scientific Aspects of Marine Pollution (GESAMP):

(a) To re-examine annually, and revise as required, its "Review of Harmful Chemical Substances", with a view to elaborating further its assessment of sources, pathways and resulting risks of marine pollutants;

(b) To assemble, having regard to other work in progress, scientific data and to provide advice on scientific aspects of marine pollution, especially those of an interdisciplinary nature.

Recommendation 89

It is recommended that the Secretary-General ensure:

(a) That mechanisms for combining world statistics on mining, production, processing, transport and use of potential marine pollutants shall be developed along with methods for identifying high-priority marine pollutants based in part on such data;

(b) That the Joint Group of Experts on the Scientific Aspects of Marine Pollution (GESAMP), in consultation with other expert groups, propose guidelines for test programmes to evaluate toxicity of potential marine pollutants;

(c) That the Food and Agriculture Organization of the United Nations, the World Health Organization, the Intergovernmental Oceanographic Commission and the International Atomic Energy Agency encourage studies of the effects of high-priority marine pollutants on man and other organisms, with appropriate emphasis on chronic, low-level exposures;

(d) That the Intergovernmental Oceanographic Commission, with the Food and Agriculture Organization of the United Nations and the World Health Organization, explore the possibility of establishing an international institute for tropical marine studies, which would undertake training as well as research.

Recommendation 90

It is recommended that the Intergovernmental Oceanographic Commission, jointly with the World Meteorological Organization and, as appropriate, in co-operation with other interested intergovernmental bodies, promote the monitoring of marine pollution, preferably within the framework of the Integrated Global Ocean Station System (IGOSS), as well as the development of methods for monitoring high-priority marine pollutants in the water, sediments and organisms, with advice from the Joint Group of Experts on the Scientific Aspects of Marine Pollution (GESAMP) on intercomparability of methodologies.

Recommendation 91

It is recommended that the Intergovernmental Oceanographic Commission:

(a) Ensure that provision shall be made in international marine research, monitoring and related activities for the exchange, dissemination, and referral to sources of data and information on baselines and on marine pollution and that attention shall be paid to the special needs of developing countries;

(b) Give full consideration, with the Food and Agriculture Organization of the United Nations, the World Meteorological Organization, the Inter-Governmental Maritime Consultative Organization, the World Health Organization, the International Atomic Energy Agency, the International Hydrographic Organization and the International Council for the Exploration of the Sea and other interested and relevant organizations, to the strengthening of on-going marine and related data and information exchange and dissemination activities;

(c) Support the concept of development of an interdisciplinary and interorganizational system primarily involving centres already in existence;

(d) Initiate an interdisciplinary marine pollution data and scientific information referral capability.

Recommendation 92

It is recommended:

(a) That Governments collectively endorse the principles set forth in paragraph 197 of Conference document A/CONF.48/8 as guiding concepts for the Conference on the Law of the Sea and the Inter-Governmental Maritime Consultative Organization (IMCO) Marine Pollution Conference scheduled to be held in 1973 and also the statement of objectives agreed on at the second session of the Intergovernmental Working Group on Marine Pollution, which reads as follows:

The marine environment and all the living organisms which it supports are of vital importance to humanity, and all people have an interest in assuring that this environment is so managed that its quality and resources are not impaired. This applies especially to coastal area resources. The capacity of the sea to assimilate wastes and render them harmless and its ability to regenerate natural resources are not unlimited. Proper management is required and measures to prevent and control marine pollution must be regarded as an essential element in this management of the oceans and seas and their natural resources;

and that, in respect of the particular interest of coastal States in the marine environment and recognizing that the resolution of this question is a matter for consideration at the Conference on the Law of the Sea, they take note of the principles on the rights of coastal States discussed but neither endorsed nor rejected at the second session of the Intergovernmental Working Group on Marine Pollution and refer those principles to the 1973 Inter-Governmental Maritime Consultative Organization Conference for information and to the 1973 Conference on the Law of -the Sea for such action as may be appropriate;

(b) That Governments take early action to adopt effective national measures for the control of all significant sources of marine pollution, including land-based sources, and concert and co-ordinate their actions regionally and where appropriate on a wider international basis;

(c) That the Secretary-General, in co-operation with appropriate international organizations, endeavour to provide guidelines which governments might wish to take into account when developing such measures.

Recommendation 93

It is recommended that any mechanism for co-ordinating and stimulating the actions of the different United Nations organs in connexion with environmental problems include among its functions over-all responsibility for ensuring that needed advice on marine pollution problems shall be provided to Governments.

Recommendation 94

It is recommended that the Secretary-General, with the co-operation of United Nations bodies, take steps to secure additional financial support to those training and other programmes of assistance that contribute to increasing the capacity of developing countries to participate in international marine research, monitoring and pollution-control programmes.

⚓ GENERAL GUIDELINES AND PRINCIPLES FOR THE PRESERVATION OF THE MARINE ENVIRONMENT

I. Definition

Marine pollution is defined as:

The introduction by man, directly or indirectly, of substances or energy into the marine environment (including estuaries), resulting in such deleterious effects as harm to living resources, hazards to human health, hindrance to marine activities including fishing, impairment of quality for use of sea water, and reduction of amenities.

II. Objectives

The marine environment and all the living organisms which it supports are of vital importance to humanity, and all people have an interest in assuring that this environment is so managed that its quality and resources are not impaired. This applies especially to coastal nations, which have a particular interest in the management of coastal area resources. The capacity of the sea to assimilate wastes and render them harmless, and its ability to regenerate natural resources, is not unlimited. Proper management is required, and measures to prevent and control marine pollution must be regarded as an essential element in this management of the oceans and seas and their natural resources.

III. Principles*

1. Every state has a duty to protect and preserve the marine environment and, in particular, to prevent pollution that may affect areas where an internationally shared resource is located.

2. Every state should adopt appropriate measures for the prevention of marine pollution, whether acting individually or in conjunction with other states under agreed international arrangements.

3. States should use the best practicable means available to them to

Proposed at the Ottawa Meeting of the Intergovernmental Working Group on Marine Pollution, November 8–12, 1971, and adopted at the United Nations Conference on the Human Environment at Stockholm in June 1972.

These guidelines and principles were derived from a working paper submitted by the Canadian delegation and revised by a working party of the whole under the chairmanship of the head of the Danish delegation.

* At the suggestion of the Chairman, the Committee agreed that the Secretariat should reorder the sequence of the principles; this has been done in the present text.

minimize the discharge of potentially hazardous substances to the sea by all routes, including land-based sources such as rivers, outfalls and pipelines within national jurisdiction, as well as dumping by or from ships, aircraft and platforms.

4. States should ensure that their national legislation provides adequate sanctions against those who infringe existing regulations on marine pollution.

5. States should assume joint responsibility for the preservation of the marine environment beyond the limits of national jurisdiction.

6. The states at higher levels of technological and scientific development should assist those nations which request it, for example by undertaking programmes either directly or through competent agencies intended to provide adequate training of the technical and scientific personnel of those countries, as well as by providing the equipment and facilities needed in areas such as research, administration, monitoring or surveillance, information, waste disposal, and others, which would improve their ability to discharge their duties consisting of protecting the marine environment.

7. States should discharge, in accordance with the principles of international law, their obligations toward other states where damage arises from pollution caused by their own activities or by organizations or individuals under their jurisdiction and should cooperate in developing procedures for dealing with such damage and the settlement of disputes.

8. Every state should cooperate with other states and competent international organizations with regard to the elaboration and implementation of internationally agreed rules, standards and procedures for the prevention of marine pollution on global, regional and national levels.

9. States should join together regionally to concert their policies and adopt measures in common to prevent the pollution of the areas which, for geographical or ecological reasons, form a natural entity and an integrated whole.

10. International guidelines and criteria should be developed, both by national Governments and through inter-governmental agencies, to provide the policy framework for control measures. A comprehensive plan for the protection of the marine environment should provide for the identification of critical pollutants and their pathways and sources, determination of exposures to these pollutants and assessment of the risks they pose, timely detection of undesirable trends, and development of detection and monitoring systems.

11. Internationally agreed criteria and standards should provide for regional and local variations in the effects of pollution and in the evaluation of these effects. Such variables should also include the ecology of

sea areas, economic and social conditions, and amenities, recreational facilities and other uses of the seas.

12. Primary protection standards and derived working levels—especially codes of practice and effluent standards—may usefully be established at national levels, and in some instances, on a regional or global basis.

13. Action to prevent and control marine pollution (particularly direct prohibitions and specific release limits) must guard against the effect of simply transferring damage or hazard from one part of the environment to another.

14. The development and implementation of control should be sufficiently flexible to reflect increasing knowledge of the marine ecosystem, pollution effects, and improvements in technological means for pollution control, and to take into account the fact that a number of new and hitherto unsuspected pollutants are bound to be brought to light.

15. Every state should cooperate with other states and with competent international organizations with a view to the development of marine environmental research and survey programmes and systems and means for monitoring changes in the marine environment, including studies of the present state of the oceans, the trends of pollution effects and the exchange of data and scientific information on the marine environment. There should be similar cooperation in the exchange of technological information on means of preventing marine pollution, including pollution that may arise from offshore resource exploration and exploitation.

16. International guidelines should also be developed to facilitate comparability in methods of detection and measurement of pollutants and their effects.

17. In addition to its responsibility for environmental protection within the limits of its territorial sea, a coastal state also has responsibility to protect adacent areas of the environment from damage that may result from activities within its territory.

18. Coastal states should ensure that adequate and appropriate resources are available to deal with pollution incidents resulting from the exploration and exploitation of seabed resources in areas within the limits of their national jurisdiction.

19. States should cooperate in the appropriate international forum to ensure that activities related to the exploration and exploitation of the seabed and the ocean floor beyond the limits of national jurisdiction shall not result in pollution of the marine environment.

20. All states should ensure that vessels under their registration comply with internationally agreed rules and standards relating to ship design and construction, operating procedures and other relevant fac-

tors.* States should cooperate in the development of such rules, standards and procedures, in the appropriate international bodies.

21. Following an accident on the high seas which may be expected to result in major deleterious consequences from pollution or threat of pollution of the sea, a coastal state facing grave and imminent danger to its coastline and related interests may take appropriate measures as may be necessary to prevent, mitigate, or eliminate such danger, in accordance with internationally agreed rules and standards.

22. Where there is a need for action by or through international agencies for the prevention, control or study of marine pollution, existing bodies, both within and outside the United Nations system, should be utilized as far as possible.

23. States should assist one another to the best of their ability, in action against marine pollution of whatever origin.

Among the Draft Proposals Submitted by the Canadian Delegation Were the Following:

1. A state may exercise special authority in areas of the sea adjacent to its territorial waters where functional controls of a continuing nature are necessary for the effective prevention of pollution which could cause damage or injury to the land or marine environment under its exclusive or sovereign authority.

2. A coastal state may prohibit any vessel which does not comply with internationally agreed rules and standards or, in their absence, with reasonable national rules and standards of the coastal state in question, from entering waters under its environmental protection authority.

3. The basis on which a state should exercise rights or powers, in addition to its sovereign rights or powers, pursuant to its special authority in areas adjacent to its territorial waters, is that such rights or powers should be deemed to be delegated to that state by the world community on behalf of humanity as a whole. The rights and powers exercised must be consistent with the state's primary responsibility for marine environmental protection in the areas concerned: they should be subject to international rules and standards and to review before an appropriate international tribunal.

A number of delegations (including those of Algeria, Argentina, Brazil, Barbados, Colombia, Chile, Cuba, Equador, Ghana, India, Spain, Iceland, Ivory Coast, Kenya, Mexico, Malta, Peru, Portugal, Guatemala,

---

* The delegation of Brazil wished to record its concern that developing countries might not be always in a position to adhere to the highest standards in this regard.

Tanzania) supported the general concept contained in these draft principles and similar suggestions by the Spanish delegation as listed in Annex
III [not reproduced here], although not necessarily their exact texts,
while others disagreed and still others considered that this forum was
not the place for their discussion and accordingly reserved their position. *

TEXT OF U.N. GENERAL ASSEMBLY RESOLUTION ON INSTITUTIONAL AND FINANCIAL ARRANGEMENTS FOR INTERNATIONAL ENVIRONMENTAL COOPERATION †

The General Assembly,

Convinced of the need for prompt and effective implementation
by Governments and the international community of measures designed
to safeguard and enhance the human environment for the benefit of
present and future generations of man,

Recognizing that responsibility for action to protect and enhance the
human environment rests primarily with Governments and, in the first
instance, can be exercised more effectively at the national and regional
levels,

Recognizing that environmental problems of broad international significance fall within the competence of the United Nations system,

Bearing in mind that international co-operative programmes in the
environment field must be undertaken with due respect to the sovereign
rights of States and in conformity with the Charter of the United Nations
and principles of international law,

Mindful of the sectoral responsibilities of the organizations of the
United Nations system,

Conscious of the significance of regional and subregional co-operation
in the field of the human environment and of the important role of the
regional economic commissions and other regional intergovernmental
organizations,

Emphasizing that problems of the human environment constitute a
new and important area for international co-operation and that the com-
plexity and interdependence of such problems require new approaches,

Recognizing that the relevant international scientific and other professional communities can make an important contribution to international co-operation in the field of the human environment,

---

* Several delegations including Belgium, France and Italy expressed formal reserva-
tions as to section II of this report. The Italian delegation expressed its reservation
on all points contained in the Principles which could in any way prejudge the Italian
position in other conferences on the law of the sea.

† Resolution No. 2997 (XXVII), December 15, 1972; passed at the Twenty-Seventh
Regular Session of the General Assembly.

Conscious of the need for processes within the United Nations system which would effectively assist developing countries to implement environmental policies and programmes compatible with their development plans, and to participate meaningfully in international environmental programmes,

Convinced that, in order to be effective, international co-operation in the field of the human environment requires additional financial and technical resources,

Aware of the urgent need for a permanent institutional arrangement within the United Nations for the protection and improvement of the human environment,

Taking note of the report of the Secretary-General on the United Nations Conference on the Human Environment (A/8783),

I

Governing Council for Environmental Programmes

1. *Decides* to establish the governing council for environmental programmes composed of 58 members elected by the United Nations General Assembly for three-year terms on the following basis:
   (a) Sixteen seats for African states;
   (b) Thirteen seats for Asian states;
   (c) Ten seats for Latin American states;
   (d) Thirteen seats for Western European and other states;
   (e) Six seats for Eastern European states;
2. *Decides further* that the Governing Council shall have the following main functions and responsibilities:
   (a) To promote international co-operation in the environment field and to recommend, as appropriate, policies to this end;
   (b) To provide general policy guidance for the direction and co-ordination of environmental programmes within the United Nations system;
   (c) To receive and review the periodic reports of the Executive Director, referred to in paragraph 5 below, on the implementation of environmental programmes within the United Nations system;
   (d) To keep under review the world environmental situation in order to ensure that emerging environmental problems of wide international significance should receive appropriate and adequate consideration by Governments;
   (e) To promote the contribution of the relevant international scientific and other professional communities to the acquisition, assessment and exchange of environmental knowledge and information

and, as appropriate, to the technical aspects of the formulation and implementation of environmental programmes within the United Nations system;

(f) To maintain under continuing review the impact of national and international environmental policies and measures on developing countries, as well as the problem of additional costs that might be incurred by developing countries in the implementation of environmental programmes and projects, to ensure that such programmes and projects shall be compatible with the development plans and priorities of those countries;

(g) To review and approve annually the programme of utilization of resources of the Environment Fund referred to in section III below;

3. *Decides further* that the Governing Council shall report annually to the General Assembly through the Economic and Social Council, which will transmit to the General Assembly such comments on the report as it may deem necessary, particularly with regard to questions of co-ordination and to the relationship of environment policies and programmes within the United Nations system to over-all economic and social policies and priorities;

II

Environment Secretariat

4. *Decides* that a small secretariat shall be established in the United Nations to serve as a focal point for environmental action and co-ordination within the United Nations system in such a way as to ensure a high degree of effective management;

5. *Decides further* that the environment secretariat shall be headed by the Executive Director, who shall be elected by the General Assembly on the nomination of the Secretary-General for a term of four years and who shall be entrusted, *inter alia*, with the following responsibilities:

(a) To provide substantive support to the Governing Council;

(b) To co-ordinate, under the guidance of the Governing Council, environment programmes within the United Nations system, to keep under review their implementation and to assess their effectiveness;

(c) To advise, as appropriate and under the guidance of the Governing Council, intergovernmental bodies of the United Nations system on the formulation and implementation of environmental programmes;

(d) To secure the effective co-operation of, and contribution from, the relevant scientific and other professional communities from all parts of the world;

(e) To provide, at the request of all parties concerned, advisory services for the promotion of international co-operation in the field of the environment;

(f) To submit to the Governing Council, on his own initiative or upon request, proposals embodying medium-range and long-range planning for United Nations programmes in the environment field;

(g) To bring to the attention of the Governing Council any matter which he deems to require consideration by it;

(h) To administer, under the authority and policy guidance of the Governing Council, the Environment Fund referred to in section III below;

(i) To report on environment matters to the Governing Council;

(j) To perform such other functions as may be entrusted to him by the Governing Council;

6. *Decides* that the costs of servicing the Governing Council and providing the small-core secretariat shall be borne by the regular budget of the United Nations and that operational programme costs, programme support and administrative costs of the Fund established in section III below shall be borne by the Fund;

III

Environment Fund

7. *Decides* that, in order to provide for additional financing for environmental programmes, a voluntary fund shall be established, with effect from 1 January 1973, in accordance with existing United Nations financial procedures;

8. *Decides further* that, in order to enable the Governing Council to fulfil its policy-guidance role for the direction and co-ordination of environmental activities, the Environment Fund shall finance wholly or partly the costs of the new environmental initiatives undertaken within the United Nations system; these will include the initiatives envisaged in the Action Plan for the Human Environment adopted by the United Nations Conference on the Human Environment, with particular attention to integrated projects, and such other environmental activities as may be decided upon by the Governing Council; and that the Governing Council shall review these initiatives with a view to taking appropriate decisions as to their continued financing;

9. *Decides* that the Fund shall be used for financing such programmes of general interest as regional and global monitoring, assessment and

data-collecting systems, including, as appropriate, costs for national counterparts; improvement of environmental quality management; environmental research; information exchange and dissemination; public education and training; assistance for national, regional and global environmental institutions; promotion of environmental research and studies for the development of industrial and other technologies best suited to a policy of economic growth compatible with adequate environmental safeguards, and such other programmes as the Governing Council may decide upon; and that in the implementation of such programmes due account should be taken of the special needs of the developing countries;

10. *Decides* that, in order to ensure that the development priorities of developing countries shall not be adversely affected, adequate measures be taken to provide additional financial resources on terms compatible with the economic situation of the recipient developing country; and that to this end, the Executive Director, in co-operation with competent organizations, shall keep this problem under continuing review;

11. *Decides* that the Fund, in pursuance of the objectives stated in paragraphs 8 and 9 above, shall be directed to the need for effective co-ordination in the implementation of international environmental programmes of the organizations of the United Nations system and other international organizations;

12. *Decides* that, in the implementation of programmes to be financed by the Fund, organizations outside the United Nations system, particularly those in the countries and regions concerned, shall also be utilized as appropriate, in accordance with the procedures established by the Governing Council; and that such organizations are invited to support the United Nations environmental programmes, by complementary initiatives and contributions;

13. *Decides* that the Governing Council shall formulate such general procedures as are necessary to govern the operations of the Fund;

IV

Co-ordination

14. *Decides* that in order to provide for the maximum efficient co-ordination of United Nations environmental programmes, an Environmental Co-ordinating Board, chaired by the Executive Director, should be established under the auspices and within the framework of the Administrative Committee on Co-ordination;

15. *Decides further* that the Environmental Co-ordinating Board shall meet periodically for the purpose of ensuring co-operation and co-ordi-

nation among all bodies concerned in the implementation of environmental programmes and that it shall report annually to the Governing Council;

16. *Invites* the organizations of the United Nations system to adopt the measures that may be required to undertake concerted and co-ordinated programmes with regard to international environmental problems, taking into account existing procedures for prior consultation, particularly on programme and budgetary matters;

17. *Invites* the regional economic commissions and the Economic and Social Office in Beirut, in co-operation where necessary with other appropriate regional bodies, to intensify further their efforts directed towards contributing to the implementation of environmental programmes in view of the particular need for rapid development of regional co-operation in this field;

18. *Invites also* other intergovernmental and those non-governmental organizations which have an interest in the field of the environment to lend their full support and collaboration to the United Nations with a view to achieving the largest possible degree of co-operation and co-ordination;

19. *Calls upon* Governments to ensure that appropriate national institutions shall be entrusted with the task of co-ordination of environmental action, both national and international;

20. *Decides* to review, as appropriate, at its thirty-first session, the above institutional arrangements, bearing in mind, *inter alia,* the responsibilities of the Economic and Social Council under the Charter of the United Nations.

BILATERAL AGREEMENTS

⚓ AGREEMENT ON COOPERATION IN THE FIELD OF ENVIRONMENTAL PROTECTION BETWEEN THE UNITED STATES OF AMERICA AND THE UNION OF SOVIET SOCIALIST REPUBLICS, MAY 23, 1972

The Government of the United States of America and the Government of the Union of Soviet Socialist Republics;

Attaching great importance to the problems of environmental protection;

Proceeding on the assumption that the proper utilization of contemporary scientific, technical and managerial achievements can, with appropriate control of their undesirable consequences, make possible the improvement of the interrelationship between man and nature;

Considering that the development of mutual cooperation in the field of environmental protection, taking into account the experience of countries with different social and economic systems, will be beneficial to the United States of America and the Union of Soviet Socialist Republics, as well as to other countries;

Considering that economic and social development for the benefit of future generations requires the protection and enhancement of the human environment today;

Desiring to facilitate the establishment of closer and long-term cooperation between interested organizations of the two countries in this field;

In accordance with the Agreement between the United States of America and the Union of Soviet Socialist Republics on Exchanges and Cooperation in Scientific, Technical, Educational, Cultural, and Other Fields in 1972-1973, signed April 11, 1972, and developing further the principles of mutually beneficial cooperation between the two countries;

Have agreed as follows:

ARTICLE 1

The Parties will develop cooperation in the field of environmental protection on the basis of equality, reciprocity, and mutual benefit.

ARTICLE 2

This cooperation will be aimed at solving the most important aspects of the problems of the environment and will be devoted to working out measures to prevent pollution, to study pollution and its effect on the environment, and to develop the basis for controlling the impact of human activities on nature.

It will be implemented, in particular, in the following areas:

—air pollution;
—water pollution;
—environmental pollution associated with agricultural production;
—enhancement of the urban environment;
—preservation of nature and the organization of preserves;
—marine pollution;
—biological and genetic consequences of environmental pollution;
—influence of environmental changes on climate;
—earthquake prediction;
—arctic and subarctic ecological systems;

—legal and administrative measures for protecting environmental quality.

In the course of this cooperation the Parties will devote special attention to joint efforts improving existing technologies and developing new technologies which do not pollute the environment, to the introduction of these new technologies into everyday use, and to the study of their economic aspects.

The Parties declare that, upon mutual agreement, they will share the results of such cooperation with other countries.

ARTICLE 3

The Parties will conduct cooperative activities in the field of environmental protection by the following means:

—exchange of scientists, experts and research scholars;
—organization of bilateral conferences, symposia and meetings of experts;
—exchange of scientific and technical information and documentation, and the results of research on environment;
—joint development and implementation of programs and projects in the field of basic and applied sciences;
—other forms of cooperation which may be agreed upon in the course of the implementation of this Agreement.

ARTICLE 4

Proceeding from the aims of this Agreement the Parties will encourage and facilitate, as appropriate, the establishment and development of direct contacts and cooperation between institutions and organizations, governmental, public and private, of the two countries, and the conclusion, where appropriate, of separate agreements and contracts.

ARTICLE 5

For the implementation of this Agreement a US-USSR Joint Committee on Cooperation in the Field of Environmental Protection shall be established. As a rule this Joint Committee shall meet once a year in Washington and Moscow, alternately. The Joint Committee shall approve concrete measures and programs of cooperation, designate the participating organizations responsible for the realization of these programs and make recommendations, as appropriate, to the two Governments.

Each Party shall designate a coordinator. These coordinators, between sessions of the Joint Committee, shall maintain contact between the United States and Soviet parts, supervise the implementation of the pertinent cooperative programs, specify the individual sections of these programs and coordinate the activities of organizations participating in environmental cooperation in accordance with this Agreement.

Article 6

Nothing in this Agreement shall be construed to prejudice other agreements concluded between the two Parties.

Article 7

This Agreement shall enter into force upon signature and shall remain in force for five years after which it shall be extended for successive five year periods unless one Party notifies the other of the termination thereof not less than six months prior to its expiration.

The termination of this Agreement shall not affect the validity of agreements and contracts between interested institutions and organizations of the two countries concluded on the basis of this Agreement.

Done on May 23, 1972 at Moscow in duplicate, in the English and Russian languages, both texts being equally authentic.

For the United States
of America:
Richard Nixon

For the Union of Soviet
Socialist Republics:
    N . V. Podgorny

✎ Memorandum of Implementation of the Agreement between the United States of America and the Union of Soviet Socialist Republics on Cooperation in the Field of Environmental Protection of May 23, 1972

The first meeting of the U.S.-Soviet Joint Committee on Cooperation in the Field of Environmental Protection was held in Moscow, September 18 to 21, 1972. The Joint Committee was established by the Agreement on Cooperation in the Field of Environmental Protection, signed in Moscow by the President of the United States Richard Nixon and Chairman of the Presidium of the Supreme Soviet N. V. Podgorny on May 23, 1972. As provided for in the Agreement, the Joint Committee approved concrete measures and programs of cooperation, and designated the participating organizations responsible for the realization of the programs.

Agreement was reached upon specific projects in the eleven subject areas named in the Agreement. Work will begin on a number of high priority projects during 1972-1973. For each project, responsible organizations were named by each side, although it was understood that other organizations from each side may participate in agreed projects, in many cases by working groups established in the specific area. It was agreed that the respective coordinators would verify the initiation of the agreed projects and remain in communication regarding the development of the program as a whole.

Agreement was reached upon the following initial projects:

I. AIR POLLUTION

1. *Air Pollution Modeling*

The metropolitan areas of St. Louis and Leningrad were designated as subjects for air pollution investigations. The methods used in the USSR and the U.S. to compute dispersal of pollutants from single and multiple sources, emission limitations and forecasts of hazardous conditions of air pollution will be compared and improved with special attention to meteorological techniques and topographic factors.

2. *Instrumentation and Methodology for Monitoring Major Air Pollutants*

The instruments and methods used in the USSR and the U.S. for measurement, data collection and processing, and analysis are to be compared and improved.

3. *Technology for Preventing Air Pollution from Industrial Enterprises*

The two sides will exchange information and explore opportunities for joint research on technology for controlling pollutants, with initial work to be done on major stationary sources such as power plants. Special emphasis will be placed on the control of sulphur oxides and particulates.

4. *Emissions from Transportation Sources*

The two sides will explore possibilities for cooperation in reducing emissions from transportation sources, including the improvement of engine design.

Two working groups will be appointed. The first, for modeling and instrumentation, will concern itself with Projects 1 and 2 and will meet in St. Louis, Missouri, and other cities in the United States before the end of 1972. The lead agency for the U.S. is the Environmental Protection Agency, and for the USSR the Hydrometeorological Service. The second working group, for control techniques, will concern itself with Projects 3 and 4 and will meet in the USSR at the beginning of 1973. The lead agency for the U.S. is the Environmental Protection Agency and for the USSR the All-Union Association of Gas Purification and Dust Cleaning.

II. WATER POLLUTION

1. Studies and Modeling of River Basin Pollution

Specific river basins in each country will be selected for a joint project on water pollution river basin modeling techniques. The Delaware and other river basin models will be examined in the United States. Rivers in the Soviet Union will be designated later. Soviet specialists will visit the U.S. in early 1973.

2. Protection and Management of Lakes and Estuaries

Both sides will designate lakes and estuaries in their country for joint projects on water pollution, including eutrophication. A Soviet Union lake will be Baikal; U.S. lakes to be considered include Lake Tahoe and one of the Great Lakes. U.S. specialists will visit the Soviet Union in the summer of 1973.

3. Effects of Pollutants upon Aquatic Ecological Systems and Permissible Levels of Pollution

Experts from both sides will exchange information and visits concerning research on the effects of pollutants on water systems and the development of water quality standards.

4. Prevention or Treatment of Discharges

The two sides will exchange visits and information on specific water pollution abatement techniques, including land disposal of both untreated municipal sewage and sludge from municipal treatment systems; reduction of pollution from industrial plants, such as manufacturers of pulp and paper; and reinjection of water from oil extraction activities, including disposal of liquid wastes in permafrost conditions in arctic and subarctic regions (collection, storage, treatment and final disposal). Visits will be made to arctic sites in both countries.

A single working group will be appointed. This group will meet in the USSR in the first quarter of 1973. There will be an exchange of visits of specialists to appropriate sites in both countries including arctic and subarctic areas. The lead agency for the U.S. is the Environmental Protection Agency and for the USSR the Hydrometeorological Service and the Ministry of Amelioration and Water Management.

III. POLLUTION RELATED TO AGRICULTURAL PRODUCTION

1. *Integrated Pest Management*

The two sides will exchange visits and information relating to programs of integrated pest management. Such programs include the use of non-chemical methods such as pest predators and pathogens, along with the limited use of pesticides. Both sides agreed to develop common programs, including the exchange of useful biological agents such as parasites and predators and plant species resistant to pests.

2. *Pollution Caused by Feedlots*

The two sides will exchange information and visits on management of wastes from large feedlots.

3. *Wind Erosion and Desiccation*

Both sides will exchange information and visits on research and management practices on control of wind erosion and dessication.

4. *Effects of Pollutants on Forests and Plants*

Both sides will exchange visits and information on the effects of air pollutants on forest and crop plants.

A single working group will be appointed. This group will meet in the U.S. in early 1973. Initial emphasis will be on integrated pest management and pollution caused by feedlots. A conference on integrated pest management will take place in the USSR during 1973. The lead agency for the U.S. is the Department of Agriculture and for the USSR the Ministry of Agriculture.

IV ENHANCEMENT OF URBAN ENVIRONMENT

1. *Urban Environment*

Both sides will designate two metropolitan areas in its country, with others added as appropriate, to serve as a means to examine jointly methods for planning and assuring a desirable environment in urban areas, with attention to planning for appropriate land use, transportation, noise abatement, solid waste management, water purification, recreation and park development, tourist zones and resorts, preservation of historic sites, etc.

The U.S. side has designated the Atlanta and San Francisco areas and the Soviet side has designated Leningrad for the initial exchange, and will designate a second city later.

2. *New Communities*

Both sides will designate new communities in each country as a means of examining the environmental, physical, social, economic and other factors considered in the design and development of satellite and free standing new communities. Among those communities to be designated are Columbia, Maryland and Reston, Virginia in the United States and Togliatti and Akademgorodok in the Soviet Union.

3. *Impact of Construction and Disposal of Wastes in Permafrost Areas*

The two sides will exchange visits and information on methods of construction in permafrost, the impact of construction on the environment in such areas and on the collection, storage and disposal of wastes in these areas.

A single working group will be appointed. This group will meet in the U.S. in November 1972, followed by a spring or summer 1973 meeting in the USSR. The lead agency for the U.S. is the Department of Housing and Urban Development and for the USSR the State Committee on Urban Construction and Architecture and, for noise abatement, the Ministry of the Automobile Industry.

V. NATURE AND PRESERVES

1. *Conservation of Rare and Endangered Species of Animals and Plants, and General Wildlife Conservation and Management*

Both sides will exchange visits and information and develop joint research for the purpose of improving understanding and protection of endangered species of plants and animals. A Soviet-American convention on conservation of rare species migrating between the USSR and the U.S. will be prepared, and both sides agreed on the importance and desirability of concluding, as soon as possible, international agreements on conservation of wildlife in need of special protection, for example polar bears and other animals. Joint projects will also include research on preservation and management of various marine and other mammals, specifically polar bears and whales of the North Pacific, involving the bowhead, gray and fin whales. They will also carry out projects on management of free-ranging wildlife for animal production, and research on and management of predators and waterfowl, including swans and other migratory birds.

A working group will be appointed that will meet initially in Moscow in December 1972. As necessary, appropriate subgroups will be organized (for example, for whales). The lead agencies for the U.S. are the Department of the Interior and the National Oceanic and Atmospheric Administration of the Department of Commerce, and for the USSR the Soviet Academy of Sciences and the Ministry of Agriculture. Some of the indicated projects, such as these for the bowhead whale and migrating swans, may be initiated prior to the working group meetings.

2. *Tundra Ecosystems and Permafrost*

The two sides will exchange visits and information on permafrost regions and tundra ecosystems, including research on stabilization of disturbed areas and other ecological research. Visits will be made by U.S. and Soviet specialists to appropriate institutes and places in each country.

3. *Reserved Areas*

Each side will exchange information and visits and develop appropriate research projects on preserves, their classification, organization and maintenance, on arid land ecology, and on parks, including a joint project involving the Yellowstone National Park (U.S.) and the Caucasian State Preserve (USSR).

A meeting of specialists in the U.S. early in 1973 will concern itself with Projects 2 and 3. The lead agency for the U.S. is the Department of the Interior and for the USSR the Ministry of Agriculture.

VI. MARINE POLLUTION

1. *Prevention and Clean-up of Oil Pollution in the Marine Environment*

The two sides agreed to exchange visits and information on technologies and techniques for the prevention and clean-up of oil discharges in the marine environment, including such areas as vessel design, traffic control, shore facilities and offshore oil drilling safeguards. The two sides also agreed to exchange visits and information on pipeline transport, particularly through permafrost areas.

2. Effect of Pollutants on Marine Organisms

The two sides will exchange visits and information on research on the chemical aspects of marine pollution and the effects of pollutants on marine organisms, including chemical and biological analyses of fish, monitoring of rare species, exchange of specimens, and rehabilitation of sea life after major pollution incidents.

A working group will be appointed to deal with the first project. It will meet in the U.S. in early 1973 with a visit of specialists to the USSR in the summer of 1973. The lead agencies for the U.S. are the Department of Transportation and the Department of the Interior and for the USSR the Ministry of Merchant Marine. A first-quarter of 1973 meeting of specialists will be held in the U.S. to discuss the second project. The lead agencies for the U.S. are the Environmental Protection Agency and the National Oceanic and Atmospheric Administration of the Department of Commerce and for the USSR the Hydrometeorological Service.

VII. Biological and Genetic Consequences

1. Comprehensive Analysis of the Environment

Both sides agree to hold a symposium in the USSR in the fall of 1973 to examine scientific methods of setting standards or limits on pollution discharges into the environment from separate sources and from large territories. The symposium would focus attention on the effect of man's activity on all organisms and the biosphere as a whole to provide guidance for protection of the environment and wise use of natural resources. The two sides will communicate with each other on the design of the conference, as necessary. The lead agency for the U.S. is the Environmental Protection Agency and for the USSR the Hydrometeorological Service.

2. Biological and Genetic Effects of Pollutants

Both sides will exchange visits and information and conduct joint research on the health effects of mutagenic compounds, radioactivity, and heavy metals; study extrapolation of animal toxicological tests to man;

and exchange visits and information on epidemiological studies. Both sides will exchange information and compare technical bases for establishing air quality standards. Specialists will meet in the U.S. during the first quarter of 1973. The lead agencies for the U.S. are the Department of Health, Education, and Welfare and the Environmental Protection Agency, and for the USSR the Ministry of Health and the Academy of Sciences.

VIII. INFLUENCE OF ENVIRONMENTAL CHANGES ON CLIMATE

1. *Effect of Changing Levels of Atmospheric Constituents on Climate*

The two sides will exchange information and participate in joint studies of the influence on climate of gaseous and particulate contaminants.

2. *Monitoring Atmospheric Constituents That Might Modify Climate*

The two sides will take steps to insure the comparability of data from their respective climate monitoring stations and cooperate in the analysis and interpretation of such data.

3. *Climate Modeling*

The two sides will exchange information and cooperate in the development and application of mathematical modeling to assess the consequences of atmospheric contamination on climate.

4. *Cooperation in Polar Research*

The two sides will explore possibilities of integrating such scientific programs as the U.S. Arctic Ice Dynamics Joint Experiment and the Soviet Polar Interaction Experiment so as to extend the fields of observation and permit more comprehensive analysis and modeling.

5. *Effects of Contamination of the Upper Atmosphere on Climate*

The two sides will exchange information and explore opportunities for cooperation in the study of the effects of perturbation of the upper atmosphere by propulsion effluents from high altitude aircraft.

A single working group will be established. It will meet in the U.S. late in 1972. A symposium will be held in the USSR in 1973. The lead agency for the U.S. is the National Oceanic and Atmospheric Administration of the Department of Commerce and for the USSR the Hydrometeorological Service.

IX. EARTHQUAKE PREDICTION

1. *Earthquake Prediction*

The San Andreas Fault area in the U.S. and the Garm-Dushanbe Region in the USSR were designated as subjects for the installation of jointly operated earthquake measurement instruments and detection equipment. Both sides will exchange visits and information with regard to earthquake prediction research, seismic risk mapping, seismicity and earthquake resistant design.

2. *Integration of U.S.-USSR Tsunami (Earthquake-Produced Tidal Waves) Warning Systems*

Both sides will exchange visits and information and will consider the possibility of the integration of the Tsunami warning systems currently being operated by the U.S. in the Hawaii area and by the USSR in the Kurile-Kamchatka area. The two systems will be integrated to provide an exchange of data produced from each one and to improve the operation of both systems.

One working group will be established. It will meet on the subject of earthquake prediction in the United States in early 1973 and later in 1973 in the USSR. The lead agencies for the United States will be the Department of the Interior for earthquake prediction activities and the National Oceanic and Atmospheric Administration of the Department of Commerce for integration of the Tsunami warning systems, and for the USSR the Academy of Sciences of the USSR.

X. ARCTIC AND SUBARCTIC ECOLOGICAL SYSTEMS

The two sides agreed to undertake a cooperative program involving arctic and subarctic areas. The specific projects agreed to will be undertaken under other areas of the agreement as follows:

1. *Prevention or Treatment of Discharges*

This project is covered under Water Pollution.

2. *Impact of Construction and Disposal of Wastes in Permafrost Environmental Areas*

This project is covered under the Urban Environment.

3. *Permafrost and Arctic Ecosystems*

This project is covered under Nature and Preserves.

4. *Prevention and Clean-up of Oil Pollution*

This project is covered under Marine Pollution.

XI. LEGAL AND ADMINISTRATIVE

Exchange of Information and Experience Regarding Legal and Administrative Measures for Protecting Enviromental Quality

The two sides will exchange information and hold conferences on legal and administrative measures for protecting environmental quality, dealing with questions of government organization, procedures to analyze environmental effects of government decisions, economic aspects of pollution and enforcement techniques, among others. Specialists from both countries will hold a meeting in the United States early in 1973. The lead agency for the U.S. is the Council on Environmental Quality and for the USSR the Academy of Sciences.

Both sides agreed that the present memorandum would enter into force as of thirty days from the date of signature, and that in the interim each side might propose changes of a minor character.

Both sides agreed that the next meeting of the Joint Committee would be held in Washington in 1973. At that meeting the progress of the program will be reviewed and plans made for further cooperation. The Chairman and coordinators will meet as necessary between sessions.

Signed in English and in Russian, both copies equally authentic, in Moscow, September 21, 1972.

RUSSELL E. TRAIN　　　　　　　　　　　　　　E. K. FEDOROV
Chairman for the　　　　　　　　　　　　　　*Chairman for the*
United States　　　　　　　　　　　　　　　*Soviet Union*

📧 UNITED STATES–CANADIAN JOINT COMMUNIQUE: ISSUED ON JULY 14, 1972

Meeting Between Mr. Train and Mr. Davis to Discuss Environmental Concerns

In Washington on July 13, the Honorable Russell E. Train, Chairman of the [U.S.] Council on Environmental Quality, and the Honourable Jack Davis, Canadian Minister of the Environment, met to discuss arrangements for the protection of boundary areas of the Pacific and Atlanic coasts from existing and foreseeable environmental threats. They recognized their common concern and responsibility for the protection and enhancement of the environment of these areas. Among the items discussed were present and projected use of these waters; conditions of navigation; environmental and ecological problems and programs; preventive and remedial measures designed to protect these waters from degradation; and legal and financial considerations in case of damage.

2. Both sides agreed that the strengthening of communications between the two governments respecting environmental matters is of utmost importance.

3. Both sides reaffirmed their support for Principle 21 of the Declaration on the Human Environment adopted by the recent Stockholm Conference, which provides that "States have, in accordance with the Charter of the United Nations and the principles of international law, . . . the responsibility to ensure that activities within their jurisdiction or control do not cause damage to the environment of other States or of areas beyond the limits of national jurisdiction." It was further acknowledged that the practical application of this principle to environmental questions which may arise between the two countries necessarily invokes the consequential principle (Principle 22) regarding cooperation between states in the development of legal arrangements respecting liability for environmental damage and for compensation for the victims of pollution.

4. It was recognized that these principles were of particular importance to activities along the common border of the two countries and their East and West coasts. It was considered that these principles provide the basis for the development of law and procedures for settlement of disputes of an environmental nature so as to ensure prompt and proper compensation for damage to either side by the activities of the other.

To this end it was agreed there should be further early consultations between the Legal Advisers of the Canadian Department of External Affairs and the United States Department of State.

5. Their discussions included a review of longer-range environmental problems in the boundary waters of both coasts. Mr. Davis and Mr. Train agreed that both countries should look for ways of further extending cooperation in the implementation of their respective programs for the protection and enhancement of the environment of these areas. They agreed that appropriate officals of both Governments should meet at an early date to exchange information on environmental matters in coastal boundary waters and to consult on future opportunities for closer cooperation in the implementation of their respective environmental protection programs in these waters. On the U.S. side, the Council on Environmental Quality will coordinate the U.S. contribution to these talks, while on the Canadian side, the Department of the Environment will have this responsibility.

6. It was noted that good progress was being made in developing joint contingency plans for the water boundary areas between the U.S. and Canada which would be available in the event of a spill of oil or of other noxious substances. Agreement had been reached on a joint contingency plan for the Great Lakes. A proposed plan for the Atlantic coast has been drafted, and a further round of discussions between officials of the responsible authorities in the two countries, including Provincial and State authorities, is to be held in Victoria, B.C., next week, to complete the drafting of contingency plan arrangements for the Pacific coast. The meeting in Victoria will complete the drafting plans prepared by a joint planning group which can then be submitted for national approval and agreement.

7. Mr. Davis and Mr. Train also reviewed the collaboration which exists between the two countries in the development of measures to improve vessel navigation systems in areas of common concern on the Pacific and Atlantic coasts, which will reduce the risk of environmental hazards from shipping accidents. It was agreed that this would continue to be pursued by the U.S. Coast Guard and the Canadian Ministry of Transport.

8. They recalled the signing of the Great Lakes Water Quality Agreement in Ottawa on April 15 by President Nixon and Prime Minister Trudeau and agreed that it represented a useful example of the effectiveness of close coordination between the two Governments in meeting the many threats, current and potential, to a common environment.

9. The United States Delegation, in addition to Mr. Train, included representatives of the Departments of State, Interior, Transportation (including the U.S. Coast Guard), Commerce (including the Maritime

Administration and the National Oceanic and Atmospheric Administration), the Council on Environmental Quality, and the Environmental Protection Agency.

10. The Canadian Delegation, in addition to Mr. Davis, included officials of the Department of External Affairs, the Department of Environment, the Ministry of Transport, and the Canadian Embassy, Washington.

11. The meeting was one of a series of Ministerial level consultations on environmental matters of mutual concern agreed to on April 15, 1972, by Mr. Davis and Mr. Train.

Suggested Reading List

Man's Impact on the Global Environment: Assessments and Recommendations for Action (Report of the Study of Critical Environmental Problems, M.I.T., 1970).

Wilson, Thomas W., *International Environmental Action* (1971).

Kay, David A., and Skolnikoff, Eugene B., eds., *World Eco-Crisis: International Organizations in Response* (1972).

Hargrove, J. L., ed., *Law, Institutions and the Global Environment* (1972).

Taubenfeld, Rita F. and Howard J., "Some International Implications of Weather Modification Activities," 23 *Int'l Organ.* 808 (1969).

Kade, G., ed., "Controlling the Human Environment," 22 *Int'l Soc. Sci. J.* No. 4 (1970).

Kneese, A. V., "Environmental Pollution: Economics and Policy," 61 *Amer. Econ.Rev.Pa. and Proc.* 153 (1971).

Jackson, C. I., "The Dimensions of International Pollution," 50 *Ore.L. Rev.* 223 (1971).

Samuels, J. W., "Prospective International Control of Weather Modification Activities," 21 *Univ. Toronto L.J.* 50 (1971).

Ozorio de Almeida, M., Beckermann, W., Sacho, I., and Corea, G., "Environment and Development" [The Founex Report], in *International Conciliation* No. 586 (January 1972).

Falk, Richard A., "Environmental Policy as a World Order Problem," 12 *Nat. Res. J.* 172 (1972).

Brownlie, Ian, "The Human Environment: Problems of Standard-Setting and Enforcement," *ibid.* 187.

Ross, Charles R., "National Sovereignty in International Environmental Decisions," *ibid.* 242.

Kirgis, F. L., Jr., "Effective Pollution Control in Industrialized Countries: International Economic Disincentives, Policy Responses, and the GATT," 70 *Mich. L.Rev.* 860 (1972).

Kennett, Wayland, "The Stockholm Conference on the Human Environment," 48 *Int. Affs.* (RIIA) 33 (1972).

Kay, D. A., and Skolnikoff, E. D., eds., "International Institutions and the Environmental Crisis," 26 *Int'l Organ.* pp. 169–478 (Spring 1972).

Kirgis, F. L., Jr., "Technological Challenge to the Shared Environment: United States Practice," 66 *Amer. J. Int'l L.* 290 (1972).

Contini, P., and Sand, P., "Methods to Expedite Environmental Protection," *ibid.* 37.

Fleischer, Carl A., "An International Convention on Environmental Cooperation Among Nations: Proposed Draft, Policies, and Goals," 7 *Texas Int'l L.J.* 73 (1972).

Dorsey, C. L., "Proposed International Agreement to Anticipate and Avoid Environmental Damage," 6 *Ind. L. Rev.* 190 (1972).

Bleicher, Samuel A. "Overview of International Environmental Regulation," 2 *Ecol.* 1 (1972).

Johnston, Douglas M., "International Environmental Law: Recent Developments and Canadian Contributions," in Macdonald, Morris and Johnston, eds., *Canadian Perspectives on International Law*, (1972–1973).

Sohn, Louis, "The Stockholm Declaration on the Human Environment," 14 *Harv. Int'l L.J.* p. 423 (1973).

PART III

Selected Issues in International Environmental Law

Introduction

It is a difficult and perhaps premature task to delimit the field of international environmental law. If one thinks of "environment" in the broad sense given to the term during preparations for the Stockholm Conference on the Human Environment, then virtually all areas of international law have environmental aspects. It seems to us, therefore, that a collection of materials on the international law of pollution should include a final section containing materials that reflect cognate issues in at least a few areas of international law that are not primarily concerned with the prevention and control of pollution but nonetheless affect the prospects of treating international pollution in an effective manner.

The principles of international law are not primitive or archaic, but their adequacy for the treatment of environmental problems such as pollution is now seriously in question. Part of the difficulty can be attributed to the absence of an intergovernmental environment agency to perform the functions of intelligence (data collection), promotion, invocation, and appraisal. Fortunately, this deficiency has recently been remedied by the decision of the General Assembly in 1972 to establish machinery and funding for these purposes. In consultation with appropriate organizations and agencies, the new U.N. Governing Council for Environmental Programmes, the Environment Secretariat, and its Executive Director are assigned a number of tasks, including consideration of measures to implement the Stockholm recommendations, some of which are reproduced in Part II of this book. With this means of coordinating and supervising the environmental activities of the pre-existing U.N. agencies and of providing leadership in these areas of policy formulation, it can be expected that new impetus will be given to efforts by other organs to prescribe more appropriate standards and policies for the world community and to apply them in particular situations.

It is likely that these efforts at policy prescription for environmental protection will become increasingly more ambitious, as partial approaches are found to be inadequate. In brief, we can anticipate an approach to international pollution problems that will be increasingly comprehensive and fully considerate of experience in similar and cognate issue areas.

This trend toward a more systematic approach to the international problems of pollution will no doubt be accompanied by a growing conviction that these problems are indivisible from the larger context of international environmental policy. This in turn will require reappraisals of earlier developments in international law, looked at anew in environmental perspective. A reappraisal somewhat along these lines is already in evidence in current efforts to "modernize" the law of the sea, but until these efforts are consummated at the third U.N. Conference on the Law of the Sea it is premature to measure the impact of environmentalism in this area of international law.

It may be expected, however, that both a broadening and a development of the principle of state responsibility will take place as improved technology places new strains on resource management, especially in the case of shareable resources located in the international domain. Second, it seems likely that environmental risks and dangers will be compared with military risks and dangers, in the hope that successful experience with one can lead to improved treatment of the other. Already an analogy has been suggested between territorial and environmental integrity. Third, we might anticipate a growing interest in the experience of safety control procedures, as environmental policy is designed in part to secure populations from hazards. Accordingly, Part Three consists of international legal materials chosen with these three points in mind which seem relevant to the systematic development of international environmental law.*

In the first section we have selected materials that reflect issues concerning access to and use of resources in internationally shared areas: the oceans, Antarctica, and outer space. Because most readers will be familiar with general developments in these areas, we have limited the

---

* It is still uncertain, for example, whether coastal states will be granted exclusive authority over marine pollution control within a designated zone, in line with the current "functionalist" trend in the law of the sea. Proposals of this kind should be compared with the concept of the "contiguous zone," with the regime of the continental shelf, with recent efforts to establish fishing zones, and with new proposals for a multi-purpose "economic zone."

choice to brief extracts that pertain more directly to pollution policy. Among the materials on the law of the sea, for example, we have included the provisions on innocent passage through the territorial sea, because they raise the issue of access to the high seas and are intimately related to the question of the coastal state's right to reduce the threat of marine pollution by controlling the conditions of right of passage. During the current preparations for the third U.N. Conference on the Law of the Sea it is often asked whether fully loaded oil tankers are not inherently incapable of "innocent passage." If so, it is difficult to see why foreign ships carrying potentially dangerous pollutants on board should be allowed to exercise the right of innocent passage. If the logic of environmental policy were carried to the extreme, a substantial proportion of cargoes would be denied that right, which would be replaced by a privilege granted by the coastal state if it were satisfied that specified precautions had been taken. Whether the privilege is withholdable at the coastal state's discretion or in accordance with a general international agreement on pollution control, the effect would be to reduce substantially the guarantee of innocent passage.

In this first section we also include materials on Antarctica, to parts of which several states have not yet abandoned territorial claims. But in practice the area is subject to a limited kind of international regime, and none of the interested states enjoys anything like the normal incidents of sovereignty that often provide an obstacle to effective international treatment of pollution problems. In contemporary perspective, however, the Antarctic Treaty may be even more significant because of its emphasis on features of environmental law: its ban on nuclear explosions and the disposal of radioactive wastes, its requirement that all Antarctic areas shall be subject at all times to inspection by observers designated by the Contracting Parties, and its provision for regular consultation in order to facilitate scientific research and cooperation.

The materials on outer space are more fully reproduced because they reflect an area of international law that has been developed, and is developing, somewhat in advance of human activities, but in which trends in technology point clearly to pollution threats arising at the periphery of the human environment. The outer-space texts go further than the Antarctic Treaty by applying environmental principles and procedures not merely to spaces not yet appropriated but to spaces declared not to be subject to appropriation. In advance of technology, it is agreed that celestial bodies are not to receive the imprint of territoriality. The protection of the extraterrestrial environment will not be complicated by pretensions of national sovereignty or national sovereign rights. Moreover, the technological powers that have the capability of causing damage from outer space to others on the surface of the earth or to aircraft in flight accept, in advance of such incident, the principle of absolute liability and that of a lesser degree of liability in other situations.

The second section contains materials on the prohibition of ecocidal weapons and weapons of mass destruction. These texts are included in the belief that the existence of such weapons represents a serious threat to the environment and their use a genuine example of pollution. It should be noted in the Stockholm Conference materials in Part II that this view was generally shared by the delegates there, although it was not agreed that Stockholm was an appropriate forum for disarmament or arms-control resolutions. The reader may find it useful to compare the problems of establishing safeguards and verification procedures in disarmament with those in pollution prevention and control.

In the third section the issues of safeguards and verification are also reflected in the materials, as well as questions of liability and the duty to compensate. The regulation of peaceful uses of atomic energy raises other kinds of issues, but we have concentrated mainly on extracts that show the variety of international attempts to protect health and safety that might be imperilled through exposure to radioactive materials. Most of these international measures are relatively early, belonging to the pre-Stockholm (nuclear) era of environmental concern, and to this extent they have an honoured place in the history of the international law of pollution.

Environmental Regulation in Internationally Shared Areas

THE OCEANS

CONVENTION ON THE HIGH SEAS

Article 2

The high seas being open to all nations, no State may validly purport to subject any part of them to its sovereignty. Freedom of the high seas

Adopted by the United Nations Conference on the Law of the Sea, April 29, 1958; entered into force on September 30, 1962. By August 1971, 71 states had become parties to the Convention.

is exercised under the conditions laid down by these articles and by the other rules of international law. It comprises, *inter alia,* both for coastal and non-coastal States:

(1) Freedom of navigation;

(2) Freedom of fishing;

(3) Freedom to lay submarine cables and pipelines;

(4) Freedom to fly over the high seas.

These freedoms, and others which are recognized by the general principles of international law, shall be exercised by all States with reasonable regard to the interests of other States in their exercise of the freedom of the high seas.

* * *

Article 24

Every State shall draw up regulations to prevent pollution of the seas by the discharge of oil from ships or pipelines or resulting from the exploitation and exploration of the seabed and its subsoil, taking account of existing treaty provisions on the subject.

Article 25

1. Every State shall take measures to prevent pollution of the seas from the dumping of radio-active waste, taking into account any standards and regulations which may be formulated by the competent international organizations.

2. All States shall co-operate with the competent international organizations in taking measures for the prevention of pollution of the seas or air space above, resulting from any activities with radio-active materials or other harmful agents.

Article 26

1. All States shall be entitled to lay submarine cables and pipelines on the bed of the high seas.

2. Subject to its right to take reasonable measures for the exploration of the continental shelf and the exploitation of its natural resources, the coastal State may not impede the laying or maintenance of such cables or pipelines.

3. When laying such cables or pipelines the State in question shall pay due regard to cables or pipelines already in position on the seabed. In particular, possibilities of repairing existing cables or pipelines shall not be prejudiced.

⚑ CONVENTION ON THE TERRITORIAL SEA AND THE CONTIGUOUS ZONE

PART I

❋ ❋ ❋

SECTION III. RIGHT OF INNOCENT PASSAGE

Sub-section A. Rules Applicable to All Ships

Article 14

1. Subject to the provisions of these articles, ships of all States, whether coastal or not, shall enjoy the right of innocent passage through the territorial sea.
2. Passage means navigation through the territorial sea for the purpose either of traversing that sea without entering internal waters, or of proceeding to internal waters, or of making for the high seas from internal waters.
3. Passage includes stopping and anchoring, but only in so far as the same are incidental to ordinary navigation or are rendered necessary by *force majeure* or by distress.
4. Passage is innocent so long as it is not prejudicial to the peace, good order or security of the coastal State. Such passage shall take place in conformity with these articles and with other rules of international law.
5. Passage of foreign fishing vessels shall not be considered innocent if they do not observe such laws and regulations as the coastal State may make and publish in order to prevent these vessels from fishing in the territorial sea.
6. Submarines are required to navigate on the surface and to show their flag.

Article 15

1. The coastal State must not hamper innocent passage through the territorial sea.
2. The coastal State is required to give appropriate publicity to any dangers to navigation, of which it has knowledge, within its territorial sea.

Adopted by the United Nations Conference on the Law of the Sea, April 29, 1958; entered into force on September 10, 1964. By August 1971, 64 states had become parties to the Convention.

Article 16

1. The coastal State may take the necessary steps in its territorial sea to prevent passage which is not innocent.
2. In the case of ships proceeding to internal waters, the coastal State shall also have the right to take the necessary steps to prevent any breach of the conditions to which admission of those ships to those waters is subject.
3. Subject to the provisions of paragraph 4, the coastal State may, without discrimination amongst foreign ships, suspend temporarily in specified areas of its territorial sea the innocent passage of foreign ships if such suspension is essential for the protection of its security. Such suspension shall take effect only after having been duly published.
4. There shall be no suspension of the innocent passage of foreign ships through straits which are used for international navigation between one part of the high seas and another part of the high seas or the territorial sea of a foreign State.

Article 17

Foreign ships exercising the right of innocent passage shall comply with the laws and regulations enacted by the coastal State in conformity with these articles and other rules of international law and, in particular, with such laws and regulations relating to transport and navigation.

Sub-section B. Rules Applicable to Merchant Ships

Article 18

1. No charge may be levied upon foreign ships by reason only of their passage through the territorial sea.
2. Charges may be levied upon a foreign ship passing through the territorial sea as payment only for specified services rendered to the ship. These charges shall be levied without discrimination.

Article 19

1. The criminal jurisdiction of the coastal State should not be exercised on board a foreign ship passing through the territorial sea to arrest any person or to conduct any investigation in connexion with any crime committed on board the ship during its passage, save only in the following cases:

(*a*) If the consequences of the crime extend to the coastal State; or

(*b*) If the crime is of a kind to disturb the peace of the country or the good order of the territorial sea; or

(*c*) If the assistance of the local authorities has been requested by the captain of the ship or by the consul of the country whose flag the ship flies; or

(*d*) If it is necessary for the suppression of illicit traffic in narcotic drugs.

2. The above provisions do not affect the right of the coastal State to take any steps authorized by its laws for the purpose of an arrest or investigation on board a foreign ship passing through the territorial sea after leaving internal waters.

3. In the cases provided for in paragraphs 1 and 2 of this article, the coastal State shall, if the captain so requests, advise the consular authority of the flag State before taking any steps, and shall facilitate contact between such authority and the ship's crew. In cases of emergency this notification may be communicated while the measures are being taken.

4. In considering whether or how an arrest should be made, the local authorities shall pay due regard to the interests of navigation.

5. The coastal State may not take any steps on board a foreign ship passing through the territorial sea to arrest any person or to conduct any investigation in connexion with any crime committed before the ship entered the territorial sea, if the ship, proceeding from a foreign port, is only passing through the territorial sea without entering internal waters.

Article 20

1. The coastal State should not stop or divert a foreign ship passing through the territorial sea for the purpose of exercising civil jurisdiction in relation to a person on board the ship.

2. The coastal State may not levy execution against or arrest the ship for the purpose of any civil proceedings, save only in respect of obligations or liabilities assumed or incurred by the ship itself in the course or for the purpose of its voyage through the waters of the coastal State.

3. The provisions of the previous paragraph are without prejudice to the right of the coastal State, in accordance with its laws, to levy execution against or to arrest, for the purpose of any civil proceedings, a foreign ship lying in the territorial sea, or passing through the territorial sea after leaving internal waters.

Sub-section C. Rules Applicable to Government Ships Other Than Warships

Article 21

The rules contained in sub-sections A and B shall also apply to government ships operated for commercial purposes.

Article 22

1. The rules contained in sub-section A and in article 18 shall apply to government ships operated for non-commercial purposes.
2. With such exceptions as are contained in the provisions referred to in the preceding paragraph, nothing in these articles affects the immunities which such ships enjoy under these articles or other rules of international law.

Sub-section D. Rules Applicable to Warships

Article 23

If any warship does not comply with the regulations of the coastal State concerning passage through the territorial sea and disregards any request for compliance which is made to it, the coastal State may require the warship to leave the territorial sea.

PART II

CONTIGUOUS ZONE

Article 24

1. In a zone of the high seas contiguous to its territorial sea, the coastal State may exercise the control necessary to:
   (a) Prevent infringement of its customs, fiscal, immigration or sanitary regulations within its territory or territorial sea;
   (b) Punish infringement of the above regulations committed within its territory or territorial sea.
2. The contiguous zone may not extend beyond twelve miles from the baseline from which the breadth of the territorial sea is measured.
3. Where the coasts of two States are opposite or adjacent to each other, neither of the two States is entitled, failing agreement between them to the contrary, to extend its contiguous zone beyond the median line every

point of which is equidistant from the nearest points on the baselines from which the breadth of the territorial seas of the two States is measured.

✄ CONVENTION ON THE CONTINENTAL SHELF

* * *

Article 4

Subject to its right to take reasonable measures for the exploration of the continental shelf and the exploitation of its natural resources, the coastal State may not impede the laying or maintenance of submarine cables or pipelines on the continental shelf.

Article 5

1. The exploration of the continental shelf and the exploitation of its natural resources must not result in any unjustifiable interference with navigation, fishing or the conservation of the living resources of the sea, nor result in any interference with fundamental oceanographic or other scientific research carried out with the intention of open publication.

2. Subject to the provisions of paragraphs 1 and 6 of this article, the coastal State is entitled to construct and maintain or operate on the continental shelf installations and other devices necessary for its exploration and the exploitation of its natural resources, and to establish safety zones around such installations and devices and to take in those zones measures necessary for their protection.

3. The safety zones referred to in paragraph 2 of this article may extend to a distance of 500 metres around the installations and other devices which have been erected, measured from each point of their outer edge. Ships of all nationalities must respect these safety zones.

4. Such installations and devices, though under the jurisdiction of the coastal State, do not possess the status of islands. They have no territorial sea of their own, and their presence does not affect the delimitation of the territorial sea of the coastal State.

5. Due notice must be given of the construction of any such installations, and permanent means for giving warning of their presence must be maintained. Any installations which are abandoned or disused must be entirely removed.

Adopted by the United Nations Conference on the Law of the Sea, April 29, 1958; entered into force on June 10, 1964. By August 1971, 68 states had become parties to the Convention.

6. Neither the installations or devices, nor the safety zones around them, may be established where interference may be caused to the use of recognized sea lanes essential to international navigation.

7. The coastal State is obliged to undertake, in the safety zones, all appropriate measures for the protection of the living resources of the sea from harmful agents.

8. The consent of the coastal States shall be obtained in respect of any research concerning the continental shelf and undertaken there. Nevertheless, the coastal State shall not normally withhold its consent if the request is submitted by a qualified institution with a view to purely scientific research into the physical or biological characteristics of the continental shelf, subject to the proviso that the coastal State shall have the right, if it so desires, to participate or to be represented in the research, and that in any event the results shall be published.

✍ CONVENTION ON FISHING CONSERVATION OF THE LIVING RESOURCES OF THE HIGH SEAS

✿ ✿ ✿

Article 6

1. A coastal State has a special interest in the maintenance of the productivity of the living resources in any area of the high seas adjacent to its territorial sea.

2. A coastal State is entitled to take part on equal footing in any system of research and regulation for purposes of conservation of the living resources of the high seas in that area, even though its nationals do not carry on fishing there. . . .

Article 7

1. Having regard to the provisions of paragraph 1 of article 6, any coastal State may, with a view to the maintenance of the productivity of the living resources of the sea, adopt unilaterial measures of conservation appropriate to any stock of fish or other marine resources in any area of the high seas adjacent to its territorial sea, provided that negotiations to that effect with the other States concerned have not led to an agreement within six months.

Adopted by the United Nations Conference on the Law of the Sea, April 29, 1958; entered into force on March 20, 1966. By August 1971, 54 states had become parties to the Convention.

2. The measures which the coastal State adopts under the previous paragraph shall be valid as to other States only if the following requirements are fulfilled:

 (*a*) That there is a need for urgent application of conservation measures in the light of the existing knowledge of the fishery;

 (*b*) That the measures adopted are based on appropriate scientific findings;

 (*c*) That such measures do not discriminate in form or in fact against foreign fishermen. . . .

✿　✿　✿

Article 9

1. Any dispute which may arise between States under articles 4, 5, 6, 7 and 8 shall, at the request of any of the parties, be submitted for settlement to a special commission of five members, unless the parties agree to seek a solution by another method of peaceful settlement, as provided for in Article 33 of the Charter of the United Nations. . . .

Article 10

1. The special commission shall, in disputes arising under article 7, apply the criteria listed in paragraph 2 of that article. In disputes under articles 4, 5, 6 and 8, the commission shall apply the following criteria, according to the issues involved in the dispute:

 (*a*) Common to the determination of disputes arising under articles 4, 5 and 6 are the requirements:

  (i)   That scientific findings demonstrate the necessity of conservation measures;

  (ii) That the specific measures are based on scientific findings and are practicable; and

  (iii) That the measures do not discriminate, in any form or in fact, against fishermen of other States;

 (*b*) Applicable to the determination of disputes arising under article 8 is the requirement that scientific findings demonstrate the necessity for conservation measures, or that the conservation programme is adequate, as the case may be.

2. The special commission may decide that pending its award the measures in dispute shall not be applied, provided that, in the case of disputes under article 7, the measures shall only be suspended when it is apparent to the commission on the basis of *prima facie* evidence that the need for the urgent application of such measures does not exist.

Article 11

The decisions of the special commission shall be binding on the States concerned and the provisions of paragraph 2 of Article 94 of the Charter of the United Nations shall be applicable to those decisions. If the decisions are accompanied by any recommendations, they shall receive the greatest possible consideration.

Article 12'

1. If the factual basis of the award of the special commission is altered by substantial changes in the conditions of the stock or stocks of fish or other living marine resources or in methods of fishing, any of the States concerned may request the other States to enter into negotiations with a view to prescribing by agreement the necessary modifications in the measures of conservation.
2. If no agreement is reached within a reasonable period of time, any of the States concerned may again resort to the procedure contemplated by article 9 provided that at least two years have elapsed from the original award.

ANTARCTICA

◢ THE ANTARCTIC TREATY

The Governments of Argentina, Australia, Belgium, Chile, the French Republic, Japan, New Zealand, Norway, the Union of South Africa, the Union of Soviet Socialist Republics, the United Kingdom of Great Britain and Northern Ireland, and the United States of America,

Recognizing that it is in the interest of all mankind that Antarctica shall continue forever to be used exclusively for peaceful purposes and shall not become the scene or object of international discord;

Acknowledging the substantial contributions to scientific knowledge resulting from international cooperation in scientific investigation in Antarctica;

Convinced that the establishment of a firm foundation for the continuation and development of such cooperation on the basis of freedom of scientific investigation in Antarctica as applied during the International

Adopted on December 1, 1959.

Geophysical Year accords with the interests of science and the progress of all mankind;

Convinced also that a treaty ensuring the use of Antarctica for peaceful purposes only and the continuance of international harmony in Antarctica will further the purposes and principles embodied in the Charter of the United Nations;

Have agreed as follows:

Article I

1. Antarctica shall be used for peaceful purposes only. There shall be prohibited, *inter alia,* any measures of a military nature, such as the establishment of military bases and fortifications, the carrying out of military maneuvers, as well as the testing of any weapons. . . .

❋ ❋ ❋

Article V

1. Any nuclear explosions in Antarctica and the disposal there of radioactive waste material shall be prohibited.

2. In the event of the conclusion of international agreements concerning the use of nuclear energy, including nuclear explosions and the disposal of radioactive waste material, to which all of the Contracting Parties whose representatives are entitled to participate in the meetings provided for under Article IX are parties, the rules established under such agreements shall apply in Antarctica.

Article VI

The provisions of the present Treaty shall apply to *the area south of 60° South Latitude, including all ice shelves* [emphasis added], but nothing in the present Treaty shall prejudice or in any way affect the rights, or the exercise of the rights, of any State under international law with regard to the high seas within that area.

Article VII

1. In order to promote the objectives and ensure the observance of the provisions of the present Treaty, each Contracting Party whose representatives are entitled to participate in the meetings referred to in Article IX of the Treaty, shall have the right to designate observers to carry out any inspection provided for by the present Article. Observers shall be nationals of the Contracting Parties which designate them. . . .

2. Each observer designated in accordance with the provisions of paragraph 1 of this Article shall have complete freedom of access at any time to any or all areas of Antarctica.

3. All areas of Antarctica, including all stations, installations, and equipment within those areas, and all ships and aircraft at points of discharging or embarking cargoes or personnel in Antarctica, shall be open at all times to inspection by any observers designated in accordance with paragraph 1 of this Article.

4. Aerial observation may be carried out at any time over any or all areas of Antarctica by any of the Contracting Parties having the right to designate observers. . . .

* * *

Article IX

1. Representatives of the Contracting Parties named in the preamble to the present Treaty shall meet at the City of Canberra within two months after the date of entry into force of the Treaty, and thereafter at suitable intervals and places, for the purpose of exchanging information, consulting together on matters of common interest pertaining to Antarctica, and formulating and considering, and recommending to their Governments, measures in furtherance of the principles and objectives of the Treaty, including measures regarding:

(a) use of Antarctica for peaceful purposes only;

(b) facilitation of scientific research in Antarctica;

(c) facilitation of international scientific cooperation in Antarctica;

(d) facilitation of the exercise of the rights of inspection provided for in Article VII of the Treaty;

(e) questions relating to the exercise of jurisdiction in Antarctica;

(f) preservation and conservation of living resources in Antarctica.

2. Each Contracting Party which has become a party to the present Treaty by accession under Article XIII shall be entitled to appoint representatives to participate in the meetings referred to in paragraph 1 of the present Article, during such time as that Contracting Party demonstrates its interest in Antarctica by conducting substantial scientific research activity there, such as the establishment of a scientific station or the despatch of a scientific expedition. . . .

Article X

Each of the Contracting Parties undertakes to exert appropriate efforts, consistent with the Charter of the United Nations, to the end that no one engages in any activity in Antarctica contrary to the principles or purposes of the present Treaty.

OUTER SPACE

▶ TEXT OF THE U.N. GENERAL ASSEMBLY RESOLUTION ON INTERNATIONAL CO-OPERATION IN THE PEACEFUL USES OF OUTER SPACE*

The General Assembly,

Recognizing the common interest of mankind in furthering the peaceful uses of outer space and the urgent need to strengthen international co-operation in this important field,

Believing that the exploration and use of outer space should be only for the betterment of mankind and to the benefit of States irrespective of the stage of their economic or scientific development,

1. *Commends* to States for their guidance in the exploration and use of outer space the following principles:

   (*a*) International law, including the Charter of the United Nations, applies to outer space and celestial bodies;

   (*b*) Outer space and celestial bodies are free for exploration and use by all States in conformity with international law and are not subject to national appropriation;

2. *Invites* the Committee on the Peaceful Uses of Outer Space to study and report on the legal problems which may arise from the exploration and use of outer space.

▶ TEXT OF THE U.N. DECLARATION OF LEGAL PRINCIPLES GOVERNING THE ACTIVITIES OF STATES IN THE EXPLORATION AND USE OF OUTER SPACE†

The General Assembly,

Inspired by the great prospects opening up before mankind as a result of man's entry into outer space,

Recognizing the common interest of all mankind in the progress of the exploration and use of outer space for peaceful purposes,

Believing that the exploration and use of outer space should be carried on for the betterment of mankind and for the benefit of States irrespective of their degree of economic or scientific development,

---

* Resolution No. 1721 (XVI), December 20, 1961; passed at the Sixteenth Regular Session of the General Assembly.

† Resolution No. 1962 (XVIII), December 13, 1963; passed by the General Assembly at its Eighteenth Regular Session.

Desiring to contribute to broad international co-operation in the scientific as well as in the legal aspects of exploration and use of outer space for peaceful purposes,

* * *

Solemnly declares that in the exploration and use of outer space States should be guided by the following principles:

1. The exploration and use of outer space shall be carried on for the benefit and in the interests of all mankind.

2. Outer space and celestial bodies are free for exploration and use by all States on a basis of equality and in accordance with international law.

3. Outer space and celestial bodies are not subject to national appropriation by claim of sovereignty, by means of use or occupation, or by any other means.

4. The activities of States in the exploration and use of outer space shall be carried on in accordance with international law, including the Charter of the United Nations, in the interest of maintaining international peace and security and promoting international co-operation and understanding.

5. States bear international responsibility for national activities in outer space, whether carried on by governmental agencies or by non-governmental entities, and for assuring that national activities are carried on in conformity with the principles set forth in the present Declaration. The activities of non-governmental entities in outer space shall require authorization and continuing supervision by the State concerned. When activities are carried on in outer space by an international organization, responsibility for compliance with the principles set forth in this Declaration shall be borne by the international organization and by the States participating in it.

6. In the exploration and use of outer space, States shall be guided by the principle of co-operation and mutual assistance and shall conduct all their activities in outer space with due regard for the corresponding interests of other States. If a State has reason to believe that an outer space activity or experiment planned by it or its nationals would cause potentially harmful interference with activities of other States in the peaceful exploration and use of outer space, it shall undertake appropriate international consultations before proceeding with any such activity or experiment. A State which has reason to believe that an outer space activity or experiment planned by another State would cause potentially harmful interference with activities in the peaceful exploration and use of outer space may request consultation concerning the activity or experiment.

⊌ TEXT OF THE U.N. GENERAL ASSEMBLY RESOLUTION ON INTERNATIONAL CO-OPERATION IN THE PEACEFUL USES OF OUTER SPACE*

The General Assembly,

Recalling its resolutions 1721 (XVI) of 20 December 1961 and 1802 (XVII) of 14 December 1962 on international co-operation in the peaceful uses of outer space,

Having considered the report submitted by the Committee on the Peaceful Uses of Outer Space,

Mindful of the benefits which all Member States would enjoy by participation in international programmes of co-operation in this field,

I

1. *Recommends* that consideration should be given to incorporating in international agreement form, in the future as appropriate, legal principles governing the activities of States in the exploration and use of outer space;

2. *Requests* the Committee on the Peaceful Uses of Outer Space to continue to study and report on legal problems which may arise in the exploration and use of outer space, and in particular to arrange for the prompt preparation of draft international agreements on liability for damage caused by objects launched into outer space and on assistance to and return of astronauts and space vehicles; . . .

⊌ TREATY ON PRINCIPLES GOVERNING THE ACTIVITIES OF STATES IN THE EXPLORATION AND USE OF OUTER SPACE, INCLUDING THE MOON AND OTHER CELESTIAL BODIES†

The States Parties to this Treaty,

Inspired by the great prospects opening up before mankind as a result of man's entry into outer space,

Recognizing the common interest of all mankind in the progress of the exploration and use of outer space for peaceful purposes,

---

* Resolution No. 1963 (XVIII), December 13, 1963; passed at the Eighteenth Regular Session of the General Assembly.
† Entered into force on October 10, 1967.

Believing that the exploration and use of outer space should be carried on for the benefit of all peoples irrespective of the degree of their economic or scientific development,

Desiring to contribute to broad international co-operation in the scientific as well as the legal aspects of the exploration and use of outer space for peaceful purposes,

Believing that such co-operation will contribute to the development of mutual understanding and to the strengthening of friendly relations between States and peoples,

Recalling resolution 1962 (XVIII), entitled 'Declaration of Legal Principles Governing the Activities of States in the Exploration and Use of Outer Space', which was adopted unanimously by the United Nations General Assembly on 13 December 1963,

* * *

Convinced that a Treaty on Principles Governing the Activities of States in the Exploration and Use of Outer Space, including the Moon and Other Celestial Bodies, will further the purposes and principles of the Charter of the United Nations,

Have agreed on the following:

Article 1

The exploration and use of outer space, including the Moon and other celestial bodies, shall be carried out for the benefit and in the interests of all countries, irrespective of their degree of economic or scientific development, and shall be the province of all mankind.

Outer space including the Moon and other celestial bodies, shall be free for exploration and use by all States without discrimination of any kind, on a basis of equality and in accordance with international law, and there shall be free access to all areas of celestial bodies.

There shall be freedom of scientific investigation in outer space, including the Moon and other celestial bodies, and States shall facilitate and encourage international co-operation in such investigation.

Article 2

Outer space, including the Moon and other celestial bodies, is not subject to national appropriation by claim of sovereignty, by means of use or occupation, or by any other means.

Article 3

States Parties to the Treaty shall carry on activities in the exploration and use of outer space, including the Moon and other celestial bodies, in accordance with international law, including the Charter of the United Nations, in the interest of maintaining international peace and security and promoting international co-operation and understanding.

Article 4

States Parties to the Treaty undertake not to place in orbit around the Earth any objects carrying nuclear weapons or any other kinds of weapons of mass destruction, install such weapons on celestial bodies, or station such weapons in outer space in any other manner.

The Moon and other celestial bodies shall be used by all States Parties to the Treaty exclusively for peaceful purposes. The establishment of military bases, installations and fortifications, the testing of any type of weapons and the conduct of military manoeuvres on celestial bodies shall be forbidden. The use of military personnel for scientific research or for any other peaceful purposes shall not be prohibited. The use of any equipment or facility necessary for peaceful exploration of the Moon and other celestial bodies shall also not be prohibited.

* * *

Article 6

States Parties to the Treaty shall bear international responsibility for national activities in outer space, including the Moon and other celestial bodies, whether such activities are carried on by governmental agencies or by non-governmental entities, and for assuring that national activities are carried out in conformity with the provisions set forth in the present Treaty. The activities of non-governmental entities in outer space, including the Moon and other celestial bodies, shall require authorization and continuing supervision by the appropriate State Party to the Treaty. When activities are carried on in outer space, including the Moon and other celestial bodies, by an international organization, responsibility for compliance with this Treaty shall be born both by the international organization and by the States Parties to the Treaty participating in such organization.

* * *

Article 9

In the exploration and use of outer space, including the Moon and other celestial bodies, States Parties to the Treaty shall be guided by the principle of co-operation and mutual assistance and shall conduct all their activities in outer space, including the Moon and other celestial bodies, with due regard to the corresponding interests of all other States Parties to the Treaty. States Parties to the Treaty shall pursue studies of outer space, including the Moon and other celestial bodies, and conduct exploration of them so as to avoid their harmful contamination and also adverse changes in the environment of the Earth resulting from the introduction of extraterrestrial matter and, where necessary, shall adopt appropriate measures for this purpose. If a State Party to the Treaty has reason to believe that an activity or experiment planned by it or its nationals in outer space, including the Moon and other celestial bodies, would cause potentially harmful interference with activities of other States Parties in the peaceful exploration and use of outer space, including the Moon and other celestial bodies, it shall undertake appropriate international consultations before proceeding with any such activity or experiment. A State Party to the Treaty which has reason to believe that an activity or experiment planned by another State Party in outer space, including the Moon and other celestial bodies, would cause potentially harmful interference with activities in the peaceful exploration, and use of outer space, including the Moon and other celestial bodies, may request consultation concerning the activity or experiment.

☙ AGREEMENT ON THE RESCUE OF ASTRONAUTS, THE RETURN OF ASTRONAUTS AND THE RETURN OF OBJECTS LAUNCHED INTO OUTER SPACE

Article 5

1. Each Contracting Party which receives information or discovers that a space object or its component parts has returned to Earth in territory under its jurisdiction or on the high seas or in any other place not under the jurisdiction of any State, shall notify the launching authority and the Secretary-General of the United Nations.

2. Each Contracting Party having jurisdiction over the territory on which a space object or its component parts has been discovered shall, upon the request of the launching authority and with assistance from that authority if requested, take such steps as it finds practicable to recover the object or component parts.

3. Upon request of the launching authority, objects launched into

Came into force on December 3, 1968, the date of deposit of the instruments of ratification by five governments, including the governments designated as Depositary governments, viz., the governments of the United Kingdom, the U.S.A., and the USSR.

outer space or their component parts found beyond the territorial limits of the launching authority shall be returned to or held at the disposal of representatives of the launching authority, which shall, upon request, furnish identifying data prior to their return.

4. Notwithstanding paragraphs 2 and 3 of this Article, a Contracting Party which has reason to believe that a space object or its component parts discovered in territory under its jurisdiction, or recovered by it elsewhere, is of a hazardous or deleterious nature may so notify the launching authority, which shall immediately take effective steps, under the direction and control of the said Contracting Party, to eliminate possible danger of harm.

5. Expenses incurred in fulfilling obligations to recover and return a space object or its component parts under paragraphs 2 and 3 of this Article shall be borne by the launching authority.

Article 6

For the purposes of this Agreement, the term "launching authority" shall refer to the State responsible for launching, or, where an international intergovernmental organization is responsible for launching, that organization, provided that that organization declares its acceptance of the rights and obligations provided for in this Agreement and a majority of the States members of that organization are Contracting Parties to this Agreement and to the Treaty on Principles Governing the Activities of States in the Exploration and Use of Outer Space, including the Moon and Other Celestial Bodies.

☙ TEXT OF THE U.N. GENERAL ASSEMBLY RESOLUTION ON INTERNATIONAL LIABILITY FOR DAMAGE CAUSED BY SPACE OBJECTS

The General Assembly,
Reaffirming the importance of international co-operation in the field of the exploration and peaceful uses of outer space, including the Moon and other celestial bodies, and of promoting the law in this new field of human endeavour,
Desiring that the rights and obligations pertaining to liability for damage as laid down in the Treaty on Principles Governing the Activities of States in the Exploration and Use of Outer Space, including the Moon

Resolution No. 2777 (XXVI), November 29, 1971; passed at the Twenty-Sixth Regular Session of the General Assembly.

and Other Celestial Bodies should be elaborated in a separate international instrument,

* * *

Recalling also that in resolution 2733 B (XXV) it urged the Committee on the Peaceful Uses of Outer Space to reach early agreement on a draft convention on liability, to be submitted to the General Assembly at its twenty-sixth session, embodying the principles of a full measure of compensation to victims and effective procedures which would lead to prompt and equitable settlement of claims,

Having considered the report of the Committee on the Peaceful Uses of Outer Space,

Taking note with appreciation of the work accomplished by the Committee on the Peaceful Uses of Outer Space, and in particular that of its Legal Sub-Committee,

1. *Commends* the Convention on International Liability for Damage Caused by Space Objects, the text of which is annexed to the present resolution;

2. *Requests* the depositary governments to open the Convention for signature and ratification at the earliest possible date;

3. *Notes* that any State may, on becoming a party to the Convention, declare that it will recognize as binding, in relation to any other State accepting the same obligation, the decision of the Claims Commission concerning any dispute to which it may become a party;

4. *Express its hope* for the widest possible adherence to this Convention.

CONVENTION ON INTERNATIONAL LIABILITY FOR DAMAGE CAUSED BY SPACE OBJECTS

The States Parties to this Convention,

Recognizing the common interest of all mankind in furthering the exploration and use of outer space for peaceful purposes

Recalling the Treaty on Principles Governing the Activities of States in the Exploration and Use of Outer Space, including the Moon and Other Celestial Bodies.

Taking into consideration that, notwithstanding the precautionary measures to be taken by States and international intergovernmental organizations involved in the launching of space objects, damage may on occasion be caused by such objects,

Entered into force on September 1, 1972.

Recognizing the need to elaborate effective international rules and procedures concerning liability for damage caused by space objects and to ensure, in particular, the prompt payment under the terms of this Convention of a full and equitable measure of compensation to victims of such damage,

Believing that the establishment of such rules and procedures will contribute to the strengthening of international co-operation in the field of the exploration and use of outer space for peaceful purposes.

Have agreed on the following:

Article I

For the purposes of this Convention:

(a) The term "damage" means loss of life, personal injury or other impairment of health; or loss of or damage to property of States or of persons, natural or juridical, or property of international intergovernmental organizations;

(b) The term "launching" includes attempted launching;

(c) The term "launching State" means:

  (i) A State which launches or procures the launching of a space object;

  (ii) A State from whose territory or facility a space object is launched;

(d) The term "space object" includes component parts of a space object as well as its launch vehicle and parts thereof.

Article II

A launching State shall be absolutely liable to pay compensation for damage caused by its space object on the surface of the earth or to aircraft in flight.

Article III

In the event of damage being caused elsewhere than on the surface of the earth to a space object of one launching State or to persons or property on board such a space object by a space object of another launching State, the latter shall be liable only if the damage is due to its fault or the fault of persons for whom it is responsible.

Article IV

1. In the event of damage being caused elsewhere than on the surface of the earth to a space object of one launching State or to persons or property on board such a space object by a space object of another

launching State, and of damage thereby being caused to a third State or to its natural or juridical persons, the first two States shall be jointly and severally liable to the third State, to the extent indicated by the following:

(*a*) If the damage has been caused to the third State on the surface of the earth or to aircraft in flight, their liability to the third State shall be absolute;

(*b*) If the damage has been caused to a space object of the third State or to persons or property on board that space object elsewhere than on the surface of the earth, their liability to the third State shall be based on the fault of either of the first two States or on the fault of persons for whom either is responsible.

2. In all cases of joint and several liability referred to in paragraph 1 of this article, the burden of compensation for the damage shall be apportioned between the first two States in accordance with the extent to which they were at fault; if the extent of the fault of each of these States cannot be established, the burden of compensation shall be apportioned equally between them. Such apportionment shall be without prejudice to the right of the third State to seek the entire compensation due under this Convention from any or all of the launching States which are jointly and severally liable.

ARTICLE V

1. Whenever two or more States jointly launch a space object, they shall be jointly and severally liable for any damage caused.

2. A launching State which has paid compensation for damage shall have the right to present a claim for indemnification to other participants in the joint launching. The participants in a joint launching may conclude agreements regarding the apportioning among themselves of the financial obligation in respect of which they are jointly and severally liable. Such agreements shall be without prejudice to the right of a State sustaining damage to seek the entire compensation due under this Convention from any or all of the launching States which are jointly and severally liable.

3. A State from whose territory or facility a space object is launched shall be regarded as a participant in a joint launching.

ARTICLE VI

1. Subject to the provisions of paragraph 2 of this article, exoneration from absolute liability shall be granted to the extent that a launching State establishes that the damage has resulted either wholly or partially from gross negligence or from an act or omission done with intent to

cause damage on the part of a claimant State or of natural or juridical persons it represents.

2. No exoneration whatever shall be granted in cases where the damage has resulted from activities conducted by a launching State which are not in conformity with international law including, in particular, the Charter of the United Nations and the Treaty on Principles Governing the Activities of States in the Exploration and Use of Outer Space, including the Moon and Other Celestial Bodies.

ARTICLE VII

The provisions of this Convention shall not apply to damage caused by a space object of a launching State to:

(a) Nationals of that launching State;

(b) Foreign nationals during such time as they are participating in the operation of that space object from the time of its launching or at any stage thereafter until its descent, or during such time as they are in the immediate vicinity of a planned launching or recovery area as the result of an invitation by that launching State.

ARTICLE VIII

1. A State which suffers damage, or whose natural or juridical persons suffer damage, may present to a launching State a claim for compensation for such damage.

2. If the State of nationality has not presented a claim, another State may, in respect of damage sustained in its territory by any natural or juridical person, present a claim to a launching State.

3. If neither the State of nationality nor the State in whose territory the damage was sustained has presented a claim or notified its intention of presenting a claim, another State may, in respect of damage sustained by its permanent residents, present a claim to a launching State.

ARTICLE IX

A claim for compensation for damage shall be presented to a launching State through diplomatic channels. If a State does not maintain diplomatic relations with the launching State concerned, it may request another State to present its claim to that launching State or otherwise represent its interests under this Convention. It may also present its claim through the Secretary-General of the United Nations, provided the claimant State and the launching State are both Members of the United Nations.

ARTICLE X

1. A claim for compensation for damage may be presented to a launch-

ing State not later than one year following the date of the occurrence of the damage or the identification of the launching State which is liable.

2. If, however, a State does not know of the occurrence of the damage or has not been able to identify the launching State which is liable, it may present a claim within one year following the date on which it learned of the aforementioned facts; however, this period shall in no event exceed one year following the date on which the State could reasonably be expected to have learned of the facts through the exercise of due diligence.

3. The time-limits specified in paragraphs 1 and 2 of this article shall apply even if the full extent of the damage may not be known. In this event, however, the claimant State shall be entitled to revise the claim and submit additional documentation after the expiration of such time-limits until one year after the full extent of the damage is known.

ARTICLE XI

1. Presentation of a claim to a launching State for compensation for damage under this Convention shall not require the prior exhaustion of any local remedies which may be available to a claimant State or to natural or juridical persons it represents.

2. Nothing in this Convention shall prevent a State, or natural or juridical persons it might represent, from pursuing a claim in the courts or administrative tribunals or agencies of a launching State. A State shall not, however, be entitled to present a claim under this Convention in respect of the same damage for which a claim is being pursued in the courts or administrative tribunals or agencies of a launching State or under another international agreement which is binding on the States concerned.

ARTICLE XII

The compensation which the launching State shall be liable to pay for damage under this Convention shall be determined in accordance with international law and the principles of justice and equity, in order to provide such reparation in respect of the damage as will restore the person, natural or juridical, State or international organization on whose behalf the claim is presented to the condition which would have existed if the damage had not occurred.

ARTICLE XIII

Unless the claimant State and the State from which compensation is due under this Convention agree on another form of compensation, the compensation shall be paid in the currency of the claimant State or, if that State so requests, in the currency of the State from which compensation is due.

Article XIV

If no settlement of a claim is arrived at through diplomatic negotiations as provided for in article IX, within one year from the date on which the claimant State notifies the launching State that it has submitted the documentation of its claim, the parties concerned shall establish a Claims Commission at the request of either party.

Suggested Reading List

Jessup, Philip C., and Taubenfeld, Howard J., *Controls for Outer Space and the Antarctic Analogy* (1959).

MacDougal, Myres S., Lasswell, Harold D., and Vlasic, Ivan A., *Law and Public Order in Space* (1963).

MacDougal, Myres S., and Burke, William T., *The Public Order of the Oceans: A Contemporary International Law of the Sea* (1962).

Johnston, Douglas M., *The International Law of Fisheries* (1965).

McWhinney, Edward, and Bradley, Martin A., eds., *New Frontiers in Space Law* (1969).

White, Irving L., *Decision-making for Space: Law and Politics in Air, Sea and Outer Space* (1970).

Note: Articles on the law of the sea are extremely numerous. It is suggested that the reader should consult the periodical literature that focuses on the extent of sovereignty (e.g., territorial sea), the extent of limited functional authority (e.g., exclusive fishing zones), marine areas that present special considerations (e.g., straits, gulfs), and questions of access (e.g., innocent passage, freedom of the high seas).

See also:

Johnson, John A., "Pollution and Contamination in Space," in Cohen, Maxwell, ed., *Law and Politics in Space*, pp. 37–53 (1964).

Hall, R. Cargill, "Comments on Salvage and Removal of Man-made Objects from Outer Space," 33 *J. Air Law and Comm.* 288 (1967).

Gorove, Stephen, "Pollution and Outer Space: A Legal Analysis and Appraisal," 5 *N.Y.U.J. Int'l L. and Politics* 53 (1972).

———, "Arms Control Provisions in the Outer Space Treaty: A Scrutinizing Reappraisal," 3 *Georgia J. Int'l and Comp. L.* 114 (1973).

Prohibition of Ecocidal Weapons and Weapons of Mass Destruction

CHEMICAL AND BACTERIOLOGICAL (BIOLOGICAL) WEAPONS

✍ THE HAGUE REGULATIONS RESPECTING THE LAWS AND CUSTOMS OF WAR ON LAND (REVISED 1907)

ARTICLE 22.

The right of belligerents to adopt means of injuring the enemy is not unlimited.

ARTICLE 23.*

In addition to the prohibitions provided by special Conventions, it is especially forbidden:

(*a*) to employ poison or poisonous weapons;

* * *

(*e*) to employ arms, projectiles, or material calculated to cause unnecessary suffering;

* * *

(*g*) to destroy or seize the enemy's property, unless such destruction or seizure be imperatively demanded by the necessities of war;

* * *

✍ PROTOCOL FOR THE PROHIBITION OF THE USE IN WAR OF ASPHYXIATING, POISONOUS OR OTHER GASES, AND OF BACTERIOLOGICAL METHODS OF WARFARE†

THE undersigned Plenipotentiaries [not reproduced here], in the name of their respective Governments:

Whereas the use in war of asphyxiating, poisonous or other gases, and

---

* For an interpretation of Article 23, see U.S. Dept. of Defense position with regard to destruction of crops through chemical agents in (1971) 10 *Int'l Legal Materials* at pp. 1300–1306.
† Adopted at Geneva on June 17, 1925.

of all analogous liquids, materials or devices, has been justly condemned by the general opinion of the civilised world; and

Whereas the prohibition of such use has been declared in Treaties to which the majority of Powers of the world are Parties; and

To the end that this prohibition shall be universally accepted as a part of International Law, binding alike the conscience and the practices of nations;

DECLARE:

That the High Contracting Parties, so far as they are not already Parties to Treaties prohibiting such use, accept this prohibition, agree to extend this prohibition to the use of bacteriological methods of warfare, and agree to be bound as between themselves according to the terms of this declaration.

☙ TEXT OF THE U.N. GENERAL ASSEMBLY RESOLUTION ON THE PROHIBITION OF THE DEVELOPMENT, PRODUCTION AND STOCKPILING OF BACTERIOLOGICAL (BIOLOGICAL) AND TOXIN WEAPONS AND ON THEIR DESTRUCTION

The General Assembly,

Recalling its resolution 2662 (XXV) of 7 December 1970,

Convinced of the importance and urgency of eliminating from the arsenals of States, through effective measures, such dangerous weapons of mass destruction as those using chemical or bacteriological (biological) agents,

Having considered the report of the Conference of the Committee on Disarmament dated 6 October 1971, and being appreciative of its work on the draft Convention on the Prohibition of the Development, Production and Stockpiling of Bacteriological (Biological) and Toxin Weapons and on Their Destruction, annexed to the report,

Recognizing the important significance of the Protocol for the Prohibition of the Use in War of Asphyxiating, Poisonous or Other Gases, and of Bacteriological Methods of Warfare, signed at Geneva on 17 June 1925, and conscious also of the contribution which the said Protocol has already made, and continues to make, to mitigating the horrors of war,

Noting that the Convention on the Prohibition of the Development, Production and Stockpiling of Bacteriological (Biological) and Toxin Weapons and on Their Destruction provides for the parties to reaffirm their adherence to the principles and objectives of that Protocol and to call upon all States to comply strictly with them,

Resolution No. 2826 (XXVI), December 16, 1971; passed at the Twenty-Sixth Regular Session of the General Assembly.

Further noting that nothing in the Convention shall be interpreted as in any way limiting or detracting from the obligations assumed by any State under the Geneva Protocol,

Determined, for the sake of all mankind, to exclude completely the possibility of bacteriological (biological) agents and toxins being used as weapons,

Recognizing that an agreement on the prohibition of bacteriological (biological) and toxin weapons represents a first possible step towards the achievement of agreement on effective measures also for the prohibition of the development, production and stockpiling of chemical weapons,

Noting that the Convention contains an affirmation of the recognized objective of effective prohibition of chemical weapons and, to this end, an undertaking to continue negotiations in good faith with a view to reaching early agreement on effective measures for the prohibition of their development, production and stockpiling and for their destruction, and on appropriate measures concerning equipment and means of delivery specifically designed for the production or use of chemical agents for weapons purposes,

Convinced that the implementation of measures in the field of disarmament should release substantial additional resources, which should promote economic and social development, particularly in the developing countries,

Convinced that the Convention will contribute to the realization of the purposes and principles of the Charter of the United Nations,

1. *Commends* the Convention on the Prohibition of the Development, Production and Stockpiling of Bacteriological (Biological) and Toxin Weapons and on Their Destruction, the text of which is annexed to the present resolution;

2. *Requests* the depositary Governments to open the Convention for signature and ratification at the earliest possible date;

3. *Expresses the hope* for the widest possible adherence to the Convention.

CONVENTION ON THE PROHIBITION OF THE DEVELOPMENT, PRODUCTION AND STOCKPILING OF BACTERIOLOGICAL (BIOLOGICAL) AND TOXIN WEAPONS AND ON THEIR DESTRUCTION

The States Parties to this Convention,

Determined to act with a view to achieving effective progress towards general and complete disarmament, including the prohibition and elim-

Not yet in force as of June 11, 1973.

ination of all types of weapons of mass destruction, and convinced that the prohibition of the development, production and stockpiling of chemical and bacteriological (biological) weapons and their elimination, through effective measures, will facilitate the achievement of general and complete disarmament under strict and effective international control,

Recognizing the important significance of the Protocol for the Prohibition of the Use in War of Asphyxiating, Poisonous or Other Gases, and of Bacteriological Methods of Warfare, signed at Geneva on 17 June 1925, and conscious also of the contribution which the said Protocol has already made, and continues to make, to mitigating the horrors of war,

Reaffirming their adherence to the principles and objectives of that Protocol and calling upon all States to comply strictly with them,

Recalling that the General Assembly of the United Nations has repeatedly condemned all actions contrary to the principles and objectives of the Geneva Protocol of 17 June 1925,

Desiring to contribute to the strengthening of confidence between peoples and the general improvement of the international atmosphere,

Desiring also to contribute to the realization of the purposes and principles of the Charter of the United Nations,

Convinced of the importance and urgency of eliminating from the arsenals of States, through effective measures, such dangerous weapons of mass destruction as those using chemical or bacteriological (biological) agents,

Recognizing that an agreement on the prohibition of bacteriological (biological) and toxin weapons represents a first possible step towards the achievement of agreement on effective measures also for the prohibition of the development, production and stocking of chemical weapons, and determined to continue negotiations to that end,

Determined, for the sake of all mankind, to exclude completely the possibility of bacteriological (biological) agents and toxins being used as weapons,

Convinced that such use would be repugnant to the conscience of mankind and that no effort should be spared to minimize this risk,

Have agreed as follows:

ARTICLE I

Each State Party to this Convention undertakes never in any circumstances to develop, produce, stockpile or otherwise acquire or retain:

(1) Microbial or other biological agents, or toxins whatever their origin or method of production, of types and in quantities that have no justification for prophylactic, protective or other peaceful purposes;

(2) Weapons, equipment or means of delivery designed to use such agents or toxins for hostile purposes or in armed conflict.

ARTICLE II

Each State Party to this Convention undertakes to destroy, or to divert to peaceful purposes, as soon as possible but not later than nine months after the entry into force of the Convention, all agents, toxins, weapons, equipment and means of delivery specified in article I of the Convention, which are in its possession or under its jurisdiction or control. In implementing the provisions of this article all necessary safety precautions shall be observed to protect populations and the environment.

ARTICLE III

Each State Party to this Convention undertakes not to transfer to any recipient whatsoever, directly or indirectly and not in any way to assist, encourage or induce any State, group of States or international organizations to manufacture or otherwise acquire any of the agents, toxins, weapons, equipment or means of delivery specified in article I of the Convention.

ARTICLE IV

Each State Party to this Convention shall, in accordance with its constitutional processes, take any necessary measures to prohibit and prevent the development, production, stockpiling, acquisition or retention of the agents, toxins, weapons, equipment and means of delivery specified in article I of the Convention, within the territory of such State, under its jurisdiction or under its control anywhere.

ARTICLE V

The States Parties to this Convention undertake to consult one another and to co-operate in solving any problems which may arise in relation to the objective of, or in the application of the provisions of, the Convention. Consultation and co-operation pursuant to this article may also be undertaken through appropriate international procedures within the framework of the United Nations and in accordance with its Charter.

ARTICLE VI

1. Any State Party to this Convention which finds that any other State Party is acting in breach of obligations deriving from the provisions of

the Convention may lodge a complaint with the Security Council of the United Nations. Such a complaint should include all possible evidence confirming its validity, as well as a request for its consideration by the Security Council.

2. Each State Party to this Convention undertakes to co-operate in carrying out any investigation which the Security Council may initiate, in accordance with the provisions of the Charter of the United Nations, on the basis of the complaint received by the Council. The Security Council shall inform the States Parties to the Convention of the results of the investigation.

ARTICLE VII

Each State Party to this Convention undertakes to provide or support assistance, in accordance with the United Nations Charter, to any Party to the Convention which so requests, if the Security Council decides that such Party has been exposed to danger as a result of violation of the Convention.

ARTICLE VIII

Nothing in this Convention shall be interpreted as in any way limiting or detracting from the obligations assumed by any State under the Protocol for the Prohibition of the Use in War of Asphyxiating, Poisonous or Other Gases, and of Bacteriological Methods of Warfare, signed at Geneva on 17 June 1925.

ARTICLE IX

Each State Party to this Convention affirms the recognized objective of effective prohibition of chemical weapons and, to this end, undertakes to continue negotiations in good faith with a view to reaching early agreement on effective measures for the prohibition of their development, production and stock-piling and for their destruction, and on appropriate measures concerning equipment and means of delivery specifically designed for the production or use of chemical agents for weapons purposes.

ARTICLE X

1. The States Parties to this Convention undertake to facilitate, and have the right to participate in, the fullest possible exchange of equipment, materials and scientific and technological information for the use

of bacteriological (biological) agents and toxins for peaceful purposes. Parties to the Convention in a position to do so shall also co-operate in contributing individually or together with other States or international organizations to the further development and application of scientific discoveries in the field of bacteriology (biology) for the prevention of disease, or for other peaceful purposes.

2. This Convention shall be implemented in a manner designed to avoid hampering the economic or technological development of States Parties to the Convention or international co-operation in the field of peaceful bacteriological (biological) activities, including the international exchange of bacteriological (biological) agents and toxins and equipment for the processing, use or production of bacteriological (biological) agents and toxins for peaceful purposes in accordance with the provisions of the Convention.

🖢 TEXT OF THE U.N. GENERAL ASSEMBLY RESOLUTION ON QUESTIONS OF CHEMICAL AND BACTERIOLOGICAL (BIOLOGICAL) WEAPONS

A

The General Assembly,

Recalling its resolution 2454 A (XXIII) of 20 December 1968, its resolution 2603 B (XXIV) of 16 December 1969, and in particular its resolution 2662 (XXV) of 7 December 1970 in which it stressed that the prospects for international peace and security, as well as the achievement of the goal of general and complete disarmament under effective international control, would be enhanced if the development, production and stockpiling of chemical and bacteriological (biological) agents for purposes of war were to end and if those agents were eliminated from all military arsenals, and commended the following basic approach for reaching an effective solution to the problem of chemical and bacteriological (biological) methods of warfare:

* * *

(a) It is urgent and important to reach agreement on the problem of chemical and bacteriological (biological) methods of warfare,

Convinced of the importance and urgency of eliminating from the

Resolution No. 2827 (XXVI), December 16, 1971; passed at the Twenty-Sixth Regular Session of the General Assembly.

arsenals of States, through effective measures, such dangerous weapons of mass destruction as those using chemical or bacteriological (biological) agents,

Having considered the report of the Conference of the Committee on Disarmament, in particular its work on the draft Convention on the Prohibition of the Development, Production and Stockpiling of Bacteriological (Biological) and Toxin Weapons and on Their Destruction and its efforts towards reaching early agreement also on the elimination of chemical weapons,

Convinced that the Convention on the Prohibition of the Development, Production and Stockpiling of Bacteriological (Biological) and Toxin Weapons and on Their Destruction is a first possible step toward the achievement of early agreement on the effective prohibition of the development, production and stockpiling of chemical weapons and on the elimination of such weapons from military arsenals of all States, and determined to continue negotiations to this end,

Recalling that the General Assembly has repeatedly condemned all actions contrary to the principles and objectives of the Protocol for the Prohibition of the Use in War of Asphyxiating, Poisonous or Other Gases, and of Bacteriological Methods of Warfare, signed at Geneva on 17 June 1925,

Noting that the Convention provides for the parties to reaffirm their adherence to the principles and objectives of that Protocol and to call upon all States to comply strictly with them,

1. *Notes with satisfaction* that the Convention on the Prohibition of the Development, Production and Stockpiling of Bacteriological (Biological) and Toxin Weapons and on Their Destruction contains an affirmation of the recognized objective of effective prohibition of chemical weapons and, to this end, an undertaking to continue negotiations in good faith with a view to reaching early agreement on effective measures for the prohibition of their development, production and stockpiling and for their destruction, and on appropriate measures concerning equipment and means of delivery specifically designed for the production or use of chemical agents for weapons purposes;

2. *Requests* the Conference of the Committee on Disarmament to continue, as a matter of high priority, its negotiations with a view to reaching early agreement on effective measures for the prohibition of the development, production and stockpiling of chemical weapons and for their elimination from the arsenals of all States;

3. *Also requests* the Conference of the Committee on Disarmament to take into account in its further work:

(a) The elements contained in the joint memorandum on the prohibition of the development, production and stockpiling of chemical weapons and on their destruction, submitted on 28 September 1971 to the Conference by Argentina, Brazil, Burma, Egypt, Ethiopia, India, Mexico, Morocco, Nigeria, Pakistan, Sweden and Yugoslavia;

(b) Other proposals, suggestions, working papers and expert views put forward in the Conference and in the First Committee;

4. *Urges* Governments to take all steps that may contribute to a successful outcome of the negotiations of the Conference of the Committee on Disarmament and that could facilitate early agreement on effective measures for the prohibition of the development, production and stockpiling of chemical weapons and the elimination of such weapons from the arsenals of all States;

5. *Reaffirms* its resolution 2162 B (XXI) of 5 December 1966 and calls anew for the strict observance by all States of the principles and objectives of the Protocol for the Prohibition of the Use in War of Asphyxiating, Poisonous or Other Gases, and of Bacteriological Methods of Warfare;

6. *Invites* all States that have not already done so to accede to or ratify the Protocol;

7. *Requests* the Conference of the Committee on Disarmament to submit a report on the results achieved to the General Assembly at its twenty-seventh session;

8. *Requests* the Secretary-General to transmit to the Conference of the Committee on Disarmament all documents and records of the First Committee relating to questions connected with the problem of chemical and bacteriological (biological) methods of warfare.

B

The General Assembly,

Noting that the Convention on the Prohibition of the Development, Production and Stockpiling of Bacteriological (Biological) and Toxin Weapons and on Their Destruction contains an undertaking to continue negotiations in good faith with a view to reaching early agreement on effective measures for the prohibition of the development, production and stockpiling of chemical weapons and for their destruction,

Believing that it is most desirable that some measures of a preliminary nature be adopted immediately,

Urges all States to undertake, pending agreement on the complete prohibition of the development, production and stockpiling of chemical weapons and their destruction, to refrain from any further development, production or stockpiling of those chemical agents for weapons purposes which, because of their degree of toxicity, have the highest lethal effects and are not usable for peaceful purposes.

NUCLEAR WEAPONS

⚓ TREATY BANNING NUCLEAR WEAPON TESTS IN THE ATMOSPHERE, IN OUTER SPACE AND UNDER WATER

The Governments of the United States of America, the United Kingdom of Great Britain and Northern Ireland, and the Union of Soviet Socialist Republics, . . .

Seeking to achieve the discontinuance of all test explosions of nuclear weapons for all time, determined to continue negotiations to this end, and desiring to put an end to the contamination of man's environment by radioactive substances,

Have agreed as follows:

Article I

1. Each of the Parties to this Treaty undertakes to prohibit, to prevent, and not to carry out any nuclear weapon test explosion, or any other nuclear explosion, at any place under its jurisdiction or control:

    (*a*) in the atmosphere; beyond its limits, including outer space; or underwater, including territorial waters or high seas; or

    (*b*) in any other environment if such explosion causes radioactive debris to be present outside the territorial limits of the State under whose jurisdiction or control such explosion is conducted. . . .

2. Each of the Parties to this Treaty undertakes furthermore to refrain from causing, encouraging, or in any way participating in, the carrying out of any nuclear weapon test explosion, or any other nuclear explosion, anywhere which would take place in any of the environments described, or have the effect referred to, in paragraph 1 of this Article.

❖ ❖ ❖

Article IV

This Treaty shall be of unlimited duration.

Each Party shall in exercising its national sovereignty have the right to withdraw from the Treaty if it decides that extraordinary events, related to the subject matter of this Treaty, have jeopardized the supreme interests of its country. It shall give notice of such withdrawal to all other Parties to the Treaty three months in advance.

Entered into force on October 10, 1963.

⚓ TREATY FOR THE PROHIBITION OF NUCLEAR WEAPONS IN LATIN AMERICA (Tlatelolco Treaty)

In the name of their peoples and faithfully interpreting their desires and aspirations, the Governments of the States which sign the Treaty for the Prohibition of Nuclear Weapons in Latin America,

Desiring to contribute, so far as lies in their power, towards ending the armaments race, especially in the field of nuclear weapons, and towards strengthening a world at peace, based on the sovereign equality of States, mutual respect and good neighbourliness,

Recalling that the United Nations General Assembly, in its Resolution 808 (IX), adopted unanimously as one of the three points of a coordinated programme of disarmament "the total prohibition of the use and manufacture of nuclear weapons and weapons of mass destruction of every type,"

Recalling United Nations General Assembly Resolution 1911 (XVIII), which established that the measures that should be agreed upon for the denuclearization of Latin America should be taken "in the light of the principles of the Charter of the United Nations and of regional agreements",

❄ ❄ ❄

Recalling United Nations General Assembly Resolution 2028 (XX), which established the principle of an acceptable balance of mutual responsibilities and duties for the nuclear and non-nuclear powers, and

Recalling that the Charter of the Organization of American States proclaims that it is an essential purpose of the Organization to strength the peace and security of the hemisphere,

Convinced:

That the incalculable destructive power of nuclear weapons has made it imperative that the legal prohibition of war should be strictly observed in practice if the survival of civilization and of mankind itself is to be assured,

That nuclear weapons, whose terrible effects are suffered, indiscriminately and inexorably, by military forces and civilian population alike, *constitute, through the persistence of the radioactivity they release, an*

Adopted at Mexico City on February 14, 1967.

attack on the integrity of the human species and ultimately may even render the whole earth uninhabitable [emphasis added],

* * *

Have agreed as follows:

Article 1

1. The Contracting Parties hereby undertake to use exclusively for peaceful purposes the nuclear material and facilities which are under their jurisdiction, and to prohibit and prevent in their respective territories:
 (a) The testing, use, manufacture, production or acquisition by any means whatsoever of any nuclear weapons, by the Parties themselves, directly or indirectly, on behalf of anyone else or in any other way, and
 (b) The receipt, storage, installation, deployment and any form of possession of any nuclear weapons, directly or indirectly, by the Parties themselves, by anyone on their behalf or in any other way.
2. The Contracting Parties also undertake to refrain from engaging in, encouraging or authorizing, directly or indirectly, or in any way participating in the testing, use, manufacture, production, possession or control of any nuclear weapon.

* * *

Article 7

1. In order to ensure compliance with the obligations of this Treaty, the Contracting Parties hereby establish an international organization to be known as the Agency for the Prohibition of Nuclear Weapons in Latin America, hereinafter referred to as "the Agency". Only the Contracting Parties shall be affected by its decisions.
2. The Agency shall be responsible for the holding of periodic or extraordinary consultations among Member States on matters relating to the purposes, measures and procedures set forth in this Treaty and to the supervision of compliance with the obligations arising therefrom.
3. The Contracting Parties agree to extend to the Agency full and prompt co-operation in accordance with the provisions of this Treaty, of any agreements they may conclude with the Agency and of any agreements the Agency may conclude with any other international organization or body.
4. The headquarters of the Agency shall be in Mexico City.

* * *

Article 14

1. The Contracting Parties shall submit to the Agency and to the International Atomic Energy Agency, for their information, semi-annual reports stating that no activity prohibited under this Treaty has occurred in their respective territories.

2. The Contracting Parties shall simultaneously transmit to the Agency a copy of any report they may submit to the International Atomic Energy Agency which relates to matters that are the subject of this Treaty and to the application of safeguards.

3. The Contracting Parties shall also transmit to the Organization of American States, for its information, any reports that may be of interest to it, in accordance with the obligations established by the Inter-American System.

Article 15

1. With the authorization of the Council, the General Secretary may request any of the Contracting Parties to provide the Agency with complementary or supplementary information regarding any event or circumstance connected with compliance with this Treaty, explaining his reasons. The Contracting Parties undertake to co-operate promptly and fully with the General Secretary.

2. The General Secretary shall inform the Council and Contracting Parties forthwith of such requests and of the respective replies.

*   *   *

Article 18

1. The Contracting Parties may carry out explosions of nuclear devices for peaceful purposes—including explosions which involve devices similar to those used in nuclear weapons—or collaborate with third parties for the same purpose, provided that they do so in accordance with the provisions of this article and the other articles of the Treaty, particularly articles 1 and 5.

2. Contracting Parties intending to carry out, or to co-operate in carrying out, such an explosion shall notify the Agency and the International Atomic Energy Agency, as far in advance as the circumstances require, of the date of the explosion and shall at the same time provide the following information:

(a) The nature of the nuclear device and the source from which it was obtained;

(b) The place and purpose of the planned explosion;

(c) The procedures which will be followed in order to comply with paragraph 3 of this article;

(d) The expected force of the device, and

(e) The fullest possible information on any possible radioactive fall-out that may result from the explosion or explosions, and measures which will be taken to avoid danger to the population, flora, fauna and territories of any other Party or Parties.

3. The General Secretary and the technical personnel designated by the Council and the International Atomic Energy Agency may observe all the preparations, including the explosion of the device, and shall have unrestricted access to any area in the vicinity of the site of the explosion in order to ascertain whether the device and the procedures followed during the explosion are in conformity with the information supplied under paragraph 2 of this article and the other provisions of this Treaty.

4. The Contracting Parties may accept the collaboration of third parties for the purpose set forth in paragraph 1 of the present article, in accordance with paragraphs 2 and 3 thereof.

⚓ TREATY ON THE NON-PROLIFERATION OF NUCLEAR WEAPONS

The States concluding this Treaty, hereinafter referred to as "Parties of the Treaty",

*   *   *

In conformity with resolutions of the United Nations General Assembly calling for the conclusion of an agreement on the prevention of wider dissemination of nuclear weapons,

Undertaking to co-operate in facilitating the application of International Atomic Energy Agency safeguards on peaceful nuclear activities,

Expressing their support for research, development and other efforts to further the application, within the framework of the International Atomic Energy Agency safeguards system, of the principle of safeguarding effectively the flow of source and special fissionable materials by use of instruments and other techniques at certain strategic points,

Affirming the principle that the benefits of peaceful applications of nuclear technology, including any technological by-products which may be derived by nuclear-weapon States from the development of nuclear explosive devices, should be available for peaceful purposes to all Parties to the Treaty, whether nuclear-weapon or non-nuclear-weapon States,

Entered into force on March 5, 1970.

Convinced that, in furtherance of this principle, all Parties to the Treaty are entitled to participate in the fullest possible exchange of scientific information for, and to contribute alone or in co-operation with other States to, the further development of the applications of atomic energy for peaceful purposes,

Declaring their intention to achieve at the earliest possible date the cessation of the nuclear arms race and to undertake effective measures in the direction of nuclear disarmament,

Urging the co-operation of all States in the attainment of this objective,

Recalling the determination expressed by the Parties to the 1963 Treaty banning nuclear weapon tests in the atmosphere, in outer space and under water in its preamble to seek to achieve the discontinuance of all test explosions of nuclear weapons for all time and to continue negotiations to this end,

*   *   *

Have agreed as follows:

Article I

Each nuclear-weapon State Party to the Treaty undertakes not to transfer to any recipient whatsoever nuclear weapons or other nuclear explosive devices, or control over such weapons or explosive devices, directly or indirectly; and not in any way to assist, encourage, or induce any non-nuclear-weapon State to manufacture or otherwise acquire nuclear weapons or other nuclear explosive devices, or control over such weapons or explosive devices.

Article II

Each non-nuclear-weapon State Party to the Treaty undertakes not to receive the transfer from any transferor whatsoever of nuclear weapons or other nuclear explosive devices, or of control over such weapons or explosive devices, directly or indirectly; not to manufacture or otherwise acquire nuclear weapons or other nuclear explosive devices; and not to seek or receive any assistance in the manufacture of nuclear weapons or other nuclear explosive devices.

Article III

1. Each non-nuclear-weapon State Party to the Treaty undertakes to accept safeguards, as set forth in an agreement to be negotiated and concluded with the International Atomic Energy Agency in accordance with

the Statute of the International Atomic Energy Agency and the Agency's safeguards system, for the exclusive purpose of verification of the fulfilment of its obligations assumed under this Treaty with a view to preventing diversion of nuclear energy from peaceful uses to nuclear weapons or other nuclear explosive devices. Procedures for the safeguards required by this article shall be followed with respect to source or special fissionable material whether it is being produced, processed or used in any principal nuclear facility or is outside any such facility. The safeguards required by this article shall be applied on all source or special fissionable material in all peaceful nuclear activities within the territory of such State, under its jurisdiction, or carried out under its control anywhere.

2. Each State Party to the Treaty undertakes not to provide: (a) source or special fissionable material, or (b) equipment or material especially designed or prepared for the processing, use or production of special fissionable material, to any non-nuclear-weapon State for peaceful purposes, unless the source or special fissionable material shall be subject to the safeguards required by this article.

3. The safeguards required by this article shall be implemented in a manner designed to comply with article IV of the Treaty, and to avoid hampering the economic or technological development of the parties or international co-operation in the field of peaceful nuclear activities, including the international exchange of nuclear material and equipment for the processing, use or production of nuclear material for peaceful purposes in accordance with the provisions of this article and the principle of safeguarding set forth in the preamble.

4. Non-nuclear-weapon States Party to the Treaty shall conclude agreements with the International Atomic Energy Agency to meet the requirements of this article either individually or together with other States in accordance with the Statute of the International Atomic Energy Agency. Negotiation of such agreements shall commence within 180 days from the original entry into force of this Treaty. For States depositing their instruments of ratification or accession after the 180-day period negotiation of such agreements shall commence not later than the date of such deposit. Such agreements shall enter into force not later than eighteen months after the date of initiation of negotiations.

Article IV

1. Nothing in this Treaty shall be interpreted as affecting the inalienable right of all the Parties to the Treaty to develop research, production and use of nuclear energy for peaceful purposes without discrimination and in conformity with articles I and II of this Treaty.

2. All the Parties to the Treaty undertake to facilitate, and have the right to participate in, the fullest possible exchange of equipment, materials and scientific and technological information for the peaceful uses of nuclear energy. Parties to the Treaty in a position to do so shall also cooperate in contributing alone or together with other States or international organizations to the further development of the applications of nuclear energy for peaceful purposes, especially in the territories of non-nuclear-weapon States Party to the Treaty, with due consideration for the needs of the developing areas of the world.

Article V

Each Party to this Treaty undertakes to take appropriate measures to ensure that, in accordance with this Treaty, under appropriate international observation and through appropriate international procedures, potential benefits from any peaceful applications of nuclear explosions will be made available to non-nuclear-weapon States Party to this Treaty on a non-discriminatory basis and that the charge to such Parties for the explosive devices used will be as low as possible and exclude any charge for research and development. Non-nuclear-weapon States Party to the Treaty shall be able to obtain such benefits pursuant to a special international agreement or agreements, through an appropriate international body with adequate representation of non-nuclear-weapon States. Negotiations on this subject shall commence as soon as possible after the Treaty enters into force. Non-nuclear-weapons States Party to the Treaty so desiring may also obtain such benefits pursuant to bilateral agreements.

Article VI

Each of the Parties to the Treaty undertakes to pursue negotiations in good faith on effective measures relating to cessation of the nuclear arms race at an early date and to nuclear disarmament, and on a treaty on general and complete disarmament under strict and effective international control.

Article VII

Nothing in this Treaty affects the right of any group of States to conclude regional treaties in order to assure the total absence nuclear weapons in their respective territories.

⚓ TEXT OF THE U.N. GENERAL ASSEMBLY RESOLUTION ON THE URGENT NEED FOR SUSPENSION OF NUCLEAR AND THERMONUCLEAR TESTS

A

The General Assembly,

Viewing with the utmost apprehension the harmful consequences of nuclear weapon tests for the acceleration of the arms race and for the health of present and future generations of mankind,

Fully conscious that world opinion has, over the years, demanded the immediate and complete cessation of all nuclear weapon tests in all environments,

Recalling that the item on the question of a comprehensive test ban has been included in the agenda of the General Assembly every year since 1957,

Deploring the fact that the General Assembly has not yet succeeded in its aim of achieving a comprehensive test ban, despite eighteen successive resolutions on the subject,

Noting with regret that all States have not yet adhered to the Treaty Banning Nuclear Weapon Tests in the Atmosphere, in Outer Space and under Water, signed in Moscow on 5 August 1963,

Deploring the fact that the determination expressed by the original parties to that Treaty to continue negotiations to achieve the discontinuance of all test explosions of nuclear weapons for all time has not so far produced the desired results,

Noting with special concern that the continuation of nuclear weapon tests in the atmosphere is a source of growing pollution and that the number and magnitude of underground tests have increased at an alarming rate since 1963,

Having considered the special report submitted by the Conference of the Committee on Disarmament in response to General Assembly resolution 2663 B (XXV) of 7 December 1970,

Recalling its resolution 1762 A (XVII) of 6 November 1962, whereby all nuclear weapon tests, without exception, were condemned,

Convinced that, whatever may be the differences on the question of verification, there is no valid reason for delaying the conclusion of a comprehensive test ban of the nature contemplated in the preamble to

Resolution No. 2828 (XXVI), December 16, 1971; passed at the Twenty-Sixth Regular Session of the General Assembly.

the Treaty Banning Nuclear Weapon Tests in the Atmosphere, in Outer Space and under Water,

1. *Reiterates solemnly and most emphatically* its condemnation of all nuclear weapon tests;

2. *Urges* the Governments of nuclear-weapon States to bring to a halt all nuclear weapon tests at the earliest possible date and, in any case, not later than 5 August 1973;

3. *Requests* the Secretary-General to transmit the present resolution to the nuclear-weapon States and to inform the General Assembly at its twenty-seventh session of any measures they have taken to implement it.

B

The General Assembly,

Noting that one of the first steps in the strengthening of international security is to dissipate world-wide fears that nuclear, thermonuclear and other weapons of mass destruction may be used by miscalculation in what could appear to be a desperate situation,

Considering that for the last few years the United Nations has been preoccupied with finding ways and means of diminishing the pollution of the earth's atmosphere,

Noting that scientists have been unanimous in the conclusion that the fall-out from nuclear tests is injurious to human and animal life and that such fall-out may poison the earth's atmosphere for many decades to come,

Taking into account that underground nuclear and thermonuclear tests may not only create serious health hazards but may also cause as yet undetermined injury to humans and animals of the region where such tests are conducted,

Recognizing that there already exist sufficient nuclear, thermonuclear and other lethal weapons of mass destruction in the arsenals of certain Powers to decimate the world's population and possibly render the earth uninhabitable,

1. *Appeals* to the nuclear Powers to desist from carrying out further nuclear and thermonuclear tests, whether underground, under water or in the earth's atmosphere;

2. *Urges* the nuclear Powers to reach an agreement without delay on the cessation of all nuclear and thermonuclear tests;

3. *Reassures* the peoples of the world that the United Nations will continue to raise its voice against nuclear and thermonuclear tests of any kind and earnestly requests the nuclear Powers not to deploy such weapons of mass destruction.

C

The General Assembly,

Recognizing the urgent need for the cessation of nuclear and thermo-nuclear weapon tests, including those carried out underground,

Recalling that this subject has been included in the agenda of the General Assembly every year since 1957,

* * *

Noting with regret that all States have not yet adhered to the Treaty Banning Nuclear Weapon Tests in the Atmosphere, in Outer Space and under Water, signed in Moscow on 5 August 1963, and that some continue to test in the atmosphere,

Taking into account the determination expressed by the parties to that Treaty to continue negotiations to achieve the discontinuance of all test explosions of nuclear weapons for all time,

Noting the appeal for progress on this issue, made by the Secretary-General in the introduction to his report on the work of the Organization,

Noting with special concern that nuclear weapon tests in the atmosphere and underground are continuing,

Having considered the special report submitted by the Conference of the Committee on Disarmament in response to General Assembly resolution 2663 B (XXV),

1. *Stresses anew* the urgency of bringing to a halt all nuclear weapon testing in all environments by all States;

2. *Urges* all States that have not yet done so to adhere without further delay to the Treaty Banning Nuclear Weapon Tests in the Atmosphere, in Outer Space and under Water and meanwhile to refrain from testing in the environments covered by that Treaty;

3. *Calls upon* all Governments that have been conducting nuclear weapon tests, particularly those of parties to the Treaty Banning Nuclear Weapon Tests in the Atmosphere, in Outer Space and under Water, immediately to undertake unilateral or negotiated measures of restraint that would suspend nuclear weapon testing or limit or reduce the size and number of nuclear weapon tests, pending the early entry into force of a comprehensive ban on all nuclear weapon tests in all environments by all States;

4. *Urges* Governments to take all possible measures to develop further, and to use more effectively, existing capabilities for the seismological identification of underground nuclear tests, in order to facilitate the monitoring of a comprehensive test ban;

5. *Requests* the Conference of the Committee on Disarmament to con-

tinue, as a matter of high priority, its deliberations on a treaty banning underground nuclear weapon tests, taking into account the suggestions already made in the Conference as well as the views expressed at the current session of the General Assembly;

6. *Requests particularly* Governments that have been carrying out nuclear tests to take an active and constructive part in developing in the Conference of the Committee on Disarmament, or in any successor body, specific proposals for an underground test ban treaty;

7. *Expresses the hope* that these ecorts will enable all States to sign, in the near future, a treaty banning underground nuclear weapon tests.

☀ TEXT OF THE U.N. GENERAL ASSEMBLY RESOLUTION ON STATUS OF THE TREATY FOR THE PROHIBITION OF NUCLEAR WEAPONS IN LATIN AMERICA (TREATY OF TLATELOLCO)

The General Assembly,

*   *   *

Recalling in particular that in its resolution 2286 (XXII) it declared that the Treaty for the Prohibition of Nuclear Weapons in Latin America (Treaty of Tlatelolco) constituted an event of historic significance in the efforts to prevent the proliferation of nuclear weapons and to promote international peace and security and that in its resolution 2666 (XXV) it repeated the appeals which on two previous occasions it had addressed to the nuclear-weapon States to sign and ratify Additional Protocol II of the Treaty as soon as possible and urged them to avoid further delay in the fulfilment of such appeals,

1. *Reaffirms its conviction* that, for the maximum effectiveness of any treaty establishing a nuclear-weapon-free zone, the co-operation of the nuclear-weapon States is necessary and that such co-operation should take the form of commitments likewise undertaken in a formal international instrument which is legally binding, such as a treaty, convention or protocol;

2. *Notes with satisfaction* that the United States of America deposited its instrument of ratification of Additional Protocol II of the Treaty for the Prohibition of Nuclear Weapons in Latin America on 12 May 1971, thus becoming a State party to the Protocol, as the United Kingdom of Great Britain and Northern Ireland has been since 11 December 1969;

Resolution No. 2830 (XXVI), December 16, 1971; passed at the Twenty-Sixth Regular Session of the General Assembly.

3. *Deplores* the fact that the other nuclear-weapon States have not yet heeded the urgent appeals which the General Assembly has made in three different resolutions and urges them once again to sign and ratify without further delay Additional Protocol II of the Treaty for the Prohibition of Nuclear Weapons in Latin America;

4. *Decides* to include in the provisional agenda of its twenty-seventh session an item entitled "Implementation of General Assembly resolution 2830 (XXVI) concerning the signature and ratification of Additional Protocol II of the Treaty for the Prohibition of Nuclear Weapons in Latin America (Treaty of Tlatelolco)";

5. *Requests* the Secretary-General to transmit the present resolution to the nuclear-weapon States and to inform the General Assembly at its twenty-seventh session of any measure adopted by them in order to implement it.

☝ TREATY ON THE PROHIBITION OF THE EMPLACEMENT OF NUCLEAR WEAPONS AND OTHER WEAPONS OF MASS DESTRUCTION ON THE SEA-BED AND THE OCEAN FLOOR AND IN THE SUBSOIL THEREOF

The States Parties to this Treaty,

Recognizing the common interest of mankind in the progress of the exploration and use of the sea-bed and the ocean floor for peaceful purposes,

Considering that the prevention of a nuclear arms race on the sea-bed and the ocean floor serves the interests of maintaining world peace, reduces international tensions and strengthens friendly relations among States,

Convinced that this Treaty constitutes a step towards the exclusion of the sea-bed, the ocean floor and the subsoil thereof from the arms race,

Convinced that this Treaty constitutes a step towards a treaty on general and complete disarmament under strict and effective international control, and determined to continue negotiations to this end,

Convinced that this Treaty will further the purposes and principles of the Charter of the United Nations, in a manner consistent with the principles of international law and without infringing the freedoms of the high seas,

Have agreed as follows:

Entered into force on May 18, 1972.

ARTICLE I

1. The States Parties to this Treaty undertake not to emplant or emplace on the sea-bed and the ocean floor and in the subsoil thereof beyond the outer limit of a sea-bed zone, as defined in article II, any nuclear weapons or any other types of weapons of mass destruction as well as structures, launching installations or any other facilities specifically designed for storing, testing or using such weapons.

2. The undertakings of paragraph 1 of this article shall also apply to the sea-bed zone referred to in the same paragraph, except that within such sea-bed zone, they shall not apply either to the coastal State or to the sea-bed beneath its territorial waters.

3. The States Parties to this Treaty undertake not to assist, encourage or induce any State to carry out activities referred to in paragraph 1 of this article and not to participate in any other way in such actions.

ARTICLE II

For the purpose of this Treaty, the outer limit of the sea-bed zone referred to in article I shall be coterminous with the twelve-mile outer limit of the zone referred to in part II of the Convention on the Territorial Sea and the Contiguous Zone, signed at Geneva on 29 April 1958, and shall be measured in accordance with the provisions of part I, section II, of that Convention and in accordance with international law.

ARTICLE III

1. In order to promote the objectives of and ensure compliance with the provisions of this Treaty, each State Party to the Treaty shall have the right to verify through observation the activities of other States Parties to the Treaty on the sea-bed and the ocean floor and in the subsoil thereof beyond the zone referred to in article I, provided that observation does not interefere with such activities.

2. If after such observation reasonable doubts remain concerning the fulfilment of the obligations assumed under the Treaty, the State Party having such doubts and the State Party that is responsible for the activities giving rise to the doubts shall consult with a view to removing the doubts. If the doubts persist, the State Party having such doubts shall notify the other States Parties, and the Parties concerned shall co-operate on such further procedures for verification as may be agreed, including

appropriate inspection of objects, structures, installations or other facilities that reasonably may be expected to be of a kind described in article I. The Parties in the region of the activities, including any coastal State, and any other Party so requesting, shall be entitled to participate in such consultation and co-operation. After completion of the further procedures for verification, an appropriate report shall be circulated to other Parties by the Party that initiated such procedures.

3. If the State responsible for the activities giving rise to the reasonable doubts is not identifiable by observation of the object, structure, installation or other facility, the State Party having such doubts shall notify and make appropriate inquiries of States Parties in the region of the activities and of any other State Party. If it is ascertained through these inquires that a particular State Party is responsible for the activities, that State Party shall consult and co-operate with other Parties as provided in paragraph 2 of this article. If the identity of the States responsible for the activities cannot be ascertained through these inquiries, then further verification procedures, including inspection, may be undertaken by the inquiring State Party, which shall invite the participation of the Parties in the region of the activities, including any coastal State, and of any other Party desiring to co-operate.

4. If consultation and co-operation pursuant to paragraphs 2 and 3 of this article have not removed the doubts concerning the activities and there remains a serious question concerning fulfilment of the obligations assumed under this Treaty, a State Party may, in accordance with the provisions of the Charter of the United Nations, refer the matter to the Security Council, which may take action in accordance with the Charter.

5. Verification pursuant to this article may be undertaken by any State Party using its own means, or with the full or partial assistance of any other State Party, or through appropriate international procedures within the framework of the United Nations and in accordance with its Charter.

6. Verification activities pursuant to this Treaty shall not interfere with activities of other States Parties and shall be conducted with due regard for rights recognized under international law, including the freedoms of the high seas and the rights of coastal States with respect to the exploration and exploitation of their continental shelves.

ARTICLE IV

Nothing in this Treaty shall be interpreted as supporting or prejudicing the position of any State Party with respect to existing international conventions, including the 1958 Convention on the Territorial Sea and the Contiguous Zone, or with respect to rights or claims which such State Party may assert, or with respect to recognition or non-recognition of rights or claims asserted by any other State, related to waters off its coasts, including, *inter alia,* territorial seas and contiguous zones, or to the sea-bed and the ocean floor, including continental shelves.

Suggested Reading List

Sherman, Michael E., *Nuclear Proliferation: The Treaty and After* (1968).

Brown, Frederic J., *Chemical Warfare: A Study in Restraints* (1968).

————, *The Control of Chemical and Biological Weapons* (Carnegie Endowment for International Peace, 1971).

————, *The Problem of Chemical and Biological Warfare* (Stockholm International Peace Research Institute, 1971),
vol. 3, *CBW and International Law.*
vol. 4, *Chemical and Biological Disarmament Negotiations, 1920–1970.*
vol. 5, *The Prevention of CBW.*

MacDougal, Myres S., and Schlei, Norbert, "The Hydrogen Bomb Tests in Perspective: Lawful Measures for Security," 64 *Yale L.J.* 648 (1955).

Mezerik, A. G., ed., "Atom Tests and Radiation Hazards," 7 *Int'l Rev. Service* No. 68 (1961).

Firmage, Edwin B., "The Treaty on the Non-Proliferation of Nuclear Weapons," 63 *Amer. J. Int'l L.* 711 (1969).

Gorove, Stephen, "Toward Denuclearization of the Ocean Floor," 7 *San Diego L. Rev.* 504 (1970).

Baxter, R. R., and Buergenthal, T., "Legal Aspects of the Geneva Protocol of 1925," 64 *Amer. J. Int'l L.* 853 (1970).

Quester, George H., "The Nuclear Non-Proliferation Treaty and the IAEA," 24 *Int'l Organ.* 163 (1970).

Robinson, D. R., "Treaty of Tlatelolco and the United States: A Latin American Nuclear Free Zone," 64 *Amer. J. Int'l L.* 282 (1970).

Coffey, J. I., "Nuclear Guarantees and Non-Proliferation," 25 *Int'l Organ.* 836 (1971).

(Note), "War, Genetics and the Law," 1 *Ecol. L.Q.* 795 (1971).

International Protection against Radiation Hazards

✍ STATUTE OF THE INTERNATIONAL
ATOMIC ENERGY AGENCY

ARTICLE I

Establishment of the Agency

The Parties hereto establish an International Atomic Energy Agency (hereinafter referred to as "the Agency") upon the terms and conditions hereinafter set forth.

ARTICLE II

Objectives

The Agency shall seek to accelerate and enlarge the contribution of atomic energy to peace, health and prosperity throughout the world. It shall ensure, so far as it is able, that assistance provided by it or at its request or under its supervision or control is not used in such a way as to further any military purpose.

ARTICLE III

Functions

A. The Agency is authorized:
1. To encourage and assist research on, and development and practical application of, atomic energy for peaceful uses throughout the world; and, if requested to do so, to act as an intermediary for the purposes of securing the performance of service or the supplying of materials, equipment, or facilities by one member of the Agency for another; and to perform any operation or service useful in research on, or development or practical application of, atomic energy for peaceful purposes;
2. To make provision, in accordance with this Statute, for materials, services, equipment, and facilities to meet the needs of research on, and

Signed on October 26, 1956.

development and practical application of, atomic energy for peaceful purposes, including the production of electric power, with due consideration for the needs of the under-developed areas of the world;

3. To foster the exchange of scientific and technical information on peaceful uses of atomic energy;

4. To encourage the exchange and training of scientists and experts in the field of peaceful uses of atomic energy;

5. To establish and administer safeguards designed to ensure that special fissionable and other materials, services, equipment, facilities, and information made available by the Agency or at its request or under its supervision or control are not used in such a way as to further any military purpose; and to apply safeguards, at the request of the parties, to any bilateral or multilateral arrangement, or, at the request of a State, to any of that State's activities in the field of atomic energy;

6. To establish or adopt, in consultation and, where appropriate, in collaboration with the competent organs of the United Nations and with the specialized agencies concerned, standards of safety for protection of health and minimization of danger to life and property (including such standards for labour conditions), and to provide for the application of these standards to its own operations as well as to the operations making use of materials, services, equipment, facilities, and information made available by the Agency or at its request or under its control or supervision; and to provide for the application of these standards, at the request of the parties, to operations under any bilateral or multilateral arrangement, or, at the request of a State, to any of that State's activities in the field of atomic energy;

7. To acquire or establish any facilities, plant and equipment useful in carrying out its authorized functions, whenever the facilities, plant, and equipment otherwise available to it in the area concerned are inadequate or available only on terms it deems unsatisfactory.

B. In carrying out its functions, the Agency shall:

1. Conduct its activities in accordance with the purposes and principles of the United Nations to promote peace and international cooperation, and in conformity with policies of the United Nations furthering the establishment of safeguarded world-wide disarmament and in conformity with any international agreements entered into pursuant to such policies;

2. Establish control over the use of special fissionable materials received by the Agency, in order to ensure that these materials are used only for peaceful purposes;

3. Allocate its resources in such a manner as to secure efficient utilization and the greatest possible general benefit in all areas of the world, bearing in mind the special needs of the under-developed areas of the world;

      *   *   *

ARTICLE IV

Membership

A. The initial members of the Agency shall be those States Members of the United Nations or of any of the specialized agencies which shall have signed this Statute within ninety days after it is opened for signature and shall have deposited an instrument of ratification.

B. Other members of the Agency shall be those States, whether or not Members of the United Nations or of any of the specialized agencies, which deposit an instrument of acceptance of this Statute after their membership has been approved by the General Conference upon the recommendation of the Board of Governors. In recommending and approving a State for membership, the Board of Governors and the General Conference shall determine that the State is able and willing to carry out the obligations of membership in the Agency, giving due consideration to its ability and willingness to act in accordance with the purposes and principles of the Charter of the United Nations.

C. The Agency is based on the principle of the sovereign equality of all its members, and all members, in order to ensure to all of them the rights and benefits resulting from membership, shall fulfil in good faith the obligations assumed by them in accordance with this Statute.

❄   ❄   ❄

ARTICLE XII

Agency Safeguards

A. With respect to any Agency project, or other arrangement where the Agency is requested by the parties concerned to apply safeguards, the Agency shall have the following rights and responsibilities to the extent relevant to the project or arrangement:

1. To examine the design of specialized equipment and facilities, including nuclear reactors, and to approve it only from the viewpoint of assuring that it will not further any military purpose, that it complies with applicable health and safety standards, and that it will permit effective application of the safeguards provided for in this article;

2. To require the observance of any health and safety measures prescribed by the Agency;

3. To require the maintenance and production of operating records to

assist in ensuring accountability for source and special fissionable materials used or produced in the project or arrangement;

4. To call for and receive progress reports;

5. To approve the means to be used for the chemical processing of irradiated materials solely to ensure that this chemical processing will not lend itself to diversion of materials for military purposes and will comply with applicable health and safety standards; to require that special fissionable materials recovered or produced as a by-product be used for peaceful purposes under continuing Agency safeguards for research or in reactors, existing or under construction, specified by the member or members concerned; and to require deposit with the Agency of any excess of any special fissionable materials recovered or produced as by-product over what is needed for the above-stated uses in order to prevent stockpiling of these materials, provided that thereafter at the request of the member or members concerned special fissionable materials so deposited with the Agency shall be returned promptly to the member or members concerned for use under the same provisions as stated above;

6. To send into the territory of the recipient State or States inspectors, designated by the Agency after consultation with the State or States concerned, who shall have access at all times to all places and data and to any person who by reason of his occupation deals with materials equipment, or facilities which are required by this Statute to be safeguarded, as necessary to account for source and special fissionable materials supplied and fissionable products and to determine whether there is compliance . . . with the health and safety measures referred to in sub-paragraph A-2 of this article, and with any other conditions prescribed in the agreement between the Agency and the State or States concerned. Inspectors designated by the Agency shall be accompanied by representatives of the authorities of the State concerned, if that State so requests, provided that the inspectors shall not thereby be delayed or otherwise impeded in the exercise of their functions;

7. In the event of non-compliance and failure by the recipient State or States to take requested corrective steps within a reasonable time, to suspend or terminate assistance and withdraw any materials and equipment made available by the Agency or a member in furtherance of the project.

B. The Agency shall, as necessary, establish a staff of inspectors. The staff of inspectors shall have the responsibility of examining all operations conducted by the Agency itself to determine whether the Agency is complying with the health and safety measures prescribed by it for application to projects subject to its approval, supervision or control, and whether the Agency is taking adequate measures to prevent the source and special fissionable materials in its custody or used or produced in its own operations from being used in furtherance of any military purpose. The Agency shall take remedial action forthwith to correct any non-compliance or failure to take adequate measures.

C. The staff of inspectors shall also have the responsibility of obtaining and verifying the accounting referred to in sub-paragraph A-6 of this article and of determining whether there is compliance with ... the measures referred to in sub-paragraph A-2 of this article, and with all other conditions of the project prescribed in the agreement between the Agency and the State or States concerned. The inspectors shall report any non-compliance to the Director General who shall thereupon transmit the report to the Board of Governors. The Board shall call upon the recipient State or States to remedy forthwith any non-compliance which it finds to have occurred. The Board shall report the non-compliance to all members and to the Security Council and General Assembly of the United Nations. In the event of failure of the recipient State or States to take fully corrective action within a reasonable time, the Board may take one or both of the following measures: direct curtailment or suspension of assistance being provided by the Agency or by a member, and call for the return of materials and equipment made available to the recipient member or group of members. The Agency may also, in accordance with article XIX, suspend any non-complying member from the exercise of the privileges and rights of membership.

*   *   *

ARTICLE XV

Privileges and Immunities

A. The Agency shall enjoy in the territory of each member such legal capacity and such privileges and immunities as are necessary for the exercise of its functions.

B. Delegates of members together with their alternates and advisers, Governors appointed to the Board together with their alternates and advisers, and the Director General and the staff of the Agency, shall enjoy such privileges and immunities as are necessary in the independent exercise of their functions in connexion with the Agency.

C. The legal capacity, privileges, and immunities referred to in this article shall be defined in a separate agreement or agreements between the Agency, represented for this purpose by the Director General acting under instructions of the Board of Governors, and the members.

*   *   *

ARTICLE XVII

Settlement of Disputes

A. Any question or dispute concerning the interpretation or application of this Statute which is not settled by negotiation shall be referred to the International Court of Justice in conformity with the Statute of the Court, unless the parties concerned agree on another mode of settlement.

B. The General Conference and the Board of Governors are separately empowered, subject to authorization from the General Assembly of the United Nations, to request the International Court of Justice to give an advisory opinion on any legal question arising within the scope of the Agency's activities.

* * *

ARTICLE XIX

Suspension of Privileges

* * *

B. A member which has persistently violated the provisions of this Statute or of any agreement entered into by it pursuant to this Statute amy be suspended from the exercise of the privileges and rights of membership by the General Conference acting by a two-thirds majority of the members present and voting upon recommendation by the Board of Governors.

TREATY FOR THE ESTABLISHMENT OF THE EUROPEAN ATOMIC ENERGY COMMUNITY (EURATOM)

HIS MAJESTY THE KING OF THE BELGIANS, THE PRESIDENT OF THE FEDERAL REPUBLIC OF GERMANY, THE PRESIDENT OF THE FRENCH REPUBLIC, THE PRESIDENT OF THE ITALIAN REPUBLIC, HER ROYAL HIGHNESS THE GRAND DUCHESS OF LUXEMBOURG, HER MAJESTY THE QUEEN OF THE NETHERLANDS,

REALISING that nuclear energy constitutes the essential resource for ensuring the expansion and invigoration of production and for effecting progress in peaceful achievement,

Executed at Rome on March 25, 1957.

CONVINCED that only a common effort undertaken without delay can lead to achievements commensurate with the creative capacities of their countries,

RESOLVED to create the conditions required for the development of a powerful nuclear industry which will provide extensive supplies of energy, lead to the modernisation of technical processes and in addition have many other applications contributing to the well-being of their peoples,

ANXIOUS to establish conditions of safety which will eliminate danger to the life and health of the people,

DESIROUS of associating other countries with them in their work and of co-operating with international organisations concerned with the peaceful development of atomic energy,

HAVE DECIDED to establish a European Atomic Energy Community (EURATOM)....

❋ ❋ ❋

Article 1

By the present Treaty, the HIGH CONTRACTING PARTIES establish among themselves a EUROPEAN ATOMIC ENERGY COMMUNITY (EURATOM).

It shall be the aim of the Community to contribute to the raising of the standard of living in Member States and to the development of commercial exchanges with other countries by the creation of conditions necessary for the speedy establishment and growth of nuclear industries.

Article 2

For the attainment of its aims the Community shall, in accordance with the provisions set out in this Treaty:

(a) develop research and ensure the dissemination of technical knowledge,

(b) establish, and ensure the application of, uniform safety standards to protect the health of workers and of the general public,

(c) facilitate investment and ensure, particularly by encouraging business enterprise, the construction of the basic facilities required for the development of nuclear energy within the Community,

(d) ensure a regular and equitable supply of ores and nuclear fuels to all users in the Community,

(e) guarantee, by appropriate measures of control, that nuclear materials are not diverted for purposes other than those for which they are intended, ...

Article 3

1. The achievement of the tasks entrusted to the Community shall be ensured by:

—an ASSEMBLY,
—a COUNCIL,
—a COMMISSION,
—a COURT OF JUSTICE.

Each of these institutions shall act within the limits of the powers conferred upon it by this Treaty.

2. The Council and the Commission shall be assisted by an Economic and Social Committee acting in a consultative capacity.

* * *

Article 8

1. The Commission shall... set up a Joint Nuclear Research Centre.
    The Centre shall ensure the implementation of the research programmes and of any other tasks entrusted to it by the Commission.
    The Centre shall also ensure the establishment of uniform nuclear terminology and of a standard system of measurements.
    It shall organise a central bureau of nuclear measurements.

2. The work of the Centre may, for geographical or operational reasons, be carried on in separate establishments.

Article 9

1. ... [T]he Commission may, within the framework of the Joint Nuclear Research Centre, set up schools for training specialists, particularly in prospecting for ores, producing nuclear materials of a high degree of purity, processing irradiated fuels, in atomic engineering, health protection and the production and use of radioactive isotopes.

    The Commission shall settle the particulars of instruction.

2. An institution at university level shall be set up; the particulars of its operation shall be settled by the Council acting by means of a qualified majority vote on a proposal of the Commission.

* * *

Article 30

Basic standards for the protection of the health of workers and of the general public from the dangers arising from ionising radiation shall be established within the Community.

The term "basic standards" shall mean:

(a) the maximum doses compatible with adequate safety;
(b) the maximum permissible degree of exposure and contamination; and
(c) the fundamental principles governing the medical supervision of workers.

Article 31

The Commission shall work out the basic standards after obtaining the opinion of a group of authorities appointed by the Scientific and Technical Committee from among the scientific experts, especially public health experts, of the Member States. The Commission shall request the opinion of the Economic and Social Committee on the basic standards thus worked out.

After consulting the Assembly, the Council, acting by means of a qualified majority vote on a proposal of the Commission which shall transmit to it the opinions received from the Committees, shall determine the basic standards.

Article 32

At the request of the Commission or of a Member State, the basic standards may be revised or supplemented according to the procedure laid down in Article 31.

The Commission shall be bound to examine any such request made by a Member State.

Article 33

Each Member State shall enact the legislative and administrative provisions required to ensure compliance with the basic standards so determined and shall take the necessary measures with regard to instruction, education and professional training.

The Commission shall make recommendations in order to ensure the harmonisation of the provisions applicable in Member States in this respect.

For this purpose, Member States shall communicate to the Commission all such provisions applicable at the time of the entry into force of this Treaty and any subsequent draft provisions of the same nature.

Any recommendations by the Commission in respect of such draft provisions shall be made within a period of three months after the date of such communication.

Article 34

Any Member State in whose territories experiments of a particularly dangerous nature are to take place shall take additional health precautions, concerning which it shall first obtain the opinion of the Commission.

The consenting opinion of the Commission shall be required when such experiments are likely to affect the territories of other Member States.

Article 35

Each Member State shall set up the facilities necessary for the permanent control of the level of radioactivity in the atmosphere, water and soil and for controlling compliance with the basic standards.

The Commission shall have right of access to such control facilities; it may examine their operation and efficiency.

Article 36

The competent authorities shall, in order that the Commission may be kept informed of the level of radioactivity likely to affect the population, report regularly to the Commission on the control provided for in Article 35.

Article 37

Each Member State shall submit to the Commission such general data concerning any plan for the disposal of any kind of radioactive waste as will enable the Commission to determine whether the implementation of such plan is likely to involve radioactive contamination of the water, soil or airspace of another Member State.

The Commission, after consulting the group of experts referred to in Article 31, shall give its opinion thereon within a period of six months.

Article 38

The Commission shall make recommendations to Member States regarding the level of radioactivity in the atmosphere, water or soil.

The Commission shall, in case of urgency, issue a directive requiring the Member State concerned to take, within a period fixed by the Commission, all measures necessary to prevent the basic standards from being exceeded and to ensure observance of any applicable provisions.

If such State does not comply with the Commission's directive within the prescribed period, the Commission or any Member State concerned may, notwithstanding the provisions of Articles 141 and 142 [not reproduced here], refer the matter to the Court of Justice immediately.

Article 39

The Commission shall establish within the Joint Nuclear Research Centre, as soon as the latter has been set up, a Section for documentation on, and the study of, health protection.

It shall be the particular task of this Section to collect the documentation and information required under Articles 33, 37 and 38, and to assist the Commission in carrying out the duties imposed upon it by the provisions of this Chapter [Articles 30–39].

*　*　*

Article 77

Within the framework of this Chapter [Articles 77–85], the Commission shall satisfy itself that in the territories of Member States:

(a) ores, source materials and special fissionable materials are not diverted from their intended uses as stated by the users; and

(b) the provisions concerning supplies and any special undertaking concerning measures of control entered into by the Community in an agreement concluded with a third country or an international organisation are observed.

*　*　*

Article 81

The Commission may send inspectors into the territories of Member States. It shall, prior to the first visit of an inspector to the territories of any State, enter into consultations, which shall cover all future visits of this inspector, with the Member State concerned.

On presentation of their credentials, inspectors shall at all times have access to all places and data and to any person who by reason of his occupation deals with materials, equipment or facilities subject to the control provided for in this Chapter, to the extent necessary to control ores, source materials and special fissionable material, and to satisfy themselves concerning the observance of Article 77. Inspectors appointed by the Commission shall be accompanied by representatives of the authorities of the State concerned, if that State so requests, provided that the inspectors shall not thereby be delayed or otherwise impeded in the exercise of their functions.

In case of opposition to the carrying out of an inspection, the Commission shall apply to the President of the Court of Justice for a warrant to enforce the carrying out of an inspection. The President of the Court of Justice shall give a decision within a period of three days.

If there is danger in delay, the Commission may itself issue a written order, in the form of a decision, to the effect that the inspection be carried out. Such order shall be submitted without delay to the President of the Court of Justice for subsequent approval.

After service of the warrant or decision, the national authorities of the State concerned shall ensure access by the inspectors to the places named in the warrant or decision.

*   *   *

Article 83

1. In the event of any infringement of the obligations imposed on persons or enterprises under the provisions of this Chapter [Articles 77–85], penalties may be imposed on them by the Commission.

These penalties, in order of gravity, shall be as follows:

(a) a warning;
(b) the withdrawal of special advantages, such as financial or technical assistance;
(c) the placing of the enterprise, for a maximum period of four months, under the administration of a person or board apointed jointly by the Commission and the State having jurisdiction over such enterprise; or
(d) the complete or partial withdrawal of source materials or special fissionable materials.

2. ... The protection of injured interests shall be guaranteed by an appropriate legal procedure.

3. The Commission may make any recommendations to Member States concerning legislative provisions designed to ensure the observance in their territories of the obligations resulting from the provisions of this Chapter.

4. Member States shall ensure the enforcement of penalties and, where applicable, the making of reparation by those responsible for any infringement.

*   *   *

Article 101

The Community may, within the limits of its competence, enter into obligations by means of the conclusion of agreements or conventions with a third country, an international organisation or a national of a third country.

Such agreements or conventions shall be negotiated by the Commission in accordance with directives issued by the Council and shall be concluded by the Commission with the approval of the Council acting by means of a qualified majority vote.

Agreements or conventions the implementation of which does not require action by the Council and can be effected within the limits of the appropriate budget shall, however, be negotiated and concluded by the Commission, provided that it keeps the Council informed thereof.

❋ ❋ ❋

Article 184

The Community shall have legal personality.

Article 185

The Community shall in each of the Member States possess the most extensive legal capacity accorded to legal persons under their respective municipal law; it may, in particular, acquire or transfer movable and immovable property and may sue and be sued in its own name. For this purpose, the Community shall be represented by the Commission.

❋ ❋ ❋

Article 188

The contractual liability of the Community shall be governed by the law applying to the contract concerned.

As regards non-contractual liability, the Community shall in accordance with the general principles common to the laws of Member States make reparation for any damage caused by its institutions or by its employees in the performance of their duties.

The personal liability of employees towards the Community shall be determined in the provisions establishing the statute of service or the conditions of employment applicable to them.

❋ ❋ ❋

Article 191

The Community shall, under conditions defined in a separate Protocol, enjoy in the territories of the Member States the privileges and immunities necessary for the achievement of its aims.

Article 192

Member States shall take all general or particular measures which are appropriate for ensuring the carrying out of the obligations arising out of this Treaty or resulting from acts of the institutions of the Community. They shall facilitate the achievement of the aims of the Community.

They shall abstain from any measures likely to jeopardise the achievement of the aims of this Treaty.

Article 193

Member States undertake not to submit a dispute concerning the interpretation or application of this Treaty to any method of settlement other than those provided for in this Treaty.

❖ ❖ ❖

Article 195

The institutions of the Community, as well as the Agency and Joint Enterprises shall, in applying this Treaty, comply with any conditions, in regard to access to ores, source materials and special fissionable materials, imposed by domestic provisions enacted for reasons of public order or public health.

✠ AGREEMENT CONCERNING THE HIGH-TEMPERATURE GAS-COOLED REACTOR PROJECT "DRAGON"

The United Kingdom Atomic Energy Authority, the Republic of Austria represented by the Federal Chancellery, the Danish Atomic Energy Commission, the Commission of the European Atomic Energy Community (EURATOM), Institutt for Atomenergi, Norway, Aktiebolaget Atomenergi in Stockholm, and the Government of the Swiss Confederation (hereinafter referred to as the "Signatories");

❖ ❖ ❖

CONSIDERING that the Signatories have decided in order to avoid the creation of a new legal personality that the legal acts relating to the carrying out of this work should be performed on their behalf by the United Kingdom Atomic Energy Authority (hereinafter referred to as the "Authority");

HAVE AGREED as follows:

Signed in Paris on March 23, 1959.

Article 1

* * *

(b) All legal acts relating to the carrying out of the joint programme shall be performed on behalf of the Signatories by the Authority which will be the owner of any experimental reactor which may be built in the United Kingdom, and the operation of any such reactor shall be carried out under the supervision and responsibility, subject to this Agreement, of the Authority and in accordance with the relevant laws, regulations and safety requirements of the United Kingdom.

* * *

Article 5

* * *

(d) The Authority shall be solely liable in respect of all actions, claims costs and expenses whatsoever arising out of the construction and operation of any experimental reactor which may be built in the United Kingdom or installations ancillary thereto, and shall indemnify the other Signatories in respect of any such actions, claims, costs and expenses which may involve the other Signatories.

CONVENTION CONCERNING THE PROTECTION OF WORKERS AGAINST IONISING RADIATIONS

The General Conference of the International Labour Organisation,

* * *

Having decided upon the adoption of certain proposals with regard to the protection of workers against ionising radiations, which is the fourth item on the agenda of the session, and

Having determined that these proposals shall take the form of an international Convention,

adopts this twenty-second day of June of the year one thousand nine hundred and sixty the following Convention, which may be cited as the Radiation Protection Convention, 1960:

PART I. GENERAL PROVISIONS

Article 1

Each Member of the International Labour Organisation which ratifies this Convention undertakes to give effect thereto by means of laws or

Adopted by the General Conference of the International Labour Organisation at its Forty-Fourth Session, Geneva, June 22, 1960; came into force on June 17, 1962.

regulations, codes of practice or other appropriate means. In applying the provisions of the Convention the competent authority shall consult with representatives of employers and workers.

Article 2

1. This Convention applies to all activities involving exposure of workers to ionising radiations in the course of their work.

2. This Convention does not apply to radioactive substances, whether sealed or unsealed, nor to apparatus generating ionising radiations which substances or aparatus, owing to the limited doses of ionising radiations which can be received from them, are exempted from its provisions by one of the methods of giving effect to the Convention mentioned in Article 1.

Article 3

1. In the light of knowledge available at the time, all appropriate steps shall be taken to ensure effective protection of workers, as regards their health and safety, against ionising radiations.

2. Rules and measures necessary for this purpose shall be adopted and data essential for effective protection shall be made available.

3. With a view to ensuring such effective protection,

(a) measures for the protection of workers against ionising radiations adopted after ratification of the Convention by the Member concerned shall comply with the provisions thereof;

(b) the Member concerned shall modify, as soon as practicable, measures adopted by it prior to the ratification of the Convention, so as to comply with the provisions thereof, and shall promote such modification of other measures existing at the time of ratification;

(c) the Member concerned shall communicate to the Director-General of the International Labour Office, when ratifying the Convention, a statement indicating the manner in which and the categories of workers to which the provisions of the Convention are applied, and shall indicate in its reports on the application of the Convention any further progress made in the matter;

(d) at the expiration of three years from the date on which this Convention first enters into force the Governing Body of the International Labour Office shall submit to the Conference a special report concerning the application of subparagraph (b) of this paragraph and containing such proposals as it may think appropriate for further action in regard to the matter.

PART II. PROTECTIVE MEASURES

Article 4

The activities referred to in Article 2 shall be so arranged and conducted as to afford the protection envisaged in this Part of the Convention.

Article 5

Every effort shall be made to restrict the exposure of workers to ionising radiations to the lowest practicable level, and any unnecessary exposure shall be avoided by all parties concerned.

Article 6

1. Maximum permissible doses of ionising radiations which may be received from sources external to or internal to the body and maximum permissible amounts of radioactive substances which can be taken into the body shall be fixed in accordance with Part I of this Convention for various categories of workers.

2. Such maximum permissible doses and amounts shall be kept under constant review in the light of current knowledge.

Article 7

1. Appropriate levels shall be fixed in accordance with Article 6 for workers who are directly engaged in radiation work and are
   (a) aged 18 and over;
   (b) under the age of 18.

2. No worker under the age of 16 shall be engaged in work involving ionising radiations.

Article 8

Appropriate levels shall be fixed in accordance with Article 6 for workers who are not directly engaged in radiation work, but who remain or pass where they may be exposed to ionising radiations or radioactive substances.

Article 9

1. Appropriate warnings shall be used to indicate the presence of hazards from ionising radiations. Any information necessary in this connection shall be supplied to the workers.

2. All workers directly engaged in radiation work shall be adequately instructed, before and during such employment, in the precautions to be taken for their protection, as regards their health and safety, and the reasons therefor.

Article 10

Laws or regulations shall require the notification in a manner prescribed thereby of work involving exposure of workers to ionising radiations in the course of their work.

Article 11

Appropriate monitoring of workers and places of work shall be carried out in order to measure the exposure of workers to ionising radiations and radioactive substances, with a view to ascertaining that the applicable levels are respected.

Article 12

All workers directly engaged in radiation work shall undergo an appropriate medical examination pri r to or shortly after taking up such work and subsequently undergo further medical examinations at appropriate intervals.

Article 13

Circumstances shall be specified, by one of the methods of giving effect to the Convention mentioned in Article 1, in which, because of the nature or degree of the exposure or a combination of both, the following action shall be taken promptly:
  (a) the worker shall undergo an appropriate medical examination;
  (b) the employer shall notify the competent authority in accordance with its requirements;
  (c) persons competent in radiation protection shall examine the conditions in which the worker's duties are performed;
  (d) the employer shall take any necessary remedial action on the basis of the technical findings and the medical advice.

Article 14

No worker shall be employed or shall continue to be employed in work by reason of which the worker could be subject to exposure to ionising radiations contrary to qualified medical advice.

Article 15

Each Member which ratifies this Convention undertakes to provide appropriate inspection services for the purpose of supervising the application of its provisions, or to satisfy itself that appropriate inspection is carried out.

⚘ PARIS CONVENTION ON THIRD PARTY LIABILITY IN THE FIELD OF NUCLEAR ENERGY

THE GOVERNMENTS of the Federal Republic of Germany, the Republic of Austria, the Kingdom of Belgium, the Kingdom of Denmark, Spain, the French Republic, the Kingdom of Greece, the Italian Republic, the Grand Duchy of Luxembourg, the Kingdom of Norway, the Kingdom of the Netherlands, the Portuguese Republic, the United Kingdom of Great Britain and Northern Ireland, the Kingdom of Sweden, the Swiss Confederation and the Turkish Republic;

CONSIDERING that the European Nuclear Energy Agency, established within the framework of the Organisation for European Economic Cooperation (hereinafter referred to as the "Organisation"), is charged with encouraging the elaboration and harmonization of legislation relating to nuclear energy in participating countries, in particular with regard to third party liability and insurance against atomic risks;

DESIROUS of ensuring adequate and equitable compensation for persons who suffer damage caused by nuclear incidents whilst taking the necessary steps to ensure that the development of the production and uses of nuclear energy for peaceful purposes is not thereby hindered;

CONVINCED of the need for unifying the basic rules applying in the various countries to the liability incurred for such damage, whilst leaving these countries free to take, on a national basis, any additional measures which they deem appropriate, including the application of the provisions of this Convention to damage caused by nuclear incidents not covered therein;

HAVE AGREED as follows:

ARTICLE 1

a) For the purposes of this Convention:
   (*i*) "A nuclear incident" means any occurence or succession of occurrences having the same origin which causes damage, provided that such occurrence or succession of occurrences, or any

Adopted at Paris on July 29, 1960.

of the damage caused, arises out of or results from the radio-active properties, or a combination of radioactive properties with toxic, explosive, or other hazardous properties of nuclear fuel or radioactive products or waste or with any of them.

(*ii*) "Nuclear installation" means reactors other than those comprised in any means of transport; factories for the manufacture or processing of nuclear substances; factories for the separation of isotopes of nuclear fuel; factories for the reprocessing of irradiated nuclear fuel; facilities for the storage of nuclear substances other than storage incidental to the carriage of such substances; and such other installations in which there are nuclear fuel or radioactive products or waste as the Steering Committee of the European Nuclear Energy Agency (hereinafter referred to as the "Steering Committee") shall from time to time determine.

(*iii*) "Nuclear fuel" means fissionable material in the form of uranium metal, alloy, or chemical compound (including natural uranium), plutonium metal, alloy, or chemical compound, and such other fissionable material as the Steering Committee shall from time to time determine.

(*iv*) "Radioactive products or waste" means any radioactive material produced in or made radioactive by exposure to the radiation incidental to the process of producing or utilizing nuclear fuel, but does not include 1. nuclear fuel, or 2. radioisotopes outside a nuclear installation which are used or intended to be used for any industrial, commercial, agricultural, medical or scientific purpose.

(*v*) "Nuclear substances" means nuclear fuel (other than natural uranium and other than depleted uranium) and radioactive products or waste.

(*vi*) "Operator" in relation to a nuclear installation means the person designated or recognised by the competent public authority as the operator of that installation.

b) The Steering Committee may, if in its view the small extent of the risks involved so warrants, exclude any nuclear installation, nuclear fuel, or nuclear substances from the application of this Convention.

Article 2

This Convention does not apply to nuclear incidents occurring in the territory of non-Contracting States or to damage suffered in such territory, unless national legislation otherwise provides and except in regard to rights of recourse referred to in Article 6 *d*).

ARTICLE 3

The operator of a nuclear installation shall be liable, in accordance with this Convention, for:

a) damage to or loss of life of any person; and

b) damage to or loss of any property other than

> (*i*) property held by the operator or in his custody or under his control in connection with, and at the site of, such installation, and
>
> (*ii*) in the cases within Article 4, the means of transport upon which the nuclear substances involved were at the time of the nuclear incident, upon proof that such damage or loss (hereinafter referred to as "damage") was caused by a nuclear incident involving either nuclear fuel or radioactive products or waste in, or nuclear substances coming from, such installation, except as otherwise provided for in Article 4.

ARTICLE 4

In the case of carriage of nuclear substances, including storage incidental thereto, without prejudice to Article 2:

a) The operator of a nuclear installation shall be liable, in accordance with this Convention, for damage upon proof that it was caused by a nuclear incident outside that installation and involving nuclear substances in the course of carriage therefrom, only if the incident occurs

> (*i*) before the nuclear substances involved have been taken in charge by another operator of a nuclear installation situated in the territory of a Contracting Party; or
>
> (*ii*) before the nuclear substances involved have been unloaded from the means of transport by which they have arrived in the territory of a non-Contracting State, if they are consigned to a person within the territory of that State.

b) The operator referred to in paragraph *a*) (*i*) of this Article shall, from his taking charge of the nuclear substances, be the operator liable in accordance with this Convention for damage caused by a nuclear incident occurring thereafter and involving the nuclear substances.

c) Where nuclear substances are sent from outside the territory of the Contracting Parties to a nuclear installation situated in such territory, with the approval of the operator of that installation, he shall be liable, in accordance with this Convention, for damage caused by a nuclear incident occurring after the nuclear substances involved have been loaded on the means of transport by which they are to be carried from the territory of the non-Contracting State.

d) The operator liable in accordance with this Convention shall provide the carrier with a certificate issued by or on behalf of the insurer or other financial guarantor furnishing the security required pursuant to Article 10. The certificate shall state the name and address of that operator and the amount, type and duration of the security, and these statements may not be disputed by the person by whom or on whose behalf the certificate was issued. The certificate shall also indicate the nuclear substances and the carriage in respect of which the security applies and shall include a statement by the competent public authority that the person named is an operator within the meaning of this Convention.

e) A Contracting Party may provide by legislation that, under such terms as may be contained therein and upon fulfilment of the requirements of Article 10 *a*), a carrier may, at his request and with the consent of an operator of a nuclear installation situated in its territory, by decision of the competent public authority, be liable in accordance with this Convention in place of that operator. In such case for all the purposes of this Convention the carrier shall be considered, in respect of nuclear incidents occurring in the course of carriage of nuclear substances, as an operator of a nuclear installation on the territory of the Contracting Party whose legislation so provides.

ARTICLE 5

a) If the nuclear fuel or radioactive products or waste involved in a nuclear incident have been in more than one nuclear installation and are in a nuclear installation at the time damage is caused, no operator of any nuclear installation in which they have previously been shall be liable for the damage. If the nuclear fuel or radioactive products or waste involved in a nuclear incident have been in more than one nuclear installation and are not in a nuclear installation at the time damage is caused, no person other than the operator of the last nuclear installation in which they were before the damage was caused or an operator who has subsequently taken them in charge shall be liable for the damage.

b) If damage gives rise to liability of more than one operator in accordance with this Convention, the liability of those operators shall be joint and several: provided that where such liability arises as a result of damage caused by a nuclear incident involving nuclear substances in the course of carriage, the maximum total amount for which such operators shall be liable shall be the highest amount established with respect to any of them pursuant to Article 7 and provided that in no case shall any one operator be required, in respect of a nuclear incident, to pay more than the amount established with respect to him pursuant to Article 7.

ARTICLE 6

a) The right to compensation for damage caused by a nuclear incident may be exercised only against an operator liable for the damage in accordance with this Convention, or, if a direct right of action against the insurer or other financial guarantor furnishing the security required pursuant to Article 10 is given by national law, against the insurer or other financial guarantor.

b) No other person shall be liable for damage caused by a nuclear incident, but this provision shall not affect the application of any international agreement in the field of transport in force or open for signature, ratification or accession at the date of this Convention.

c) Any person who is liable for damage caused by a nuclear incident under any international agreement referred to in paragraph *b*) of this Article or under any legislation of a non-Contracting State shall have a right of recourse, within the limitation of the amount of liability established pursuant to Article 7, against the operator liable for that damage in accordance with this Convention.

d) Where a nuclear incident occurs in the territory of a non-Contracting State or damage is suffered in such territory, any person who has his principal place of business in the territory of a Contracting Party or who is the servant of such a person shall have a right of recourse for any sums which he is liable to pay in respect of such incident or damage, within the limitation of liability established pursuant to Article 7, against the operator, who, but for the provisions of Article 2, would have been liable.

e) The Council of the Organisation may decide that carriers whose principal place of business is in the territory of a non-Contracting State should benefit from the provisions of paragraph *d*) of this Article. In taking its decision, the Council shall give due consideration to the general provisions on third party liability in the field of nuclear energy in such non-Contracting State and the extent to which these provisions are available to the benefit of nationals of, and persons whose principal place of business is in the territory of, the Contracting Parties.

f) The operator shall have a right of recourse only
   (*i*) if the damage caused by a nuclear incident results from an act or omission done with intent to cause damage, against the individual acting or omitting to act with such intent;
   (*ii*) if and to the extent that it is so provided expressly by contract;
   (*iii*) if and to the extent that he is liable pursuant to Article 7 *e*) for an amount over and above that established with respect to him pursuant to Article 7 *b*), in respect of a nuclear incident occurring in the course of transit of nuclear substances carried out without his consent, against the carrier of the nuclear sub-

stances, except where such transit is for the purpose of saving or attempting to save life or property or is caused by circumstances beyond the control of such carrier.

g) If the operator has a right of recourse to any extent pursuant to paragraph *f*) of this Article against any person, that person shall not, to that extent, have a right of recourse against the operator under paragraphs *c*) and *d*) of this Article.

h) Where provisions of national health insurance, social security, workmen's compensation or occupational disease compensation systems include compensation for damage caused by a nuclear incident, rights of beneficiaries of such systems and rights of recourse by virtue of such systems shall be determined by the law of the Contracting Party having established such systems.

ARTICLE 7

a) The aggregate of compensation required to be paid in respect of damage caused by a nuclear incident shall not exceed the maximum liability established in accordance with this Article,

b) The maximum liability of the operator in respect of damage caused by a nuclear incident shall be 15,000,000 European Monetary Agreement units of account as defined at the date of this Convention (hereinafter referred to as "units of account"): provided that any Contracting Party, taking into account the possibilities for the operator of obtaining the insurance or other financial security required pursuant to Article 10, may establish by legislation a greater or less amount, but in no event less than 5,000,000 units of account. The sums mentioned above may be converted into national currency in round figures.

c) Any Contracting Party may by legislation provide that the exception in Article 3 *b*) (*ii*) shall not apply; provided that, in no case, shall the inclusion of damage to the means of transport result in reducing the liability of the operator in respect of other damage to an amount less than 5,000,000 units of account.

d) The amount of the liability of operators of nuclear installations in the territory of a Contracting Party established in accordance with paragraph *b*) of this Article, as well as the provisions of any legislation of a Contracting Party pursuant to paragraph *c*) of this Article, shall apply to the liability of such operators wherever the nuclear incident occurs.

e) A Contracting Party may subject the transit of nuclear substances through its territory to the condition that the maximum amount of liability of the foreign operator concerned be increased, if it considers that such amount does not adequately cover the risks of a nuclear incident in the course of the transit: provided that the maximum amount thus increased shall not exceed the maximum amount of liability of operators of nuclear installations situated in its territory.

f) The provisions of paragraph *e*) of this Article shall not apply

(*i*) to carriage by sea where, under international law, there is a right of entry in cases of urgent distress into the ports of such Contracting Party or a right of innocent passage through its territory; or

(*ii*) to carriage by air where, by agreement or under international law, there is a right to fly over or land on the territory of such Contracting Party.

g) Any interest and costs awarded by a court in actions for compensation under this Convention shall not be considered to be compensation for the purposes of this Convention and shall be payable by the operator in addition to any sum for which he is liable in accordance with this Article.

Article 8

a) The right of compensation under this Convention shall be extinguished if an action is not brought within ten years from the date of the nuclear incident. In the case of damage caused by a nuclear incident involving nuclear fuel or radioactive products or waste which, at the time of the incident, have been stolen, lost, or abandoned and have not yet been recovered, the period for the extinction of the right shall be ten years from the date of the theft, loss, or abandonment. National legislation may, however, establish a period of not less than two years for the extinction of the right or as a period of limitation either from the date at which the person suffering damage has knowledge or from the date at which he ought reasonably to have known of both the damage and the operator liable: provided that the period of ten years shall not be exceeded except in accordance with paragraph *c*) of this Article.

b) Where the provisions of Article 13 *d*) (*i*) 2, or (*ii*) are applicable, the right of compensation shall not, however, be extinguished if, within the time provided for in paragraph *a*) of this Article,

(*i*) prior to the determination by the Tribunal referred to in Article 17, an action has been brought before any of the courts from which the Tribunal can choose; if the Tribunal determines that the competent court is a court other than that before which such action has already been brought, it may fix a date by which such action has to be brought before the competent court so determined; or

(*ii*) a request has been made to a Contracting Party to initiate a determination by the Tribunal of the competent court pursuant to Article 13 *d*) (*i*) 2, or (*ii*) and an action is brought subsequent to such determination within such time as may be fixed by the Tribunal.

c) National legislation may establish a period longer than ten years if measures have been taken to cover the liability of the operator in respect of any actions for compensation begun after the expiry of the period of ten years.

d) Unless national law provides to the contrary, any person suffering damage caused by a nuclear incident who has brought an action for compensation within the period provided for in this Article may amend his claim in respect of any aggravation of the damage after the expiry of such period provided that final judgment has not been entered by the competent court.

ARTICLE 9

Except in so far as national legislation may provide to the contrary, the operator shall not be liable for damage caused by a nuclear incident due to an act of armed conflict, invasion, civil war, insurrection, or a grave natural disaster of an exceptional character.

ARTICLE 10

a) To cover the liability under this Convention, the operator shall be required to have and maintain insurance or other financial security of the amount established pursuant to Article 7 and of such type and terms as the competent public authority shall specify.

b) No insurer or other financial guarantor shall suspend or cancel the insurance or other financial security provided for in paragraph *a*) of this Article without giving notice in writng of at least two months to the competent publc authority or in so far as such insurance or other financial security relates to the carriage of nuclear substances, during the period of the carriage in question.

c) The sums provided as insurance, reinsurance, or other financial security may be drawn upon only for compensation for damage caused by a nuclear incident.

ARTICLE 11

The nature, form and extent of the compensation, within the limits of this Convention, as well as the equitable distribution thereof, shall be governed by national law.

❈   ❈   ❈

ARTICLE 13

a) Jurisdiction over actions under Article 3, 6 *a*), 6 *c*) and 6 *d*) shall lie only with the courts competent in accordance with the legislation of the Contracting Party in whose territory the nuclear installation of the operator liable is situated.

b) In the case of a nuclear incident occurring in the course of carriage, jurisdiction shall, except as otherwise provided in paragraph *c*) of this Article, lie only with the courts competent in accordance with the legislation of the Contracting Party in whose territory the nuclear substances involved were at the time of the nuclear incident.

c) If a nuclear incident occurs outside the territory of the Contracting Parties in the course of carriage, or if the place where the nuclear substances involved were at the time of the nuclear incident cannot be determined, or if the nuclear substances involved were in territory under the jurisdiction of more than one Contracting Party at the time of the nuclear incident, jurisdiction shall lie only with the courts competent in accordance with the legislation of the Contracting Party in whose territory the nuclear installation of the operator liable is situated.

d) Where jurisdiction would lie with the courts of more than one Contracting Party by virtue of paragraphs *a*) or *c*) of this Article, jurisdiction shall lie,

> (*i*) in the case of a nuclear incident occurring in the course of carriage of nuclear substances,
>> 1. with the courts competent in accordance with the legislation of the Contracting Party at the place in its territory where the means of transport upon which the nuclear substances involved were at the time of the nuclear incident is registered, provided that they are competent under paragraph *c*) of this Article; or
>> 2. if there is no such court, with that one of the courts which is competent under paragraph *c*) of this Article, determined, at the request of a Contracting Party concerned, by the Tribunal referred to in Article 17 as being the most closely related to the case in question;
> (*ii*) in any other case, with the courts competent in accordance with the legislation of the Contracting Party determined, at the request of a Contracting Party concerned, by the said Tribunal as being the most closely related to the case in question,

e) Judgments entered by the competent court under this Article after trial, or by default, shall, when they have become enforceable under the law applied by that court, become enforceable in the territory of any of the other Contracting Parties as soon as the formalities required by the Contracting Party concerned have been complied with. The merits of the case shall not be the subject of further proceedings. The foregoing provisions shall not apply to interim judgments.

f) If an action is brought against a Contracting Party as an operator liable under this Convention, such Contracting Party may not invoke any jurisdictional immunities before the court competent in accordance with this Article.

ARTICLE 14

a) This Convention shall be applied without any discrimination based upon nationality, domicile, or residence.

b) "National law" and "national legislation" mean the national law or the national legislation of the court having jurisdiction under this Convention over claims arising out of a nuclear incident, and that law or legislation shall apply to all matters both substantive and procedural not specifically governed by this Convention.

c) That law and legislation shall be applied without any discrimination based upon nationality, domicile, or residence.

* * *

ARTICLE 17

Any dispute arising between two or more Contracting Parties concerning the interpretation or application of this Convention shall be examined by the Steering Committee and in the absence of friendly settlement shall, upon the request of a Contracting Party concerned, be submitted to the Tribunal established by the Convention of 20th December, 1957, on the Establishment of a Security Control in the Field of Nuclear Energy.

EXCHANGE OF NOTES CONSTITUTING AN AGREEMENT BETWEEN THE UNITED STATES OF AMERICA AND AUSTRALIA RELATING TO SAMPLING OF RADIOACTIVITY OF UPPER ATMOSPHERE BY MEANS OF BALLOONS

The American Embassy to the Australian Department of External Affairs

EMBASSY OF THE UNITED STATES OF AMERICA

The Embassy of the United States of America presents its compliments to the Department of External Affairs and has the honor to inform the

Signed at Canberra on May 9, 1961.

Department that the Government of the United States of America desires to enlist the cooperation of the Government of the Commonwealth of Australia in the program outlined hereunder to sample by means of balloons the radioactivity of the upper atmosphere. The objective of this program is to provide valuable data on the distribution of radioactivity in the Southern Hemisphere which will contribute to mutual scientific knowledge of this subject.

It is proposed that this program be carried out in accordance with the following understandings:

1. The program will be conducted by cooperating agencies of the two governments. On the part of the Government of the United States of America, the cooperating agency will be the United States Atomic Energy Commission, which may act through a contractor of its own selection. On the part of the Government of the Commonwealth of Australia, the cooperating agency will be the Department of Supply.

2. (a) The cooperating agencies are agreed that the airport at Mildura, Australia meets the need for a large, flat, hard-surfaced balloon site possessing communications and transportation facilities and terrain suitable for recovery operations extending a few hundred miles downwind. The Australian cooperating agency will provide the balloon site on terms to be agreed and, on a reimbursable basis, equipment for meteorological recovery purposes as may be mutually agreed.

(b) The United States cooperating agency will provide, inter alia, large plastic balloons of the order of 10,000 to 12,000 cubic [feet] of lifting gas and a flight package consisting of sampling devices, power supply control mechanism, communication facilities and all necessary equipment constituting a ground control station.

(c) The United States cooperating agency will bear the cost of conducting the program, including the support of operating personnel and the installation, operation, and maintenance of the equipment.

(d) The program will be carried out in accordance with the safety requirements of the Australian cooperating agency.

3. The United States cooperating agency will assume responsibility for the training of such personnel, including Australians, as are required for the installation, operation, and maintenance of the program.

4. The results of all studies under this program shall be available to both cooperating agencies.

❉   ❉   ❉

10. To the extent the Commonwealth of Australia is not compensated by other financial protection, the United States cooperating agency will indemnify the Commonwealth of Australia against (a) claims, in the form of judgments rendered or settlements approved in advance by the

United States cooperating agency, for public liability arising out of or in connection with the program, and (*b*) the reasonable costs of investigating and settling such claims, and defending suits for damage for such public liability provided, however, that this indemnification is subject to the availability of appropriated funds to the United States cooperating agency

CONVENTION ON THE LIABILITY OF OPERATORS OF NUCLEAR SHIPS

THE CONTRACTING PARTIES,

HAVING RECOGNIZED the desirability of determining by agreement certain uniform rules concerning the liability of operators of nuclear ships,

HAVE DECIDED to conclude a Convention for this purpose, and thereto have agreed as follows:

ARTICLE I

For the purposes of this Convention:

1. "Nuclear ship" means any ship equipped with a nuclear power plant.

2. "Licensing State" means the Contracting State which operates or which has authorized the operation of a nuclear ship under its flag.

3. "Person" means any individual or partnership, or any public or private body whether corporate or not, including a State or any of its constituent subdivisions.

4. "Operator" means the person authorized by the licensing State to operate a nuclear ship, or where a Contracting State operates a nuclear ship, that State.

5. "Nuclear fuel" means any material which is capable of producing energy by a self-sustaining process of nuclear fission and which is used or intended for use in a nuclear ship.

6. "Radioactive products or waste" means any material, including nuclear fuel, made radioactive by neutron irradiation incidental to the utilization of nuclear fuel in a nuclear ship.

7. "Nuclear damage" means loss of life or personal injury and loss or damage to property which arises out of or results from the radioactive properties or a combination of radioactive properties with toxic, explosive or other hazardous properties of nuclear fuel or of radioactive products

Signed at Brussels on May 25, 1962.

or waste; any other loss, damage or expense so arising or resulting shall be included only if and to the extent that the applicable national law so provides.

8. "Nuclear incident" means any occurrence or series of occurrences having the same origin which causes nuclear damage.

9. "Nuclear power plant" means any power plant in which a nuclear reactor is, or is to be used as, the source of power, whether for propulsion of the ship or for any other purpose.

10. "Nuclear reactor" means any installation containing nuclear fuel in such an arrangement that a self-sustained chain process of nuclear fission can occur therein without an additional source of neutrons.

11. "Warship" means any ship belonging to the naval forces of a State and bearing the external marks distinguishing warships of its nationality, under the command of an officer duly commissioned by the Government of such State and whose name appears in the Navy List, and manned by a crew who are under regular naval discipline.

12. "Applicable national law" means the national law of the court having jurisdiction under the Convention including any rules of such national law relating to conflict of laws.

Article II

1. The operator of a nuclear ship shall be absolutely liable for any nuclear damage upon proof that such damage has been caused by a nuclear incident involving the nuclear fuel of, or radioactive products or waste produced in, such ship.

2. Except as otherwise provided in this Convention no person other than the operator shall be liable for such nuclear damage.

3. Nuclear damage suffered by the nuclear ship itself, its equipment, fuel or stores shall not be covered by the operator's liability as defined in this Convention.

4. The operator shall not be liable with respect to nuclear incidents occurring before the nuclear fuel has been taken in charge by him or after the nuclear fuel or radioactive products or waste have been taken in charge by another person duly authorized by law and liable for any nuclear damage that may be caused by them.

5. If the operator proves that the nuclear damage resulted wholly or partially from an act or omission done with intent to cause damage by the individual who suffered the damage, the competent courts may exonerate the operator wholly or partially from his liability to such individual.

6. Notwithstanding the provisions of paragraph 1 of this Article, the operator shall have a right of recourse:

(a) If the nuclear incident results from a personal act or omission done with intent to cause damage, in which event recourse shall lie against the individual who has acted, or omitted to act, with such intent;

(b) If the nuclear incident occurred as a consequence of any wreck-raising operation, against the person or persons who carried out such operation without the authority of the operator or of the State having licensed the sunken ship or of the State in whose waters the wreck is situated;

(c) If recourse is expressly provided for by contract.

ARTICLE III

1. The liability of the operator as regards one nuclear ship shall be limited to 1500 million francs in respect of any one nuclear incident, notwithstanding that the nuclear incident may have resulted from any fault or privity of that operator; such limit shall include neither any interest nor costs awarded by a court in actions for compensation under this Convention.

2. The operator shall be required to maintain insurance, or other financial security covering his liability for nuclear damage, in such amount, of such type and in such terms as the licensing State shall specify. The licensing State shall ensure the payment of claims for compensation for nuclear damage established against the operator by providing the necessary funds up to the limit laid down in paragraph 1 of this Article to the extent that the yield of the insurance or the financial security is inadequate to satisfy such claims.

3. However, nothing in paragraph 2 of this Article shall require any Contracting State or any of its constituent subdivisions, such as States, Republics or Cantons, to maintain insurance or other financial security to cover their liability as operators of nuclear ships.

4. The franc mentioned in paragraph 1 of this Article is a unit of account constituted by sixty-five and one half milligrams of gold of millesimal fineness nine hundred. The amount awarded may be converted into each national currency in round figures. Conversion into national currencies other than gold shall be effected on the basis of their gold value at the date of payment.

ARTICLE IV

Whenever both nuclear damage and damage other than nuclear damage have been caused by a nuclear incident or jointly by a nuclear incident and one or more other occurrences and the nuclear damage and such other damage are not reasonably separable, the entire damage shall, for the purposes of this Convention, be deemed to be nuclear damage exclusively caused by the nuclear incident. However, where damage is caused jointly by a nuclear incident covered by this Convention and by an emission of ionizing radiation or by an emission of ionizing radiation in combination with the toxic, explosive or other hazardous properties of the source of radiation not covered by it, nothing in this Convention shall limit or otherwise affect the liability, either as regards the victims or by way of recourse or contribution, of any person who may be held liable in connection with the emission of ionizing radiation or by the toxic, explosive or other hazardous properties of the source of radiation not covered by this Convention.

Article V

1. Rights of compensation under this Convention shall be extinguished if an action is not brought within ten years from the date of the nuclear incident. If, however, under the law of the licensing State the liability of the operator is covered by insurance or other financial security or State indemnification for a period longer than ten years, the applicable national law may provide that rights of compensation against the operator shall only be extinguished after a period which may be longer than ten years but shall not be longer than the period for which his liability is so covered under the law of the licensing State. However, such extension of the extinction period shall in no case affect the right of compensation under this Convention of any person who has brought an action for loss of life or personal injury against the operator before the expiry of the aforesaid period of ten years.

2. Where nuclear damage is caused by nuclear fuel, radioactive products or waste which were stolen, lost, jettisoned, or abandoned, the period established under paragraph 1 of this Article shall be computed from the date of the nuclear incident causing the nuclear damage, but the period shall in no case exceed a period of twenty years from the date of the theft, loss, jettison or abandonment.

3. The applicable national law may establish a period of extinction or prescription of not less than three years from the date on which the person who claims to have suffered nuclear damage had knowledge or ought reasonably to have had knowledge of the damage and of the person responsible for the damage, provided that the period established under paragraphs 1 and 2 of this Article shall not be exceeded.

4. Any person who claims to have suffered nuclear damage and who has brought an action for compensation within the period applicable under this Article may amend his claim to take into account any aggrava-

tion of the damage, even after the expiry of that period, provided that final judgment has not been entered.

ARTICLE VI

Where provisions of national health insurance, social insurance, social security, workmen's compensation or occupational disease compensation systems include compensation for nuclear damage, rights of beneficiaries under such systems and rights of subrogation, or of recourse against the operator, by virtue of such systems, shall be determined by the law of the Contracting State having established such systems. However, if the law of such Contracting State allows claims of beneficiaries of such systems and such rights of subrogation and recourse to be brought against the operator in conformity with the terms of this Convention, this shall not result in the liability of the operator exceeding the amount specified in paragraph 1 of Article III.

* * *

ARTICLE X

1. Any action for compensation shall be brought, at the option of the claimant, either before the courts of the licensing State or before the courts of the Contracting State or States in whose territory nuclear damage has been sustained.

2. If the licensing State has been or might be called upon to ensure the payment of claims for compensation in accordance with paragraph 2 of Article III of this Convention, it may intervene as party in any proceedings brought against the operator.

3. Any immunity from legal processes pursuant to rules of national or international law shall be waived with respect to duties or obligations arising under, or for the purpose of, this Convention. Nothing in this Convention shall make warships or other State-owned or State-operated ships on non-commercial service liable to arrest, attachment or seizure or confer jurisdiction in respect of warships on the courts of any foreign State.

* * *

ARTICLE XII

1. The Contracting States undertake to adopt such measures as are necessary to ensure implementation of the provisions of this Convention, including any appropriate measures for the prompt and equitable distribution of the sums available for compensation for nuclear damage.

2. The Contracting States undertake to adopt such measures as are necessary to ensure that insurance and reinsurance premiums and sums provided by insurance, reinsurance or other financial security, or provided by them in accordance with paragraph 2 of Article III, shall be freely transferable into the currency of the Contracting State in which the damage was sustained, of the Contracting State in which the claimant is habitually resident or, as regards insurance and reinsurance premiums and payments, in the currencies specified in the insurance or reinsurance contract.

3. This Convention shall be applied without discrimination based upon nationality, domicile or residence.

Article XIII

This Convention applies to nuclear damage caused by a nuclear incident occurring in any part of the world and involving the nuclear fuel of, or radioactive products of waste produced in, a nuclear ship flying the flag of a Contracting State.

*   *   *

Article XV

1. Each Contracting State undertakes to take all measures necessary to prevent a nuclear ship flying its flag from being operated without a license or authority granted by it.

2. In the event of nuclear damage involving the nuclear fuel of, or radioactive products or waste produced in, a nuclear ship flying the flag of a Contracting State, the operation of which was not at the time of the nuclear incident licensed or authorized by such Contracting State, the owner of the nuclear ship at the time of the nuclear incident shall be deemed to be the operator of the nuclear ship for all the purposes of this Convention, except that his liability shall not be limited in amount.

3. In such an event, the Contracting State whose flag the nuclear ship flies shall be deemed to be the licensing State for all the purposes of this Convention and shall, in particular, be liable for compensation for victims in accordance with the obligations imposed on a licensing State by Article III and up to the limit laid down therein.

4. Each Contracting State undertakes not to grant a license or other authority to operate a nuclear ship flying the flag of another State. However, nothing in this paragraph shall prevent a Contracting State from implementing the requirements of its national law concerning the operation of a nuclear ship within its internal waters and territorial sea.

☙ CONVENTION OF 31ST JANUARY, 1963,
SUPPLEMENTARY TO THE PARIS CONVENTION
OF 29TH JULY, 1960, ON THIRD PARTY LIABILITY
IN THE FIELD OF NUCLEAR ENERGY

THE GOVERNMENTS of the Federal Republic of Germany, the Republic of Austria, the Kingdom of Belgium, the Kingdom of Denmark, Spain, the French Republic, the Italian Republic, the Grand Duchy of Luxembourg, the Kingdom of Norway, the Kingdom of the Netherlands, the United Kingdom of Great Britain and Northern Ireland, the Kingdom of Sweden and the Swiss Confederation;

BEING PARTIES to the Convention of 29th July, 1960, on Third Party Liability in the Field of Nuclear Energy concluded within the framework of the Organisation for European Economic Co-operation, now the Organisation for Economic Co-operation and Development (hereinafter referred to as the "Paris Convention");

DESIROUS of supplementing the measures provided in that Convention with a view to increasing the amount of compensation for damage which might result from the use of nuclear energy for peaceful purposes:

HAVE AGREED as follows:

ARTICLE 1

The system instituted by this Convention is supplementary to that of the Paris Convention, shall be subject to the provisions of the Paris Convention, and shall be applied in accordance with the following Articles.

ARTICLE 2

a) The system of this Convention shall apply to damage caused by nuclear incidents, other than those occurring entirely in the territory of a State which is not a Party to this Convention:

(i) for which an operator of a nuclear installation, used for peaceful purposes, situated in the territory of a Contracting Party to this Convention (hereinafter referred to as a "Contracting Party"), and which appears on the list established and kept up to date in accordance with the terms of article 13, is liable under the Paris Convention, and

(ii) suffered

1. in the territory of a Contracting Party; or
2. on or over the high seas on board a ship or aircraft registered in the territory of a Contracting Party; or

3. on or over the high seas by a national of a Contracting Party, provided that, in the case of damage to a ship or an aircraft, the ship or aircraft is registered in the territory of a Contracting Party;

provided that the courts of a Contracting Party have jurisdiction pursuant to the Paris Convention.

b) Any Signatory or acceding Government may, at the time of signature of or accession to this Convention or on the deposit of its instrument of ratification, declare that, for the purposes of the application of paragraph a) (ii) of this Article, individuals or certain categories thereof, considered under its law as having their habitual residence in its territory, are assimilated to its own nationals.

c) In this Article, the expression "a national of a Contracting Party" shall include a Contracting Party or any of its constitutent sub-divisions, or a partnership, or any public or private body whether corporate or not established in the territory of a Contracting Party.

ARTICLE 3

a) Under the conditions established by this Convention, the Contracting Parties undertake that compensation in respect of the damage referred to in Article 2 shall be provided up to the amount of 120 million units of account per incident.

b) Such compensation shall be provided:

(i) up to an amount of at least 5 million units of account, out of funds provided by insurance or other financial security, such amount to be established by the legislation of the Contracting Party in whose territory the nuclear installation of the operator liable is situated;

(ii) between this amount and 70 million units of account, out of public funds to be made available by the Contracting Party in whose territory the nuclear installation of the operator liable is situated;

(iii) between 70 million and 120 million units of account, out of public funds to be made available by the Contracting Parties according to the formula for contributions specified in Article 12.

c) For this purpose, each Contracting Party shall either:

(i) establish the maximum liability of the operator, pursuant to Article 7 of the Paris Convention, at 120 million units of account, and provide that such liability shall be covered by all the funds referred to in paragraph b) of this Article; or

(ii) establish the maximum liability of the operator at an amount at least equal to that established pursuant to paragraph b) (i) of this Article and provide that, in excess of such amount and up to 120 million units of account, the public funds referred to in paragraph *b*) (*ii*) and (*iii*) of this Article shall be made available by some means other than as cover for the liability of the operator, provided that the rules of substance and procedure laid down in this Convention are not thereby affected.

d) The obligation of the operator to pay compensation, interest or costs out of public funds made available pursuant to paragraphs *b*) (*ii*) and (*iii*), and *f*) of this Article shall only be enforceable against the operator as and when such funds are in fact made available.

❋ ❋ ❋

f) The interest and costs referred to in Article 7 *g*) of the Paris Convention are payable in addition to the amounts referred to in paragraph *b*) of this Article and shall be borne in so far as they are awarded in respect of compensation payable out of the funds referred to in:

(*i*) paragraph *b*) (*i*) of this Article, by the operator liable;

(*ii*) paragraph *b*) (*ii*) of this Article, by the Contracting Party in whose territory the nuclear installation of that operator is situated;

(*iii*) paragraph *b*) (*iii*) of this Article, by the Contracting Parties together.

❋ ❋ ❋

ARTICLE 5

a) Where the operator liable has a right of recourse pursuant to Article 6 *f*) of the Paris Convention, the Contracting Party in whose territory the nuclear installation of that operator is situated shall take such legislative measures as are necessary to enable both that Contracting Party and the other Contracting Parties to benefit from this recourse to the extent that public funds have been made available pursuant to Article 3 *b*) (*ii*) and (*iii*), and *f*).

b) Such legislation may provide for the recovery of public funds made available pursuant to Article 3 *b*) (*ii*) an (*iii*), and *f*) from such operator if the damage results from fault on his part.

❋ ❋ ❋

ARTICLE 8

Any person who is entitled to benefit from the provisions of this Convention shall have the right to full compensation in accordance with national law for damage suffered, provided that, where the amount of damage exceeds or is likely to exceed:

(i) 120 million units of account; or

(ii) if there is aggregate liability under Article 5 *b*) of the Paris Convention and a higher sum results therefrom, such higher sum,

any Contracting Party may establish equitable criteria for apportionment. Such criteria shall be applied whatever the origin of the funds and, subject to the provisions of Article 2, without discrimination based on the nationality, domicile or residence of the person suffering the damage.

ARTICLE 9

a) The system of disbursements by which the public funds required under Article 3 *b*) (*ii*) and (*iii*), and *f*) are to be made available shall be that of the Contracting Party whose courts have jurisdiction.

b) Each Contracting Party shall ensure that persons suffering damage may enforce their rights to compensation without having to bring separate proceedings according to the origin of the funds provided for such compensation.

c) No Contracting Party shall be required to make available the public funds referred to in Article 3 *b*) (*ii*) and (*iii*) so long as any of the funds referred to in Article 3 *b*) (*i*) remain available.

ARTICLE 10

a) The Contracting Party whose courts have jurisdiction shall be required to inform the other Contracting Parties of a nuclear incident and its circumstances as soon as it appears that the damage caused by such incident exceeds, or is likely to exceed, 70 million units of account. The Contracting Parties shall without delay make all the necessary arrangements to settle the procedure for their relations in this connection.

b) Only the Contracting Party whose courts have jurisdiction shall be entitled to request the other Contracting Parties to make available the public funds required under Article 3 *b*) (*iii*) and *f*) and shall have exclusive competence to disburse such funds.

ARTICLE 11

a) If the courts having jurisdiction are those of a Contracting Party other than the Contracting Party in whose territory the nuclear installation of the operator liable is situated, the public funds required under Article 3 *b*) (*ii*) and *f*) shall be made available by the first-named Contracting Party. The Contracting Party in whose territory the nuclear installation of the operator liable is situated shall reimburse to the other Contracting Party the sums paid. These two Contracting Parties shall agree on the procedure for reimbursement.

b) In adopting all legislative, regulatory or administrative provisions, after the nuclear incident has occurred, concerning the nature, form and extent of the compensation, the procedure for making available the public funds required under Article 3 *b*) (*ii*) and, if necessary, the criteria for the apportionment of such funds, the Contracting Party whose courts have jurisdiction shall consult the Contracting Party in whose territory the nuclear installation of the operator liable is situated. It shall further take all measures necessary to enable the latter to intervene in proceedings and to participate in any settlement concerning compensation.

ARTICLE 12

a) The formula for contributions according to which the Contracting Parties shall make available the public funds referred to in Article 3 *b*) (*iii*) shall be determined as follows:

   (*i*) as to 50%, on the basis of the ratio between the gross national product at current prices of each Contracting Party and the total of the gross national products at current prices of all Contracting Parties as shown by the official statistics published by the Organisation for Economic Co-operation and Development for the year preceding the year in which the nuclear incident occurs;

   (*ii*) as to 50%, on the basis of the ratio between the thermal power of the reactors situated in the territory of each Contracting Party and the total thermal power of the reactors situated in the territories of all the Contracting Parties. This calculation shall be made on the basis of the thermal power of the reactors shown at the date of the nuclear incident in the list referred to in Article 2 *a*) (*i*): provided that a reactor shall only be taken into consideration for the purposes of this calculations as from the date when it first reaches criticality.

b) For the purposes of this Convention, "thermal power" means

   (*i*) before the issue of a final operating licence, the planned thermal power;

   (*ii*) after the issue of such licence, the thermal power authorized by the competent national authorities.

ARTICLE 13

a) Each Contracting Party shall ensure that all nuclear installations used for peaceful purposes situated in its territory and falling within the definition in Article 1 of the Paris Convention, appear in the list referred to in Article 2 *a*) (*i*).

b) For this purpose, each Signatory or acceding Government shall, on the deposit of its instrument of ratification or accession, communicate to the Belgian Government full particulars of such installations.

c) Such particulars shall indicate:

(*i*) in the case of all installations not yet completed, the expected date on which the risk of a nuclear incident will exist;

(*ii*) and further, in the case of reactors, the expected date on which they will first reach criticality, and also their thermal power.

d) Each Contracting Party shall also communicate to the Belgian Government the exact date of the existence of the risk of a nuclear incident and, in the case of reactors, the date on which they first reached criticality.

e) Each Contracting Party shall also be communicate to the Belgian Government all modifications to be made to the list. Where such modifications include the addition of a nuclear installation, the communication must be made at least three months before the expected date on which the risk of a nuclear incident will exist. . . .

ARTICLE 14

a) Except insofar as this Convention otherwise provides, each Contracting Party may exercise the powers vested in it by virtue of the Paris Convention, and any provisions made thereunder may be invoked against the other Contracting Parties in order that the public funds referred to in Article 3 *b*) (*ii*) and (*iii*) be made available.

b) Any such provisions made by a Contracting Party pursuant to Articles 2, 7 *c*) and 9 of the Paris Convention as a result of which the public funds referred to in Article 3 *b*) (*ii*) and (*iii*) are required to be made available may not be invoked against any other Contracting Party unless it has consented thereto.

c) Nothing in this Convention shall prevent a Contracting Party from making provisions outside the scope of the Paris Convention and of this Convention, provided that such provisions shall not involve any further obligation on the part of the other Contracting Parties insofar as their public funds are concerned.

ARTICLE 15

a) Any Contracting Party may conclude an agreement with a State which is not a Party to this Convention concerning compensation out of public funds for damage caused by a nuclear incident. . . .

❀ ❀ ❀

ARTICLE 17

Any dispute arising between two or more Contracting Parties concerning the interpretation or application of this Convention shall, upon the request of a Contracting Party concerned, be submitted to the European Nuclear Energy Tribunal established by the Convention of 20th December, 1957, on the Establishment of a Security Control in the Field of Nuclear Energy.

* * *

✠ VIENNA CONVENTION ON CIVIL LIABILITY FOR NUCLEAR DAMAGE

THE CONTRACTING PARTIES,

HAVING RECOGNIZED the desirability of establishing some minimum standards to provide financial protection against damage resulting from certain peaceful uses of nuclear energy,

BELIEVING that a convention on civil liability for nuclear damage would also contribute to the development of friendly relations among nations, irrespective of their differing constitutional and social systems,

HAVE DECIDED to conclude a convention for such purposes, and thereto have agreed as follows—

ARTICLE I

1. For the purposes of this Convention—

* * *

(e) "Law of the competent court" means the law of the court having jurisdiction under this Convention, including any rules of such law relating to conflict of laws.

* * *

(g) "Radioactive products or waste" means any radioactive material produced in, or any material made radioactive by exposure to the radiation incidental to, the production or utilization of nuclear fuel, but does not include radioisotopes which have reached the final stage of fabrication so as to be usable for any scientific, medical, agricultural, commercial or industrial purpose.

(h) "Nuclear material" means—

    (i) Nuclear fuel, other than natural uranium and depleted ura-

Adopted at Vienna on May 19, 1963.

nium, capable of producing energy by a self-sustaining chain process of nuclear fission outside a nuclear reactor, either alone or in combination with some other material; and
    (ii) Radioactive products or waste.

* * *

(k) "Nuclear damage" means—
    (i) Loss of life, any personal injury or any loss of, or damage to, property which arises out of or results from the radioactive properties or a combination of radioactive properties with toxic, explosive or other hazardous properties of nuclear fuel or radioactive products or waste in, or of nuclear material coming from, originating in, or sent to, a nuclear installation;
    (ii) Any other loss or damage so arising resulting if and to the extent that the law of the competent court so provides; and
    (iii) If the law of the Installation State so provides, loss of life, any personal injury or any loss of, or damage to, property which arises out of or results from other ionizing radiation emitted by any other source of radiation inside a nuclear installation.
(1) "Nuclear incident" means any occurrence or series of occurrences having the same origin which causes nuclear damage.

* * *

ARTICLE II

1. The operator of a nuclear installation shall be liable for nuclear damage upon proof that such damage has been caused by a nuclear incident—
    (a) In his nuclear installation; or
    (b) Involving nuclear material coming from or orignating in his nuclear installation, and occurring—
        (i) Before liability with regard to nuclear incidents involving the nuclear material has been assumed, pursuant to the express terms of a contract in writing, by the operator of another nuclear installation;
        (ii) In the absence of such express terms, before the operator of another nuclear installation has taken charge of the nuclear material; or
        (iii) Where the nuclear material is intended to be used in a nuclear reactor with which a means of transport is equipped for use as a source of power, whether for propulsion thereof or for any other purpose, before the person duly authorized to

operate such reactor has taken charge of the nuclear material; but

(iv) Where the nuclear material has been sent to a person within the territory of a non-contracting State, before it has been unloaded from the means of transport by which it has arrived in the territory of that non-contracting State;

(c) Involving nuclear material sent to his nuclear installation, and occurring—

(i) After liability with regard to nuclear incidents involving the nuclear material has been assumed by him, pursuant to the express terms of a contract in writing, from the operator of another nuclear installation;

(ii) In the absence of such express terms, after he has taken charge of the nuclear material; or

(iii) After he has taken charge of the nuclear material from a person operating a nuclear reactor with which a means of transport is equipped for use as a source of power, whether for propulsion thereof or for any other purpose; but

(iv) Where the nuclear material has, with the written consent of the operator, been sent from a person within the territory of a non-Contracting State, only after it has been loaded on the means of transport by which it is to be carried from the territory of that State;

provided that, if nuclear damage is caused by a nuclear incident occurring in a nuclear installation and involving nuclear material stored therein incidentally to the carriage of such material, the provisions of sub-paragraph (a) of this paragraph shall not apply where another operator or person is solely liable pursuant to the provisions of sub-paragraph (b) or (c) of this paragraph.

2. The Installation State may provide by legislation that, in accordance with such terms as may be specified therein, a carrier of nuclear material or a person handling radioactive waste may, at his request and with the consent of the operator concerned, be designated or recognized as operator in the place of that operator in respect of such nuclear material or radioactive waste respectively. In this case such carrier or such person shall be considered, for all the purposes of this Convention, as an operator of a nuclear installation situated within the territory of that State.

3. (a) Where nuclear damage engages the liability of more than one operator, the operators involved shall, in so far as the damage attributable to each operator is not reasonably separable, be jointly and severally liable.

(b) Where a nuclear incident occurs in the course of carriage of nuclear material, either in one and the same means of transport, or, in the case of storage incidental to the carriage, in one and the same nuclear installation, and causes nuclear damage which engages the liability of more than one operator, the total liability shall not exceed the highest amount applicable with respect to any one of them pursuant to Article V.

(c) In neither of the cases referred to in sub-paragraphs (a) and (b) of this paragraph shall the liability of any one operator exceed the amount applicable with respect to him pursuant to Article V.

4. Subject to the provisions of paragraph 3 of this Article, where several nuclear installations of one and the same operator are involved in one nuclear incident, such operator shall be liable in respect of each nuclear installation involved up to the amount applicable with respect to him pursuant to Article V.

5. Except as otherwise provided in this Convention, no person other than the operator shall be liable for nuclear damage. This, however, shall not affect the application of any international convention in the field of transport in force or open for signature, ratification or accession at the date on which this Convention is opened for signature.

6. No person shall be liable for any loss or damage which is not nuclear damage pursuant to sub-paragraph (k) of paragraph 1 of Article I but which could have been included as such pursuant to sub-paragraph (k) (ii) of that paragraph.

7. Direct action shall lie against the person furnishing financial security pursuant to Article VII, if the law of the competent court so provides.

ARTICLE III

The operator liable in accordance with this Convention shall provide the carrier with a certificate issued by or on behalf of the insurer or other financial guarantor furnishing the financial security required pursuant to Article VII. The certificate shall state the name and address of that operator and the amount, type and duration of the security, and these statements may not be disputed by the person by whom or on whose behalf the certificate was issued. The certificate shall also indicate the nuclear material in respect of which the security applies and shall include a statement by the competent public authority of the Installation State that the person named is an operator within the meaning of this Convention.

ARTICLE IV

1. The liability of the operator for nuclear damage under this Convention shall be absolute.

2. If the operator proves that the nuclear damage resulted wholly or partly either from the gross negligence of the person suffering the damage or from an act or omission of such person done with intent to cause damage, the competent court may, if its law so provides, relieve the operator wholly or partly from his obligation to pay compensation in respect of the damage suffered by such person.

3. (a) No liability under this Convention shall attach to an operator for nuclear damage caused by a nuclear incident directly due to an act of armed conflict, hostilities, civil war or insurrection.

   (b) Except in so far as the law of the Installation State may provide to the contrary, the operator shall not be liable for nuclear damage caused by a nuclear incident directly due to a grave natural disaster of an exceptional character.

4. Whenever both nuclear damage and damage other than nuclear damage have been caused by a nuclear incident or jointly by a nuclear incident and one or more other occurrences, such other damage shall, to the extent that it is not reasonably separable from the nuclear damage, be deemed, for the purposes of this Convention, to be nuclear damage caused by that nuclear incident. Where, however, damage is caused jointly by a nuclear incident covered by this Convention and by an emission of ionizing radiation not covered by it, nothing in this Convention shall limit or otherwise affect the liability, either as regards any person suffering nuclear damage or by way of recourse or contribution, of any person who may be held liable in connection with that emission of ionizing radiation.

5. The operator shall not be liable under this Convention for nuclear damage—

   (a) To the nuclear installation itself or to any property on the site of that installation which is used or to be used in connection with that installation; or

   (b) To the means of transport upon which the nuclear material involved was at the time of the nuclear incident.

6. Any Installation State may provide by legislation that sub-paragraph (b) of paragraph 5 of this Article shall not apply, provided that in no case shall the liability of the operator in respect of nuclear damage, other than nuclear damage to the means of transport, be reduced to less than US $5 million for any one nuclear incident.

7. Nothing in this Convention shall affect—

   (a) The liability of any individual for nuclear damage for which the operator, by virtue of paragraph 3 or 5 of this Article, is not liable under this Convention and which that individual caused by an act or omission done with intent to cause damage; or

   (b) The liability outside this Convention of the operator for nuclear damage for which, by virtue of sub-paragraph (b) of paragraph 5 of this Article, he is not liable under this Convention.

ARTICLE V

1. The liability of the operator may be limited by the Installation State to not less than US $ 5 million for any one nuclear incident.
2. Any limits of liability which may be established pursuant to this Article shall not include any interest or costs awarded by a court in actions for compensation of nuclear damage.
3. The United States dollar referred to in this Convention is a unit of account equivalent to the value of the United States dollar in terms of gold on 29 April 1963, that is to say, US $35 per one troy ounce of fine gold.
4. The sum mentioned in paragraph 6 of Article IV and in paragraph 1 of this Article may be converted into national currency in round figures.

ARTICLE VI

1. Rights of compensation under this Convention shall be extinguished if an action is not brought within ten years from the date of the nuclear incident. If, however, under the law of the Installation State the liability of the operator is covered by insurance or other financial security or by State funds for a period longer than ten years, the law of the competent court may provide that rights of compensation against the operator shall only be extinguished after a period which may be longer than ten years, but shall not be longer than the period for which his liability is so covered under the law of the Installation State. Such extension of the extinction period shall in no case affect rights of compensation under this Convention of any person who has brought an action for loss of life or personal injury against the operator before the expiry of the aforesaid period of ten years.
2. Where nuclear damage is caused by a nuclear incident involving nuclear material which at the time of the nuclear incident was stolen, lost, jettisoned or abandoned, the period established pursuant to paragraph 1 of this Article shall be computed from the date of that nuclear incident, but the period shall in no case exceed a period of twenty years from the date of the theft, loss, jettison or abandonment.
3. The law of the competent court may establish a period of extinction or prescription of less than three years from the date on which the person suffering nuclear damage had knowledge or should have had knowledge of the damage and of the operator liable for the damage, provided that the period established pursuant to paragraphs 1 and 2 of this Article shall not be exceeded.

4. Unless the law of the competent court otherwise provides, any person who claims to have suffered nuclear damage and who has brought an action for compensation within the period applicable pursuant to this Article may amend his claim to take into account any aggravation of the damage, even after the expiry of that period, provided that final judgment has not been entered.

5. Where jurisdiction is to be determined pursuant to sub-paragraph (b) of paragraph 3 of Article XI and a request has been made within the period applicable pursuant to this Article to any one of the Contracting Parties empowered so to determine, but the time remaining after such determination is less than six months, the period within which an action may be brought shall be six months, reckoned from the date of such determination.

ARTICLE VII

1. The operator shall be required to maintain insurance or other financial security covering his liability for nuclear damage in such amount, of such type and in such terms as the Installation State shall specify. The Installation State shall ensure the payment of claims for compensation for nuclear damage which have been established against the operator by providing the necessary funds to the extent that the yield of insurance or other financial security is inadequate to satisfy such claims, but not in excess of the limit, if any, established pursuant to Article V.

2. Nothing in paragraph 1 of this Article shall require a Contracting Party or any of its constituent sub-divisions, such as States or Republics, to maintain insurance or other financial security to cover their liability as operators.

3. The funds provided by insurance, by other financial security or by the Installation State pursuant to paragraph 1 of this Article shall be exclusively available for compensation due under this Convention.

4. No insurer or other financial guarantor shall suspend or cancel the insurance or other financial security provided pursuant to paragraph 1 of this Article without giving notice in writing of at least two months to the competent public authority or, in so far as such insurance or other financial security relates to the carriage of nuclear material, during the period of the carriage in question.

ARTICLE VIII

Subject to the provisions of this Convention, the nature, form and extent of the compensation, as well as the equitable distribution thereof, shall be governed by the law of the competent court.

ARTICLE IX

1. Where provisions of national or public health insurance, social insurance, social security, workmen's compensation or occupational disease compensation systems include compensation for nuclear damage, rights of beneficiaries of such systems to obtain compensation under this Convention and rights of recourse by virtue of such systems against the operator liable shall be determined, subject to the provisions of this Convention, by the law of the Contracting Party in which such systems have been established, or by the regulations of the intergovernmental organization which has established such systems.

2. (a) If a person who is a national of a Contracting Party, other than the operator, has paid compensation for nuclear damage under an international convention or under the law of a non-contracting State, such person shall, up to the amount which he has paid, acquire by subrogation the rights under this Convention of the person so compensated. No right shall be so acquired by any person to the extent that the operator has a right of recourse against such person under this Convention.

(b) Nothing in this Convention shall preclude an operator who has paid compensation for nuclear damage out of funds other than those provided pursuant to paragraph 1 of Article VII from recovering from the person providing financial security pursuant to that paragraph or from the Installation State, up to the amount he has paid, the sum which the person so compensated would have obtained under this Convention.

* * *

ARTICLE XI

1. Except as otherwise provided in this Article, jurisdiction over actions under Article II shall lie only with the courts of the Contracting Party within whose territory the nuclear incident occurred.

2. Where the nuclear incident occurred outside the territory of any Contracting Party, or where the place of the nuclear incident cannot be determined with certainty, jurisdiction over such actions shall lie with the courts of the Installation State of the operator liable.

3. Where under paragraph 1 or 2 of this Article, jurisdiction would lie with the courts of more than one Contracting Party, jurisdiction shall lie -

(a) If the nuclear incident occurred partly outside the territory of any Contracting Party, and partly within the territory of a single Contracting Party, with the courts of the latter; and

(b) In any other case, with the courts of that Contracting Party which is determined by agreement between the Contracting Parties whose courts would be competent under paragraph 1 or 2 of this Article.

* * *

ARTICLE XIII

This Convention and the national law applicable thereunder shall be applied without any discrimination based upon nationality, domicile or residence.

ARTICLE XIV

Except in respect of measures of execution, jurisdictional immunities under rules of national or international law shall not be invoked in actions under this Convention before the courts competent pursuant to Article XI.

* * *

ARTICLE XVI

No person shall be entitled to recover compensation under this Convention to the extent that he has recovered compensation in respect of the same nuclear damage under another international convention on civil liability in the field of nuclear energy.

ARTICLE XVII

This Convention shall not, as between the parties to them, affect the application of any international agreements or international conventions on civil liability in the field of nuclear energy in force, or open for signature, ratification or accession at the date of which this Convention is opened for signature.

ARTICLE XVIII

This Convention shall not be construed as affecting the rights, if any, of a Contracting Party under the general rules of public international law in respect to nuclear damage.

OPTIONAL PROTOCOL
CONCERNING THE COMPULSORY SETTLEMENT OF DISPUTES

The States Parties to the present Protocol and to the Vienna Convention on Civil Liability for Nuclear Damage hereinafter referred to as "the

Convention" adopted by the International Conference held at Vienna from 29 April to 19 May 1963,

EXPRESSING THEIR WISH to resort in all matters concerning them in respect of any dispute arising out of the interpretation or application of the Convention to the compulsory jurisdiction of the International Court of Justice, unless some other form of settlement has been agreed upon by the parties within a reasonable period,

HAVE AGREED as follows—

ARTICLE I

Disputes arising out of the interpretation or application of the Convention shall lie within the compulsory jurisdiction of the International Court of Justice and may accordingly be brought before the Court by an application made by any party to a dispute being a Party to the present Protocol.

ARTICLE II

The parties to a dispute may agree, within a period of two months after one party has notified its opinion to the other that a dispute exists, to resort not to the International Court of Justice but to an arbitral tribunal. After the expiry of the said period, either party may bring the dispute before the Court by an application.

ARTICLE III

1. Within the same period of two months, the parties may agree to adopt a conciliation procedure before resorting to the International Court of Justice.
2. The conciliation commission shall make its recommendations within five months after its appointment. If its recommendations are not accepted by the parties to the dispute within two months after they have been delivered, either party may bring the dispute before the Court by an application.

AGREEMENT FOR CO-OPERATION BETWEEN THE GOVERNMENT OF THE UNITED STATES OF AMERICA AND THE GOVERNMENT OF THE UNITED STATES OF BRAZIL CONCERNING CIVIL USES OF ATOMIC ENERGY

Whereas the peaceful uses of atomic energy hold great promise for all mankind; and

Signed at Washington on July 8, 1965.

Whereas the Government of the United States of America and the Government of the United States of Brazil desire to cooperate with each other in the development of such peaceful uses of atomic energy; and

Whereas there is well advanced the design and development of several types of research reactors . . .; and

Whereas research reactors are useful in the production of research quantities of radioisotopes, in medical therapy and in numerous other research activities, and at the same time are a means of affording valuable training and experience in nuclear science and engineering useful in the development of other peaceful uses of atomic energy including civilian nuclear power; and

Whereas the Government of the United States of Brazil desires to pursue a research and development program looking toward the realization of the peaceful and humanitarian uses of atomic energy and desires to obtain assistance from the Government of the United States of America and United States industry with respect to this program; and

Whereas the Government of the United States of America, represented by the United States Atomic Energy Commission (hereinafter referred to as the "Commission"), desires to assist the Government of the United States of Brazil in such a program;

The Parties therefore agree as follows:

Article I

A. Subject to the limitations of Article V, the Parties hereto will exchange information in the following fields:

1. Design, construction and operation of research reactors and their use as research, development, and engineering tools and in medical therapy;
2. Health and safety problems related to the operation and use of research reactors;
3. The use of radioactive isotopes in physical and biological research, medical therapy, agriculture, and industry.

B. The application or use of any information or data of any kind whatsoever, including design drawings and specifications, exchanged under this Agreement shall be the responsibility of the Party which receives and uses such information or data, and it is understood that the other cooperating Party does not warrant the accuracy, completeness, or suitability of such information or data for any particular use or application.

* * *

Article V

Restricted Data shall not be communicated under this Agreement, and no materials or equipment and devices shall be transferred and no

services shall be furnished under this Agreement to the Government of
the United States of Brazil or authorized persons under its jurisdiction if
the transfer of any such materials or equipment and devices or the furnishing of any such services involves the communication of Restricted
Data.

Article VI

A. The Government of the United States of America and the Government of the United States of Brazil emphasize their common interest in
ensuring that any material, equipment, or device made available to the
Government of the United States of Brazil pursuant to this Agreement
shall be used solely for civil purposes.

B. Except to the extent that the safeguards provided for in this Agreement are supplanted, ... by safeguards of the International Atomic
Energy Agency, the Government of the United States of America, notwithstanding any other provisions of this Agreement, shall have the following rights:

* * *

(6) To consult with the Government of the United States of Brazil in
    the matter of health and safety.

✍ AGREEMENT BETWEEN THE INTERNATIONAL ATOMIC ENERGY AGENCY AND THE GOVERNMENT OF IRAN FOR ASSISTANCE BY THE AGENCY TO IRAN IN ESTABLISHING A RESEARCH REACTOR PROJECT

WHEREAS the Government of Iran (hereinafter called "Iran"), desiring
to establish a project for research on, and development and practical
application of, atomic energy for peaceful purposes, has requested the
assistance of the International Atomic Energy Agency (hereinafter called
the "Agency") in securing the special fissionable material necessary for
a training and research reactor;

WHEREAS the Board of Governors of the Agency approved the project
on 21 February 1967;

WHEREAS the Agency and the Government of the United States of
America (hereinafter called the "United States" on 11 May 1959 concluded an Agreement for Co-operation (hereinafter called the "Co-
operation Agreement") under which the United States undertook to make

Signed at Vienna on March 15, 1967, and at Teheran on May 10, 1967.

available to the Agency pursuant to its Statute certain quantities of special fissionable material; and

WHEREAS the Agency, Iran and the United States Atomic Energy Commission acting on behalf of the United States are this day concluding a contract (hereinafter called the "Supply Agreement") for the transfer of enriched uranium and plutonium for the research reactor;

Now, THEREFORE, the Agency and Iran hereby agree as follows:

Article I

DEFINITION OF THE PROJECT

Section 1. The project to which this Agreement relates is the establishment of a five-megawatt pool-type research reactor (hereinafter called the "reactor") to be operated by the Iranian National Atomic Energy Commission at the Teheran Nuclear Centre of the University of Teheran.

❊   ❊   ❊

Article V

HEALTH AND SAFETY MEASURES

Section 6. The health and safety measures specified in Annex B shall be applied to the project.

❊   ❊   ❊

ANNEX B

HEALTH AND SAFETY MEASURES

1. The health and safety measures applicable to the project shall be those set forth in Agency document INFCIRC/18 (hereinafter called the "Health and Safety Document"), as specified below.

2. Iran shall apply the Agency's Basic Safety Standards and relevant provisions of the Agency's Regulations for the Safe Transport of Radioactive Materials, as these Standards and Regulations are revised from time to time, and shall as far as possible apply them also to any shipment of supplied material outside Iran. Iran shall endeavour to ensure safety conditions as recommended in the relevant parts of the Agency's codes of practice.

3. Iran shall arrange for the submission to the Agency, at least 60 days before the proposed transfer of any of the supplied material to the jurisdiction of Iran, of a detailed health hazards report containing the information specified in paragraph 29 of the Health and Safety Document, with particular reference to the following types of operation, to the extent that such information is relevant and not yet available to the Agency:

(a) Receipt and handling of supplied material;

(b) Loading of fuel into the reactor;

(c) Start-up and pre-operational testing of the reactor with the supplied material;

(d) Experimental programme and procedures involving the reactor;

(e) Unloading of fuel from the reactor;

(f) Handling and storage of fuel after unloading.

The transfer shall not take place until the Agency has determined that the safety measures, as described in the report, are acceptable. The Agency may require further safety measures in accordance with paragraph 30 of the Health and Safety Document. Should Iran desire to make substantial modifications to the procedures with respect to which information was submitted, or to perform any operations with the reactor (including finally closing it down) or the supplied material as to which operation no such information was submitted, it shall submit to the Agency all relevant information as specified in paragraph 29 of the Health and Safety Document in sufficient time to enable the Agency to perform its task in accordance with paragraph 30 of the Document before such modified procedures or additional operations are carried out.

4. Iran shall arrange for the submission of the reports specified in paragraph 25 of the Health and Safety Document, the first report to be submitted not later than twelve months after the entry into force of this Agreement. In addition, the reports specified in paragraphs 26 and 27 of the Document shall be submitted.

5. The Agency may inspect the reactor, in accordance with the paragraphs 33–35 of the Health and Safety Document, at the time of initial start-up with the supplied material, once during the first year of operation, and thereafter not more than once a year, provided that special inspections may be carried out in the circumstances specified in paragraph 32 of the Document.

6. Changes may be made in the safety measures referred to in paragraph 3 of this Annex, in accordance with paragraphs 38 and 39 of the Health and Safety Document.

✍ PROJECT AGREEMENT BETWEEN THE INTERNATIONAL ATOMIC ENERGY AGENCY AND THE GOVERNMENT OF IRAQ REGARDING ARRANGEMENTS FOR THE TRANSFER OF RADIOTHERAPY EQUIPMENT

WHEREAS the Government of Iraq (hereinafter called "Iraq"), desiring to expand the facilities for radiotherapy at the Mosul Teaching Hospital,

Signed at Vienna on September 15 and 21, 1967.

has requested the assistance of the International Atomic Energy Agency (hereinafter called the "Agency") in securing radioisotopes and radiotherapy equipment therefor;

WHEREAS the Government of the Union of Soviet Socialist Republics (hereinafter called the "Soviet Union") has offered to make available to the Agency free of charge equipment for radiotherapy centres;

WHEREAS Iraq has informed the Agency that the equipment offered by the Soviet Union would meet its requirements;

WHEREAS the Soviet Union has informed the Agency of its readiness, pursuant to a decision by the Board of Governors of the Agency, to deliver that equipment to Iraq; and

WHEREAS the Board of Governors of the Agency approved the project on 24 February 1966, and authorized the Director General to conclude with Iraq a Project Agreement;

The Agency and Iraq hereby agree as follows:

Article I

Section 1. The Agency will facilitate arrangements for the transfer to Iraq of the following equipment: a Rum-7 short-focus X-ray unit and a 4000-curie Luch radiocobalt unit (together hereinafter called the "supplied equipment").

Section 2. The supplied equipment will be installed at the Mosul Teaching Hospital.

Article II

Section 3. The arrangements for the delivery and installation of the supplied equipment will be made between Iraq and the Soviet Union. These arrangements shall provide:

(a) That title to the supplied equipment shall pass directly from the Soviet Union to Iraq (or the designated organ of either) upon the dispatch of the supplied equipment from the Soviet Union;

(b) That the transportation of the supplied equipment from the Soviet Union to Iraq shall be, as far as possible, subject to the Agency's Regulations for the Safe Transport of Radioactive Materials; and

(c) For the settlement of any disputes between Iraq and the Soviet Union.

Article III

Section 4. Iraq undertakes that the supplied equipment shall not be used in such a way as to further any military purpose.

Article IV

Section 5. The health and safety measures applicable to the project shall be those set forth in Agency document INFCIRC/18 (hereinafter called the "Health and Safety Document").

Section 6. Iraq shall apply to operations involving the supplied equipment the Agency's Basic Safety Standards and shall endeavour to ensure safety conditions as recommended in the relevant parts of the Agency's Codes of Practice.

Section 7. Iraq shall submit the reports specified in paragraphs 25(a), 26 and 27 of the Health and Safety Document.

Section 8. The Agency shall be given the opportunity to carry out an inspection after the supplied equipment has been installed and before it is put into operation and may also carry out special inspections under the circumstances specified in paragraph 32 of the Health and Safety Document.

Section 9. Iraq shall apply the relevant provisions of the Annex to Agency document GC(V)/INF/39 and of the Agreement on the Privileges and Immunities of the Agency to the Agency's inspectors and to any property used by them in performing their functions.

Article V

Section 10. Pursuant to paragraph B of Article VIII of the Statute of the Agency, Iraq shall make available to the Agency without charge all scientific information developed as a result of the assistance extended by the Agency with respect to this project.

Section 11. The Agency does not claim any right in any inventions or discoveries arising from the implementation of the project. The Agency may, however, be granted licences under any patents upon terms to be agreed.

Article VI

Section 12. The Agency shall at no time bear any responsibility for the transfer, the installation, the safe handling or the use of the supplied equipment, or for any defect in the equipment.

Article VII

Section 13. Any dispute arising out of or relating to this Agreement, which is not settled by negotiations or as may otherwise be agreed, shall be submitted to an arbitral tribunal at the request of either Party.

Section 14. Each Party shall designate an arbitrator, and the two arbitrators so designated shall elect a third, who shall be the Chairman. If within thirty days of the request for arbitration either Party has not designated an arbitrator, or if within thirty days of the designation of the second arbitrator the third arbitrator has not been elected, either Party may request the President of the International Court of Justice to make the relevant appointment.

Section 15. The arbitral tribunal shall make decisions by majority vote. The arbitral procedure shall be established by the tribunal whose decisions, including all rulings concerning its constitution, procedure, jurisdiction and the division of expenses of arbitration between the Parties, shall be binding on the Parties.

Section 16. The remuneration of the arbitrators shall be determined on the same basis as that of *ad hoc* judges of the International Court of Justice.

Article VIII

Section 17. This Agreement shall enter into force upon signature by or for the Director General of the Agency and by the authorized representative of Iraq.

TEXT OF THE U.N. GENERAL ASSEMBLY RESOLUTION ON THE ESTABLISHMENT WITHIN THE FRAMEWORK OF THE INTERNATIONAL ATOMIC ENERGY AGENCY OF AN INTERNATIONAL SERVICE FOR NUCLEAR EXPLOSIONS FOR PEACEFUL PURPOSES UNDER APPROPRIATE INTERNATIONAL CONTROL

The General Assembly,

Recalling its resolution 2665 (XXV) of 7 December 1970,

Having considered the report of the International Atomic Energy Agency on the establishment, within its framework, of an international service for nuclear explosions for peaceful purposes under appropriate international control,

Noting with satisfaction that the International Atomic Energy Agency has demonstrated its efficiency with regard to promoting co-operation in the peaceful uses of nuclear energy,

Noting further that the International Atomic Energy Agency, in ac-

Resolution No. 2829 (XXVI), December 16, 1971; passed at the Twenty-Sixth Regular Session of the General Assembly.

cordance with its statute, is an appropriate organ to exercise the functions of an international service for nuclear explosions for peaceful purposes, taking into account the relevant provisions of the Treaty on the Non-Proliferation of Nuclear Weapons,

1. *Commends* the International Atomic Energy Agency for its intensive work on problems in connexion with nuclear explosions for peaceful purposes;

2. *Requests* the International Atomic Energy Agency to continue its activities in this field and to study ways and means of establishing, within its framework, an international service for nuclear explosions for peaceful purposes under appropriate international control;

3. *Invites* the Director-General of the International Atomic Energy Agency to submit, in his annual report to the General Assembly, information on further developments and on the progress made in this regard.

⚑ CONVENTION RELATING TO CIVIL LIABILITY IN THE FIELD OF MARITIME CARRIAGE OF NUCLEAR MATERIAL

The High Contracting Parties,

Considering that the Paris Convention of 29 July 1960 on Third Party Liability in the Field of Nuclear Energy and its Additional Protocol of 28 January 1964 (hereinafter referred to as "the Paris Convention") and the Vienna Convention of 21 May 1963 on Civil Liability for Nuclear Damage (hereinafter referred to as "the Vienna Convention") provide that, in the case of damage caused by a nuclear incident occurring in the course of maritime carriage of nuclear material covered by such Conventions, the operator of a nuclear installation is the person liable for such damage,

Considering that similar provisions exist in the national law in force in certain States,

Considering that the application of any preceding international convention in the field of maritime transport is however maintained,

Executed at Brussels on December 17, 1971.

Under Article 5 of this Convention, it remained open for signature until December 31, 1972, and thereafter remained open for accession. Under Article 6, the Convention enters into force on the ninetieth day following the date on which five states have either signed it without reservation as to ratification, acceptance or approval or have deposited instruments of ratification, acceptance, approval or accession with the Secretary-General of the International Maritime Consultative Organization. The Convention was the result of the Conference on Maritime Carriage of Nuclear Substances which was held at Brussels from November 29 to December 2, 1971, on the basis of decisions and cooperative measures taken in IMCO, IAEA, and the European Nuclear Energy Agency of OECD.

Desirous of ensuring that the operator of a nuclear installation will be exclusively liable for damage caused by a nuclear incident occurring in the course of maritime carriage of nuclear material,

Have agreed as follows:

ARTICLE 1

Any person who by virtue of an international convention or national law applicable in the field of maritime transport might be held liable for damage caused by a nuclear incident shall be exonerated from such liability:

- (a) if the operator of a nuclear installation is liable for such damage under either the Paris or the Vienna Convention, or
- (b) if the operator of a nuclear installation is liable for such damage by virtue of a national law governing the liability for such damage, provided that such law is in all respects as favourable to persons who may suffer damage as either the Paris or the Vienna Convention.

ARTICLE 2

1. The exoneration provided for in Article 1 shall also apply in respect of damage caused by a nuclear incident:

- (a) to the nuclear installation itself or to any property on the site of that installation which is used or to be used in connexion with that installation, or
- (b) to the means of transport upon which the nuclear material involved was at the time of the nuclear incident,

for which the operator of the nuclear installation is not liable because his liability for such damage has been excluded pursuant to the provisions of either the Paris or the Vienna Convention, or, in cases referred to in Article 1(b), by equivalent provisions of the national law referred to therein.

2. The provisions of paragraph 1 shall not, however, affect the liability of any individual who has caused the damage by an act or omission done with intent to cause damage.

ARTICLE 3

No provision of the present Convention shall affect the liability of the operator of a nuclear ship in respect of damage caused by a nuclear incident involving the nuclear fuel of or radioactive products or waste produced in such ship.

ARTICLE 4

The present Convention shall supersede any international conventions in the field of maritime transport which, at the date on which the present Convention is opened for signature, are in force or open for signature, ratification or accession but only to the extent that such conventions would be in conflict with it; however, nothing in this Article shall affect the obligations of the Contracting Parties to the present Convention to non-Contracting States arising under such international conventions.

＊ ＊ ＊

ARTICLE 8

1. The United Nations where it is the administering authority for a territory, or any Contracting Party to the present Convention responsible for the international relations of a territory, may at any time by notification in writing to the Secretary-General of the Organization declare that the present Convention shall extend to such territory. . . .

Suggested Reading List

Environmental Aspects of Atomic Energy and Waste Management, Proceedings of Third International Conference on Peaceful Uses of Atomic Energy, 1964, Vol. 14 (1965).

Smyth, H. D., "International Cooperation on Nuclear Power," *ibid.,* Vol. 1, pp. 287–293 (1965).

Morokhov, I. D., et al., "International Cooperation in the Field of Nuclear Energy," *ibid.* 302 (abstract in English).

Mezerik, A. G., ed., "The International Atomic Energy Agency," *Int'l Rev. Service* (Jan. 1957).

Hardy, M. J. L., "International Protection Against Nuclear Risks," 10 *Int'l and Comp. L.Q.* 739 (1961).

International Atomic Energy Agency, *IAEA: What It Is and What It Does* (1961).

Szasz, Paul C., "The Convention on the Liability of Operators of Nuclear Ships," 2 *J. Mar. L. and Comm.* 541 (1970–71).

Postface

In preparing this collection of materials, we have made no effort to provide a conceptual framework for systematic inquiries into all aspects of the international legal process for the prevention and control of pollution. It may be in order, however, to offer a few comments on the difficulties that would be involved in such a task.

The chief problem lies in balancing the need for conceptual integrity against the demand for practical utility. More than ever before, legal scholars are endeavoring to accept a more creative role by reappraising the modes and objectives of legal analysis and by experimenting within comprehensive frameworks of inquiry. Confronted with a formidable tangle of complexities in the social context of environmental issues, the legal scholar will have little to contribute creatively if he limits himself to "traditional exercises in derivational logic." On the contrary, he may find it increasingly useful and sensible to follow the more ambitious example of Myres McDougal and Harold Lasswell, the pioneers of policy science, who address themselves to a range of tasks arising out of questions relating to the interplay between law and social process: the clarification of community policy, the description of past trends in decision, the analysis of factors affecting decision, the projection of future trends in decision, and the invention and evaluation of policy alternatives.*

The focus on "policy" and "decision" provides much wider limits of inquiry for the legal scholar than those provided by the traditional focus on "law," conceived as a "frozen set of pre-existing rules or ar-

* For a recent discussion, see Myres S. McDougal, "Legal Bases for Securing the Integrity of the Earth-Space Environment," 184 *Annals of N.Y. Acad. Sciences* 375 at 379–80 (1971).

rangements." Yet the decisional focus saves him from assuming un-manageable undertakings that would involve all the data and tech-niques of the environmental sciences. The policy science approach in environmental studies is comprehensive, but it is disciplined by virtue of the lawyer's systematic concern with past, present, and pro-jected features of the law-making process.

When the process in question is not just that of national society, but the much more complicated process of the world community, there is a danger that the decisional focus may not save the legal scholar from creating a framework so gigantic that it fails the most relevant tests of practical utility. If a policy science framework is to be workable for international environmental policy studies, it may be necessary for practical reasons to reduce the scale of the concept of "environmental policy."

A totalistic yet practically useful policy science study of international environmental law that attempts to comprehend all problems involved in the preservation of the human environment is difficult to envisage, but such a study would be perfectly feasible if limited, for example, to the problems of marine pollution caused by ship-generated wastes. The feasibility of the undertaking is much more questionable if the selected problem is stretched to embrace all forms of threats to the preservation of the marine environment, especially if such threats are defined to include the overuse as well as the misuse of marine re-sources. Such an interpretation would require the policy-science scholar to investigate marine resource policy and practice in great detail in order to deal systematically with all the questions suggested by it. A reasonably restrictive interpretation of the marine pollution concept is a matter of prerogative. Whether overfishing, for example, con-tributes to the deterioration of the marine environment can be de-termined by the way one defines one's terms!

In a sense, these comments are intended to justify our editorial policy, which might be regarded as fairly relaxed about structure. Most of the problems reflected in these pages are pollution problems, in a generally accepted sense. We believe the pollution materials reflect the most important developments so far in the field of inter-national environmental law and present them, more or less, in histori-cal sequence. The non-pollution materials, mostly in Part Three, are added as a kind of compromise between the competing claims of con-ceptual integrity and practical utility. We believe they will help the reader, especially the more advanced student of international law, to identify parallels and analogies that may be useful in developing the international law of pollution control. In this unstructured way, we hope that Part Three contributes in a modest degree to the larger purpose of truly systematic inquiry.

Index